1990 SUPPLEMENT TO TEXT, CASES AND MATERIALS ON
SEX–BASED DISCRIMINATION
Third Edition

By

Herma Hill Kay
Richard W. Jennings Professor of Law
University of California at Berkeley

AMERICAN CASEBOOK SERIES®

WEST PUBLISHING CO.
ST. PAUL, MINN., 1990

American Casebook Series, the key number appearing on the front cover and the WP symbol are registered trademarks of West Publishing Co. Registered in U.S. Patent and Trademark Office.

COPYRIGHT © 1990 By WEST PUBLISHING CO.
50 West Kellogg Boulevard
P.O. Box 64526
St. Paul, MN 55164–0526

All rights reserved
Printed in the United States of America

ISBN 0–314–76483–6

Author's Note and Acknowledgements

This 1990 Supplement covers the two year period since July 1988. It reflects renewed struggle over issues once believed settled: for example, the constitutionality of a woman's right to choose whether to bear children; the meaning and implementation of statutory guarantees of non-discrimination; and the appropriateness of affirmative efforts to ensure equality. An emerging conservative consensus on the United States Supreme Court has reopened these old problems by signaling its willingness to grant greater latitude to state legislatures seeking to regulate procreation and by its restrictive reinterpretation of Title VII and 42 U.S.C. § 1981. In response to the Court's new mood, confrontations over abortion have engulfed the state legislatures, and more than one Governor has been forced to ponder appropriate veto messages. As this Supplement goes to press, a newly constituted liberal coalition in the Congress is seeking to restore the prior statutory understanding by enacting The Civil Rights Restoration Act of 1990 in face of the threat of a Presidential veto.

Even as these old battles are being refought at the state and federal political levels, new and more subtle legal issues concerning the meaning of and remedies for discrimination make their appearance on the Supreme Court's agenda. During its past two terms, the Court recognized the damaging influence of sexual stereotyping in employment decisions; it rejected a university's claim that academic freedom provided an exception from Title VII investigative procedures; and it upheld an administrative agency's determination that diversity in broadcasting could be implemented by racial preferences. The Court will rule this term on the question of whether an employer, invoking business necessity, can exclude women of childbearing age from working in toxic environments. Justice Brennan's clear vision on this and other vexed questions of sex-based discrimination will be sorely missed.

As the final decade of the 20th century opens, the American legal system continues to debate the meaning of the essential human dignity of women, racial minorities, homosexuals, and other marginalized groups. This Supplement continues to document that debate, and to invite critical examination of its direction and ultimate outcome.

I am grateful to my Research Assistant, Nancy Kim, and to my Secretary, Erika Liskamm, for their assistance.

HHK

July, 1990

Table of Contents

	Page
AUTHOR'S NOTE AND ACKNOWLEDGEMENTS	iii
TABLE OF CASES	vii

Chapter I. Constitutional Limits on Sex–Based Discrimination 1
B. The New Direction 1
C. Identifying the Victims of Discrimination 2
D. First Amendment Constraints on Sex Discrimination Claims 3
E. Equal Protection or Equal Rights as the Appropriate Constitutional Basis for Abolishing Sex Discrimination 4

Chapter II. Sexual Interaction Within the Family 6
A. Marriage and Family Life 6
   1. The Marriage Contract 6
      a. Traditional Marriage and its Consequences for Women 6
         i. Age at Marriage, Married Name, Domicile 6
            In re Laura Beth Lamb on Disbarment 6
         ii. Support of Spouse and Children 11
      b. Rethinking the Marriage Contract 12
         ii. Same–Sex Marriage 12
   2. Dissolution of Marriage 12
      a. Grounds 12
      b. Financial Provisions 12
      c. Custody and Support of Children 13
B. Family Life Without Marriage 15
   1. Barriers Against the Unwed Family 15
   2. The Unwed Parent 18
      Michael H. v. Gerald D. 18
D. Family Planning: Who Controls the Reproductive Process? 44
   1. Contraception 44
   2. Abortion 45
      Webster v. Reproductive Health Services 45

Chapter III. Women and Employment 111
A. Title VII of the Civil Rights Act of 1964 111
   1. The Statutory Definition of Sex Discrimination in Employment 111
      a. Coverage: What Is Sex Discrimination? 111
      b. Scope: What Does Non-discrimination Entail? 113

	Page
A. Title VII of the Civil Rights Act of 1964—Continued	
2. The Evidentiary Framework for Title VII Litigation	114
a. Proving Discrimination: The Prima Facie Case	114
i. Disparate Impact	114
Wards Cove Packing Co., Inc. v. Atonio	114
b. Rebutting the Prima Facie Case: Some Defense Strategies	132
i. The BFOQ and Business Necessity Defenses in Sex Discrimination Cases	132
International Union, UAW v. Johnson Controls, Inc.	132
ii. Articulating Legitimate and Nondiscriminatory Reasons	161
c. The Plaintiff's Ultimate Burden of Persuasion	162
3. Title VII and "Upper Level" Jobs	162
Price Waterhouse v. Hopkins	162
University of Pennsylvania v. E.E.O.C.	195
4. Wage Discrimination	205
5. Title VII Remedies	206
a. Introductory Note	206
Martin v. Wilks	207
b. Voluntary Affirmative Action: Reverse Discrimination Under Title VII?	216
B. Constitutional Prohibitions Against Intentional Discrimination in Employment	217
Patterson v. McLean Credit Union	217
C. The Equal Pay Act of 1963	235
D. Executive Order 11246	236
Chapter IV. Educational Opportunity	243
A. Sex Segregation in Educational Institutions	243
1. Admission Barriers: Single–Sex and Sex Quota Schools	243
2. The Right to Equal Play: Sex Segregation in Athletic Programs	244
B. Legal Remedies for Sex Discrimination in Educational Institutions	244
C. Sexism and Sexuality in Academic Life	249
1. Sexual Harassment	249
D. Law Schools	251
Chapter V. Women and Crime	253
A. Rape	253
1. Statutory Rape	253
2. Forcible Rape	253
The Florida Star v. B.J.F.	253
C. Women and the Criminal Justice System	268
1. Women as Defendants	268

Table of Cases

The principal cases are in bold type. Cases cited or discussed in the text are roman type. References are to pages. Cases cited in principal cases and within other quoted materials are not included.

AFSCME v. Washington, 205
Agg v. Flanagan, 15
Anderson v. Hewlett–Packard Corp., 112

Baird v. Bellotti, 109
Bakke, University of California v., 239
Birdwhistle v. Kansas Power and Light Co., 235
Board of Directors of Rotary Intern. v. Rotary Club of Duarte, 3
Bobb v. Municipal Court of California, Monterey County, 10
Bobo v. Jewell, 11
Booth v. Terminix Intern., Inc., 234
Bougher v. University of Pittsburgh, 882 F.2d 74, p. 251
Bougher v. University of Pittsburgh, 713 F.Supp. 139, p. 249
Braschi v. Stahl Associates Co., 15
Brown v. Board of Education, 216
Brown v. Trustees of Boston University, 205

California Federal Sav. and Loan Ass'n v. Guerra, 113, 159, 160
California State Employees' Ass'n (CSEA) v. California, 205
Chicago, City of, United States v., 206
City of (see name of city)
Clark v. Arizona Interscholastic Ass'n (Clark II), 244
Clark v. Arizona Interscholastic Ass'n (Clark I), 244
Craft v. Hodel, 1
Craig v. Boren, 1, 2, 244
Croteau v. Fair, 244

Davis v. City and County of San Francisco, 161, 215
Davis v. Davis, 13
DeCintio v. Westchester County Medical Center, 111
Degraffenreid v. General Motors Assembly Div., 161
Doe v. University of Michigan, 4
Donahue v. Donahue, 12
Douglass, In re, 11
Dworkin v. Hustler Magazine, Inc., 4

Elias v. United States Dept. of State, 1
Ex parte (see name of party)

Florida v. Long, 111
Fowler v. McCrory Corp., 235
Fullilove v. Klutznick, 236, 238

Greenfield v. Greenfield, 13
Griggs v. Duke Power Co., 131

Hodgson v. Minnesota, 73, 108, 109
Hopkins v. Price Waterhouse, 195, 206

In re (see name of party)
International Union, UAW v. Johnson Controls, Inc., 111, 113, **132,** 159, 160, 161

Jaffee v. United States, 2
Jefferies v. Harris County Community Action Ass'n, 162
Jett v. Dallas Independent School Dist., 235
Johnson v. Uncle Ben's, Inc., 161
Johnson Controls, Inc. v. California Fair Employment and Housing Com'n, 159
Jones v. Wesco Investments, Inc., 112

Katcoff v. Marsh, 2

Laura Beth Lamb on Disbarment, In re, 10
Lehr v. Robertson, 42
Lewis v. United States Army, 2
Lorance v. AT & T Technologies, Inc., 241, 242
Lynn v. Regents of University of California, 204

Mahoney v. Mahoney, 12
Marriage of (see name of party)
Martin v. Wilks, 207, 215
Martinez v. Martinez, 12, 13
Massachusetts v. Bowen, 105
Massachusetts v. Secretary of Health and Human Services, 106
Metro Broadcasting, Inc. v. F.C.C., 217, 238
Michael H. v. Gerald D., 18, 42, 43, 44

TABLE OF CASES

Monell v. Department of Social Services, 235
Moore v. Hughes Helicopters, Inc., 161

Namenwirth v. Board of Regents of University of Wisconsin System, 204
New York v. Sullivan, 106
New York State Nat. Organization for Women v. Terry, 109
Northeast Women's Center, Inc. v. McMonagle, 110

Ohio v. Akron Center for Reproductive Health, 109
Olesen v. Board of Educ. of School Dist. No. 228, p. 1

Parrillo v. Parrillo, 13
Patterson v. McLean Credit Union, 217, 234, 235
Plessy v. Ferguson, 240
Presse, Ex parte, 43
Price Waterhouse v. Hopkins, 162, 194

Quinn v. Millsap, 1

Radich v. Goode, 110
Regan v. Taxation with Representation of Washington, 106
Richmond, City of v. J.A. Croson Co., 216, 217, 236, 238, 239, 244
Rivera v. AT & T Information Systems, Inc., 235
Roberts v. United States Jaycees, 3
Roe v. Wade, 105, 106, 108
Rostker v. Goldberg, 2
Rowley v. Board of Educ. of St. Vrain Valley School Dist., 244
Rust v. Sullivan, 106

Schiffman, In re, 10, 11
Sharif by Salahuddin v. New York State Educ. Dept., 244, 248
Smith v. Cole, 44

Texas Dept. of Community Affairs v. Burdine, 161
The Florida Star v. B.J.F., 253

United States v. ___(see opposing party)
United States Catholic Conference, In re, 109
United States Postal Service Bd. of Governors v. Aikens, 162, 194
University of California v. Bakke, 239
University of Pennsylvania v. E.E.O.C., 195, 204, 205

Van Pool v. City and County of San Francisco, 215, 216

Walls v. City of Petersburg, 130, 131
Wards Cove Packing Co., Inc. v. Atonio, 114, 130, 131, 159, 161, 162, 194, 205, 248
Watson v. Fort Worth Bank and Trust, 129, 130
Webster v. Reproductive Health Services, 45, 105, 106, 107, 108
Will v. Michigan Dept. of State Police, 235

Yellow Freight System, Inc. v. Donnelly, 159

Chapter I

CONSTITUTIONAL LIMITS ON SEX-BASED DISCRIMINATION

B. THE NEW DIRECTION

Text Note

An Overview of Equal Protection Analysis

Page 20. Add to final paragraph:

In Quinn v. Millsap, 491 U.S. ___, 109 S.Ct. 2324, 105 L.Ed.2d 74 (1989), the Court invalidated a Missouri state constitutional provision authorizing a "board of freeholders" composed only of property owners to draft a governmental reorganization plan to be submitted to voters, explaining that the provision constituted invidious discrimination against non-property owners that could not survive review under the rational basis standard. The Court also rejected the Missouri Supreme Court's view that the provision was not subject to scrutiny under the Equal Protection clause because the board exercised no general governmental powers, noting that this rationale "would render the Equal Protection Clause inapplicable even to a requirement that all members of the board be white males." Id., 491 U.S. at ___, 109 S.Ct. at 2331, 105 L.Ed.2d at 88.

Page 49. Add new Note 6:

6. How would you apply the *Craig* standard to the following cases? (a) A Board of Education rule forbids male high school students from wearing gang symbols or jewelry, including earrings, to school; female students are not prohibited from wearing earrings (see Olesen v. Board of Education of School Dist. No. 228, 676 F.Supp. 820, 823 (N.D.Ill.1987)); (b) A National Park Service regulation prohibits the public exposure of female breasts, but not male chests, at the Cape Cod National Seashore (see Craft v. Hodel, 683 F.Supp. 289, 299–301 (D.Mass.1988)); (c) a former provision of the Immigration and Nationality Act that conferred citizenship upon children born abroad whose fathers, but not mothers, were United States citizens (see Elias v. United States Department of State, 721 F.Supp. 243 (N.D.Cal.1989)).

C. IDENTIFYING THE VICTIMS OF DISCRIMINATION

Page 108. Add new Note 4:

4. Did the *Goldberg* majority use the *Craig* standard? When he was called upon to review the validity of an Army enlistment policy that permits men who have not graduated from high school but who have obtained a General Educational Development (GED) certificate to enlist but prohibits women from so doing, Judge Newcomer inferred from *Goldberg* and two Court of Appeal decisions, Jaffe v. United States, 663 F.2d 1226 (3d Cir.1981) and Katcoff v. Marsh, 755 F.2d 223 (2d Cir.1985), that "the standard outlined in *Craig* is not applicable to gender-based equal protection claims raised in the context of military affairs." Lewis v. United States Army, 697 F.Supp. 1385, 1390 n. 5 (E.D.Pa.1988). Instead, Judge Newcomer tested the Army policy "using a standard of review that asks whether the regulations are reasonably relevant and necessary to the national defense, with any doubt as to constitutionality resolved in favor of deference to the military's exercise of its discretion." Id., at 1390. The Army relied on studies showing that high school graduates are more likely than GED holders to complete their initial enlistment term and to reenlist; thus, it would prefer to impose the high school diploma requirement on all recruits. Because of its policy barring women from combat, however, the Army felt it needed to enlist a "much greater number of men than women" and accordingly could not afford to impose the high school diploma restriction on men. Not surprisingly, under Judge Newcomer's standard plaintiff Vivian Lewis lost her case. Would she have won under *Craig*?

Text Note

Women in the Military

Page 110. Add to text following footnote 15:

Kristin M. Baker, the daughter of an Army colonel who describes herself as an "Army brat," became the First Captain of the Corps of Cadets at West Point in 1989. The New York Times, August 9, 1989, at A1, col. 2.

Page 113. Add new paragraphs to text after discussion of *Hill*:

In November, 1988, after reviewing the report of the Task Force on Women in the Military, the Pentagon announced that a number of noncombat occupations previously closed to women would be opened; a move that could make as many as 11,138 jobs available to Army women. The New York Times, November 15, 1988, at A16, col. 1.

As the new decade began, the question of women in combat was reopened by the disclosure that a woman, Captain Linda L. Bray, had led U.S. troops in combat during the United States invasion of Panama in December, 1989. Captain Bray, the Commander of an Army Military Police Unit of 30 soldiers, was assigned to capture a kennel holding guard dogs that was mistakenly thought not to be defended by Panamanian soldiers. The New York Times called the event "a 'First' for [the] Army."

The New York Times, January 4, 1990, at A1, col. 3. Military spokespersons sought to calm the furor that followed this account by announcing that Captain Bray had commanded the initial attack from a command center about a half mile away from the kennel, arriving on the scene in person when the enemy was escaping to lead her troops under sniper fire, but after the heavy firing had ended. The New York Times, January 9, 1990, at A6, col. 1. The wide-spread public discussion of the incident prompted Representative Patricia Schroeder to introduce legislation in Congress directing the Secretary of the Army to carry out a four-year test program to examine the implications of the removal of limitations on the assignment of female members of the Army to combat and combat-support positions. Addressing the House in support of H.R. 3868 (101st Cong. 2d Sess.), Representative Schroeder said,

> Mr. Speaker, have you seen the Army's latest commercial asking women to be all that they can be? The commercial portrays a woman in a communications van obviously handling the communications for manuvers. Assuming that our enemy is intelligent, that woman would be the first hit in a strike. It's always smart to destroy your enemy's lines of communications first. So let me see if I have this straight. Army policy allows women to be shot first, but they can't be the first to shoot. The logic eludes me.

136 Cong.Rec. H 5 (Jan. 23, 1990). The bill's chances of enactment appear slim, but Representative Schroeder plans to continue to push it, if only to make a statement. Galvin & Weiss, "Proposal for Women in Combat is Running into Flak on Hill," 48 CQ 762 (No. 10, Mar. 10, 1990). What statement might that be?

D. FIRST AMENDMENT CONSTRAINTS ON SEX DISCRIMINATION CLAIMS

Page 157. Add at end of Note 2:

Rhode has indicated more recently that she finds the holdings in *Jaycees, Rotary,* and *New York Clubs* "quite limited." She points out that these cases

> * * * permitted states to bar gender discrimination by certain organizations, but fell short of creating a constitutional remedy for such discrimination or of clarifying the organizations subject to regulation. These limitations in the Court's approach reflect more fundamental limitations in its public-private dichotomy. Such an approach obscures how women's exclusion from spheres conventionally classified as private contributes to their exclusion from spheres uniformly understood as public.

D. Rhode, Justice and Gender 283 (1990).

Page 159. Add at end of Note 5:

As you might expect, Hustler Magazine did not stand idly by while MacKinnon and Dworkin waged their battle on one of its steady sources of income, the pornography industry. In its February, March, and December, 1984 issues, Hustler published features that mentioned Dworkin's name in a derogatory manner. Dworkin sued Hustler for libel, invasion of privacy, intentional infliction of emotional injury, and outrage, but Hustler won a motion for summary judgment. See Dworkin v. Hustler Magazine, Inc., 668 F.Supp. 1408 (C.D.Cal.1987), affirmed 867 F.2d 1188 (9th Cir.1989), certiorari denied ___ U.S. ___, 110 S.Ct. 59, 107 L.Ed.2d 26 (1989).

Page 161. Add at end of Note 7:

See Spaulding, Anti–Pornography Laws as a Claim for Equal Respect: Feminism, Liberalism & Community, 4 Berkeley Wom.L.J. 128 (1988–89) (a thoughtful re-examination of the pornography debate from the perspective of the feminist as social critic, which offers a broader notion of equal respect as membership in the sense of belonging and acceptance); see generally, Symposium, 21 U.Mich.J. of L.Reform 1 (1987–88).

Page 161. Add new Note 8:

8. Does the First Amendment permit a state university to adopt a policy subjecting persons to discipline for engaging in "[a]ny behavior, verbal or physical, that stigmatizes or victimizes an individual on the basis of race, ethnicity, religion, sex, sexual orientation, creed, national origin, ancestry, age, marital status, handicap or Vietnam-era veteran status, and that (a) involves an express or implied threat to an individual's academic efforts, employment, participation in University sponsored extra-curricular activities or personal safety; or (b) has the purpose or reasonably foreseeable effect of interfering with an individual's academic efforts, employment, participation in University sponsored extra-curricular activities or personal safety"? See Doe v. University of Michigan, 721 F.Supp. 852 (E.D. Mich.1989).

E. EQUAL PROTECTION OR EQUAL RIGHTS AS THE APPROPRIATE CONSTITUTIONAL BASIS FOR ABOLISHING SEX DISCRIMINATION

Page 165. Add following quote from Rhode:

See also D. Rhode, Gender and Justice 63–80 (1990).

Text Note

The Equal Protection Principle Versus the Equal Rights Amendment as a Means of Establishing Equality of Rights and Responsibilities Under the Law for Women and Men

Page 166. Add following quotation from Ginsburg:

In a revisionist interpretation of the Fourteenth Amendment, Nina Morais argues that the framers contemplated that "women's rights, short of suffrage, were * * * within the reach of the Fourteenth Amendment." Note, Sex Discrimination and the Fourteenth Amendment: Lost History, 97 Yale L.J. 1153, 1158 (1988). In support of her argument, Morais points to the presence of suffragists at the Congressional debates on the amendment and on the textual difference between the first section, which refers to "persons" and "citizens," and the second section, which redressed the denial of the vote only to males. Are you convinced?

Page 183. Add at end of Note 7:

See also Kovacic, Remedying Underinclusive Statutes, 33 Wayne L.Rev. 39 (1986).

Chapter II

SEXUAL INTERACTION WITHIN THE FAMILY

A. MARRIAGE AND FAMILY LIFE

1. THE MARRIAGE CONTRACT

a. *Traditional Marriage and its Consequences for Women*

i. *Age at Marriage, Married Name, Domicile*

Page 190. Add following *Bobb*:

IN RE LAURA BETH LAMB ON DISBARMENT

Supreme Court of California, 1989.
49 Cal.3d 239, 260 Cal.Rptr. 856, 776 P.2d 765.

BY THE COURT:

Petitioner Laura Beth Lamb was admitted to practice in December 1983. She has no prior record of discipline. On November 13, 1986, she pled nolo contendere to two felony counts of false personation to obtain a benefit. (Pen.Code, § 529, subd. 3.) The charges arose from allegations that petitioner took the July 1985 bar examination for her husband.

Upon receiving the record of conviction, we referred the matter to the State Bar for a determination whether the misconduct involved moral turpitude and, if so, what discipline should be imposed. Among other things, the parties stipulated before the State Bar Court that moral turpitude was involved. The hearing officer proposed disbarment, and the review department concurred. Petitioner sought review.

Petitioner's case has sympathetic aspects, and her expressions of contrition seem genuine. Nonetheless, her deceitful crime was exceptionally serious. Considering the public danger inherent in bar exam cheating, and the criminal dishonesty and moral turpitude involved, "[o]nly * * * the most compelling mitigating circumstances" could prevent disbarment. (See Rules Proc. of State Bar, div. V, Stds. for Atty. Sanctions for Prof. Misconduct, std. 3.2.) Moreover, despite her intellectual promise, the psychological problems which led to petitioner's moral misjudgment cast continuing doubt upon her fitness to practice law. Under the circumstances, we adopt the State Bar Court's proposal and disbar petitioner.

* * *

DISCUSSION

The only issue is the appropriate discipline. On that score we must examine the record independently and exercise our own judgment.

* * *

* * *

As the State Bar suggests on review, because petitioner's criminal breach of professional standards was so morally serious and so dangerous, only the most overwhelming evidence of mitigation could prevent her disbarment in the public interest. Petitioner fails to sustain that heavy burden.

* * *

Petitioner emphasizes that she has ended the marriage which contributed to her acute stress. She also points out that diabetes, though sometimes controllable, cannot be cured. Thus, she urges, she has done everything possible to eliminate the causes of her misconduct.

However, the consensus of mental health professionals was that petitioner suffered a *chronic emotional disability, independent* of her marital and physical problems, which contributed substantially to her disastrous misjudgment. As noted, we have no convincing evidence that her susceptibility in this regard has ended.

* * *

Despite our sympathetic feelings, our paramount duty is to protect the public, the courts, and the profession. Accordingly we, like the State Bar Court, believe that reinstatement proceedings are the means by which petitioner should demonstrate her clear rehabilitation after "the passage of considerable time." (Std. 1.2(e)(viii).) We therefore adopt the State Bar Court's recommendation that petitioner be disbarred.

* * *

KAUFMAN, JUSTICE, dissenting.

I dissent.

There was public danger inherent in petitioner's serious misconduct, but the circumstances that gave rise to that misconduct were unique and no longer exist. Contrary to the majority's premise, there is no danger to the public or anyone else from petitioner's one-time, aberrational conduct stemming from circumstances that no longer exist and as to which there is not the slightest possibility of recurrence. Thus, while disbarment in this case will doubtlessly be applauded in some circles, it is wholly unwarranted. It serves only to punish an apparently talented lawyer whose misconduct resulted from the most desperate, life-threatening circumstances. Indeed, such drastic discipline serves the public interest *less* well than would a long period of probation on appropriate conditions, including proof of fitness before returning to the practice of law.

The record discloses the following uncontroverted facts: After adamantly refusing several times her then-husband's insistent demands that she take the bar examination for him, petitioner eventually did so only when she was so desperately physically ill and overwhelmingly mentally intimidated by his barbaric threats and conduct that she felt she had no alternative but to do so, or lose the unborn child with which she was then many months pregnant. The child has long since been born and petitioner's marriage to her former husband has been dissolved. The circumstances were absolutely unique and could not possibly recur.

Petitioner is an insulin-dependent diabetic. When she became pregnant, her physician advised her the pregnancy and its anticipated complications would be life threatening and recommended that she have the pregnancy aborted. She refused. What ensued was nightmarish.

* * *

In addition to the overwhelming physical and emotional problems of her pregnancy, petitioner's marriage and home life had become nothing short of a disaster.

Petitioner had met Morgan Lamb in law school. In 1983, after their graduation from law school, Morgan accepted employment at a prestigious law firm in Houston. Petitioner joined Morgan in Houston and they were married in October 1983. After passing the California bar examination, petitioner was hired as an attorney in the Houston office of the Securities and Exchange Commission (SEC). Soon after, however, things began to fall apart.

Morgan failed the Texas bar examination. He began to act depressed and moody. He would cry, hide in bed, or watch television. He also became violently argumentative.

Morgan retook the Texas bar examination. He was so convinced he would fail again that he became hysterical. Although he did pass, he was fired by his law firm. His reactions became more extreme, violent and unpredictable. He would shout and throw things, and even abused petitioner physically.

After these setbacks, petitioner and her husband attempted a new start. They moved to Los Angeles where Morgan had secured a position with a prominent law firm. Petitioner was able to transfer to the Los Angeles office of the SEC.

Morgan sat for the February 1985 California bar examination. By this time, petitioner was pregnant and already so ill she had to take a leave of absence from her job. Then, within a short space of time, Morgan was fired from his position with the Los Angeles law firm and he received a letter notifying him that he had failed the California bar examination. After that, he lost any semblance of self-control. He threw heavy objects and furniture. He smashed large lamps and tore down the curtain rods. He screamed at petitioner and pushed her violently. He threatened to kill himself. He threatened to kill petitioner and the baby. Petitioner was so frightened she removed a gun he kept near the bed. Members of petitioner's family who visited her saw broken glass on the floor, smashed lamps, holes in the wall and bits of food plastered on the wall. Petitioner lived in fear of her husband's violent tantrums.

Petitioner desperately wanted to save her marriage and the lives of herself and her baby. The stress of her home situation placed an intolerable stress on the unborn baby because of petitioner's extremely high blood pressure and physical illnesses. Her doctors told her she had to alleviate the stress or risk the life of her baby or herself. Petitioner was required to lie still because of her dangerous protein deficiency. At times, however, Morgan would shake her and force her to get up and do housework and take care of him.

Morgan became convinced he could not pass the bar examination and repeatedly importuned petitioner to take it for him. She refused numerous times, although she was afraid of what he might do to her or to himself if she did not relent. Each time she refused he would fly into a rage. Finally, in her weak and confused state, petitioner gave in to her husband's demands that she take the exam for him because she could not think of any way to refuse without endangering herself or the baby. She submitted her photograph with his application to take the July 1985 bar examination. Even thereafter, she attempted to convince her husband to take the examination himself and studied with him so that he would be prepared for the examination. For a short time, that plan seemed to be working, but then Morgan began to find more and more excuses not to study. Ultimately, petitioner succumbed to the overwhelming pressures and took the examination posing as her husband.

Immediately upon completing the bar examination, petitioner entered the hospital, where her doctors urged her to have the baby delivered at once or risk the death of both herself and her baby. Petitioner refused because the baby's lungs were too underdeveloped for it to survive outside her body. Petitioner underwent experimental treatments to help the baby's lungs develop. She herself was on the verge of death and required intensive care. After ten days, labor was induced and a healthy baby girl was born, two months prematurely.

Discussion

Petitioner does not claim that her conduct was justified or legally excused by these circumstances. She in fact stipulated her conduct involved moral turpitude and accepts responsibility for it. Rather, the issue is what discipline is appropriate for petitioner's conduct.

In fastening upon disbarment as the appropriate discipline the majority give insufficient consideration to the mitigating circumstances in this case. * * *

Petitioner's "long term" psychological problems relate to her childhood in a dysfunctional family where one parent abused drugs and all the family members became withdrawn and isolated. Yet it is uncontroverted that, despite the psychological shortcomings attributable to her past, petitioner had always been able to conform her conduct to the highest ethical standards. The record shows that the conduct leading to this offense was completely aberrational and out of character. It was only in the unique combination of situational circumstances here, in which she was on the verge of complete physical, mental and emotional collapse, that she engaged in these bizarre acts.

Petitioner has shown, not only clearly and convincingly, but beyond question, that she has done everything possible to eliminate the extreme emotional and physical difficulties that led to the misconduct. She is, of course, no longer pregnant and no longer suffers the dire complications brought on by the combination of pregnancy and her diabetes. She has ended her marriage to Morgan Lamb. Though she cannot change the fact of her diabetes, she has brought it under control. And she has committed to voluntary, long-term therapy to overcome her problems. * * *

* * *

* * * Disbarment here serves only to punish petitioner. An alternative is available which would, in my view, far better serve the public, the profession and the courts. To the extent necessary, we may impose conditions of probation which will ensure that the attorney is rehabilitated and the public is protected. I would impose a lengthy probation, with a substantial term of actual suspension and with appropriate probationary conditions, including continued therapy and a demonstration of fitness before returning to the practice of law.

Notes on Lamb:

1. Do you think that Laura Beth Lamb should have been disbarred? What would Justice Kaufman have done if she had remained married to Morgan Lamb?

2. Do the facts of *Lamb* lend support to the *Bobb* Trial Court's voir dire examination of Carolyn Bobb? (See casebook at p. 186.)

Text Note

The Married Woman's Loss of Identity

Page 202. Add to text following footnote 45:

Schiffman was extended to apply to a case where the mother and father disagreed about what surname should be recorded on the child's birth certificate. Cynthia Lesher and Bruce S. Douglass married on July 18, 1986; Cynthia assumed her husband's surname as her marital name.

They separated one month later, on August 21, 1986. Cynthia was pregnant at the time of separation. After the separation, she resumed her birth name of Lesher (also the name used by her two sons by a prior marriage who were in her custody). Bruce had physical custody of two children by a prior marriage; their surname was Douglass. Their son, David Thomas, was born on March 19, 1987, and was placed in the temporary custody of his mother. Bruce wanted their son's surname to be recorded on the birth certificate as Douglass; Cynthia wanted it to be Lesher. The trial court ordered the child's surname entered on the birth certificate as David Thomas Douglass–Lesher, but provided that he shall be known as Lesher for all other purposes. Bruce appealed, arguing that *Schiffman* was limited to name changes because the California Supreme Court had indicated that it had no intention of changing the "established practice" and "prevalent custom" of giving a child born in wedlock the paternal surname on the birth certificate. The appellate court dismissed this argument as "a distinction without a difference," going on to hold that the *Schiffman* best interest standard applied to parental disputes over initial naming as well as name changes. The best interests standard led the court to affirm the trial judge's "Solomon-like determination that the birth certificate should state both surnames in a hyphenated form" on the ground that "[i]t meets and satisfies the concerns of both parents in establishing an identity with both parents and their respective family members." In re Douglass, 205 Cal.App.3d 1046, 1055, 252 Cal.Rptr. 839, 844–45 (1988).

Page 202. Add to footnote 46:

See also Bobo v. Jewell, 38 Ohio St.3d 330, 528 N.E.2d 180 (1988), following *Schiffman* in adopting a best interests standard to reverse an order changing the name of an illegitimate child in the custody of his mother from her surname to that of his father in the context of a proceeding to establish the father's paternity.

Page 203. Add to text at end of first full paragraph:

Priscilla Ruth MacDougall concludes in her authoritative article, The Right of Women to Name Their Children, 3 Law & Inequality 91, 159 (1985), that *Schiffman* "should become a guiding light for the future in order for women to have any bona fide right to name their children." Do you think this will happen?

ii. Support of Spouse and Children

Text Note

Support of Spouse and Children During Marriage

Page 221. Add to footnote 52:

See Becker, Obscuring the Struggle: Sex Discrimination, Social Security, and Stone, Seidman, Sunstein & Tushnet's *Constitutional Law,* 89 Colum.L.Rev. 264, 276–88 (1989).

b. Rethinking the Marriage Contract

ii. Same–Sex Marriage

Page 259. Add to end of Note 2:

See Lewis, From This Day Forward: A Feminine Moral Discourse on Homosexual Marriage, 97 Yale L.J. 1783, 1797 (1988) (arguing that a feminine vision of equality "mandates that if marriage is a primary unit of community and that community strives to treat all individuals with equal care, then homosexuals have an equal right to establish a connection to the community as a whole through the institution of marriage").

Page 262. Add to Note 9:

In Maryland, a gay account executive who won a company-paid vacation for two in Hawaii was told that he could take along a wife or female companion, but not his male companion with whom he had lived since 1984. After the ACLU filed suit on the executive's behalf under the Montgomery County Human Relations Act, however, the company agreed to pay the expenses of both men. The New York Times, November 3, 1989, at A8, col. 4. See generally, Friedman, The Necessity for State Recognition of Same–Sex Marriage: Constitutional Requirements and Evolving Notions of Family, 3 Berkeley Wom.L.J. 134 (1987–88).

2. DISSOLUTION OF MARRIAGE

a. Grounds

Page 263. Add to footnote 8:

Compare Scott, Rational Decisionmaking About Marriage and Divorce, 76 Va.L.Rev. 9 (1990) (applying "precommitment theory" to the marital relationship and reexamining the role of fault from that perspective).

b. Financial Provisions

Page 286. Add to end of Note 3:

See generally, Marcus, Locked In and Locked Out: Reflections on the History of Divorce Law Reform in New York State, 37 Buff.L.Rev. 375 (1989).

Page 287. Add to end of Note 4:

See generally Ellman, The Theory of Alimony, 77 Calif.L.Rev. 1 (1989); O'Connell, Alimony After No–Fault: A Practice in Search of a Theory, 23 N.E.L.Rev. 437 (1988).

Page 289. Add to Note 7 following discussion of *Mahoney*:

The Supreme Court of South Carolina followed *Mahoney* to adopt the concept of reimbursement alimony in Donahue v. Donahue, 299 S.C. 353, 384 S.E.2d 741, 747–48 (1989).

Page 290. Add to end of Note 7:

Move sentence discussing *Martinez* to end of Note 7, following discussion of *Reiss*. The Utah Supreme Court granted certiorari in *Martinez:* see

Martinez v. Martinez, 765 P.2d 1277 (1988) (Table). The court has not yet handed down an opinion in the case.

Text Note

Spousal Support and Division of Property Following Divorce

Page 292. Add to footnote 14:

Hoffman and Duncan claim that Weitzman's findings on this point "are almost certainly in error." See Hoffman & Duncan, What Are The Economic Consequences of Divorce?, 25 Demography, No. 4, at 641 (November, 1988).

c. Custody and Support of Children

Page 308. Add to Note 1:

See O'Hanlon & Workman, Beyond the Best Interest of the Child: The Primary Caretaker Doctrine in West Virginia, 92 W.Va.L.Rev. 355, 380–88 (1990), detailing West Virginia's experience with the doctrine. See also Davis v. Davis, 749 P.2d 647 (Utah 1988), awarding custody of a three year old boy to his father under the primary caretaker rule in a case where the boy had lived with the father in the family home for one year pursuant to a divorce decree that was set aside three days after its entry because of the mother's emotional instability. The Utah Supreme Court disregarded the mother's argument that the trial court's order was improper because it had the effect of rewarding the father's exploitative conduct in securing the earlier hurried divorce and custody order, pointing out that the mother's difficulties in caring for the child were in part responsible for the divorce. Is *Davis* a proper application of the primary caretaker doctrine?

Page 315. Add to Note 8:

Compare with the *Greenfield* court's approach the decision in Parrillo v. Parrillo, 554 A.2d 1043 (R.I.1989), certiorari denied ___ U.S. ___, 110 S.Ct. 364, 107 L.Ed.2d 351 (1989). Carla Parrillo divorced Justin Parrillo in mid-May 1986. She was given custody of the three children. In early June, she sought to fix Justin's visitation schedule; he responded with a request for an order restraining Carla from permitting unrelated males to stay overnight at her residence. Carla admitted that she was dating Joseph DiPippo, and that occasionally he stayed overnight in the family home. The opinion indicates how the trial court handled the dispute:

> Carla told the trial justice that Justin began to harass her once he learned she was dating Joseph. Carla acknowledged that Joseph would remain overnight "[o]nce or twice a week behind closed doors." Carla saw no risk to the children, who were present when Joseph was staying overnight, because, she explained, the daughters slept in separate bedrooms about twenty feet away from her bedroom and the son's bedroom was downstairs. When asked if Joseph wore his pajamas in front of the children, Carla explained that when Joseph stayed overnight, he wore a jogging suit. She explained to the trial justice that the children liked Joseph but that she had no intention of marrying him in the near future.

Justin began to reduce his support payments once he learned that Joseph was making his nocturnal visitations.

With the consent and in the presence of counsel, the trial justice met with the three children in his chambers. All the children said they got along well with Joseph, although the son did say that there were times when he did not like him.

In a bench decision given immediately after the presentation of the evidence, the trial justice stated that the children "appear to be well cared for" and that he could not fault the mother's care of her children. However, he did observe that Joseph's overnight visits, in the presence of the children, were not conducive to their general wellbeing, at least in terms of their psychological welfare. The trial justice did observe that if Carla married Joseph, he would become the children's stepfather and the cohabitation [1] issue would become moot.

The trial justice directed Carla to refrain from allowing any "unrelated males" to stay overnight at her residence when the children were present.

Id., 554 A.2d at 1044. On appeal, Justice Kelleher affirmed the trial court's order, pointing out that:

This court, in Vieira v. Vieira, 98 R.I. 454, 204 A.2d 431 (1964), approved a change of custody from the mother to the father because six days after granting the father's petition for a divorce on the grounds of gross misbehavior, the mother and the children spent the night at a New Hampshire motor lodge. Present at the lodge was the male whose association with the mother caused the divorce. This court, in commenting on the trial justice's action, observed "it cannot seriously be questioned that the best interests of these children could no longer be served by continuing their custody in their mother. The harmful effect of her conduct on children of tender years and at impressionable ages cannot be doubted." Id. at 458, 204 A.2d at 433.

However, in this dispute no change in custody has been ordered by the Family Court. In entering the order that was without question directed at Joseph, the trial justice, in simple and direct language, ordered the mother to forgo any overnight visitations with Joseph on those occasions when the children are present. We cannot fault the trial justice's actions. Joseph may still visit the marital domicile overnight, with the exception of those times when the children are with their mother. Notwithstanding the views of Carla's appellate counsel to the contrary, we see no great constitutional issue in this controversy.

Id., 554 A.2d at 1045. Justice Kelleher was right about the absence of any "great constitutional issue" in the case, wasn't he? Do you think the United States Supreme Court should have granted certiorari? If so, how and why should the case have been decided?

1. In using the term "cohabitation," we are referring to sexual relations.

Text Note

Child Custody and Support

Page 328. Add to text following discussion of *Carter*:

See also Agg v. Flanagan, 855 F.2d 336 (6th Cir.1988), rejecting the equal protection claims of a class of male litigants who were or would be subjected to wage assignments, garnishments, or wage attachments under Ohio child support procedures. Characterizing the argument as "essentially a 'reverse discrimination' claim, based on the disparate impact on men of Ohio's child support procedures", the court held that plaintiffs were required to prove intentional discrimination to make out their case. Judge Kennedy pointed out that "[i]t is fairly obvious that the disparate impact on men, insofar as we may characterize the law's effect in that way, is a result of the fact that men generally have higher incomes than women, and that society wants some of that income used to support their children. * * * Ohio, like other states, has attempted to redress the unequal burden of supporting the children of divorced parents between the custodial and non-custodial parents, according to their ability to pay." Id., 855 F.2d at 342.

B. FAMILY LIFE WITHOUT MARRIAGE

1. BARRIERS AGAINST THE UNWED FAMILY

Page 358. Add to Note 9:

See also Law, Homosexuality and the Social Meaning of Gender, 1988 Wis. L.Rev. 187, defending the thesis "that contemporary legal and cultural contempt for lesbian women and gay men serves primarily to preserve and reinforce the social meaning attached to gender."

Page 359. Add to Note 10:

In Braschi v. Stahl Associates Co., 74 N.Y.2d 201, 544 N.Y.S.2d 784, 543 N.E.2d 49 (1989), the New York Court of Appeals upheld a preliminary injunction preventing the eviction of Miguel Braschi from the rent-controlled apartment he had shared with Leslie Blanchard for eleven years. A plurality of the court, led by Judge Titone and joined by Judges Kaye and Alexander, interpreted New York City Rent and Eviction Regulations § 2204.6(d), which provides that "[n]o occupant of housing accommodations shall be evicted under this section where the occupant is either the surviving spouse of the deceased tenant or some other member of the deceased tenant's family who has been living with the tenant," to include same-sex couples. Judge Titone reasoned that:

> * * * we conclude that the term family, as used in 9 NYCRR 2204.6(d), should not be rigidly restricted to those people who have formalized their relationship by obtaining, for instance, a marriage certificate or an adoption order. The intended protection against sudden eviction should not rest on fictitious legal distinctions or genetic history, but instead should find its foundation in the reality of family life. In the context of eviction, a more realistic, and certainly

> equally valid, view of a family includes two adult lifetime partners whose relationship is long term and characterized by an emotional and financial commitment and interdependence. This view comports both with our society's traditional concept of "family" and with the expectations of individuals who live in such nuclear units (see, also, 829 Seventh Ave. Co. v. Reider, 67 N.Y.2d 930, 931–932, 502 N.Y.S.2d 715, 493 N.E.2d 939 [interpreting 9 NYCRR 2204.6(d)'s additional "living with" requirement to mean living with the named tenant "in a *family unit,* which in turn connotes an arrangement, whatever its duration, bearing some indicia of permanence or continuity" (emphasis supplied)]). In fact, Webster's Dictionary defines "family" *first* as "a group of people united by certain convictions or common affiliation" (Webster's Ninth New Collegiate Dictionary 448 [1984]; see, Ballantine's Law Dictionary 456 [3d ed. 1969] ["family" defined as "(p)rimarily, the collective body of persons who live in one house and under one head or management"]; Black's Law Dictionary 543 [Special Deluxe 5th ed. 1979]). Hence, it is reasonable to conclude that, in using the term "family," the Legislature intended to extend protection to those who reside in households having all of the normal familial characteristics. Appellant Braschi should therefore be afforded the opportunity to prove that he and Blanchard had such a household.
>
> This definition of "family" is consistent with both of the competing purposes of the rent-control laws: the protection of individuals from sudden dislocation and the gradual transition to a free market system. Family members, whether or not related by blood, or law who have always treated the apartment as their family home will be protected against the hardship of eviction following the death of the named tenant, thereby furthering the Legislature's goals of preventing dislocation and preserving family units which might otherwise be broken apart upon eviction. This approach will foster the transition from rent control to rent stabilization by drawing a distinction between those individuals who are, in fact, genuine family members, and those who are mere roommates (see, Real Property Law § 235-f; Yorkshire Towers Co. v. Harpster, 134 Misc.2d 384, 510 N.Y.S.2d 976) or newly discovered relatives hoping to inherit the rent-controlled apartment after the existing tenant's death.

Id., 74 N.Y.2d at 211, 544 N.Y.S.2d at 788–89, 543 N.E.2d at 53–54. Judge Bellacosa, concurring, saw no reason to choose between the differing definitions of "family" advocated by the plurality and the dissent. In his view, it was enough that irreparable harm would result from the eviction:

> The plurality opinion favors the petitioner's side by invoking the nomenclature of "nuclear"/"normal"/"genuine" family versus the "traditional"/"legally recognizable" family selected by the dissenting opinion in favor of the landlord. I eschew both polar camps because I see no valid reason for deciding so broadly; indeed, there are cogent reasons not to yaw towards either end of the spectrum.
>
> The application of the governing word and statute to reach a decision in this case can be accomplished on a narrow and legitimate jurisprudential track. The enacting body has selected an unqualified

> word for a socially remedial statute, intended as a protection against one of the harshest decrees known to the law—eviction from one's home. Traditionally, in such circumstances, generous construction is favored. Petitioner has made his shared home in the affected apartment for 10 years. The only other occupant of that rent-controlled apartment over that same extended period of time was the tenant-in-law who has now died, precipitating this battle for the apartment. The best guidance available to the regulatory agency for correctly applying the rule in such circumstances is that it would be irrational not to include this petitioner and it is a more reasonable reflection of the intention behind the regulation to protect a person such as petitioner as within the regulation's class of "family". In that respect, he qualifies as a tenant in fact for purposes of the interlocking provisions and policies of the rent-control law. Therefore, under CPLR 6301, there would unquestionably be irreparable harm by not upholding the preliminary relief Supreme Court has decreed; the likelihood of success seems quite good since four Judges of this court, albeit by different rationales, agree at least that petitioner fits under the beneficial umbrella of the regulation; and the balance of equities would appear to favor petitioner.

Id., 74 N.Y.2d at 215, 544 N.Y.S.2d at 791, 543 N.E.2d at 56. Judges Simons and Hancock, in dissent, interpreted the regulation as limited to persons related to the decedent by blood, marriage, or adoption:

> Central to any interpretation of the regulatory language is a determination of its purpose. There can be little doubt that the purpose of section 2204.6(d) was to create succession rights to a possessory interest in real property where the tenant of record has died or vacated the apartment * * *. It creates a new tenancy for every surviving family member living with decedent at the time of death who then becomes a new statutory tenant until death or until he or she vacates the apartment. The State concerns underlying this provision include the orderly and just succession of property interests (which includes protecting a deceased's spouse and family from loss of their longtime home) and the professed State objective that there be a gradual transition from government regulation to a normal market of free bargaining between landlord and tenant. Those objectives require a weighing of the interests of certain individuals living with the tenant of record at his or her death and the interests of the landlord in regaining possession of its property and rerenting it under the less onerous rent-stabilization laws. The interests are properly balanced if the regulation's exception is applied by using objectively verifiable relationships based on blood, marriage and adoption, as the State has historically done in the estate succession laws, family court acts and similar legislation * * *. The distinction is warranted because members of families, so defined, assume certain legal obligations to each other and to third persons, such as creditors, which are not imposed on unrelated individuals and this legal interdependency is worthy of consideration in determining which individuals are entitled to succeed to the interest of the statutory tenant in rent-controlled premises. Moreover, such an interpretation promotes certainty and consistency

in the law and obviates the need for drawn out hearings and litigation focusing on such intangibles as the strength and duration of the relationship and the extent of the emotional and financial interdependency * * *. So limited, the regulation may be viewed as a tempered response, balancing the rights of landlords with those of the tenant. To come within that protected class, individuals must comply with State laws relating to marriage or adoption. Plaintiff cannot avail himself of these institutions, of course, but that only points up the need for a legislative solution, not a judicial one * * *.

Id., 74 N.Y.2d at 218–19, 544 N.Y.S.2d at 793, 543 N.E.2d at 58. Which of the three opinions has it right? The New York Times editorialized that:

> Judge Titone's view is humane; it is also impractical and illustrates how a warm heart can sometimes turn the law upside down. There may be strong reasons for legislators to broaden the legal definition of family. But absent such change, case-by-case judicial redefinition risks unanticipated grief. In this case, for instance, Judge Titone risks turning more landlords into spies.

The New York Times, July 11, 1989, at A18, col. 1. Do you agree? Should New York City "broaden the legal definition of family" by permitting gay and lesbian couples to register as domestic partners? Denmark created the status of domestic partnership, a legal relationship that is said to be the functional equivalent of marriage, except that adoption is not permitted, and the State Lutheran Church is not required to recognize it. San Francisco Chronicle, May 27 1989, at A15, col. 3. Eleven gay couples were "married" under the new law on October 1, 1989. San Francisco Chronicle, October 2, 1989, at A14, col. 1. In San Francisco, where voters rejected a much more limited domestic partners ordinance in November, 1988, the Mayor's Family Policy Task Force recommended extending health and child care benefits to unmarried partners of city workers, as well as creating a mechanism to register domestic relationships. San Francisco Chronicle, March 29, 1990, at A1, col. 1.

2. THE UNWED PARENT

Page 375. Delete Note 6 and add *Michael H.*:

MICHAEL H. v. GERALD D.
Supreme Court of the United States, 1989.
491 U.S. ___, 109 S.Ct. 2333, 105 L.Ed.2d 91.
Rehearing denied ___ U.S. ___, 110 S.Ct. 22, 106 L.Ed.2d 634 (1989).

JUSTICE SCALIA announced the judgment of the Court and delivered an opinion, in which THE CHIEF JUSTICE joins, and in all but note 6 of which JUSTICE O'CONNOR and JUSTICE KENNEDY join.

Under California law, a child born to a married woman living with her husband is presumed to be a child of the marriage. Cal.Evid.Code Ann. § 621 (West Supp.1989). The presumption of legitimacy may be rebutted only by the husband or wife, and then only in limited circumstances. *Ibid.* The instant appeal presents the claim that this presumption infringes upon the due process rights of a man who wishes to establish his paternity of a child born to the wife of another man, and the claim that it infringes upon the constitutional right of the child to maintain a relationship with her natural father.

I

The facts of this case are, we must hope, extraordinary. On May 9, 1976, in Las Vegas, Nevada, Carole D., an international model, and Gerald D., a top executive in a French oil company, were married. The couple established a home in Playa del Rey, California in which they resided as husband and wife when one or the other was not out of the country on business. In the summer of 1978, Carole became involved in an adulterous affair with a neighbor, Michael H. In September 1980, she conceived a child, Victoria D., who was born on May 11, 1981. Gerald was listed as father on the birth certificate and has always held Victoria out to the world as his daughter. Soon after delivery of the child, however, Carole informed Michael that she believed he might be the father.

In the first three years of her life, Victoria remained always with Carole, but found herself within a variety of quasi-family units. In October 1981, Gerald moved to New York City to pursue his business interests, but Carole chose to remain in California. The end of that month, Carole and Michael had blood tests of themselves and Victoria, which showed a 98.07% probability that Michael was Victoria's father. In January 1982, Carole visited Michael in St. Thomas, where his primary business interests were based. There Michael held Victoria out as his child. In March, however, Carole left Michael and returned to California, where she took up residence with yet another man, Scott K. Later that spring, and again in the summer, Carole and Victoria spent time with Gerald in New York City, as well as on vacation in Europe. In the fall, they returned to Scott in California.

In November 1982, rebuffed in his attempts to visit Victoria, Michael filed a filiation action in California Superior Court to establish his paternity and right to visitation. In March 1983, the court appointed an attorney and guardian ad litem to represent Victoria's interests. Victoria then filed a cross-complaint asserting that if she had more than one psychological or *de facto* father, she was entitled to maintain her filial relationship, with all of the attendant rights, duties, and obligations, with both. In May 1983, Carole filed a motion for summary judgment. During this period, from March through July of 1983, Carole was again living with Gerald in New York. In August, however, she returned to California, became involved once again with Michael, and instructed her attorneys to remove the summary judgment motion from the calendar.

For the ensuing eight months, when Michael was not in St. Thomas he lived with Carole and Victoria in Carole's apartment in Los Angeles, and held Victoria out as his daughter. In April 1984, Carole and Michael signed a stipulation that Michael was Victoria's natural father. Carole left Michael the next month, however, and instructed her attorneys not to file the stipulation. In June 1984, Carole reconciled with Gerald and joined him in New York, where they now live with Victoria and two other children since born into the marriage.

In May 1984, Michael and Victoria, through her guardian ad litem, sought visitation rights for Michael *pendente lite*. To assist in determining whether visitation would be in Victoria's best interests, the Superior Court appointed a psychologist to evaluate Victoria, Gerald, Michael, and Carole. The psychologist recommended that Carole retain sole custody, but that Michael be allowed continued contact with Victoria pursuant to a restricted visitation schedule. The court concurred and ordered that Michael be provided with limited visitation privileges *pendente lite*.

On October 19, 1984, Gerald, who had intervened in the action, moved for summary judgment on the ground that under Cal.Evid.Code § 621 there were no triable issues of fact as to Victoria's paternity. This law provides that "the issue of a wife cohabiting with her husband, who is not impotent or sterile, is conclusively presumed to be a child of the marriage." Cal.Evid.Code Ann. § 621(a) (Supp.1989). The presumption may be rebutted by blood tests, but only if a motion for such tests is made, within two years from the date of the child's birth, either by the husband or, if the natural father has filed an affidavit acknowledging paternity, by the wife. §§ 621(c) and (d).

On January 28, 1985, having found that affidavits submitted by Carole and Gerald sufficed to demonstrate that the two were cohabiting at conception and birth and that Gerald was neither sterile nor impotent, the Superior Court granted Gerald's motion for summary judgment, rejecting Michael's and Victoria's challenges to the constitutionality of § 621. The court also denied their motions for continued visitation pending the appeal under Cal.Civ.Code § 4601, which provides that a court may, in its discretion, grant "reasonable visitation rights * * * to any * * * person having an interest in the welfare of the child." Cal.Civ.Code Ann. § 4601 (West Supp.1989). It found that allowing such visitation would "violat[e] the intention of the Legislature by impugning the integrity of the family unit."

* * * After submission of briefs and a hearing, the California Court of Appeal affirmed the judgment of the Superior Court and upheld the constitutionality of the statute. * * *

The Court of Appeal denied Michael's and Victoria's petitions for rehearing and, on July 30, 1987, the California Supreme Court denied discretionary review. On February 29, 1988, we noted probable jurisdiction of the present appeal. * * * Before us, Michael and Victoria both raise equal protection and due process challenges. We do not reach Michael's equal protection claim, however, as it was neither raised nor passed upon below. See *Bankers Life & Casualty Co. v. Crenshaw*, 486 U.S. 71, 108 S.Ct. 1645, 100 L.Ed.2d 62 (1988).

II

The California statute that is the subject of this litigation is, in substance, more than a century old. * * * In their present form, the substantive provisions of the statute are as follows:

"§ 621. Child of the marriage; notice of motion for blood tests

"(a) Except as provided in subdivision (b), the issue of a wife cohabiting with her husband, who is not impotent or sterile, is conclusively presumed to be a child of the marriage.

"(b) Notwithstanding the provisions of subdivision (a), if the court finds that the conclusions of all the experts, as disclosed by the evidence based upon blood tests performed pursuant to Chapter 2 (commencing with Section 890) of Division 7 are that the husband is not the father of the child, the question of paternity of the husband shall be resolved accordingly.

"(c) The notice of motion for blood tests under subdivision (b) may be raised by the husband not later than two years from the child's date of birth.

"(d) The notice of motion for blood tests under subdivision (b) may be raised by the mother of the child not later than two years from the child's date of birth if the child's biological father has filed an affidavit with the court acknowledging paternity of the child.

"(e) The provisions of subdivision (b) shall not apply to any case coming within the provisions of Section 7005 of the Civil Code [dealing with artificial insemination] or to any case in which the wife, with the consent of the husband, conceived by means of a surgical procedure."

III

We address first the claims of Michael. At the outset, it is necessary to clarify what he sought and what he was denied. California law, like nature itself, makes no provision for dual fatherhood. Michael was seeking to be declared *the* father of Victoria. The immediate benefit he evidently sought to obtain from that status was visitation rights. * * * But if Michael were successful in being declared the father, other rights would follow—most importantly, the right to be considered as the parent who should have custody, * * *. All parental rights, including visitation, were automatically denied by denying Michael status as the father. While Cal.Civ.Code Ann. § 4601 places it within the discretionary power of a court to award visitation rights to a nonparent, the Superior Court here, affirmed by the Court of Appeal, held that California law denies visitation, against the wishes of the mother, to a putative father who has been prevented by § 621 from establishing his paternity. * * *

Michael raises two related challenges to the constitutionality of § 621. First, he asserts that requirements of procedural due process prevent the State from terminating his liberty interest in his relationship with his child without affording him an opportunity to demonstrate his paternity in an evidentiary hearing. * * *

This Court has struck down as illegitimate certain "irrebuttable presumptions." See, *e.g., Stanley v. Illinois,* 405 U.S. 645, 92 S.Ct. 1208, 31 L.Ed.2d 551 (1972); *Vlandis v. Kline,* 412 U.S. 441, 93 S.Ct. 2230, 37 L.Ed.2d 63 (1973); *Cleveland Board of Education v. LaFleur,* 414 U.S. 632, 94 S.Ct. 791, 39 L.Ed.2d 52 (1974). Those holdings did not, however, rest upon *procedural* due process. A conclusive presumption does, of course, foreclose the person against whom it is invoked from demonstrating, in a particularized proceeding, that applying the presumption to him will in fact not further the lawful governmental policy the presumption is designed to effectuate. But the same can be said of any legal rule that establishes general classifications, whether framed in terms of a presumption or not. In this respect there is no difference between a rule which says that the marital husband shall be irrebuttably presumed to be the father, and a rule which says that the adulterous natural father shall not be recognized as the legal father. *Both* rules deny someone in Michael's situation a hearing on whether, in the particular circumstances of his case, California's policies would best be served by giving him parental rights. Thus, as many commentators have observed, * * * our "irrebuttable presumption" cases must ultimately be analyzed as calling into question not the adequacy of procedures but—like our cases involving classifications framed in other terms, see, *e.g., Craig v. Boren,* 429 U.S. 190, 97 S.Ct. 451, 50 L.Ed. 2d 397 (1976); *Carrington v. Rash,* 380 U.S. 89, 85 S.Ct. 775, 13 L.Ed.2d 675 (1965)—the adequacy of the "fit" between the classification and the policy that the classification serves. * * * We therefore reject Michael's procedural due process challenge and proceed to his substantive claim.

Michael contends as a matter of substantive due process that because he has established a parental relationship with Victoria, protection of Gerald's and Carole's marital union is an insufficient state interest to support termination of that relationship. This argument is, of course, predicated on the assertion that Michael has a constitutionally protected liberty interest in his relationship with Victoria.

It is an established part of our constitutional jurisprudence that the term "liberty" in the Due Process Clause extends beyond freedom from physical restraint. See, *e.g., Pierce v. Society of Sisters,* 268 U.S. 510, 45 S.Ct. 571, 69 L.Ed. 1070 (1925); *Meyer v. Nebraska,* 262 U.S. 390, 43 S.Ct. 625, 67 L.Ed. 1042 (1923). Without that core textual meaning as a limitation, defining the scope of the Due Process Clause "has at times been a treacherous field for this Court," giving "reason for concern lest the only limits to * * * judicial intervention become the predilections of those who happen at the time to be Members of this Court." *Moore v. East Cleveland,* 431 U.S. 494, 502, 97 S.Ct. 1932, 1937, 52 L.Ed.2d 531 (1977). * * * In an attempt to limit and guide interpretation of the

Clause, we have insisted not merely that the interest denominated as a "liberty" be "fundamental" (a concept that, in isolation, is hard to objectify), but also that it be an interest traditionally protected by our society.[2] As we have put it, the Due Process Clause affords only those protections "so rooted in the traditions and conscience of our people as to be ranked as fundamental." *Snyder v. Massachusetts,* 291 U.S. 97, 105, 54 S.Ct. 330, 332, 78 L.Ed. 674 (1934) (Cardozo, J.). Our cases reflect "continual insistence upon respect for the teachings of history [and] solid recognition of the basic values that underlie our society * * *." *Griswold v. Connecticut,* 381 U.S. 479, 501, 85 S.Ct. 1678, 1690, 14 L.Ed.2d 510 (1965) (Harlan, J., concurring in judgment).

This insistence that the asserted liberty interest be rooted in history and tradition is evident, as elsewhere, in our cases according constitutional protection to certain parental rights. Michael reads the landmark case of *Stanley v. Illinois,* * * * and the subsequent cases of *Quilloin v. Walcott,* * * * *Caban v. Mohammed,* * * * and *Lehr v. Robertson,* * * * as establishing that a liberty interest is created by biological fatherhood plus an established parental relationship—factors that exist in the present case as well. We think that distorts the rationale of those cases. As we view them, they rest not upon such isolated factors but upon the historic respect—indeed, sanctity would not be too strong a term—traditionally accorded to the relationships that develop within the unitary family.[3] * * * In *Stanley,* for example, we forbade the destruction of such a family when, upon the death of the mother, the state had sought to remove children from the custody of a father who had lived with and supported them and their mother for 18 years. As Justice Powell stated for the plurality in *Moore v. East Cleveland, supra,* 431 U.S., at 503, 97 S.Ct., at 1938: "Our decisions establish that the Constitution protects the sanctity of the family precisely because the institution of the family is deeply rooted in this Nation's history and tradition."

2. We do not understand what Justice Brennan has in mind by an interest "that society traditionally has thought important * * * without protecting it." * * * The protection need not take the form of an explicit constitutional provision or statutory guarantee, but it must at least exclude (all that is necessary to decide the present case) a societal tradition of enacting laws *denying* the interest. Nor do we understand why our practice of limiting the Due Process Clause to traditionally protected interests turns the clause "into a redundancy," * * *. Its purpose is to prevent future generations from lightly casting aside important traditional values—not to enable this Court to invent new ones.

3. Justice Brennan asserts that only "a pinched conception of 'the family'" would exclude Michael, Carole and Victoria from protection. * * * We disagree. The family unit accorded traditional respect in our society, which we have referred to as the "unitary family," is typified, of course, by the marital family, but also includes the household of unmarried parents and their children. Perhaps the concept can be expanded even beyond this, but it will bear no resemblance to traditionally respected relationships—and will thus cease to have any constitutional significance—if it is stretched so far as to include the relationship established between a married woman, her lover and their child, during a three-month sojourn in St. Thomas, or during a subsequent 8-month period when, if he happened to be in Los Angeles, he stayed with her and the child.

Thus, the legal issue in the present case reduces to whether the relationship between persons in the situation of Michael and Victoria has been treated as a protected family unit under the historic practices of our society, or whether on any other basis it has been accorded special protection. We think it impossible to find that it has. In fact, quite to the contrary, our traditions have protected the marital family (Gerald, Carole, and the child they acknowledge to be theirs) against the sort of claim Michael asserts.[4]

The presumption of legitimacy was a fundamental principle of the common law. H. Nicholas, Adulturine Bastardy 1 (1836). Traditionally, that presumption could be rebutted only by proof that a husband was incapable of procreation or had had no access to his wife during the relevant period. *Id.,* at 9–10 (citing Bracton, De Legibus et Consuetudinibus Angliae, bk. i, ch. 9, p. 6; bk. ii, ch. 29, p. 63, ch. 32, p. 70 (1569)). As explained by Blackstone, nonaccess could only be proved "if the husband be out of the kingdom of England (or, as the law somewhat loosely phrases it, *extra quatuor maria* [beyond the four seas]) for above nine months * * *." 1 Blackstone's Commentaries 456 (Chitty ed. 1826). And, under the common law both in England and here, "neither husband nor wife [could] be a witness to prove access or nonaccess." J. Schouler, Law of the Domestic Relations § 225, p. 306 (3d ed.1882); R. Graveson & F. Crane, A Century of Family Law: 1857–1957, p. 158 (1957). The primary policy rationale underlying the common law's severe restrictions on rebuttal of the presumption appears to have been an aversion to declaring children illegitimate, see Schouler, *supra,* § 225, at 306–307; M. Grossberg, Governing the Hearth 201 (1985), thereby depriving them of rights of inheritance and succession, 2 Kent's Commentaries 175 (1827), and likely making them wards of the state. A secondary policy concern was the interest in promoting the "peace and tranquillity of States and families," Schouler, *supra,* § 225, at 304, quoting Boullenois, Traité des Status, bk. 1, p. 62, a goal that is obviously impaired by facilitating suits against husband and wife asserting that their children are illegitimate. Even though, as bastardy laws became less harsh, "[j]udges in both [England and the United States] gradually widened the acceptable range of evidence that could be offered by spouses, and placed restraints on the 'four seas rule' * * * [,] the law retained a strong bias against ruling the children of married women illegitimate." Grossberg, *supra,* at 202.

---

4. Justice Brennan insists that in determining whether a liberty interest exists we must look at Michael's relationship with Victoria in isolation, without reference to the circumstance that Victoria's mother was married to someone else when the child was conceived, and that that woman and her husband wish to raise the child as their own. * * * We cannot imagine what compels this strange procedure of looking at the act which is assertedly the subject of a liberty interest in isolation from its effect upon other people—rather like inquiring whether there is a liberty interest in firing a gun where the case at hand happens to involve its discharge into another person's body. The logic of Justice Brennan's position leads to the conclusion that if Michael had begotten Victoria by rape, that fact would in no way affect his possession of a liberty interest in his relationship with her.

We have found nothing in the older sources, nor in the older cases, addressing specifically the power of the natural father to assert parental rights over a child born into a woman's existing marriage with another man. Since it is Michael's burden to establish that such a power (at least where the natural father has established a relationship with the child) is so deeply embedded within our traditions as to be a fundamental right, the lack of evidence alone might defeat his case. But the evidence shows that even in modern times—when, as we have noted, the rigid protection of the marital family has in other respects been relaxed—the ability of a person in Michael's position to claim paternity has not been generally acknowledged. For example, a 1957 annotation on the subject: "Who may dispute presumption of legitimacy of child conceived or born during wedlock," 53 ALR2d 572, shows three States (including California) with statutes limiting standing to the husband or wife and their descendants, one State (Louisiana) with a statute limiting it to the husband, two States (Florida and Texas) with judicial decisions limiting standing to the husband, and two States (Illinois and New York) with judicial decisions denying standing even to the mother. Not a single decision is set forth specifically according standing to the natural father, and "express indications of the nonexistence of any * * * limitation" upon standing were found only "in a few jurisdictions." *Id.*, at 579.

Moreover, even if it were clear that one in Michael's position generally possesses, and has generally always possessed, standing to challenge the marital child's legitimacy, that would still not establish Michael's case. As noted earlier, what is at issue here is not entitlement to a state pronouncement that Victoria was begotten by Michael. It is no conceivable denial of constitutional right for a State to decline to declare facts unless some legal consequence hinges upon the requested declaration. What Michael asserts here is a right to have himself declared the natural father *and thereby to obtain parental prerogatives*.[5] What he must establish, therefore, is not that our society has traditionally allowed a natural father in his circumstances to establish paternity, but that it has traditionally accorded such a father parental rights, or at least has not traditionally denied them. Even if the law in all States had always been that the entire world could challenge the marital presumption and obtain a declaration as to who was the natural father, that would not advance Michael's claim. Thus, it is ultimately irrelevant, even for purposes of determining *current* social attitudes towards the alleged substantive right Michael asserts, that

---

5. According to Justice Brennan, Michael does not claim—and in order to prevail here need not claim—a substantive right to maintain a parental relationship with Victoria, but merely the right to "a hearing on the issue" of his paternity. *Post,* at * * * n. 12. "Michael's challenge * * * does not depend," we are told, "on his ability ultimately to obtain visitation rights." * * * To be sure it does not depend upon his ability ultimately to *obtain* those rights, but it surely depends upon his *asserting a claim* to those rights, which is precisely what Justice Brennan denies. We cannot grasp the concept of a "right to a hearing" on the part of a person who claims no substantive entitlement that the hearing will assertedly vindicate.

the present law in a number of States appears to allow the natural father—including the natural father who has not established a relationship with the child—the theoretical power to rebut the marital presumption, see Note, Rebutting the Marital Presumption: A Developed Relationship Test, 88 Col.L.Rev. 369, 373 (1988). What counts is whether the States in fact award substantive parental rights to the natural father of a child conceived within and born into an extant marital union that wishes to embrace the child. We are not aware of a single case, old or new, that has done so. This is not the stuff of which fundamental rights qualifying as liberty interests are made.[6]

6. Justice Brennan criticizes our methodology in using historical traditions specifically relating to the rights of an adulterous natural father, rather than inquiring more generally "whether parenthood is an interest that historically has received our attention and protection." * * * There seems to us no basis for the contention that this methodology is "nove[l]," * * *. For example, in *Bowers v. Hardwick,* 478 U.S. 186, 106 S.Ct. 2841, 92 L.Ed.2d 140 (1986), we noted that at the time the Fourteenth Amendment was ratified all but 5 of the 37 States had criminal sodomy laws, that all 50 of the States had such laws prior to 1961, and that 24 States and the District of Columbia continued to have them; and we concluded from that record, regarding that very specific aspect of sexual conduct, that "to claim that a right to engage in such conduct is 'deeply rooted in this Nation's history and tradition' or 'implicit in the concept of ordered liberty' is, at best, facetious." *Id.,* at 194, 106 S Ct. at 2845. In *Roe v. Wade,* 410 U.S. 113, 93 S.Ct. 705, 35 L.Ed.2d 147 (1973), we spent about a fifth of our opinion negating the proposition that there was a long-standing tradition of laws proscribing abortion. *Id.,* at 129–141, 93 S.Ct., at 715–721.

We do not understand why, having rejected our focus upon the societal tradition regarding the natural father's rights vis-à-vis a child whose mother is married to another man, Justice Brennan would choose to focus instead upon "parenthood." Why should the relevant category not be even more general—perhaps "family relationships"; or "personal relationships"; or even "emotional attachments in general"? Though the dissent has no basis for the level of generality it would select, we do: We refer to the most specific level at which a relevant tradition protecting, or denying protection to, the asserted right can be identified. If, for example, there were no societal tradition, either way, regarding the rights of the natural father of a child adulterously conceived, we would have to consult, and (if possible) reason from, the traditions regarding natural fathers in general. But there is such a more specific tradition, and it unqualifiedly denies protection to such a parent.

One would think that Justice Brennan would appreciate the value of consulting the most specific tradition available, since he acknowledges that "[e]ven if we can agree * * * that 'family' and 'parenthood' are part of the good life, it is absurd to assume that we can agree on the content of those terms and destructive to pretend that we do." * * * Because such general traditions provide such imprecise guidance, they permit judges to dictate rather than discern the society's views. The need, if arbitrary decision-making is to be avoided, to adopt the most specific tradition as the point of reference—or at least to announce, as Justice Brennan declines to do, some other criterion for selecting among the innumerable relevant traditions that could be consulted—is well enough exemplified by the fact that in the present case Justice Brennan's opinion and Justice O'Connor's opinion, which disapproves this footnote, *both* appeal to tradition, but on the basis of the tradition they select reach opposite results. Although assuredly having the virtue (if it be that) of leaving judges free to decide as they think best when the unanticipated occurs, a rule of law that binds neither by text nor by any particular, identifiable tradition, is no rule of law at all.

Finally, we may note that this analysis is not inconsistent with the result in cases such as *Griswold v. Connecticut,* 381 U.S. 479, 85 S.Ct. 1678, 14 L.Ed.2d 510 (1965), or *Eisenstadt v. Baird,* 405 U.S. 438, 92 S.Ct. 1029, 31 L.Ed.2d 349 (1972). None of those cases acknowledged a longstanding and still extant societal tradition withholding the very right pronounced to be the subject of a liberty interest and then rejected it. Justice Brennan must do so here. In this case, the existence of such a tradition, continuing to the present day, refutes any

In *Lehr v. Robertson,* a case involving a natural father's attempt to block his child's adoption by the unwed mother's new husband, we observed that "[t]he significance of the biological connection is that it offers the natural father an opportunity that no other male possesses to develop a relationship with his offspring," 463 U.S., at 262, 103 S.Ct., at 2993, and we assumed that the Constitution might require some protection of that opportunity, *id.,* at 262–265, 103 S.Ct., at 2993–2995. Where, however, the child is born into an extant marital family, the natural father's unique opportunity conflicts with the similarly unique opportunity of the husband of the marriage; and it is not unconstitutional for the State to give categorical preference to the latter. In *Lehr* we quoted approvingly from Justice Stewart's dissent in *Caban v. Mohammed,* 441 U.S., at 397, 99 S.Ct., at 1770, to the effect that although "'[i]n some circumstances the actual relationship between father and child may suffice to create in the unwed father parental interests comparable to those of the married father,'" "'the absence of a legal tie with the mother may in such circumstances appropriately place a limit on whatever substantive constitutional claims might otherwise exist.'" 463 U.S., at 260, n. 16, 103 S.Ct., at 2993, n. 16. In accord with our traditions, a limit is also imposed by the circumstance that the mother is, at the time of the child's conception and birth, married to and cohabiting with another man, both of whom wish to raise the child as the offspring of their union.[7] It is a question of legislative policy and not constitutional law whether California will allow the presumed parenthood of a couple desiring to retain a child conceived within and born into their marriage to be rebutted.

We do not accept Justice Brennan's criticism that this result "squashes" the liberty that consists of "the freedom not to conform," * * *. It seems to us that reflects the erroneous view that there is only one side to this controversy—that one disposition can expand a "liberty" of sorts without contracting an equivalent "liberty" on the other side. Such a happy choice is rarely available. Here, to *provide* protection to an adulterous natural father is to *deny* protection to a

possible contention that the alleged right is "so rooted in the traditions and conscience of our people as to be ranked as fundamental," *Snyder v. Massachusetts,* 291 U.S. 97, 105, 54 S.Ct. 330, 332, 78 L.Ed. 674 (1934), or "implicit in the concept of ordered liberty," *Palko v. Connecticut,* 302 U.S. 319, 325, 58 S.Ct. 149, 152, 82 L.Ed. 288 (1937).

7. Justice Brennan chides us for thus limiting our holding to situations in which, as here, the husband and wife wish to raise her child jointly. The dissent believes that without this limitation we would be unable to "rely on the State's asserted interest in protecting the 'unitary family' in denying that Michael and Victoria have been deprived of liberty." * * *. As we have sought to make clear, however, and as the dissent elsewhere seems to understand, * * * we rest our decision not upon our independent "balancing" of such interests, but upon the absence of any constitutionally protected right to legal parentage on the part of an adulterous natural father in Michael's situation, as evidenced by long tradition. That tradition reflects a "balancing" that has already been made by society itself. We limit our pronouncement to the relevant facts of this case because it is at least possible that our traditions lead to a different conclusion with regard to adulterous fathering of a child whom the marital parents do not wish to raise as their own. It seems unfair for those who disagree with our holding to include among their criticisms that we have not extended the holding more broadly.

marital father, and vice versa. If Michael has a "freedom not to conform" (whatever that means), Gerald must equivalently have a "freedom to conform." One of them will pay a price for asserting that "freedom"—Michael by being unable to act as father of the child he has adulterously begotten, or Gerald by being unable to preserve the integrity of the traditional family unit he and Victoria have established. Our disposition does not choose between these two "freedoms," but leaves that to the people of California. Justice Brennan's approach chooses one of them as the constitutional imperative, on no apparent basis except that the unconventional is to be preferred.

IV

* * *

The judgment of the California Court of Appeal is

Affirmed.

JUSTICE O'CONNOR, with whom JUSTICE KENNEDY joins, concurring in part.

I concur in all but footnote 6 of Justice Scalia's opinion. This footnote sketches a mode of historical analysis to be used when identifying liberty interests protected by the Due Process Clause of the Fourteenth Amendment that may be somewhat inconsistent with our past decisions in this area. See *Griswold v. Connecticut,* 381 U.S. 479, 85 S.Ct. 1678, 14 L.Ed.2d 510 (1965); *Eisenstadt v. Baird,* 405 U.S. 438, 92 S.Ct. 1029, 31 L.Ed.2d 349 (1972). On occasion the Court has characterized relevant traditions protecting asserted rights at levels of generality that might not be "the most specific level" available. * * * See *Loving v. Virginia,* 388 U.S. 1, 12, 87 S.Ct. 1817, 1823, 18 L.Ed.2d 1010 (1967); *Turner v. Safley,* 482 U.S. 78, 94, 107 S.Ct. 2254, 2265, 96 L.Ed. 2d 64 (1987); cf. *United States v. Stanley,* 483 U.S. 669, 709, 107 S.Ct. 3054, ___, 97 L.Ed.2d 550 (1987) (opinion concurring in part and dissenting in part). I would not foreclose the unanticipated by the prior imposition of a single mode of historical analysis. *Poe v. Ullman,* 367 U.S. 497, 542, 544, 81 S.Ct. 1752, 1776, 1777, 6 L.Ed.2d 989 (1961) (Harlan, J., dissenting).

JUSTICE STEVENS, concurring in the judgment.

As I understand this case, it raises two different questions about the validity of California's statutory scheme. First, is Cal.Evid.Code Ann. § 621 (West Supp.1989) unconstitutional because it prevents Michael and Victoria from obtaining a judicial determination that he is her biological father—even if no legal rights would be affected by that determination? Second, does the California statute deny appellants a fair opportunity to prove that Victoria's best interests would be served by granting Michael visitation rights?

On the first issue I agree with Justice Scalia that the Federal Constitution imposes no obligation upon a State to "declare facts unless some legal consequence hinges upon the requested declaration." * * * "The actions of judges neither create nor sever genetic bonds."

Lehr v. Robertson, 463 U.S. 248, 261, 103 S.Ct. 2985, 2993, 77 L.Ed.2d 614 (1983).

On the second issue I do not agree with Justice Scalia's analysis. He seems to reject the possibility that a natural father might ever have a constitutionally protected interest in his relationship with a child whose mother was married to and cohabiting with another man at the time of the child's conception and birth. I think cases like *Stanley v. Illinois,* 405 U.S. 645, 92 S.Ct. 1208, 31 L.Ed.2d 551 (1972) and *Caban v. Mohammed,* 441 U.S. 380, 99 S.Ct. 1760, 60 L.Ed.2d 297 (1979), demonstrate that enduring "family" relationships may develop in unconventional settings. I therefore would not foreclose the possibility that a constitutionally protected relationship between a natural father and his child might exist in a case like this. Indeed, I am willing to assume for the purpose of deciding this case that Michael's relationship with Victoria is strong enough to give him a constitutional right to try to convince a trial judge that Victoria's best interest would be served by granting him visitation rights. I am satisfied, however, that the California statute, as applied in this case, gave him that opportunity.

Section 4601 of the California Civil Code Annotated (West Supp. 1989) provides:

> "[R]easonable visitation rights [shall be awarded] to a parent unless it is shown that the visitation would be detrimental to the best interests of the child. In the discretion of the court, reasonable visitation rights may be granted *to any other person having an interest in the welfare of the child.*" (Emphasis added.)

The presumption established by § 621 denied Michael the benefit of the first sentence of § 4601 because, as a matter of law, he is not a "parent." It does not, however, prevent him from proving that he is an "other person having an interest in the welfare of the child." On its face, therefore, the statute plainly gave the trial judge the authority to grant Michael "reasonable visitation rights."

I recognize that my colleagues have interpreted § 621 as creating an absolute bar that would prevent a California trial judge from regarding the natural father as either a "parent" within the meaning of the first sentence of § 4601 *or* as "any other person" within the meaning of the second sentence. * * * (BRENNAN, J., dissenting). That is not only an unnatural reading of the statute's plain language, but it is also not consistent with the California courts' reading of the statute. * * *

* * * [I]n this case, the trial judge not only found the conclusive presumption applicable, but also separately considered the effect of § 4601 and expressly found "that, at the present time, it is not in the best interests of the child that the Plaintiff have visitation. The Court believes that the existence of two (2) 'fathers' as male authority figures will confuse the child and be counter-productive to her best interests."

* * *

Under the circumstances of the case before us, Michael was given a fair opportunity to show that he is Victoria's natural father, that he had developed a relationship with her, and that her interests would be served by granting him visitation rights. On the other hand, the record also shows that after its rather shaky start, the marriage between Carole and Gerald developed a stability that now provides Victoria with a loving and harmonious family home. In the circumstances of this case, I find nothing fundamentally unfair about the exercise of a judge's discretion that, in the end, allows the mother to decide whether her child's best interest would be served by allowing the natural father visitation privileges. Because I am convinced that the trial judge had the authority under state law both to hear Michael's plea for visitation rights and to grant him such rights if Victoria's best interests so warranted, I am satisfied that the California statutory scheme is consistent with the Due Process Clause of the Fourteenth Amendment.

I therefore concur in the Court's judgment of affirmance.

JUSTICE BRENNAN, with whom JUSTICE MARSHALL and JUSTICE BLACKMUN join, dissenting.

In a case that has yielded so many opinions as has this one, it is fruitful to begin by emphasizing the common ground shared by a majority of this Court. Five Members of the Court refuse to foreclose "the possibility that a natural father might ever have a constitutionally protected interest in his relationship with a child whose mother was married to and cohabiting with another man at the time of the child's conception and birth." * * * (Stevens, J., concurring in judgment). Five Justices agree that the flaw inhering in a conclusive presumption that terminates a constitutionally protected interest without any hearing whatsoever is a *procedural* one. * * * (White, J., dissenting); * * * (Stevens, J., concurring in judgment). Four Members of the Court agree that Michael H. has a liberty interest in his relationship with Victoria, * * * (White, J., dissenting), and one assumes for purposes of this case that he does, * * * (Stevens, J., concurring in judgment).

In contrast, only two Members of the Court fully endorse Justice Scalia's view of the proper method of analyzing questions arising under the Due Process Clause. * * * (O'Connor, J., concurring in part). Nevertheless, because the plurality opinion's exclusively historical analysis portends a significant and unfortunate departure from our prior cases and from sound constitutional decisionmaking, I devote a substantial portion of my discussion to it.

I

Once we recognized that the "liberty" protected by the Due Process Clause of the Fourteenth Amendment encompasses more than freedom from bodily restraint, today's plurality opinion emphasizes, the concept was cut loose from one natural limitation on its meaning. This innovation paved the way, so the plurality hints, for judges to substitute their own preferences for those of elected officials. Dissatisfied with this supposedly unbridled and uncertain state of affairs, the plurality casts about for another limitation on the concept of liberty.

It finds this limitation in "tradition." Apparently oblivious to the fact that this concept can be as malleable and as elusive as "liberty" itself, the plurality pretends that tradition places a discernible border around the Constitution. The pretense is seductive; it would be comforting to believe that a search for "tradition" involves nothing more idiosyncratic or complicated than poring through dusty volumes on American history. Yet, as Justice White observed in his dissent in *Moore v. East Cleveland*, 431 U.S. 494, 549, 97 S.Ct. 1932, 1961, 52 L.Ed. 2d 531 (1977): "What the deeply rooted traditions of the country are is arguable." Indeed, wherever I would begin to look for an interest "deeply rooted in the country's traditions," one thing is certain: I would not stop (as does the plurality) at Bracton, or Blackstone, or Kent, or even the American Law Reports in conducting my search. Because reasonable people can disagree about the content of particular traditions, and because they can disagree even about which traditions are relevant to the definition of "liberty," the plurality has not found the objective boundary that it seeks.

Even if we could agree, moreover, on the content and significance of particular traditions, we still would be forced to identify the point at which a tradition becomes firm enough to be relevant to our definition of liberty and the moment at which it becomes too obsolete to be relevant any longer. The plurality supplies no objective means by which we might make these determinations. Indeed, as soon as the plurality sees signs that the tradition upon which it bases its decision (the laws denying putative fathers like Michael standing to assert paternity) is crumbling, it shifts ground and says that the case has nothing to do with that tradition, after all. "What is at issue here," the plurality asserts after canvassing the law on paternity suits, "is not entitlement to a state pronouncement that Victoria was begotten by Michael." * * * But that is precisely what is at issue here, and the plurality's last-minute denial of this fact dramatically illustrates the subjectivity of its own analysis.

* * *

It is not that tradition has been irrelevant to our prior decisions. Throughout our decisionmaking in this important area runs the theme that certain interests and practices—freedom from physical restraint, marriage, childbearing, childrearing, and others—form the core of our definition of "liberty." Our solicitude for these interests is partly the result of the fact that the Due Process Clause would seem an empty promise if it did not protect them, and partly the result of the historical and traditional importance of these interests in our society. In deciding cases arising under the Due Process Clause, therefore, we have considered whether the concrete limitation under consideration impermissibly impinges upon one of these more generalized interests.

Today's plurality, however, does not ask whether parenthood is an interest that historically has received our attention and protection; the answer to that question is too clear for dispute. Instead, the plurality asks whether the specific variety of parenthood under consideration—a natural father's relationship with a child whose mother is married to another man—has enjoyed such protection.

If we had looked to tradition with such specificity in past cases, many a decision would have reached a different result. Surely the use of contraceptives by unmarried couples, *Eisenstadt v. Baird,* 405 U.S. 438, 92 S.Ct. 1029, 31 L.Ed.2d 349 (1972), or even by married couples, *Griswold v. Connecticut,* 381 U.S. 479, 85 S.Ct. 1678, 14 L.Ed.2d 510 (1965); the freedom from corporal punishment in schools, *Ingraham v. Wright,* 430 U.S. 651, 97 S.Ct. 1401, 51 L.Ed.2d 711 (1977); the freedom from an arbitrary transfer from a prison to a psychiatric institution, *Vitek v. Jones,* 445 U.S. 480, 100 S.Ct. 1254, 63 L.Ed.2d 552 (1980); and even the right to raise one's natural but illegitimate children, *Stanley v. Illinois,* 405 U.S. 645, 92 S.Ct. 1208, 31 L.Ed.2d 551 (1972), were not "interest[s] traditionally protected by our society," * * * at the time of their consideration by this Court. If we had asked, therefore, in *Eisenstadt, Griswold, Ingraham, Vitek,* or *Stanley* itself whether the specific interest under consideration had been traditionally protected, the answer would have been a resounding "no." That we did not ask this question in those cases highlights the novelty of the interpretive method that the plurality opinion employs today.

The plurality's interpretive method is more than novel; it is misguided. It ignores the good reasons for limiting the role of "tradition" in interpreting the Constitution's deliberately capacious language. In the plurality's constitutional universe, we may not take notice of the fact that the original reasons for the conclusive presumption of paternity are out of place in a world in which blood tests can prove virtually beyond a shadow of a doubt who sired a particular child and in which the fact of illegitimacy no longer plays the burdensome and stigmatizing role it once did. Nor, in the plurality's world, may we deny "tradition" its full scope by pointing out that the rationale for the conventional rule has changed over the years, as has the rationale for Cal.Evid.Code Ann. § 621 (West Supp.1989);[1] instead, our task is simply to identify a rule denying the asserted interest and not to ask whether the basis for that rule—which is the true reflection of the values undergirding it—has changed too often or too recently to call the rule embodying that rationale a "tradition." Moreover, by describing the decisive question as whether Michael and Victoria's interest is one that has been "traditionally *protected by* our society," * * * (emphasis added), rather than one that society traditionally has thought

---

1. See *In re Marriage of Stephen and Sharyne B.,* 124 Cal.App.3d 524, 528–531, 177 Cal.Rptr. 429, 431–433 (1981) (noting that California courts initially justified conclusive presumption of paternity on the ground that biological paternity was impossible to prove, but that the preservation of family integrity became the rule's paramount justification when paternity tests became reliable).

important (with or without protecting it), and by suggesting that our sole function is to "*discern* the society's views," * * *, n. 6 (emphasis added), the plurality acts as if the only purpose of the Due Process Clause is to confirm the importance of interests already protected by a majority of the States. Transforming the protection afforded by the Due Process Clause into a redundancy mocks those who, with care and purpose, wrote the Fourteenth Amendment.

In construing the Fourteenth Amendment to offer shelter only to those interests specifically protected by historical practice, moreover, the plurality ignores the kind of society in which our Constitution exists. We are not an assimilative, homogeneous society, but a facilitative, pluralistic one, in which we must be willing to abide someone else's unfamiliar or even repellant practice because the same tolerant impulse protects our own idiosyncracies. Even if we can agree, therefore, that "family" and "parenthood" are part of the good life, it is absurd to assume that we can agree on the content of those terms and destructive to pretend that we do. In a community such as ours, "liberty" must include the freedom not to conform. The plurality today squashes this freedom by requiring specific approval from history before protecting anything in the name of liberty.

The document that the plurality construes today is unfamiliar to me. It is not the living charter that I have taken to be our Constitution; it is instead a stagnant, archaic, hidebound document steeped in the prejudices and superstitions of a time long past. *This* Constitution does not recognize that times change, does not see that sometimes a practice or rule outlives its foundations. I cannot accept an interpretive method that does such violence to the charter that I am bound by oath to uphold.

II

The plurality's reworking of our interpretive approach is all the more troubling because it is unnecessary. This is not a case in which we face a "new" kind of interest, one that requires us to consider for the first time whether the Constitution protects it. On the contrary, we confront an interest—that of a parent and child in their relationship with each other—that was among the first that this Court acknowledged in its cases defining the "liberty" protected by the Constitution, * * * and I think I am safe in saying that no one doubts the wisdom or validity of those decisions. Where the interest under consideration is a parent-child relationship, we need not ask, over and over again, whether that interest is one that society traditionally protects.

* * *

On four prior occasions, we have considered whether unwed fathers have a constitutionally protected interest in their relationships with their children. See *Stanley v. Illinois*, * * * *Quilloin v. Walcott*, * * * *Caban v. Mohammed*, * * * and *Lehr v. Robertson*, * * *. Though different in factual and legal circumstances, these cases have produced a unifying theme: although an unwed father's biological link to his child does not, in and of itself, guarantee him a constitutional stake in his relationship with that child, such a link combined with a substantial parent-child relationship will do so.[2] "When an unwed father demonstrates a full commitment to the responsibilities of parenthood by 'com[ing] forward to participate in the rearing of his child,' * * * his interest in personal contact with his child acquires substantial protection under the Due Process Clause. At that point it may be said that he 'act[s] as a father toward his children.'" *Lehr v. Robertson, supra*, at 261, 103 S.Ct., at 2993, quoting *Caban v. Mohammed, supra*, 441 U.S., at 392, 389, n. 7, 99 S.Ct., at 1768, 1766, n. 7. This commitment is why Mr. Stanley and Mr. Caban won; why Mr. Quilloin and Mr. Lehr lost; and why Michael H. should prevail today. Michael H. is almost certainly Victoria D.'s natural father, has lived with her as her father, has contributed to her support, and has from the beginning sought to strengthen and maintain his relationship with her.

Claiming that the intent of these cases was to protect the "unitary family," * * * the plurality waves *Stanley, Quilloin, Caban,* and *Lehr* aside. In evaluating the plurality's dismissal of these precedents, it is essential to identify its conception of the "unitary family." If, by acknowledging that *Stanley, et al.*, sought to protect "the relationships that develop within the unitary family," * * * the plurality meant only to describe the kinds of relationships that develop when parents and children live together (formally or informally) as a family, then the plurality's vision of these cases would be correct. But that is not the plurality's message. Though it pays lip service to the idea that marriage is not the crucial fact in denying constitutional protection to the relationship between Michael and Victoria, *ante*, at * * * n. 3, the plurality cannot mean what it says.

The evidence is undisputed that Michael, Victoria, and Carole did live together as a family; that is, they shared the same household, Victoria called Michael "Daddy," Michael contributed to Victoria's support, and he is eager to continue his relationship with her. Yet they are not, in the plurality's view, a "unitary family," whereas Gerald, Carole, and Victoria do compose such a family. The only difference between these two sets of relationships, however, is the fact of marriage. The plurality, indeed, expressly recognizes that marriage is the critical fact in denying Michael a constitutionally protected stake in his relationship with Victoria: no fewer than six times, the plurality refers to Michael as the "*adulterous* natural father." * * * However, the very premise of *Stanley* and the cases following it is that marriage is not decisive in answering the question whether the Constitution protects the parental relationship under consideration. These cases are, after all, important precisely because they involve the rights of

---

2. The plurality's claim that "the logic of [my] position leads to the conclusion that if Michael had begotten Victoria by rape, that fact would in no way affect his possession of a liberty interest in his relationship with her," *ante*, at * * * n. 4, ignores my observation that a mere biological connection is insufficient to establish a liberty interest on the part of an unwed father.

unwed fathers. It is important to remember, moreover, that in *Quilloin, Caban,* and *Lehr,* the putative father's demands would have disrupted a "unitary family" as the plurality defines it; in each case, the husband of the child's mother sought to adopt the child over the objections of the natural father. Significantly, our decisions in those cases in no way relied on the need to protect the marital family. Hence the plurality's claim that *Stanley, Quilloin, Caban,* and *Lehr* were about the "unitary family," as that family is defined by today's plurality, is surprising indeed.

The plurality's exclusive rather than inclusive definition of the "unitary family" is out of step with other decisions as well. This pinched conception of "the family," crucial as it is in rejecting Michael and Victoria's claim of a liberty interest, is jarring in light of our many cases preventing the States from denying important interests or statuses to those whose situations do not fit the government's narrow view of the family. From *Loving v. Virginia,* 388 U.S. 1, 87 S.Ct. 1817, 18 L.Ed.2d 1010 (1967), to *Levy v. Louisiana,* 391 U.S. 68, 88 S.Ct. 1509, 20 L.Ed.2d 436 (1968), and *Glona v. American Guarantee & Liability Ins. Co.,* 391 U.S. 73, 88 S.Ct. 1515, 20 L.Ed.2d 441 (1968), and from *Gomez v. Perez,* 409 U.S. 535, 93 S.Ct. 872, 35 L.Ed.2d 56 (1973), to *Moore v. East Cleveland,* 431 U.S. 494, 97 S.Ct. 1932, 52 L.Ed.2d 531 (1977), we have declined to respect a State's notion, as manifested in its allocation of privileges and burdens, of what the family should be. Today's rhapsody on the "unitary family" is out of tune with such decisions.

The plurality's focus on the "unitary family" is misdirected for another reason. It conflates the question whether a liberty interest exists with the question what procedures may be used to terminate or curtail it. It is no coincidence that we never before have looked at the relationship that the unwed father seeks to disrupt, rather than the one he seeks to preserve, in determining whether he has a liberty interest in his relationship with his child. To do otherwise is to allow the State's interest in terminating the relationship to play a role in defining the "liberty" that is protected by the Constitution. According to our established framework under the Due Process Clause, however, we first ask whether the person claiming constitutional protection has an interest that the Constitution recognizes; if we find that she does, we next consider the State's interest in limiting the extent of the procedures that will attend the deprivation of that interest. See, *e.g., Logan v. Zimmerman Brush Co.,* 455 U.S. 422, 428, 102 S.Ct. 1148, 1153, 71 L.Ed.2d 265 (1982). By stressing the need to preserve the "unitary family" and by focusing not just on the relationship between Michael and Victoria but on their "situation" as well, * * * today's plurality opinion takes both of these steps at once.

The plurality's premature consideration of California's interests is evident from its careful limitation of its holding to those cases in which "the mother is, at the time of the child's conception and birth, married to and cohabiting with another man, *both of whom wish to raise the child as the offspring of their union."* * * * (emphasis added). See also * * * (describing Michael's liberty interest as the "substantive parental rights [of] the natural father of a child conceived within and born into an *extant marital union that wishes to embrace the child* "). The high-lighted language suggests that if Carole or Gerald alone wished to raise Victoria, or if both were dead and the State wished to raise her, Michael and Victoria might be found to have a liberty interest in their relationship with each other. But that would be to say that whether Michael and Victoria have a liberty interest varies with the State's interest in recognizing that interest, for it is the State's interest in protecting the marital family—and not Michael and Victoria's interest in their relationship with each other—that varies with the status of Carole and Gerald's relationship. It is a bad day for due process when the State's interest in terminating a parent-child relationship is reason to conclude that that relationship is not part of the "liberty" protected by the Fourteenth Amendment.

The plurality has wedged itself between a rock and a hard place. If it limits its holding to those situations in which a wife and husband wish to raise the child together, then it necessarily takes the State's interest into account in defining "liberty"; yet if it extends that approach to circumstances in which the marital union already has been dissolved, then it may no longer rely on the State's asserted interest in protecting the "unitary family" in denying that Michael and Victoria have been deprived of liberty.

The plurality's confusion about the proper analysis of claims involving procedural due process also becomes obvious when one examines the plurality's shift in emphasis from the putative father's standing to his ability to obtain parental prerogatives. * * * In announcing that what matters is not the father's ability to claim paternity, but his ability to obtain "substantive parental rights," * * * the plurality turns procedural due process upside down. Michael's challenge in this Court does not depend on his ability ultimately to obtain visitation rights; it would be strange indeed if, before one could be granted a hearing, one were required to prove that one would prevail on the merits. The point of procedural due process is to give the litigant a fair chance at prevailing, not to ensure a particular substantive outcome. Nor does Michael's challenge depend on the success of fathers like him in obtaining parental rights in past cases; procedural due process is, by and large, an individual guarantee, not one that should depend on the success or failure of prior cases having little or nothing to do with the claimant's own suit.

III

Because the plurality decides that Michael and Victoria have no liberty interest in their relationship with each other, it need consider neither the effect of § 621 on their relationship nor the State's interest in bringing about that effect. It is obvious, however, that the effect of § 621 is to terminate the relationship between Michael and Victoria before affording any hearing whatsoever on the issue whether Michael is Victoria's father. This refusal to hold a hearing is properly analyzed under our procedural due process cases, which instruct us to consider the State's interest in curtailing the procedures accompanying the termination of a constitutionally protected interest. California's interest, minute in comparison with a father's interest in his relationship with his child, cannot justify its refusal to hear Michael out on his claim that he is Victoria's father.

A

We must first understand the nature of the challenged statute: it is a law that stubbornly insists that Gerald is Victoria's father, in the face of evidence showing a 98 percent probability that her father is Michael.[6] What Michael wants is a chance to show that he is Victoria's father. By depriving him of this opportunity, California prevents Michael from taking advantage of the best-interest standard embodied in § 4601 of California's Civil Code, which directs that *parents* be given visitation rights unless "the visitation would be detrimental to the best interests of the child." Cal.Civ.Code Ann. § 4601 (West Supp.1989).

As interpreted by the California courts, however, § 621 not only deprives Michael of the benefits of the best-interest standard; it also deprives him of any chance of maintaining his relationship with the child he claims to be his own.

* * *

Section 621 as construed by the California courts thus cuts off the relationship between Michael and Victoria—a liberty interest protected by the Due Process Clause—without affording the least bit of process. This case, in other words, involves a conclusive presumption that is used to terminate a constitutionally protected interest—the kind of rule that our preoccupation with procedural fairness has caused us to condemn. See, *e.g., Vlandis v. Kline,* 412 U.S. 441, 93 S.Ct. 2230, 37 L.Ed.2d 63 (1973); *Cleveland Board of Education v. LaFleur,* 414 U.S. 632, 94 S.Ct. 791, 39 L.Ed.2d 52 (1974); *Weinberger v. Salfi,* 422 U.S. 749, 770–772, 95 S.Ct. 2457, 2469–2470, 45 L.Ed.2d 522 (1975).

Gerald D. and the plurality turn a blind eye to the true nature of § 621 by protesting that, instead of being a conclusive presumption, it is a "substantive rule of law." * * * This facile observation cannot save § 621. It may be that all conclusive presumptions are, in a sense, substantive rules of law; but § 621 then belongs in that special category of substantive rules that presumes a fact relevant to a certain class of litigation, and it is that feature that renders § 621 suspect under our prior cases. To put the point differently, a conclusive presumption takes the form of "no X's are Y's," and is typically accompanied by a rule such as, " * * * and only Y's may obtain a driver's license."

---

6. Justice Stevens' claim that "Michael was given a fair opportunity to show that he is Victoria's natural father," * * * ignores the fact that this case is before us precisely because California law refuses to allow men like Michael such an opportunity.

(There would be no need for the presumption unless something hinged on the fact presumed.) Ignoring the fact that § 621 takes the form of "no X's are Y's," Gerald D. and the plurality fix upon the rule following § 621—only Y's may assert parental rights—and call § 621 a substantive rule of law. This strategy ignores both the form and the effect of § 621.

* * *

B

The question before us, therefore, is whether California has an interest so powerful that it justifies granting Michael *no* hearing before terminating his parental rights.

* * *

The purported state interests here, * * * stem primarily from the State's antagonism to Michael and Victoria's constitutionally protected interest in their relationship with each other * * *. Gerald D. explains that § 621 promotes marriage, maintains the relationship between the child and presumed father, and protects the integrity and privacy of the matrimonial family. * * * It is not, however, § 621, but the best-interest principle, that protects a stable marital relationship and maintains the relationship between the child and presumed father. These interests are implicated by the determination of who gets parental rights, *not* by the determination of who is the father; in the hearing that Michael seeks, parental rights are not the issue. Of the objectives that Gerald stresses, therefore, only the preservation of family privacy is promoted by the refusal to hold a hearing itself. Yet § 621 furthers even this objective only partially.

Gerald D. gives generous proportions to the privacy protected by § 621 asserting that this provision protects a couple like Gerald and Carole from answering questions on such matters as "their sexual habits and practices with each other and outside their marriage, their finances, and their thoughts, beliefs, and opinions concerning their relationship with each other and with Victoria." * * * Yet invalidation of § 621 would not, as Gerald suggests, subject Gerald and Carole to public scrutiny of all of these private matters. Family finances and family dynamics are relevant, not to paternity, but to the best interests of the child—and the child's best interests are not, as I have stressed, in issue at the hearing that Michael seeks. The only private matter touching on the paternity presumed by § 621 is the married couple's sex life. Even there, § 621 as interpreted by California's intermediate appellate courts pre-empts inquiry into a couple's sexual relations, since "cohabitation" consists simply of living under the same roof together; the wife and husband need not even share the same bed. See, *e.g., Vincent B. v. Joan R.,* 126 Cal.App.3d 619, 179 Cal.Rptr. 9 (1982). Admittedly, § 621 does not foreclose inquiry into the husband's fertility or virility—matters that are ordinarily thought of as the couple's private business. In this day and age, however, proving paternity by asking intimate and detailed questions about a couple's relationship would be decidedly anachronistic. Who on earth would choose this method of establishing fatherhood when blood tests prove it with far more certainty and far less fuss? The State's purported interest in protecting matrimonial privacy thus does not measure up to Michael and Victoria's interest in maintaining their relationship with each other.

Make no mistake: to say that the State must provide Michael with a hearing to prove his paternity is not to express any opinion of the ultimate state of affairs between Michael and Victoria and Carole and Gerald. In order to change the current situation among these people, Michael first must convince a court that he is Victoria's father, and even if he is able to do this, he will be denied visitation rights if that would be in Victoria's best interests. See Cal.Civ.Code Ann. § 4601 (West Supp.1989). It is elementary that a determination that a State must afford procedures before it terminates a given right is not a prediction about the end result of those procedures.[12]

IV

The atmosphere surrounding today's decision is one of make-believe. Beginning with the suggestion that the situation confronting us here does not repeat itself every day in every corner of the country, * * * moving on to the claim that it is tradition alone that supplies the details of the liberty that the Constitution protects, and passing finally to the notion that the Court always has recognized a cramped vision of "the family," today's decision lets stand California's pronouncement that Michael—whom blood tests show to a 98 percent probability to be Victoria's father—is not Victoria's father. When and if the Court awakes to reality, it will find a world very different from the one it expects.

JUSTICE WHITE, with whom JUSTICE BRENNAN joins, dissenting.

California law, as the plurality describes it, * * * tells us that, except in limited circumstances, California declares it to be "*irrelevant* for paternity purposes whether a child conceived during and born into a lawful marriage was begotten by someone other than the husband," (emphasis in original). This I do not accept, for the fact that Michael H. is the biological father of Victoria is to me highly relevant to

---

12. The plurality's failure to see this point causes it to misstate Michael's claim in the following way: "Michael contends as a matter of substantive due process that because he has established a parental relationship with Victoria, protection of Gerald's and Carole's marital union is an insufficient state interest to support termination of that relationship." * * * Michael does not claim that the State may not, under any circumstance, terminate his relationship with Victoria; instead, he simply claims that the State may not do so without affording him a hearing on the issue—paternity—that it deems vital to the question whether their relationship may be discontinued. The plurality makes Michael's claim easier to knock down by turning it into such a big target.

The plurality's misunderstanding of Michael's claim also leads to its assertion that "to *provide* protection to an adulterous natural father is to *deny* protection to a marital father." * * * To allow Michael a chance to prove his paternity, however, in no way guarantees that Gerald's relationship with Victoria will be changed.

whether he has rights, as a father or otherwise, with respect to the child. Because I believe that Michael H. has a liberty interest that cannot be denied without due process of the law, I must dissent.

I

Like Justices Brennan, Marshall, Blackmun and Stevens, I do not agree with the plurality opinion's conclusion that a natural father can never "have a constitutionally protected interest in his relationship with a child whose mother was married to and cohabiting with another man at the time of the child's conception and birth." * * * Prior cases here have recognized the liberty interest of a father in his relationship with his child. In none of these cases did we indicate that the fathers' rights were dependent on the marital status of the mother or biological father. The basic principle enunciated in the Court's unwed father cases is that an unwed father who has demonstrated a sufficient commitment to his paternity by way of personal, financial, or custodial responsibilities has a protected liberty interest in a relationship with his child.

* * *

In the case now before us, Michael H. is not a father unwilling to assume his responsibilities as a parent. To the contrary, he is a father who has asserted his interests in raising and providing for his child since the very time of the child's birth. In contrast to the father in *Lehr,* Michael H. had begun to develop a relationship with his daughter. There is no dispute on this point. Michael contributed to the child's support. Michael and Victoria lived together (albeit intermittently, given Carole's itinerant lifestyle.) There is a personal and emotional relationship between Michael and Victoria, who grew up calling him "Daddy." Michael H. held Victoria out as his daughter and contributed to the child's financial support. (Even appellee concedes that Michael has "made greater efforts and had more success in establishing a father-child relationship" than did Mr. Lehr. * * * The mother has never denied, and indeed has admitted that Michael H. is Victoria's father. *Lehr* was predicated on the absence of a substantial relationship between the man and the child and emphasized the "difference between the developed parent-child relationship that was implicated in *Stanley* and *Caban,* and the potential relationship involved in *Quilloin* and [*Lehr*]." * * * The facts in this case satisfy the *Lehr* criteria, which focused on the relationship between father and child, not on the relationship between father and mother. Under *Lehr* a "mere biological relationship" is not enough, but in light of Carole's vicissitudes, what more could Michael H. have done? It is clear enough that Michael H. more than meets the mark in establishing the constitutionally protected liberty interest discussed in *Lehr* and recognized in *Stanley v. Illinois, supra,* and *Caban v. Mohammed, supra.* He therefore has a liberty interest entitled to protection under the Due Process Clause of the Fourteenth Amendment.

II

California plainly denies Michael this protection, by refusing him the opportunity to rebut the State's presumption that the mother's husband is the father of the child. California law not only deprives Michael H. of a legal parent-child relationship with his daughter Victoria but even denies him the opportunity to introduce blood-test evidence to rebut the demonstrable fiction that Gerald is Victoria's father. Unlike *Lehr,* Michael H. has not been denied notice. He has, most definitely, however, been denied any real opportunity to be heard.
* * * The Court gives its blessing to § 621 by relying on the State's asserted interests in the integrity of the family (defined as Carole and Gerald) and in protecting Victoria from the stigma of illegitimacy and by balancing away Michael's interest in establishing that he is the father of the child.

The interest in protecting a child from the social stigma of illegitimacy lacks any real connection to the facts of a case where a father is seeking to establish, rather than repudiate, paternity. The "stigma of illegitimacy" argument harks back to ancient common law when there were no blood tests to ascertain that the husband could not "by the laws of nature" be the child's father. Judicial process refused to declare that a child born in wedlock was illegitimate unless the proof was positive. The only such proof was physical absence or impotency. But we have now clearly recognized the use of blood tests as an authoritative means of evaluating allegations of paternity. See, *e.g., Little v. Streater,* 452 U.S. 1, 6–7, 101 S.Ct. 2202, 2205–2206, 68 L.Ed.2d 627 (1981). I see no reason to debate the plurality's multilingual explorations into "spousal nonaccess" and ancient policy concerns behind bastardy laws. It may be true that a child conceived in an extramarital relationship would be considered a "bastard" in the literal sense of the word, but whatever stigma remains in today's society is far less compelling in the context of a child of a married mother, especially when there is a father asserting paternity and seeking a relationship with his child. It is hardly rare in this world of divorce and remarriage for a child to live with the "father" to whom her mother is married, and still have a relationship with her biological father.

The State's professed interest in the preservation of the existing marital unit is a more significant concern. To be sure, the intrusion of an outsider asserting that he is the father of a child whom the husband believes to be his own would be disruptive to say the least. On the facts of this case, however, Gerald was well aware of the liaison between Carole and Michael. The conclusive presumption of evidentiary rule § 621 virtually eliminates the putative father's chances of succeeding in his effort to establish paternity, but it by no means prevents him from asserting the claim. It may serve as a deterrent to such claims but does not eliminate the threat. Further, the argument that the conclusive presumption preserved the sanctity of the marital unit had more sway in a time when the husband was similarly prevented from challenging paternity.

"The emphasis of the Due Process Clause is on 'process.'" *Moore v. East Cleveland,* 431 U.S. 494, 542, 97 S.Ct. 1932, 1957, 52 L.Ed.2d 531 (1977) (WHITE, J., dissenting). I fail to see the fairness in the process established by the State of California and endorsed by the Court today. Michael H. has evidence which demonstrates that he is the father of young Victoria. Yet he is blocked by the State from presenting that evidence to a court. As a result, he is foreclosed from establishing his paternity and is ultimately precluded, by the State, from developing a relationship with his child. "A fundamental requirement of due process is 'the opportunity to be heard.' *Grannis v. Ordean,* 234 U.S. 385, 394 [34 S.Ct. 779, 783, 58 L.Ed. 1363 (1914)]. It is an opportunity which must be granted at a meaningful time and in a meaningful manner." *Armstrong v. Manzo,* 380 U.S. 545, 552, 85 S.Ct. 1187, 1191, 14 L.Ed.2d 62 (1965). I fail to see how appellant was granted any meaningful opportunity to be heard when he was precluded at the very outset from introducing evidence which would support his assertion of paternity. Michael H. has never been afforded an opportunity to present his case in any meaningful manner.

As the Court has said: "The significance of the biological connection is that it offers the natural father an opportunity that no other male possesses to develop a relationship with his offspring. If he grasps that opportunity and accepts some measure of responsibility for the child's future, he may enjoy the blessings of the parent-child relationship and make uniquely valuable contributions to the child's development." *Lehr,* 463 U.S., at 262, 103 S.Ct., at 2993. It is as if this passage was addressed to Michael H. Yet the plurality today recants. Michael H. eagerly grasped the opportunity to have a relationship with his daughter (he lived with her; he declared her to be his child; he provided financial support for her) and still, with today's opinion, his opportunity has vanished. He has been rendered a stranger to his child.

Because Cal.Evid.Code Ann. § 621, as applied, should be held unconstitutional under the Due Process Clause of the Fourteenth Amendment, I respectfully dissent.

Notes on Michael H.:

1. All of the United States Supreme Court cases dealing with the rights of natural fathers prior to *Michael H.* involved children born out of wedlock. Victoria D., by contrast, was born during the marriage of her mother, Carole D., to Gerald D. Should this single fact make a constitutional difference in the rights of her natural father, Michael H.? What weight does Justice Scalia give to the fact that, as he points out in distinguishing *Lehr,* Victoria was "born into an extant marital family"? Does Justice Stevens concur in this distinction? Does Justice Brennan give it any significance at all? What is Justice White's position? What are the

rights of natural fathers of children born to married women cohabiting with their husbands after *Michael H.*? In Ex Parte Presse, 554 So.2d 406 (Ala.1989), the Alabama Supreme Court cited *Michael H.* in support of its interpretation of the Uniform Parentage Act (UPA) to deny a natural father the right to challenge the husband's paternity even though the father had subsequently married the child's mother after she divorced her first husband and the child, who was in her mother's custody, lived in their home. Justice Jones reasoned as follows:

> Admittedly, this case and the case of *Michael H. v. Gerald D., supra,* have some factual differences, notably the fact that Michael was not married to and living with the mother and child when he brought his suit seeking visitation rights. Nevertheless, the applicable rules of law are the same. In this case, as in *Michael H.*, the legal question is whether a man has standing to bring an action seeking to declare a child illegitimate and to have himself declared the father of that child. This is not permitted under the UPA, as long as there is a presumed father, pursuant to § 26–17–5(a)(1), who has not disclaimed his status as the child's father, consequently, another man, though he later marries the mother and lives with the mother and child, has no standing to challenge the presumed paternity of that child. Put another way, so long as the presumed father persists in maintaining his paternal status, not even the subsequent marriage of the child's mother to another man can create standing in the other man to challenge the presumed father's parental relationship.
>
> The record before us shows that despite divorce, physical separation, and painful assertions that he is not the true father of Shelly, Norman J. Presse has provided her with unconditional love, financial support, and companionship. The Court, therefore, is of the opinion that to sever or curtail this father-child relationship would frustrate the benevolent purpose of the legislative expression of public policy. Koenemann's interest in judicially establishing his claimed biological relationship is outweighed by the substantial state interest in the psychological stability and general welfare of the child and the state's overriding interest in affording legitimacy to children whenever possible, all of which are obvious objectives of Alabama's UPA.

Id., 554 So.2d at 417–18. Justice Maddox, in dissent, charged the majority with creating an irrebutable presumption favoring the mother's husband that "sets back the law regarding paternity issues 100 years" and asked the majority to answer the following question:

> Why does a biological father not have standing to establish his paternity of a child when the mother of the child says he is the father, when the scientific tests show that he is the father, and when he is now married to the child's mother and the child lives in his home and calls him "Daddy."

Id., at 418 (dissenting opinion of Justice Maddox). Do you agree that *Michael H.* supports the majority's interpretation of the Uniform Parentage Act?

2. When the natural father's responsibility for child support, rather than his right to visit the child is at stake, however, the shoe appears to be

on the other foot. In Smith v. Cole, 553 So.2d 847 (La.1989), the Louisiana Supreme Court held that its doctrine of dual paternity meant that a child conceived and born during the mother's marriage but after she separated from her husband was the husband's legitimate daughter, a fact that did not excuse the biological father from being ordered to support the child. As Justice Cole put it, "[l]egitimate children cannot be bastardized by succeeding proof of actual parentage." Id., at 854. Is this result consistent with *Michael H.*? Note that the California statute applied in *Michael H.* would not have required a different result, since the conclusive presumption of legitimacy applies only when the child is conceived during the mother's cohabitation with her husband, and when he is not impotent or sterile. Under Justice Scalia's analysis, are these distinctions relevant?

3. What do you make of the historical "methodology" that Justice Scalia announces in footnote 6 of his opinion in *Michael H.*? If this methodology is accepted by a majority of the Court, what would be its likely impact on the future development of sex discrimination claims? See The Supreme Court—1988 Term: Leading Cases, 103 Harv.L.Rev. 137, 183 (1989):

> The plurality's due process methodology dramatically departs from past due process decisions, which relied on general principles rather than specific historical practices supporting or proscribing the particular interest alleged. By abandoning the attempt to effectuate general rights when challenged by specific historical practices, the plurality's analysis chips away at the already shaky foundations of substantive due process jurisprudence. Moreover, although packaged as an objectively precise method of avoiding judicial arbitrariness, the plurality's approach is prone to the same problems of judicial subjectivity that Justice Scalia so vigorously decries.

See also Sunstein, Sexual Orientation and the Constitution: A Note on the Relationship Between Due Process and Equal Protection, 55 U.Chi.L. Rev. 1161 (1988), discussing the different functions performed by the two clauses.

D. FAMILY PLANNING: WHO CONTROLS THE REPRODUCTIVE PROCESS?

1. CONTRACEPTION

Page 414. Add new Note 6:

6. Research and development leading to new and innovative approaches to contraception has slowed in the United States since the birth control pill was introduced in the early 1960s. According to Stanford professor Carl Djerassi, this situation is the result of a combination of factors: social and political opposition to new postcoital birth control techniques; the reluctance of the pharmaceutical industry to incur litigation risks associated with the introduction of new products; and the shift of medical research interests from contraception to infertility. Djerassi, The Bitter Pill, 245 Science 356 (28 July 1989). One bright exception to this forecast is RU 486, the drug developed in France by Dr. Etienne-Emile and

manufactured by Roussel–Uclaf. Djerassi calls RU 486 "the most significant research achievement of the 1980s in new practical fertility control." Id., at 359. RU 486 taken in conjunction with prostaglandins terminates pregnancy within the first nine weeks of gestation. See Stopping the Process of Pregnancy, 245 Science 1320 (22 September 1989). The drug provides an alternative to surgical abortion that can be self-administered in the privacy of a woman's home. As Djerassi notes, "[s]uch a method would not be acceptable or suitable for every woman, but to many such a one-pill regimen would represent an enormous improvement: at a maximum, a woman would be taking 12 pills annually, rather than the present 250 or more." Id., at 359. Anti-choice activists view RU 486 as "the death pill" and they have so far lobbied successfully to prevent its importation into the United States. In early 1990, the Feminist Majority Foundation launched a counter-offensive to bring RU 486 to this country. Will RU 486, if made freely available in the United States, effectively silence the abortion controversy?

2. ABORTION

Page 463. Add before Notes:

WEBSTER v. REPRODUCTIVE HEALTH SERVICES

Supreme Court of the United States, 1989.
492 U.S. ___, 109 S.Ct. 3040, 106 L.Ed.2d 410.

CHIEF JUSTICE REHNQUIST announced the judgment of the Court and delivered the opinion of the Court with respect to Parts I, II–A, II–B, and II–C, and an opinion with respect to Parts II–D and III, in which JUSTICE WHITE and JUSTICE KENNEDY join.

This appeal concerns the constitutionality of a Missouri statute regulating the performance of abortions. * * *

II

Decision of this case requires us to address four sections of the Missouri Act: (a) the preamble; (b) the prohibition on the use of public facilities or employees to perform abortions; (c) the prohibition on public funding of abortion counseling; and (d) the requirement that physicians conduct viability tests prior to performing abortions. We address these *seriatim.*

A

The Act's preamble, as noted, sets forth "findings" by the Missouri legislature that "[t]he life of each human being begins at conception," and that "[u]nborn children have protectable interests in life, health, and well-being." * * * The Act then mandates that state laws be interpreted to provide unborn children with "all the rights, privileges, and immunities available to other persons, citizens, and residents of this state," subject to the Constitution and this Court's precedents.[4] In

---

4. Section 1.205 provides in full:

"1. The general assembly of this state finds that:

"(1) The life of each human being begins at conception;

invalidating the preamble, the Court of Appeals relied on this Court's dictum that "'a State may not adopt one theory of when life begins to justify its regulation of abortions.'" quoting *Akron v. Akron Center for Reproductive Health, Inc.,* * * *, in turn citing *Roe v. Wade,* * * *. It rejected Missouri's claim that the preamble was "abortion-neutral," and "merely determine[d] when life begins in a nonabortion context, a traditional state prerogative." * * * The court thought that "[t]he only plausible inference" from the fact that "every remaining section of the bill save one regulates the performance of abortions" was that "the state intended its abortion regulations to be understood against the backdrop of its theory of life."

* * *

In our view, the Court of Appeals misconceived the meaning of the *Akron* dictum, which was only that a State could not "justify" an abortion regulation otherwise invalid under *Roe v. Wade* on the ground that it embodied the State's view about when life begins. Certainly the preamble does not by its terms regulate abortion or any other aspect of appellees' medical practice. The Court has emphasized that *Roe v. Wade* "implies no limitation on the authority of a State to make a value judgment favoring childbirth over abortion." *Maher v. Roe,* * * *. The preamble can be read simply to express that sort of value judgment.

We think the extent to which the preamble's language might be used to interpret other state statutes or regulations is something that only the courts of Missouri can definitively decide. * * * It will be time enough for federal courts to address the meaning of the preamble should it be applied to restrict the activities of appellees in some concrete way. * * * We therefore need not pass on the constitutionality of the Act's preamble.

B

Section 188.210 provides that "[i]t shall be unlawful for any public employee within the scope of his employment to perform or assist an abortion, not necessary to save the life of the mother," while § 188.215 makes it "unlawful for any public facility to be used for the purpose of

"(2) Unborn children have protectable interests in life, health, and well-being;

"(3) The natural parents of unborn children have protectable interests in the life, health, and well-being of their unborn child.

"2. Effective January 1, 1988, the laws of this state shall be interpreted and construed to acknowledge on behalf of the unborn child at every stage of development, all the rights, privileges, and immunities available to other persons, citizens, and residents of this state, subject only to the Constitution of the United States, and decisional interpretations thereof by the United States Supreme Court and specific provisions to the contrary in the statutes and constitution of this state.

"3. As used in this section, the term 'unborn children' or 'unborn child' shall include all unborn child or [*sic*] children or the offspring of human beings from the moment of conception until birth at every stage of biological development.

"4. Nothing in this section shall be interpreted as creating a cause of action against a woman for indirectly harming her unborn child by failing to properly care for herself or by failing to follow any particular program of prenatal care."

performing or assisting an abortion not necessary to save the life of the mother." [7] The Court of Appeals held that these provisions contravened this Court's abortion decisions. * * * We take the contrary view.

As we said earlier this Term in *DeShaney v. Winnebago County Dept. of Social Services,* 489 U.S. ___, ___, 109 S.Ct. 998, 1003, 103 L.Ed. 2d 249 (1989), "our cases have recognized that the Due Process Clauses generally confer no affirmative right to governmental aid, even where such aid may be necessary to secure life, liberty, or property interests of which the government itself may not deprive the individual." In *Maher v. Roe, supra,* the Court upheld a Connecticut welfare regulation under which Medicaid recipients received payments for medical services related to childbirth, but not for nontherapeutic abortions. The Court rejected the claim that this unequal subsidization of childbirth and abortion was impermissible under *Roe v. Wade.* * * * Relying on *Maher,* the Court in *Poelker v. Doe,* * * * held that the city of St. Louis committed "no constitutional violation * * * in electing, as a policy choice, to provide publicly financed hospital services for childbirth without providing corresponding services for nontherapeutic abortions."

More recently, in *Harris v. McRae,* * * *, the Court upheld "the most restrictive version of the Hyde Amendment," * * * which withheld from States federal funds under the Medicaid program to reimburse the costs of abortions, " 'except where the life of the mother would be endangered if the fetus were carried to term.' " * * * As in *Maher* and *Poelker,* the Court required only a showing that Congress' authorization of "reimbursement for medically necessary services generally, but not for certain medically necessary abortions" was rationally related to the legitimate governmental goal of encouraging childbirth. * * *

The Court of Appeals distinguished these cases on the ground that "[t]o prevent access to a public facility does more than demonstrate a political choice in favor of childbirth; it clearly narrows and in some cases forecloses the availability of abortion to women." * * * The court reasoned that the ban on the use of public facilities "could prevent a woman's chosen doctor from performing an abortion because of his unprivileged status at other hospitals or because a private hospital adopted a similar anti-abortion stance." *Ibid.* It also thought that "[s]uch a rule could increase the cost of obtaining an abortion and delay the timing of it as well."

We think that this analysis is much like that which we rejected in *Maher, Poelker,* and *McRae.* As in those cases, the State's decision here to use public facilities and staff to encourage childbirth over

---

7. The statute defines "public employee" to mean "any person employed by this state or any agency or political subdivision thereof." Mo.Rev.Stat. § 188.200(1) (1986). "Public facility" is defined as "any public institution, public facility, public equipment, or any physical asset owned, leased, or controlled by this state or any agency or political subdivisions thereof." § 188.200(2).

abortion "places no governmental obstacle in the path of a woman who chooses to terminate her pregnancy." *McRae*, * * *. Just as Congress' refusal to fund abortions in *McRae* left "an indigent woman with at least the same range of choice in deciding whether to obtain a medically necessary abortion as she would have had if Congress had chosen to subsidize no health care costs at all," * * *. Missouri's refusal to allow public employees to perform abortions in public hospitals leaves a pregnant woman with the same choices as if the State had chosen not to operate any public hospitals at all. The challenged provisions only restrict a woman's ability to obtain an abortion to the extent that she chooses to use a physician affiliated with a public hospital. This circumstance is more easily remedied, and thus considerably less burdensome, than indigency, which "may make it difficult—and in some cases, perhaps, impossible—for some women to have abortions" without public funding. *Maher*, * * *. Having held that the State's refusal to fund abortions does not violate *Roe v. Wade*, it strains logic to reach a contrary result for the use of public facilities and employees. If the State may "make a value judgment favoring childbirth over abortion and * * * implement that judgment by the allocation of public funds," *Maher*, * * *, surely it may do so through the allocation of other public resources, such as hospitals and medical staff.

The Court of Appeals sought to distinguish our cases on the additional ground that "[t]he evidence here showed that all of the public facility's costs in providing abortion services are recouped when the patient pays." * * * Absent any expenditure of public funds, the court thought that Missouri was "expressing" more than "its preference for childbirth over abortions," but rather was creating an "obstacle to exercise of the right to choose an abortion [that could not] stand absent a compelling state interest." * * * We disagree.

"Constitutional concerns are greatest," we said in *Maher*, * * * "when the State attempts to impose its will by the force of law; the State's power to encourage actions deemed to be in the public interest is necessarily far broader." Nothing in the Constitution requires States to enter or remain in the business of performing abortions. Nor, as appellees suggest, do private physicians and their patients have some kind of constitutional right of access to public facilities for the performance of abortions. * * * Indeed, if the State does recoup all of its costs in performing abortions, and no state subsidy, direct or indirect, is available, it is difficult to see how any procreational choice is burdened by the State's ban on the use of its facilities or employees for performing abortions.[8]

8. A different analysis might apply if a particular State had socialized medicine and all of its hospitals and physicians were publicly funded. This case might also be different if the State barred doctors who performed abortions in private facilities from the use of public facilities for any purpose. See *Harris v. McRae*, 448 U.S. 297, 317, n. 19, 100 S.Ct. 2671, 2688, n. 19, 65 L.Ed.2d 784 (1980).

Maher, Poelker, and *McRae* all support the view that the State need not commit any resources to facilitating abortions, even if it can turn a profit by doing so. In *Poelker,* the suit was filed by an indigent who could not afford to pay for an abortion, but the ban on the performance of nontherapeutic abortions in city-owned hospitals applied whether or not the pregnant woman could pay. * * * The Court emphasized that the Mayor's decision to prohibit abortions in city hospitals was "subject to public debate and approval or disapproval at the polls," and that "the Constitution does not forbid a State or city, pursuant to democratic processes, from expressing a preference for normal childbirth as St. Louis has done." *Id.,* at 521, 97 S.Ct., at 2392. Thus we uphold the Act's restrictions on the use of public employees and facilities for the performance or assistance of nontherapeutic abortions.

C

The Missouri Act contains three provisions relating to "encouraging or counseling a woman to have an abortion not necessary to save her life." Section 188.205 states that no public funds can be used for this purpose; § 188.210 states that public employees cannot, within the scope of their employment, engage in such speech; and § 188.215 forbids such speech in public facilities. * * *

Missouri has chosen only to appeal the Court of Appeals' invalidation of the public funding provision, § 188.205. * * * A majority of the Court agrees with appellees that the controversy over § 188.205 is now moot, * * *.

D

Section 188.029 of the Missouri Act provides:

"Before a physician performs an abortion on a woman he has reason to believe is carrying an unborn child of twenty or more weeks gestational age, the physician shall first determine if the unborn child is viable by using and exercising that degree of care, skill, and proficiency commonly exercised by the ordinarily skillful, careful, and prudent physician engaged in similar practice under the same or similar conditions. In making this determination of viability, the physician shall perform or cause to be performed such medical examinations and tests as are necessary to make a finding of the gestational age, weight, and lung maturity of the unborn child and shall enter such findings and determination of viability in the medical record of the mother." [12]

As with the preamble, the parties disagree over the meaning of this statutory provision. The State emphasizes the language of the first sentence, which speaks in terms of the physician's determination of viability being made by the standards of ordinary skill in the medical profession. * * * Appellees stress the language of the second sen-

---

12. The Act's penalty provision provides that "[a]ny person who contrary to the provisions of sections 188.010 to 188.085 knowingly performs * * * any abortion or knowingly fails to perform any action required by [these] sections * * * shall be guilty of a class A misdemeanor." Mo.Rev.Stat. § 188.075 (1986).

tence, which prescribes such "tests as are necessary" to make a finding of gestational age, fetal weight, and lung maturity. * * *

The Court of Appeals read § 188.029 as requiring that after 20 weeks "doctors *must* perform tests to find gestational age, fetal weight and lung maturity." * * * The court indicated that the tests needed to determine fetal weight at 20 weeks are "unreliable and inaccurate" and would add $125 to $250 to the cost of an abortion. * * * It also stated that "amniocentesis, the only method available to determine lung maturity, is contrary to accepted medical practice until 28–30 weeks of gestation, expensive, and imposes significant health risks for both the pregnant woman and the fetus." * * *

We must first determine the meaning of § 188.029 under Missouri law. Our usual practice is to defer to the lower court's construction of a state statute, but we believe the Court of Appeals has "fallen into plain error" in this case. * * *

We think the viability-testing provision makes sense only if the second sentence is read to require only those tests that are useful to making subsidiary findings as to viability. If we construe this provision to require a physician to perform those tests needed to make the three specified findings *in all circumstances,* including when the physician's reasonable professional judgment indicates that the tests would be irrelevant to determining viability or even dangerous to the mother and the fetus, the second sentence of § 188.029 would conflict with the first sentence's *requirement* that a physician apply his reasonable professional skill and judgment. It would also be incongruous to read this provision, especially the word "necessary," to require the performance of tests irrelevant to the expressed statutory purpose of determining viability. It thus seems clear to us that the Court of Appeals' construction of § 188.029 violates well-accepted canons of statutory interpretation used in the Missouri courts, * * *.

The viability-testing provision of the Missouri Act is concerned with promoting the State's interest in potential human life rather than in maternal health. Section 188.029 creates what is essentially a presumption of viability at 20 weeks, which the physician must rebut with tests indicating that the fetus is not viable prior to performing an abortion. It also directs the physician's determination as to viability by specifying consideration, if feasible, of gestational age, fetal weight, and lung capacity. The District Court found that "the medical evidence is uncontradicted that a 20–week fetus is *not* viable," and that "23½ to 24 weeks gestation is the earliest point in pregnancy where a reasonable possibility of viability exists." * * * But it also found that there may be a 4–week error in estimating gestational age, * * * which supports testing at 20 weeks.

In *Roe v. Wade,* the Court recognized that the State has "important and legitimate" interests in protecting maternal health and in the potentiality of human life. * * * During the second trimester, the State "may, if it chooses, regulate the abortion procedure in ways that are reasonably related to maternal health." * * * After viability, when the State's interest in potential human life was held to become compelling, the State "may, if it chooses, regulate, and even proscribe, abortion except where it is necessary, in appropriate medical judgment, for the preservation of the life or health of the mother." * * *

In *Colautti v. Franklin,* * * * upon which appellees rely, the Court held that a Pennsylvania statute regulating the standard of care to be used by a physician performing an abortion of a possibly viable fetus was void for vagueness. * * * But in the course of reaching that conclusion, the Court reaffirmed its earlier statement in *Planned Parenthood of Central Missouri v. Danforth,* * * * that " 'the determination of whether a particular fetus is viable is, and must be, a matter for the judgment of the responsible attending physician.' " * * * The dissent, *post,* at * * * n. 6, ignores the statement in *Colautti* that "neither the legislature nor the courts may proclaim one of the elements entering into the ascertainment of viability—be it weeks of gestation or fetal weight or any other single factor—as the determinant of when the State has a compelling interest in the life or health of the fetus." * * * To the extent that § 188.029 regulates the method for determining viability, it undoubtedly does superimpose state regulation on the medical determination of whether a particular fetus is viable. The Court of Appeals and the District Court thought it unconstitutional for this reason. * * * To the extent that the viability tests increase the cost of what are in fact second-trimester abortions, their validity may also be questioned under *Akron,* * * * where the Court held that a requirement that second trimester abortions must be performed in hospitals was invalid because it substantially increased the expense of those procedures.

We think that the doubt cast upon the Missouri statute by these cases is not so much a flaw in the statute as it is a reflection of the fact that the rigid trimester analysis of the course of a pregnancy enunciated in *Roe* has resulted in subsequent cases like *Colautti* and *Akron* making constitutional law in this area a virtual Procrustean bed. Statutes specifying elements of informed consent to be provided abortion patients, for example, were invalidated if they were thought to "structur[e] * * * the dialogue between the woman and her physician." *Thornburgh v. American College of Obstetricians and Gynecologists,* * * *. As the dissenters in *Thornburgh* pointed out, such a statute would have been sustained under any traditional standard of judicial review, * * * (WHITE, J., dissenting), or for any other surgical procedure except abortion. * * * (Burger, C.J., dissenting).

Stare decisis is a cornerstone of our legal system, but it has less power in constitutional cases, where, save for constitutional amendments, this Court is the only body able to make needed changes. * * * We have not refrained from reconsideration of a prior construction of the Constitution that has proved "unsound in principle and unworkable in practice." * * * We think the *Roe* trimester framework falls into that category.

In the first place, the rigid *Roe* framework is hardly consistent with the notion of a Constitution cast in general terms, as ours is, and usually speaking in general principles, as ours does. The key elements of the *Roe* framework—trimesters and viability—are not found in the text of the Constitution or in any place else one would expect to find a constitutional principle. Since the bounds of the inquiry are essentially indeterminate, the result has been a web of legal rules that have become increasingly intricate, resembling a code of regulations rather than a body of constitutional doctrine.[15] As Justice White has put it, the trimester framework has left this Court to serve as the country's "*ex officio* medical board with powers to approve or disapprove medical and operative practices and standards throughout the United States." *Planned Parenthood of Central Missouri v. Danforth,* * * *.

In the second place, we do not see why the State's interest in protecting potential human life should come into existence only at the point of viability, and that there should therefore be a rigid line allowing state regulation after viability but prohibiting it before viability. The dissenters in *Thornburgh,* writing in the context of the *Roe* trimester analysis, would have recognized this fact by positing against the "fundamental right" recognized in *Roe* the State's "compelling interest" in protecting potential human life throughout pregnancy. "[T]he State's interest, if compelling after viability, is equally compelling before viability." *Thornburgh,* * * * (WHITE, J., dissenting); * * * (O'CONNOR, J., dissenting) ("State has compelling interests in ensuring maternal health and in protecting potential human life, and these interests exist 'throughout pregnancy'") (citation omitted).

The tests that § 188.029 requires the physician to perform are designed to determine viability. The State here has chosen viability as the point at which its interest in potential human life must be safeguarded. See Mo.Rev.Stat. § 188.030 (1986) ("No abortion of a viable unborn child shall be performed unless necessary to preserve the life or health of the woman"). It is true that the tests in question increase the expense of abortion, and regulate the discretion of the physician in

---

15. For example, the Court has held that a State may require that certain information be given to a woman by a physician or his assistant, *Akron v. Akron Center for Reproductive Health, Inc.,* 462 U.S., at 448, 103 S.Ct., at 2502, but that it may not require that such information be furnished to her only by the physician himself. *Id.,* at 449, 103 S.Ct., at 2502–03. Likewise, a State may require that abortions in the second trimester be performed in clinics, *Simopoulos v. Virginia,* 462 U.S. 506, 103 S.Ct. 2532, 76 L.Ed.2d 755 (1983), but it may not require that such abortions be performed only in hospitals. *Akron, supra,* 462 U.S., at 437–439, 103 S.Ct., at 2496–97. We do not think these distinctions are of any constitutional import in view of our abandonment of the trimester framework. The dissent's claim, *post,* at 3068–3069, n. 1, that the State goes too far, even under *Maher v. Roe,* 432 U.S. 464, 97 S.Ct. 2376, 53 L.Ed.2d 484 (1977); *Poelker v. Doe,* 432 U.S. 519, 97 S.Ct. 2391, 53 L.Ed.2d 528 (1977); and *Harris v. McRae,* 448 U.S. 297, 100 S.Ct. 2671, 65 L.Ed.2d 784 (1980), by refusing to permit the use of public facilities, as defined in Mo.Rev.Stat. § 188.200, for the performance of abortions is another example of the fine distinctions endemic in the *Roe* framework.

viability test v. 1st/2nd trimester distinction

determining the viability of the fetus. Since the tests will undoubtedly show in many cases that the fetus is not viable, the tests will have been performed for what were in fact second-trimester abortions. But we are satisfied that the requirement of these tests permissibly furthers the State's interest in protecting potential human life, and we therefore believe § 188.029 to be constitutional.

The dissent takes us to task for our failure to join in a "great issues" debate as to whether the Constitution includes an "unenumerated" general right to privacy as recognized in cases such as *Griswold v. Connecticut,* * * * and *Roe.* But *Griswold v. Connecticut,* unlike *Roe,* did not purport to adopt a whole framework, complete with detailed rules and distinctions, to govern the cases in which the asserted liberty interest would apply. As such, it was far different from the opinion, if not the holding, of *Roe v. Wade,* which sought to establish a constitutional framework for judging state regulation of abortion during the entire term of pregnancy. That framework sought to deal with areas of medical practice traditionally subject to state regulation, and it sought to balance once and for all by reference only to the calendar the claims of the State to protect the fetus as a form of human life against the claims of a woman to decide for herself whether or not to abort a fetus she was carrying. The experience of the Court in applying *Roe v. Wade* in later cases, see *supra,* at * * * n. 15, suggests to us that there is wisdom in not unnecessarily attempting to elaborate the abstract differences between a "fundamental right" to abortion, as the Court described it in *Akron,* * * *, a "limited fundamental constitutional right," which Justice Blackmun's dissent today treats *Roe* as having established, * * * or a liberty interest protected by the Due Process Clause, which we believe it to be. The Missouri testing requirement here is reasonably designed to ensure that abortions are not performed where the fetus is viable—an end which all concede is legitimate—and that is sufficient to sustain its constitutionality.

The dissent also accuses us, *inter alia,* of cowardice and illegitimacy in dealing with "the most politically divisive domestic legal issue of our time." * * * There is no doubt that our holding today will allow some governmental regulation of abortion that would have been prohibited under the language of cases such as *Colautti v. Franklin,* * * * and *Akron v. Akron Center for Reproductive Health, Inc., supra.* But the goal of constitutional adjudication is surely not to remove inexorably "politically divisive" issues from the ambit of the legislative process, whereby the people through their elected representatives deal with matters of concern to them. The goal of constitutional adjudication is to hold true the balance between that which the Constitution puts beyond the reach of the democratic process and that which it does not. We think we have done that today. The dissent's suggestion, * * * that legislative bodies, in a Nation where more than half of our population is women, will treat our decision today as an invitation to enact abortion regulation reminiscent of the dark ages not only misreads our views but does scant justice to those who serve in such bodies and the people who elect them.

III

Both appellants and the United States as *Amicus Curiae* have urged that we overrule our decision in *Roe v. Wade.* * * * The facts of the present case, however, differ from those at issue in *Roe*. Here, Missouri has determined that viability is the point at which its interest in potential human life must be safeguarded. In *Roe,* on the other hand, the Texas statute criminalized the performance of *all* abortions, except when the mother's life was at stake. * * * This case therefore affords us no occasion to revisit the holding of *Roe,* which was that the Texas statute unconstitutionally infringed the right to an abortion derived from the Due Process Clause, * * * and we leave it undisturbed. To the extent indicated in our opinion, we would modify and narrow *Roe* and succeeding cases.

Because none of the challenged provisions of the Missouri Act properly before us conflict with the Constitution, the judgment of the Court of Appeals is

Reversed.

JUSTICE O'CONNOR, concurring in part and concurring in the judgment.

I concur in Parts I, II–A, II–B, and II–C of the Court's opinion.

I

Nothing in the record before us or the opinions below indicates that subsections 1(1) and 1(2) of the preamble to Missouri's abortion regulation statute will affect a woman's decision to have an abortion. Justice Stevens, following appellees, * * * suggests that the preamble may also "interfere[ ] with contraceptive choices," * * *, because certain contraceptive devices act on a female ovum after it has been fertilized by a male sperm. The Missouri Act defines "conception" as "the fertilization of the ovum of a female by a sperm of a male," * * * and invests "unborn children" with "protectable interests in life, health, and well-being," * * * from "the moment of conception * * *". * * * Justice Stevens asserts that any possible interference with a woman's right to use such post-fertilization contraceptive devices would be unconstitutional under *Griswold v. Connecticut,* * * * and our subsequent contraception cases. * * * Similarly, certain *amici* suggest that the Missouri Act's preamble may prohibit the developing technology of *in vitro* fertilization, a technique used to aid couples otherwise unable to bear children in which a number of ova are removed from the woman and fertilized by male sperm. This process often produces excess fertilized ova ("unborn children" under the Missouri Act's definition) that are discarded rather than reinserted into the woman's uterus. Brief for Association of Reproductive Health Professionals et al. as *Amici Curiae* 38. It may be correct that the use of postfertilization contraceptive devices is constitutionally protected by

Griswold and its progeny but, as with a woman's abortion decision, nothing in the record or the opinions below indicates that the preamble will affect a woman's decision to practice contraception. For that matter, nothing in appellees' original complaint, * * * or their motion *in limine* to limit testimony and evidence on their challenge to the preamble, * * * indicates that appellees sought to enjoin potential violations of *Griswold*. Neither is there any indication of the possibility that the preamble might be applied to prohibit the performance of *in vitro* fertilization. I agree with the Court, therefore, that all of these intimations of unconstitutionality are simply too hypothetical to support the use of declaratory judgment procedures and injunctive remedies in this case.

Similarly, it seems to me to follow directly from our previous decisions concerning state or federal funding of abortions, * * * that appellees' facial challenge to the constitutionality of Missouri's ban on the utilization of public facilities and the participation of public employees in the performance of abortions not necessary to save the life of the mother * * * cannot succeed. Given Missouri's definition of "public facility" as "any public institution, public facility, public equipment, or any physical asset owned, leased, or controlled by this state or any agency or political subdivisions thereof," * * * there may be conceivable applications of the ban on the use of public facilities that would be unconstitutional. Appellees and *amici* suggest that the State could try to enforce the ban against private hospitals using public water and sewage lines, or against private hospitals leasing state-owned equipment or state land. See Brief for Appellees 49–50; Brief for National Association of Public Hospitals as *Amicus Curiae* 9–12. Whether some or all of these or other applications of § 188.215 would be constitutional need not be decided here. *Maher, Poelker,* and *McRae* stand for the proposition that some quite straightforward applications of the Missouri ban on the use of public facilities for performing abortions would be constitutional and that is enough to defeat appellees' assertion that the ban is facially unconstitutional. * * *

I also agree with the Court that, under the interpretation of § 188.205 urged by the State and adopted by the Court, there is no longer a case or controversy before us over the constitutionality of that provision. * * *

II

In its interpretation of Missouri's "determination of viability" provision, * * * the plurality has proceeded in a manner unnecessary to deciding the question at hand. I agree with the plurality that it was plain error for the Court of Appeals to interpret the second sentence of Mo.Rev.Stat. § 188.029 as meaning that "doctors *must* perform tests to find gestational age, fetal weight and lung maturity." * * * When read together with the first sentence of § 188.029—which requires a physician to "determine if the unborn child is viable by using and exercising that degree of care, skill, and proficiency commonly exercised by the ordinary skillful, careful, and prudent physician engaged in similar practice under the same or similar conditions"—it would be contradictory nonsense to read the second sentence as requiring a physician to perform viability examinations and tests in situations where it would be careless and imprudent to do so. The plurality is quite correct: "the viability-testing provision makes sense only if the second sentence is read to require only those tests that are useful to making subsidiary findings as to viability," * * *, and, I would add, only those examinations and tests that it would not be imprudent or careless to perform in the particular medical situation before the physician.

Unlike the plurality, I do not understand these viability testing requirements to conflict with any of the Court's past decisions concerning state regulation of abortion. Therefore, there is no necessity to accept the State's invitation to reexamine the constitutional validity of *Roe v. Wade,* * * *. The Court today has accepted the State's every interpretation of its abortion statute and has upheld, under our existing precedents, every provision of that statute which is properly before us. * * * When the constitutional invalidity of a State's abortion statute actually turns on the constitutional validity of *Roe v. Wade,* there will be time enough to reexamine *Roe.* And to do so carefully.

In assessing § 188.029 it is especially important to recognize that appellees did not appeal the District Court's ruling that the first sentence of § 188.029 is constitutional. * * * There is, accordingly, no dispute between the parties before us over the constitutionality of the "presumption of viability at 20 weeks," * * * created by the first sentence of § 188.029. If anything might arguably conflict with the Court's previous decisions concerning the determination of viability, I would think it is the introduction of this presumption. * * * The 20-week presumption of viability in the first sentence of § 188.029, it could be argued (though, I would think, unsuccessfully), restricts "the judgment of the responsible attending physician," by imposing on that physician the burden of overcoming the presumption. This presumption may be a "superimpos[ition] [of] state regulation on the medical determination of whether a particular fetus is viable," * * * but, if so, it is a restriction on the physician's judgment that is not before us. As the plurality properly interprets the second sentence of § 188.029, it does nothing more than delineate means by which the unchallenged 20-week presumption of viability may be overcome if those means are useful in doing so and can be prudently employed. Contrary to the plurality's suggestion, * * * the District Court did not think the second sentence of § 188.029 unconstitutional for this reason. Rather, both the District Court and the Court of Appeals thought the second sentence to be unconstitutional precisely because they interpreted that sentence to impose state regulation on the determination of viability that it does not impose.

Appellees suggest that the interpretation of § 188.029 urged by the State may "virtually eliminat[e] the constitutional issue in this case." * * * Appellees therefore propose that we should abstain from deciding that provision's constitutionality "in order to allow the state courts to render the saving construction the State has proposed." * * * Where the lower court has so clearly fallen into error I do not think abstention is necessary or prudent. Accordingly, I consider the constitutionality of the second sentence of § 188.029, as interpreted by the State, to determine whether the constitutional issue is actually eliminated.

I do not think the second sentence of § 188.029, as interpreted by the Court, imposes a degree of state regulation on the medical determination of viability that in any way conflicts with prior decisions of this Court. As the plurality recognizes, the requirement that, where not imprudent, physicians perform examinations and tests useful to making subsidiary findings to determine viability "promot[es] the State's interest in potential human life rather than in maternal health." * * * No decision of this Court has held that the State may not directly promote its interest in potential life when viability is possible. Quite the contrary. In *Thornburgh v. American College of Obstetricians and Gynecologists,* * * * the Court considered a constitutional challenge to a Pennsylvania statute requiring that a second physician be present during an abortion performed "when viability is possible." * * * For guidance, the Court looked to the earlier decision in *Planned Parenthood Assn. of Kansas City, Missouri, Inc. v. Ashcroft,* * * * upholding a Missouri statute requiring the presence of a second physician during an abortion performed after viability. * * * The *Thornburgh* majority struck down the Pennsylvania statute merely because the statute had no exception for emergency situations and not because it found a constitutional difference between the State's promotion of its interest in potential life when viability is possible and when viability is certain. * * * Despite the clear recognition by the *Thornburgh* majority that the Pennsylvania and Missouri statutes differed in this respect, there is no hint in the opinion of the *Thornburgh* Court that the State's interest in potential life differs depending whether it seeks to further that interest postviability or when viability is possible. Thus, all nine Members of the *Thornburgh* Court appear to have agreed that it is not constitutionally impermissible for the State to enact regulations designed to protect the State's interest in potential life when viability is possible. * * * That is exactly what Missouri has done in § 188.029.

Similarly, the basis for reliance by the District Court and the Court of Appeals below on *Colautti v. Franklin,* * * * disappears when § 188.029 is properly interpreted. * * * All the second sentence of § 188.029 does is to require, when not imprudent, the performance of "those tests that are useful to making *subsidiary* findings as to viability." * * * Thus, consistent with *Colautti*, viability remains the "critical point" under § 188.029.

Finally, and rather half-heartedly, the plurality suggests that the marginal increase in the cost of an abortion created by Missouri's viability testing provision may make § 188.029, even as interpreted, suspect under this Court's decision in *Akron,* * * * striking down a second-trimester hospitalization requirement. * * * I dissented from the Court's opinion in *Akron* because it was my view that, even apart from *Roe's* trimester framework which I continue to consider problematic, see *Thornburgh,* * * * the *Akron* majority had distorted and misapplied its own standard for evaluating state regulation of abortion which the Court had applied with fair consistency in the past: that, previability, "a regulation imposed on a lawful abortion is not unconstitutional unless it unduly burdens the right to seek an abortion." * * *

It is clear to me that requiring the performance of examinations and tests useful to determining whether a fetus is viable, when viability is possible, and when it would not be medically imprudent to do so, does not impose an undue burden on a woman's abortion decision. On this ground alone I would reject the suggestion that § 188.029 as interpreted is unconstitutional. More to the point, however, just as I see no conflict between § 188.029 and *Colautti* or any decision of this Court concerning a State's ability to give effect to its interest in potential life, I see no conflict between § 188.029 and the Court's opinion in *Akron.* The second-trimester hospitalization requirement struck down in *Akron* imposed, in the majority's view, "a heavy, and unnecessary, burden," * * * more than doubling the cost of "women's access to a relatively inexpensive, otherwise accessible, and safe abortion procedure." * * * By contrast, the cost of examinations and tests that could usefully and prudently be performed when a woman is 20–24 weeks pregnant to determine whether the fetus is viable would only marginally, if at all, increase the cost of an abortion. See Brief for American Association of Prolife Obstetricians and Gynecologists et al. as *Amici Curiae* 3 ("At twenty weeks gestation, an ultrasound examination to determine gestational age is standard medical practice. It is routinely provided by the plaintiff clinics. An ultrasound examination can effectively provide all three designated findings of sec. 188.029"); *id.,* at 22 ("A finding of fetal weight can be obtained from the same ultrasound test used to determine gestational age"); *id.,* at 25 ("There are a number of different methods in standard medical practice to determine fetal lung maturity at twenty or more weeks gestation. The most simple and most obvious is by inference. It is well known that fetal lungs do not mature until 33–34 weeks gestation * * *. If an assessment of the gestational age indicates that the child is less than thirty-three weeks, a general finding can be made that the fetal lungs are not mature. This finding can then be used by the physician in making his determination of viability under section 188.029"); cf. Brief for American Medical Association et al. as *Amici Curiae* 42 (no suggestion that fetal weight and gestational age cannot be determined from the same sonogram); *id.,* at 43 (another clinical test for gestational age and, by inference, fetal weight and lung maturity, is an accurate report of the last menstrual period), citing Smith, Frey, & Johnson, Assessing Gestational Age, 33 Am.Fam.Physician 215, 219–220 (1986).

Moreover, the examinations and tests required by § 188.029 are to be performed when viability is possible. This feature of § 188.029 distinguishes it from the second-trimester hospitalization requirement struck down by the *Akron* majority. As the Court recognized in *Thornburgh,* the State's compelling interest in potential life postviability renders its interest in determining the critical point of viability equally compelling. * * * Under the Court's precedents, the same cannot be said for the *Akron* second-trimester hospitalization requirement. As I understand the Court's opinion in *Akron,* therefore, the plurality's suggestion today that *Akron* casts doubt on the validity of § 188.029, even as the Court has interpreted it, is without foundation and cannot provide a basis for reevaluating *Roe.* Accordingly, because the Court of Appeals misinterpreted Mo.Rev.Stat. § 188.029, and because, properly interpreted, § 188.029 is not inconsistent with any of this Court's prior precedents, I would reverse the decision of the Court of Appeals.

In sum, I concur in Parts I, II–A, II–B, and II–C of the Court's opinion and concur in the judgment of Part II–D.

JUSTICE SCALIA, concurring in part and concurring in the judgment.

I join Parts I, II–A, II–B, and II–C of the opinion of The Chief Justice. As to Part II–D, I share Justice Blackmun's view, * * * that it effectively would overrule *Roe v. Wade,* * * *. I think that should be done, but would do it more explicitly. Since today we contrive to avoid doing it, and indeed to avoid almost any decision of national import, I need not set forth my reasons, some of which have been well recited in dissents of my colleagues in other cases. * * *

The outcome of today's case will doubtless be heralded as a triumph of judicial statesmanship. It is not that, unless it is statesmanlike needlessly to prolong this Court's self-awarded sovereignty over a field where it has little proper business since the answers to most of the cruel questions posed are political and not juridical—a sovereignty which therefore quite properly, but to the great damage of the Court, makes it the object of the sort of organized public pressure that political institutions in a democracy ought to receive.

Justice O'Connor's assertion, * * * that a " 'fundamental rule of judicial restraint' " requires us to avoid reconsidering *Roe,* cannot be taken seriously. By finessing *Roe* we do not, as she suggests, * * * adhere to the strict and venerable rule that we should avoid " 'decid[ing] questions of a constitutional nature.' " We have not disposed of this case on some statutory or procedural ground, but have decided, and could not avoid deciding, whether the Missouri statute meets the requirements of the United States Constitution. The only choice available is whether, in deciding that constitutional question, we should use *Roe v. Wade* as the benchmark, or something else. What is involved, therefore, is not the rule of avoiding constitutional issues where possible, but the quite separate principle that we will not " 'formulate a rule of constitutional law broader than is required by the precise facts to which it is to be applied.' " * * * The latter is a sound general principle, but one often departed from when good reason exists. * * *

The Court has often spoken more broadly than needed in precisely the fashion at issue here, announcing a new rule of constitutional law when it could have reached the identical result by applying the rule thereby displaced. * * *

The real question, then, is whether there are valid reasons to go beyond the most stingy possible holding today. It seems to me there are not only valid but compelling ones. Ordinarily, speaking no more broadly than is absolutely required avoids throwing settled law into confusion; doing so today preserves a chaos that is evident to anyone who can read and count. Alone sufficient to justify a broad holding is the fact that our retaining control, through *Roe*, of what I believe to be, and many of our citizens recognize to be, a political issue, continuously distorts the public perception of the role of this Court. We can now look forward to at least another Term with carts full of mail from the public, and streets full of demonstrators, urging us—their unelected and life-tenured judges who have been awarded those extraordinary, undemocratic characteristics precisely in order that we might follow the law despite the popular will—to follow the popular will. Indeed, I expect we can look forward to even more of that than before, given our indecisive decision today. And if these reasons for taking the unexceptional course of reaching a broader holding are not enough, then consider the nature of the constitutional question we avoid: In most cases, we do no harm by not speaking more broadly than the decision requires. Anyone affected by the conduct that the avoided holding would have prohibited will be able to challenge it himself, and have his day in court to make the argument. Not so with respect to the harm that many States believed, pre-*Roe*, and many may continue to believe, is caused by largely unrestricted abortion. That will continue to occur if the States have the constitutional power to prohibit it, and would do so, but we skillfully avoid telling them so. Perhaps those abortions cannot constitutionally be proscribed. That is surely an arguable question, the question that reconsideration of *Roe v. Wade* entails. But what is not at all arguable, it seems to me, is that we should decide now and not insist that we be run into a corner before we grudgingly yield up our judgment. The only sound reason for the latter course is to prevent a change in the law—but to think that desirable begs the question to be decided.

It was an arguable question today whether § 188.029 of the Missouri law contravened this Court's understanding of *Roe v. Wade,* and I would have examined *Roe* rather than examining the contravention. Given the Court's newly contracted abstemiousness, what will it take, one must wonder, to permit us to reach that fundamental question? The result of our vote today is that we will not reconsider that prior opinion, even if most of the Justices think it is wrong, unless we have before us a statute that in fact contradicts it—and even then (under our newly discovered "no-broader-than-necessary" requirement) only minor problematical aspects of *Roe* will be reconsidered, unless one expects State legislatures to adopt provisions whose compliance with *Roe* cannot even be argued with a straight face. It thus appears that the mansion of constitutionalized abortion-law, constructed overnight in *Roe v. Wade,* must be disassembled door-jamb by door-jamb, and never entirely brought down, no matter how wrong it may be.

Of the four courses we might have chosen today—to reaffirm *Roe,* to overrule it explicitly, to overrule it *sub silentio,* or to avoid the question—the last is the least responsible. On the question of the constitutionality of § 188.029, I concur in the judgment of the Court and strongly dissent from the manner in which it has been reached.

JUSTICE BLACKMUN, with whom JUSTICE BRENNAN and JUSTICE MARSHALL join, concurring in part and dissenting in part.

Today, *Roe v. Wade,* * * * and the fundamental constitutional right of women to decide whether to terminate a pregnancy, survive but are not secure. Although the Court extricates itself from this case without making a single, even incremental, change in the law of abortion, the plurality and Justice Scalia would overrule *Roe* (the first silently, the other explicitly) and would return to the States virtually unfettered authority to control the quintessentially intimate, personal, and life-directing decision whether to carry a fetus to term. Although today, no less than yesterday, the Constitution and the decisions of this Court prohibit a State from enacting laws that inhibit women from the meaningful exercise of that right, a plurality of this Court implicitly invites every state legislature to enact more and more restrictive abortion regulations in order to provoke more and more test cases, in the hope that sometime down the line the Court will return the law of procreative freedom to the severe limitations that generally prevailed in this country before January 22, 1973. Never in my memory has a plurality announced a judgment of this Court that so foments disregard for the law and for our standing decisions.

Nor in my memory has a plurality gone about its business in such a deceptive fashion. At every level of its review, from its effort to read the real meaning out of the Missouri statute, to its intended evisceration of precedents and its deafening silence about the constitutional protections that it would jettison, the plurality obscures the portent of its analysis. With feigned restraint, the plurality announces that its analysis leaves *Roe* "undisturbed," albeit "modif[ied] and narrow[ed]." * * * But this disclaimer is totally meaningless. The plurality opinion is filled with winks, and nods, and knowing glances to those who would do away with *Roe* explicitly, but turns a stone face to anyone in search of what the plurality conceives as the scope of a woman's right under the Due Process Clause to terminate a pregnancy free from the coercive and brooding influence of the State. The simple truth is that *Roe* would not survive the plurality's analysis, and that the plurality provides no substitute for *Roe's* protective umbrella.

I fear for the future. I fear for the liberty and equality of the millions of women who have lived and come of age in the 16 years since *Roe* was decided. I fear for the integrity of, and public esteem for, this Court.

I dissent.

I

The plurality parades through the four challenged sections of the Missouri statute *seriatim*. I shall not do this, but shall relegate most of my comments as to those sections to the margin. Although I disagree with the plurality's consideration of §§ 1.205, 188.210, and 188.215, and am especially disturbed by its misapplication of our past decisions in upholding Missouri's ban on the performance of abortions at "public facilities," the plurality's discussion of these provisions is merely prologue to its consideration of the statute's viability-testing requirement, § 188.029—the only section of the Missouri statute that the plurality construes as implicating *Roe* itself. There, tucked away at the end of its opinion, the plurality suggests a radical reversal of the law of abortion; and there, primarily, I direct my attention.

In the plurality's view, the viability-testing provision imposes a burden on second-trimester abortions as a way of furthering the State's interest in protecting the potential life of the fetus. Since under the *Roe* framework, the State may not fully regulate abortion in the interest of potential life (as opposed to maternal health) until the third trimester, the plurality finds it necessary, in order to save the Missouri testing provision, to throw out *Roe's* trimester framework. * * * In flat contradiction to *Roe,* * * * the plurality concludes that the State's interest in potential life is compelling before viability, and upholds the testing provision because it "permissibly furthers" that state interest. * * *

A

At the outset, I note that in its haste to limit abortion rights, the plurality compounds the errors of its analysis by needlessly reaching out to address constitutional questions that are not actually presented. The conflict between § 188.029 and *Roe's* trimester framework, which purportedly drives the plurality to reconsider our past decisions, is a contrived conflict: the product of an aggressive misreading of the viability-testing requirement and a needlessly wooden application of the *Roe* framework.

* * *

Had the plurality read the statute as written, it would have had no cause to reconsider the *Roe* framework. As properly construed, the viability-testing provision does not pass constitutional muster under even a rational-basis standard, the least restrictive level of review applied by this Court. * * * By mandating tests to determine fetal weight and lung maturity for every fetus thought to be more than 20 weeks gestational age, the statute requires physicians to undertake procedures, such as amniocentesis, that, in the situation presented, have no medical justification, impose significant additional health risks on both the pregnant woman and the fetus, and bear no rational relation to the State's interest in protecting fetal life.[3] As written, § 188.029 is an arbitrary imposition of discomfort, risk, and expense, furthering no discernible interest except to make the procurement of an abortion as arduous and difficult as possible. Thus, were it not for the plurality's tortured effort to avoid the plain import of § 188.029, it could have struck down the testing provision as patently irrational irrespective of the *Roe* framework.

The plurality eschews this straightforward resolution, in the hope of precipitating a constitutional crisis. Far from avoiding constitutional difficulty, the plurality attempts to engineer a dramatic retrenchment in our jurisprudence by exaggerating the conflict between its untenable construction of § 188.029 and the *Roe* trimester framework.

No one contests that under the *Roe* framework the State, in order to promote its interest in potential human life, may regulate and even proscribe non-therapeutic abortions once the fetus becomes viable. * * * If, as the plurality appears to hold, the testing provision simply requires a physician to use appropriate and medically sound tests to determine whether the fetus is actually viable when the estimated gestational age is greater than 20 weeks (and therefore within what the District Court found to be the margin of error for viability, * * *), then I see little or no conflict with *Roe*. Nothing in *Roe*, or any of its progeny, holds that a State may not effectuate its compelling interest in the potential life of a viable fetus by seeking to ensure that no viable fetus is mistakenly aborted because of the inherent lack of precision in estimates of gestational age. A requirement that a physician make a finding of viability, one way or the other, for every fetus that falls within the range of possible viability does no more than preserve the State's recognized authority. Although, as the plurality correctly points out, such a testing requirement would have the effect of imposing additional costs on second-trimester abortions where the tests indicated that the fetus was not viable, these costs would be merely incidental to, and a necessary accommodation of, the State's unques-

---

3. The District Court found that "the only method to evaluate [fetal] lung maturity is by amniocentesis," a procedure that "imposes additional significant health risks for both the pregnant woman and the fetus." 662 F.Supp. 407, 422 (W.D. Mo.1987). Yet the medical literature establishes that to require amniocentesis for all abortions after 20 weeks would be contrary to sound medical practice and, moreover, would be useless for the purpose of determining lung maturity until no earlier than between 28 and 30 weeks gestational age. *Ibid;* see also Brief for American Medical Association, et al., as *Amici Curiae* 41. Thus, were § 188.029 read to require a finding of lung maturity, it would require physicians to perform a highly intrusive procedure of risk that would yield no result relevant to the question of viability.

tioned right to prohibit non-therapeutic abortions after the point of viability. In short, the testing provision, as construed by the plurality is consistent with the *Roe* framework and could be upheld effortlessly under current doctrine.

* * *

B

Having set up the conflict between § 188.029 and the *Roe* trimester framework, the plurality summarily discards *Roe's* analytic core as "'unsound in principle and unworkable in practice.'" * * * This is so, the plurality claims, because the key elements of the framework do not appear in the text of the Constitution, because the framework more closely resembles a regulatory code than a body of constitutional doctrine, and because under the framework the State's interest in potential human life is considered compelling only after viability, when, in fact, that interest is equally compelling throughout pregnancy. * * * The plurality does not bother to explain these alleged flaws in *Roe*. Bald assertion masquerades as reasoning. The object, quite clearly, is not to persuade, but to prevail.

1

The plurality opinion is far more remarkable for the arguments that it does not advance than for those that it does. The plurality does not even mention, much less join, the true jurisprudential debate underlying this case: whether the Constitution includes an "unenumerated" general right to privacy as recognized in many of our decisions, most notably *Griswold v. Connecticut,* * * * and *Roe,* and, more specifically, whether and to what extent such a right to privacy extends to matters of childbearing and family life, including abortion. * * * These are questions of unsurpassed significance in this Court's interpretation of the Constitution, and mark the battleground upon which this case was fought, by the parties, by the Solicitor General as *amicus* on behalf of petitioners, and by an unprecedented number of *amici*. On these grounds, abandoned by the plurality, the Court should decide this case.

But rather than arguing that the text of the Constitution makes no mention of the right to privacy, the plurality complains that the critical elements of the *Roe* framework—trimesters and viability—do not appear in the Constitution and are, therefore, somehow inconsistent with a Constitution cast in general terms. * * * Were this a true concern, we would have to abandon most of our constitutional jurisprudence. As the plurality well knows, or should know, the "critical elements" of countless constitutional doctrines nowhere appear in the Constitution's text. The Constitution makes no mention, for example, of the First Amendment's "actual malice" standard for proving certain libels, see *New York Times v. Sullivan,* 376 U.S. 254, 84 S.Ct. 710, 11 L.Ed.2d 686 (1964), or of the standard for determining when speech is obscene. See *Miller v. California,* 413 U.S. 15, 93 S.Ct. 2607, 37 L.Ed.2d 419 (1973).

Similarly, the Constitution makes no mention of the rational-basis test, or the specific verbal formulations of intermediate and strict scrutiny by which this Court evaluates claims under the Equal Protection Clause. The reason is simple. Like the *Roe* framework, these tests or standards are not, and do not purport to be, rights protected by the Constitution. Rather, they are judge-made methods for evaluating and measuring the strength and scope of constitutional rights or for balancing the constitutional rights of individuals against the competing interests of government.

With respect to the *Roe* framework, the general constitutional principle, indeed the fundamental constitutional right, for which it was developed is the right to privacy, * * * a species of "liberty" protected by the Due Process Clause, which under our past decisions safeguards the right of women to exercise some control over their own role in procreation. * * * The trimester framework simply defines and limits that right to privacy in the abortion context to accommodate, not destroy, a State's legitimate interest in protecting the health of pregnant women and in preserving potential human life. * * * Fashioning such accommodations between individual rights and the legitimate interests of government, establishing benchmarks and standards with which to evaluate the competing claims of individuals and government, lies at the very heart of constitutional adjudication. To the extent that the trimester framework is useful in this enterprise, it is not only consistent with constitutional interpretation, but necessary to the wise and just exercise of this Court's paramount authority to define the scope of constitutional rights.

2

The plurality next alleges that the result of the trimester framework has "been a web of legal rules that have become increasingly intricate, resembling a code of regulations rather than a body of constitutional doctrine." * * * Again, if this were a true and genuine concern, we would have to abandon vast areas of our constitutional jurisprudence. * * *

That numerous constitutional doctrines result in narrow differentiations between similar circumstances does not mean that this Court has abandoned adjudication in favor of regulation. Rather, these careful distinctions reflect the process of constitutional adjudication itself, which is often highly fact-specific, requiring such determinations as whether state laws are "unduly burdensome" or "reasonable" or bear a "rational" or "necessary" relation to asserted state interests. * * *

* * *

3

Finally, the plurality asserts that the trimester framework cannot stand because the State's interest in potential life is compelling throughout pregnancy, not merely after viability. * * * The opinion contains not one word of rationale for its view of the State's interest. This "it-is-so-because-we-say-so" jurisprudence constitutes nothing other than an attempted exercise of brute force; reason, much less persuasion, has no place.

In answering the plurality's claim that the State's interest in the fetus is uniform and compelling throughout pregnancy, I cannot improve upon what Justice Stevens has written:

> "I should think it obvious that the State's interest in the protection of an embryo—even if that interest is defined as 'protecting those who will be citizens' * * *—increases progressively and dramatically as the organism's capacity to feel pain, to experience pleasure, to survive, and to react to its surroundings increases day by day. The development of a fetus—and pregnancy itself—are not static conditions, and the assertion that the government's interest is static simply ignores this reality * * *. [U]nless the religious view that a fetus is a 'person' is adopted * * * there is a fundamental and well-recognized difference between a fetus and a human being; indeed, if there is not such a difference, the permissibility of terminating the life of a fetus could scarcely be left to the will of the state legislatures. And if distinctions may be drawn between a fetus and a human being in terms of the state interest in their protection—even though the fetus represents one of 'those who will be citizens'—it seems to me quite odd to argue that distinctions may not also be drawn between the state interest in protecting the freshly fertilized egg and the state interest in protecting the 9-month-gestated, fully sentient fetus on the eve of birth. Recognition of this distinction is supported not only by logic, but also by history and by our shared experiences." *Thornburgh,* * * *.

For my own part, I remain convinced, as six other Members of this Court 16 years ago were convinced, that the *Roe* framework, and the viability standard in particular, fairly, sensibly, and effectively functions to safeguard the constitutional liberties of pregnant women while recognizing and accommodating the State's interest in potential human life. The viability line reflects the biological facts and truths of fetal development; it marks that threshold moment prior to which a fetus cannot survive separate from the woman and cannot reasonably and objectively be regarded as a subject of rights or interests distinct from, or paramount to, those of the pregnant woman. At the same time, the viability standard takes account of the undeniable fact that as the fetus evolves into its postnatal form, and as it loses its dependence on the uterine environment, the State's interest in the fetus' potential human life, and in fostering a regard for human life in general, becomes compelling. As a practical matter, because viability follows "quickening"—the point at which a woman feels movement in her womb—and because viability occurs no earlier than 23 weeks gestational age, it establishes an easily applicable standard for regulating abortion while providing a pregnant woman ample time to exercise her fundamental right with her responsible physician to terminate her pregnancy.[9] Although I have stated previously for a majority of this Court that "[c]onstitutional rights do not always have easily ascertainable boundaries," to seek and establish those boundaries remains the special responsibility of this Court. *Thornburgh,* * * *. In *Roe,* we discharged that responsibility as logic and science compelled. The plurality today advances not one reasonable argument as to why our judgment in that case was wrong and should be abandoned.

C

Having contrived an opportunity to reconsider the *Roe* framework, and then having discarded that framework, the plurality finds the testing provision unobjectionable because it "permissibly furthers the State's interest in protecting potential human life." * * * This newly minted standard is circular and totally meaningless. Whether a challenged abortion regulation "permissibly furthers" a legitimate state interest is the *question* that courts must answer in abortion cases, not the standard for courts to apply. In keeping with the rest of its opinion, the plurality makes no attempt to explain or to justify its new standard, either in the abstract or as applied in this case. Nor could it. The "permissibly furthers" standard has no independent meaning, and consists of nothing other than what a majority of this Court may believe at any given moment in any given case. The plurality's novel test appears to be nothing more than a dressed-up version of rational-basis review, this Court's most lenient level of scrutiny. One thing is clear, however: were the plurality's "permissibly furthers" standard adopted by the Court, for all practical purposes, *Roe* would be overruled.[10]

9. Notably, neither the plurality nor Justice O'Connor advance the now-familiar catch-phrase criticism of the *Roe* framework that because the point of viability will recede with advances in medical technology, *Roe* "is clearly on a collision course with itself." See *Akron,* 462 U.S., at 458, 103 S.Ct., at 2507 (dissenting opinion). This critique has no medical foundation. As the medical literature and the *amicus* briefs filed in this case conclusively demonstrate, "there is an 'anatomic threshold' for fetal viability of about 23–24 weeks gestation." Brief for American Medical Association, et al., as *Amici Curiae* 7. Prior to that time, the crucial organs are not sufficiently mature to provide the mutually sustaining functions that are prerequisite to extrauterine survival, or viability. Moreover, "no technology exists to bridge the development gap between the three-day embryo culture and the 24th week of gestation." Fetal Extrauterine Survivability, Report to the New York State Task Force on Life and Law 10 (1988). Nor does the medical community believe that the development of any such technology is possible in the foreseeable future. *Id.,* at 12. In other words, the threshold of fetal viability is, and will remain, no different from what it was at the time *Roe* was decided. Predictions to the contrary are pure science fiction. See Brief for A Group of American Law Professors as *Amici Curiae* 23–25.

10. Writing for the Court in *Akron,* Justice Powell observed the same phenomenon, though in hypothetical response to the dissent in that case: "In sum, it appears that the dissent would uphold virtually any abortion regulation under a rational-basis test. It also appears that even where heightened scrutiny is deemed appropriate, the dissent would uphold virtually any abortion-inhibiting regulation because of the State's interest in preserving potential human life. * * * This analysis is wholly incompatible with the existence of the fundamental right recognized in *Roe v. Wade.*" * * *

The "permissibly furthers" standard completely disregards the irreducible minimum of *Roe:* the Court's recognition that a woman has a limited fundamental constitutional right to decide whether to terminate a pregnancy. That right receives no meaningful recognition in the plurality's written opinion. Since, in the plurality's view, the State's interest in potential life is compelling as of the moment of conception, and is therefore served only if abortion is abolished, every hindrance to a woman's ability to obtain an abortion must be "permissible." Indeed, the more severe the hindrance, the more effectively (and permissibly) the State's interest would be furthered. A tax on abortions or a criminal prohibition would both satisfy the plurality's standard. So, for that matter, would a requirement that a pregnant woman memorize and recite today's plurality opinion before seeking an abortion.

The plurality pretends that *Roe* survives, explaining that the facts of this case differ from those in *Roe:* here, Missouri has chosen to assert its interest in potential life only at the point of viability, whereas, in *Roe,* Texas had asserted that interest from the point of conception, criminalizing all abortions, except where the life of the mother was at stake. * * * This, of course, is a distinction without a difference. The plurality repudiates every principle for which *Roe* stands; in good conscience, it cannot possibly believe that *Roe* lies "undisturbed" merely because this case does not call upon the Court to reconsider the Texas statute, or one like it. If the Constitution permits a State to enact any statute that reasonably furthers its interest in potential life, and if that interest arises as of conception, why would the Texas statute fail to pass muster? One suspects that the plurality agrees. It is impossible to read the plurality opinion and especially its final paragraph, without recognizing its implicit invitation to every State to enact more and more restrictive abortion laws, and to assert their interest in potential life as of the moment of conception. All these laws will satisfy the plurality's non-scrutiny, until sometime, a new regime of old dissenters and new appointees will declare what the plurality intends: that *Roe* is no longer good law.[11]

---

11. The plurality claims that its treatment of *Roe,* and a woman's right to decide whether to terminate a pregnancy, "hold[s] true the balance between that which the Constitution puts beyond the reach of the democratic process and that which it does not." * * * This is unadulterated nonsense. The plurality's balance matches a lead weight (the State's allegedly compelling interest in fetal life as of the moment of conception) against a feather (a "liberty interest" of the pregnant woman that the plurality barely mentions, much less describes). The plurality's balance—no balance at all—places nothing, or virtually nothing, beyond the reach of the democratic process.

Justice Scalia candidly argues that this is all for the best. * * * I cannot agree. "The very purpose of a Bill of Rights was to withdraw certain subjects from the vicissitudes of political controversy, to place them beyond the reach of majorities and officials and to establish them as legal principles to be applied by the Courts. One's right to life, liberty, and property * * * may not be submitted to vote; they depend on the outcome of no election." *West Virginia Board of Education v. Barnette,* 319 U.S. 624, 638, 63 S.Ct. 1178, 1185, 87 L.Ed. 1628 (1943). In a Nation that cherishes liberty, the ability of a woman to control the biological operation of her body and to determine with her re-

D

Thus, "not with a bang, but a whimper," the plurality discards a landmark case of the last generation, and casts into darkness the hopes and visions of every woman in this country who had come to believe that the Constitution guaranteed her the right to exercise some control over her unique ability to bear children. The plurality does so either oblivious or insensitive to the fact that millions of women, and their families, have ordered their lives around the right to reproductive choice, and that this right has become vital to the full participation of women in the economic and political walks of American life. The plurality would clear the way once again for government to force upon women the physical labor and specific and direct medical and psychological harms that may accompany carrying a fetus to term. The plurality would clear the way again for the State to conscript a woman's body and to force upon her a "distressful life and future."

* * *

The result, as we know from experience, see Cates & Rocket, Illegal Abortions in the United States: 1972–1974, 8 Family Planning Perspectives 86, 92 (1976), would be that every year hundreds of thousands of women, in desperation, would defy the law, and place their health and safety in the unclean and unsympathetic hands of back-alley abortionists, or they would attempt to perform abortions upon themselves, with disastrous results. Every year, many women, especially poor and minority women, would die or suffer debilitating physical trauma, all in the name of enforced morality or religious dictates or lack of compassion, as it may be.

Of the aspirations and settled understandings of American women, of the inevitable and brutal consequences of what it is doing, the tough-approach plurality utters not a word. This silence is callous. It is also profoundly destructive of this Court as an institution. To overturn a constitutional decision is a rare and grave undertaking. To overturn a constitutional decision that secured a fundamental personal liberty to millions of persons would be unprecedented in our 200 years of constitutional history. Although the doctrine of *stare decisis* applies with somewhat diminished force in constitutional cases generally, * * * even in ordinary constitutional cases "any departure from *stare decisis* demands special justification." *Arizona v. Rumsey,* 467 U.S. 203, 212, 104 S.Ct. 2305, 2310, 81 L.Ed.2d 164 (1984). * * * This requirement of justification applies with unique force where, as here, the Court's abrogation of precedent would destroy people's firm belief, based on past decisions of this Court, that they possess an unabridgeable right to undertake certain conduct.

sponsible physician whether or not to carry a fetus to term, must fall within that limited sphere of individual autonomy that lies beyond the will or the power of any transient majority. This Court stands as the ultimate guarantor of that zone of privacy, regardless of the bitter disputes to which our decisions may give rise. In *Roe,* and our numerous cases reaffirming *Roe,* we did no more than discharge our constitutional duty.

As discussed at perhaps too great length above, the plurality makes no serious attempt to carry "the heavy burden of persuading * * * that changes in society or in the law dictate" the abandonment of *Roe* and its numerous progeny, * * * much less the greater burden of explaining the abrogation of a fundamental personal freedom. Instead, the plurality pretends that it leaves *Roe* standing, and refuses even to discuss the real issue underlying this case: whether the Constitution includes an unenumerated right to privacy that encompasses a woman's right to decide whether to terminate a pregnancy. To the extent that the plurality does criticize the *Roe* framework, these criticisms are pure *ipse dixit*.

This comes at a cost. The doctrine of *stare decisis* "permits society to presume that bedrock principles are founded in the law rather than in the proclivities of individuals, and thereby contributes to the integrity of our constitutional system of government, both in appearance and in fact." * * * Today's decision involves the most politically divisive domestic legal issue of our time. By refusing to explain or to justify its proposed revolutionary revision in the law of abortion, and by refusing to abide not only by our precedents, but also by our canons for reconsidering those precedents, the plurality invites charges of cowardice and illegitimacy to our door. I cannot say that these would be undeserved.

II

For today, at least, the law of abortion stands undisturbed. For today, the women of this Nation still retain the liberty to control their destinies. But the signs are evident and very ominous, and a chill wind blows.

I dissent.

JUSTICE STEVENS, concurring in part and dissenting in part.

* * * The reasons why I would also affirm that court's invalidation of § 188.029, the viability testing provision, and §§ 1.205.1(1), (2) of the preamble require separate explanation.

I

It seems to me that in Part II–D of its opinion, the plurality strains to place a construction on § 188.029 that enables it to conclude, "[W]e would modify and narrow *Roe* and succeeding cases," * * *. That statement is ill-advised because there is no need to modify even slightly the holdings of prior cases in order to uphold § 188.029. * * *

* * * In this case, I agree with the Court of Appeals, * * * and the District Court, * * * that the meaning of the second sentence of § 188.029 is too plain to be ignored. The sentence twice uses the mandatory term "shall," and contains no qualifying language. If it is implicitly limited to tests that are useful in determining viability, it adds nothing to the requirement imposed by the preceding sentence.

My interpretation of the plain language is supported by the structure of the statute as a whole, particularly the preamble, which "finds" that life "begins at conception" and further commands that state laws shall be construed to provide the maximum protection to "the unborn child at every stage of development." * * * I agree with the District Court that "[o]bviously, the purpose of this law is to protect the potential life of the fetus, rather than to safeguard maternal health." * * * A literal reading of the statute tends to accomplish that goal. Thus it is not "incongruous," * * * to assume that the Missouri Legislature was trying to protect the potential human life of nonviable fetuses by making the abortion decision more costly. On the contrary, I am satisfied that the Court of Appeals, as well as the District Court, correctly concluded that the Missouri Legislature meant exactly what it said in the second sentence of § 188.029. I am also satisfied, for the reasons stated by Justice Blackmun, that the testing provision is manifestly unconstitutional under *Williamson v. Lee Optical Co.,* 348 U.S. 483, 75 S.Ct. 461, 99 L.Ed. 563 (1955), "irrespective of the *Roe* * * * framework." * * *.

II

The Missouri statute defines "conception" as "the fertilization of the ovum of a female by a sperm of a male," * * * even though standard medical texts equate "conception" with implantation in the uterus, occurring about six days after fertilization. Missouri's declaration therefore implies regulation not only of previability abortions, but also of common forms of contraception such as the IUD and the morning-after pill. Because the preamble, read in context, threatens serious encroachments upon the liberty of the pregnant woman and the health professional, I am persuaded that these plaintiffs, appellees before us, have standing to challenge its constitutionality. * * *

To the extent that the Missouri statute interferes with contraceptive choices, I have no doubt that it is unconstitutional under the Court's holdings in *Griswold v. Connecticut,* * * * *Eisenstadt v. Baird,* * * * and *Carey v. Population Services International,* * * *.

* * *

One might argue that the *Griswold* holding applies to devices "preventing conception," * * * —that is, fertilization—but not to those preventing implantation, and therefore, that *Griswold* does not protect a woman's choice to use an IUD or take a morning-after pill. There is unquestionably a theological basis for such an argument, just as there was unquestionably a theological basis for the Connecticut statute that the Court invalidated in *Griswold.* Our jurisprudence, however, has consistently required a secular basis for valid legislation. * * * Because I am not aware of any secular basis for differentiating between contraceptive procedures that are effective immediately before and those that are effective immediately after fertilization, I believe it inescapably follows that the preamble to the Missouri statute is invalid under *Griswold* and its progeny.

Indeed, I am persuaded that the absence of any secular purpose for the legislative declarations that life begins at conception and that conception occurs at fertilization makes the relevant portion of the preamble invalid under the Establishment Clause of the First Amendment to the Federal Constitution. This conclusion does not, and could not, rest on the fact that the statement happens to coincide with the tenets of certain religions, * * * or on the fact that the legislators who voted to enact it may have been motivated by religious considerations, * * *. Rather, it rests on the fact that the preamble, an unequivocal endorsement of a religious tenet of some but by no means all Christian faiths serves no identifiable secular purpose. That fact alone compels a conclusion that the statute violates the Establishment Clause. * * *

* * *

* * * The preamble to the Missouri statute endorses the theological position that there is the same secular interest in preserving the life of a fetus during the first 40 or 80 days of pregnancy as there is after viability—indeed, after the time when the fetus has become a "person" with legal rights protected by the Constitution.[13] To sustain that position as a matter of law, I believe Missouri has the burden of identifying the secular interests that differentiate the first 40 days of pregnancy from the period immediately before or after fertilization when, as *Griswold* and related cases establish, the Constitution allows the use of contraceptive procedures to prevent potential life from developing into full personhood. Focusing our attention on the first several weeks of pregnancy is especially appropriate because that is the period when the vast majority of abortions are actually performed.

As a secular matter, there is an obvious difference between the state interest in protecting the freshly fertilized egg and the state interest in protecting a 9–month–gestated, fully sentient fetus on the eve of birth. There can be no interest in protecting the newly fertilized egg from physical pain or mental anguish, because the capacity for such suffering does not yet exist; respecting a developed fetus, however, that interest is valid. * * *

* * *

Bolstering my conclusion that the preamble violates the First Amendment is the fact that the intensely divisive character of much of the national debate over the abortion issue reflects the deeply held religious convictions of many participants in the debate. The Missouri Legislature may not inject its endorsement of a particular religious

---

13. No Member of this Court has ever questioned the holding in *Roe,* * * * that a fetus is not a "person" within the meaning of the Fourteenth Amendment. Even the dissenters in *Roe* implicitly endorsed that holding by arguing that state legislatures should decide whether to prohibit or to authorize abortions. * * * (Rehnquist, J., dissenting) (arguing that the Fourteenth Amendment did not "withdraw from the States the power to legislate with respect to this matter"); *Doe v. Bolton,* * * * (White, J., dissenting jointly in *Doe* and *Roe*). By characterizing the basic question as "a political issue," * * * (concurring in part and concurring in judgment), Justice Scalia likewise implicitly accepts this holding.

tradition into this debate, for "[t]he Establishment Clause does not allow public bodies to foment such disagreement." See *Allegheny County v. Greater Pittsburgh ACLU,* ___ U.S. ___, ___, 109 S.Ct. 3086, 3132, 106 L.Ed.2d 472 (STEVENS, J., concurring in part and dissenting in part).

In my opinion the preamble to the Missouri statute is unconstitutional for two reasons. To the extent that it has substantive impact on the freedom to use contraceptive procedures, it is inconsistent with the central holding in *Griswold*. To the extent that it merely makes "legislative findings without operative effect," as the State argues, * * * it violates the Establishment Clause of the First Amendment. Contrary to the theological "finding" of the Missouri Legislature, a woman's constitutionally protected liberty encompasses the right to act on her own belief that—to paraphrase St. Thomas Aquinas—until a seed has acquired the powers of sensation and movement, the life of a human being has not yet begun.

HODGSON v. MINNESOTA

Supreme Court of the United States, 1990.
___ U.S. ___, 110 S.Ct. ___, ___ L.Ed.2d ___.

JUSTICE STEVENS announced the judgment of the Court and delivered the opinion of the Court with respect to Parts I, II, IV, and VII, an opinion with respect to Part III in which JUSTICE BRENNAN joins, an opinion with respect to Parts V and VI in which JUSTICE O'CONNOR joins, and a dissenting opinion with respect to Part VIII.

A Minnesota statute, Minn.Stat. §§ 144.343(2)–(7) (1988), provides, with certain exceptions, that no abortion shall be performed on a woman under 18 years of age until at least 48 hours after both of her parents have been notified. In subdivisions 2–4 of the statute the notice is mandatory unless (1) the attending physician certifies that an immediate abortion is necessary to prevent the woman's death and there is insufficient time to provide the required notice; (2) both of her parents have consented in writing; or (3) the woman declares that she is a victim of parental abuse or neglect, in which event notice of her declaration must be given to the proper authorities. * * * Subdivision 6 of the same statute provides that if a court enjoins the enforcement of subdivision 2, the same notice requirement shall be effective unless the pregnant woman obtains a court order permitting the abortion to proceed. * * *

For reasons that follow, we now conclude that the requirement of notice to both of the pregnant minor's parents is not reasonably related to legitimate state interests and that subdivision 2 is unconstitutional. A different majority of the Court, for reasons stated in separate opinions, concludes that subdivision 6 is constitutional. * * *

I

The parental notice statute was enacted in 1981 as an amendment to the Minors' Consent to Health Services Act. * * *

The 1981 amendment qualified the authority of an "unemancipated minor"[3] to give effective consent to an abortion by requiring that either her physician or an agent notify "the parent" personally or by certified mail at least 48 hours before the procedure is performed. The term "parent" is defined in subdivision 3 to mean "both parents of the pregnant woman if they are both living." No exception is made for a divorced parent, a noncustodial parent, or a biological parent who never married or lived with the pregnant woman's mother.[5] The statute does provide, however, that if only one parent is living, or "if the second one cannot be located through reasonably diligent effort," notice to one parent is sufficient. It also makes exceptions for cases in which emergency treatment prior to notice "is necessary to prevent the woman's

---

3. Although there is no statutory definition of emancipation in Minnesota, see *Streitz v. Streitz*, 363 N.W.2d 135, 137 (Minn.App.1985), we have no reason to question the State's representation that Minn.Stat. §§ 144.341 and 144.342 (1988) apply to the minor's decision to terminate her pregnancy. Brief for Respondents in No. 88–1125, p. 2, n. 2. Those sections provide that a minor who is living separate and apart from her parents or who is either married or has borne a child may give effective consent to medical services without the consent of any other person.

The notification statute also applies to a woman for whom a guardian or conservator has been appointed because of a finding of incompetency. § 144.343(2). This portion of the statute is not challenged in this case.

5. The Minnesota statute is the most intrusive in the Nation. Of the 38 States that require parental participation in the minor's decision to terminate her pregnancy, 27 make express that the participation of only one parent is required. An additional three States, Idaho, Tennessee, and Utah, require an unmarried minor to notify "the parents or guardian" but do not specify whether "parents" refers to either member of the parental unit or whether notice to one parent constitutes constructive notice to both. See Idaho Code § 18–609(6) (1987); Tenn.Code Ann. § 39–15–202(f) (Supp.1989); Utah Code Ann. § 76–7–304(2) (1990). In contrast, Arkansas does require an unmarried minor to notify both parents but provides exceptions where the second parent "cannot be located through reasonably diligent effort," or a parent's "whereabouts are unknown," the parent has not been in contact with the minor's custodial parent or the minor for at least one year, or the parent is guilty of sexual abuse. Ark.Code Ann. §§ 20–16–802, 20–16–808 (Supp.1989). Delaware requires the consent only of parents who are residing in the same household; if the minor is not living with both of her parents, the consent of one parent is sufficient. Del.Code Ann. Tit. 24, § 1790(b)(3) (1987). Illinois law does not require the consent of a parent who has deserted the family or is not available. Ill.Rev.Stat., ch. 38 ¶81–54(3) (1989). Kentucky requires an unmarried minor to obtain the consent of a legal guardian or "both parents, if available," but provides that if both parents are not available, the consent of the available parent shall suffice. Ky.Rev.Stat.Ann. §§ 311.732(2)(a), (b) (Michie 1990). Under Massachusetts law, an unmarried minor need obtain the consent of only one parent if the other parent "is unavailable to the physician within a reasonable time and in a reasonable manner," or if the parents are divorced and the other parent does not have custody. Mass.Gen. Laws § 112, § 12S (1988). Mississippi law requires only the consent of the parent with primary custody, care and control of the minor if the parents are divorced or unmarried and living apart and, in all other cases, the consent of only one parent if the other parent is not available in a reasonable time or manner. Miss.Code Ann. § 41–41–53(2) (Supp.1989). Finally, North Dakota requires only the consent of the custodial parent if the parents are separated and divorced, or the legal guardian if the minor is subject to guardianship. N.D.Cent. Code § 14–02.1–03.1 (1981).

death," both parents have already given their consent in writing, or the proper authorities are advised that the minor is a victim of sexual or physical abuse. The statute subjects a person performing an abortion in violation of its terms to criminal sanctions and to civil liability in an action brought by any person "wrongfully denied notification."

Subdivision 6 authorizes a judicial bypass of the two-parent notice requirement if subdivision 2 is ever "temporarily or permanently" enjoined by judicial order. If the pregnant minor can convince "any judge of a court of competent jurisdiction" that she is "mature and capable of giving informed consent to the proposed abortion," or that an abortion without notice to both parents would be in her best interest, the court can authorize the physician to proceed without notice. The statute provides that the bypass procedure shall be confidential, that it shall be expedited, that the minor has a right to court-appointed counsel, and that she shall be afforded free access to the court "24 hours a day, seven days a week." An order denying an abortion can be appealed on an expedited basis, but an order authorizing an abortion without notification is not subject to appeal.

The statute contains a severability provision, but it does not include a statement of its purposes. The Minnesota Attorney General has advised us that those purposes are apparent from the statutory text and that they "include the recognition and fostering of parent-child relationships, promoting counsel to a child in a difficult and traumatic choice, and providing for notice to those who are naturally most concerned for the child's welfare." The District Court found that the primary purpose of the legislation was to protect the well-being of minors by encouraging them to discuss with their parents the decision whether to terminate their pregnancies. It also found that the legislature was motivated by a desire to deter and dissuade minors from choosing to terminate their pregnancies. The Attorney General, however, disclaims any reliance on this purpose.

* * *

III

There is a natural difference between men and women: only women have the capacity to bear children. A woman's decision to beget or to bear a child is a component of her liberty that is protected by the Due Process Clause of the Fourteenth Amendment to the Constitution. See *Harris v. McRae,* * * *; *Carey v. Population Services International,* * * *; *Cleveland Board of Education v. LaFleur,* * * *; *Roe v. Wade,* * * *; *id.,* at 168–170 (Stewart, J., concurring); *Eisenstadt v. Baird,* * * *; *Griswold v. Connecticut,* * * * (White, J., concurring in judgment). That Clause, as interpreted in those cases, protects the woman's right to make such decisions independently and privately, see *Whalen v. Roe,* * * * free of unwarranted governmental intrusion.

"Moreover, the potentially severe detriment facing a pregnant woman, see *Roe v. Wade,* * * * is not mitigated by her minority.

Indeed, considering her probable education, employment skills, financial resources, and emotional maturity, unwanted motherhood may be exceptionally burdensome for a minor. In addition, the fact of having a child brings with it adult legal responsibility, for parenthood, like attainment of the age of majority, is one of the traditional criteria for the termination of the legal disabilities of minority. In sum, there are few situations in which denying a minor the right to make an important decision will have consequences so grave and indelible." * * * (*Bellotti II*).

As we stated in *Planned Parenthood of Central Missouri v. Danforth,* * * * the right to make this decision "do[es] not mature and come into being magically only when one attains the state-defined age of majority." Thus, the constitutional protection against unjustified state intrusion into the process of deciding whether or not to bear a child extends to pregnant minors as well as adult women.

In cases involving abortion, as in cases involving the right to travel or the right to marry, the identification of the constitutionally protected interest is merely the beginning of the analysis. State regulation of travel and of marriage is obviously permissible even though a State may not categorically exclude nonresidents from its borders, *Shapiro v. Thompson,* * * * or deny prisoners the right to marry, *Turner v. Safley,* * * *. But the regulation of constitutionally protected decisions, such as where a person shall reside or whom he or she shall marry, must be predicated on legitimate state concerns other than disagreement with the choice the individual has made. Cf. *Turner v. Safley, supra; Loving v. Virginia,* * * *. In the abortion area, a State may have no obligation to spend its own money, or use its own facilities, to subsidize nontherapeutic abortions for minors or adults. See, *e.g., Maher v. Roe,* * * *; cf. *Webster v. Reproductive Health Services,* * * * (plurality opinion); *id.,* at ___ (O'CONNOR, J., concurring in part and concurring in judgment). A State's value judgment favoring childbirth over abortion may provide adequate support for decisions involving such allocation of public funds, but not for simply substituting a state decision for an individual decision that a woman has a right to make for herself. Otherwise, the interest in liberty protected by the Due Process Clause would be a nullity. A state policy favoring childbirth over abortion is not in itself a sufficient justification for overriding the woman's decision or for placing "obstacles—absolute or otherwise—in the pregnant woman's path to an abortion." *Maher,* * * *; see also *Harris v. McRae,* * * *.

In these cases the State of Minnesota does not rest its defense of this statute on any such value judgment. Indeed, it affirmatively disavows that state interest as a basis for upholding this law. Moreover, it is clear that the state judges who have interpreted the statute in over 3,000 decisions implementing its bypass procedures have found no legislative intent to disfavor the decision to terminate a pregnancy. On the contrary, in all but a handful of cases they have approved such decisions.[21] Because the Minnesota statute unquestionably places obstacles in the pregnant minor's path to an abortion, the State has the burden of establishing its constitutionality. Under any analysis, the Minnesota statute cannot be sustained if the obstacles it imposes are not reasonably related to legitimate state interests. Cf. *Turner v. Safley*, 482 U.S., at 97; *Carey v. Population Services International*, 431 U.S., at 704 (opinion of Powell, J.); *Doe v. Bolton*, 410 U.S. 179, 194–195, 199 (1973).

IV

The Court has considered the constitutionality of statutes providing for parental consent or parental notification in six abortion cases decided during the last 14 years. Although the Massachusetts statute reviewed in *Bellotti v. Baird*, * * * (*Bellotti I*), and *Bellotti II* required the consent of both parents, and the Utah statute reviewed in *H.L. v. Matheson*, 450 U.S. 398 (1981), required notice to "the parents,"[23] none of the opinions in any of those cases focused on the possible significance of making the consent or the notice requirement applicable to both parents instead of just one. In contrast, the arguments in these cases, as well as the extensive findings of the District Court, are directed primarily at that distinction. It is therefore appropriate to summarize these findings before addressing the constitutionality of the 48-hour waiting period or the two-parent notification requirement, particularly since none of the findings has been challenged in either this Court or the Court of Appeals.

Approximately one out of every two marriages ends in divorce. * * * Unrebutted evidence indicates that only 50% of minors in the State of Minnesota reside with both biological parents. * * * This conclusion is substantially corroborated by a study indicating that 9% of the minors in Minnesota live with neither parent and 33% live with only one parent.[24] * * *

21. The District Court found:

"During the period for which statistics have been compiled, 3,573 bypass petitions were filed in Minnesota courts. Six petitions were withdrawn before decision. Nine petitions were denied and 3,558 were granted." Finding No. 55, 648 F.Supp., at 765.

23. The Utah statute reviewed in *Matheson* required the physician to "[n]otify, if possible, the parents or guardian of the woman upon whom the abortion is to be performed." Utah Code Ann. § 76–7–304(2) (1990). Unlike the Minnesota statute under review today, the Utah statute did not define the term "parents." The statute is ambiguous as to whether the term refers to each parent individually or rather to the parental unit, which could be represented by either the mother or the father, and neither the argument nor the discussion in *Matheson* indicated that notice to both parents was required. State law, to the extent it addresses the issue, is to the contrary: Although Utah law provides that a noncustodial parent retains the right to consent to marriage, enlistment, and the performance of major medical or surgical treatment, the right to notice of the minor's abortion is not among the parent's specific residual rights and duties. Utah Code Ann. § 78–3a–2(13) (Supp.1989).

24. The figures are not dissimilar to those throughout the Nation. See *e.g.*, Brief for American Psychological Association et al. as *Amici Curiae* 12–13 ("It is estimated that by age 17, 70 percent of white children born in 1980 will have spent at least some time with only one parent, and 94 percent of black children will have lived in one-parent homes") (citing Hofferth, Updating Children's Life Course, 47 J. Marriage and Fam. 93 (1985)).

The District Court found—on the basis of extensive testimony at trial—that the two-parent notification requirement had particularly harmful effects on both the minor and the custodial parent when the parents were divorced or separated. Relations between the minor and absent parent were not reestablished as a result of the forced notification thereby often producing disappointment in the minor "when an anticipated reestablishment of her relationship with the absent parent d[id] not occur." Moreover, "[t]he reaction of the custodial parent to the requirement of forced notification is often one of anger, resentment and frustration at the intrusion of the absent parent," and fear that notification will threaten the custody rights of the parent or otherwise promote intrafamily violence. Tragically, those fears were often realized:

> "Involuntary involvement of the second biological parent is especially detrimental when the minor comes from an abusive, dysfunctional family. Notification of the minor's pregnancy and abortion decision can provoke violence, even where the parents are divorced or separated. Studies have shown that violence and harassment may continue well beyond the divorce, especially when children are involved.
>
> "* * * Furthermore, a mother's perception in a dysfunctional family that there will be violence if the father learns of the daughter's pregnancy is likely to be an accurate perception." * * *

The District Court further found:

> "Twenty to twenty-five percent of the minors who go to court either are accompanied by one parent who knows and consents to the abortion or have already told one parent of their intent to terminate their pregnancy. The vast majority of these voluntarily informed parents are women who are divorced or separated from spouses whom they have not seen in years. Going to court to avoid notifying the other parent burdens the privacy of both the minor and the accompanying parent. The custodial parents are angry that their consent is not sufficient and fear that notification will bring the absent parent back into the family in an intrusive and abusive way." * * *

The District Court also found that the two-parent notification requirement had adverse effects in families in which the minor lives with both parents. These effects were particularly pronounced in the distressingly large number of cases in which family violence is a serious problem. The court found that many minors in Minnesota "live in fear of violence by family members" and "are, in fact, victims of rape, incest, neglect and violence."[25] The District Court found that few

---

25. "Studies indicating that family violence occurs in two million families in the United States substantially underestimate the actual number of such families. In Minnesota alone, reports indicate that there are an average of 31,200 incidents of assault on women by their partners each year. Based on these statistics, state officials suggest that the 'battering' of women by their partners 'has come to be recognized as perhaps the most frequently committed violent crime in the state' of Minnesota. These numbers do not include incidents of psychological or sexual abuse, low-level physical abuse, abuse of any sort of the child of a batterer, or those incidents which are not reported. Many minors in Minnesota live in fear of violence by family

minors can take advantage of the exception for a minor who declares that she is a victim of sexual or physical abuse because of the obligation to report the information to the authorities and the attendant loss of privacy. See Findings 46 and 47, * * *.[26] This concern about family violence helps to explain why the District Court found that in many instances the requirement that both parents be notified actually impairs family communication. Minors who otherwise would inform one parent were unwilling to do so when such notification likely would also involve the parent in the torturous ordeal of explaining to a court why the second parent should not be notified. The court found:

> "Minors who ordinarily would notify one parent may be dissuaded from doing so by the two-parent requirement. A minor who must go to court for authorization in any event may elect not to tell either parent. In these instances, the requirement that minors notify both biological parents actually reduces parent-child communication." * * *

The great majority of bypass petitions are filed in the three metropolitan counties in Minnesota, where courts schedule bypass hearings on a regular basis and have in place procedures for hearing emergency petitions. * * * Courts in the nonmetropolitan areas are acquainted with the statute and, for the most part, apply it conscientiously, but a number of counties are served by judges who are unwilling to hear bypass petitions. * * * Aside from the unavoidable notification of court officials, the confidentiality of minors has been maintained. * * *

During the period between August 1, 1981, and March 1, 1986, 3,573 judicial bypass petitions were filed in Minnesota courts. All but 15 were granted. The judges who adjudicated over 90% of these petitions testified; none of them identified any positive effects of the law. The court experience produced fear, tension, anxiety, and shame among minors, causing some who were mature, and some whose best interests would have been served by an abortion, to "forgo the bypass option and either notify their parents or carry to term." * * * Among parents who supported their daughters in the bypass proceedings, the court experience evoked similar reactions.

Scheduling petitions in the Minnesota court typically required minors to wait only two or three days for hearings. The District Court found, however, that the statutory waiting period of 48 hours was

---

members; many of them are, in fact, victims of rape, incest, neglect and violence. It is impossible to accurately assess the magnitude of the problem of family violence in Minnesota because members of dysfunctional families are characteristically secretive about such matters and minors are particularly reluctant to reveal violence or abuse in their families. Thus the incidence of such family violence is dramatically underreported." * * *

26. "Minors who are victims of sexual or physical abuse often are reluctant to reveal the existence of the abuse to those outside the home. More importantly, notification to government authorities creates a substantial risk that the confidentiality of the minor's decision to terminate her pregnancy will be lost. Thus, few minors choose to declare they are victims of sexual or physical abuse despite the prevalence of such abuse in Minnesota, as elsewhere." * * *

frequently compounded by a number of other factors that "commonly" created a delay of 72 hours, * * * and, "in many cases" a delay of a week or more in effecting a decision to terminate a pregnancy. * * * A delay of that magnitude increased the medical risk associated with the abortion procedure to "a statistically significant degree." * * * While recognizing that a mandatory delay following the notice to a minor's parent served the State's interest in protecting pregnant minors, the court found that that interest could be served by a shorter waiting period. * * *

At least 37 witnesses testified to the issue whether the statute furthered the State's interest in protecting pregnant minors. Only two witnesses testified that a two-parent notification statute did minors more good than harm; neither of these witnesses had direct experience with the Minnesota statute. * * *

Focusing specifically on the statutory requirement that both parents be notified, the District Court concluded:

"The court finds that this requirement places a significant burden upon pregnant minors who do not live with both parents. Particularly in these cases, notification of an abusive, or even a disinterested, absent parent has the effect of reintroducing that parent's disruptive or unhelpful participation into the family at a time of acute stress. Similarly, the two-parent notification requirement places a significant obstacle in the path of minors in two-parent homes who voluntarily have consulted with one parent but not with the other out of fear of psychological, sexual, or physical abuse toward either the minor or the notified parent. In either case, the alternative of going to court to seek authorization to proceed without notifying the second parent introduces a traumatic distraction into her relationship with the parent whom the minor has notified. The anxiety attending either option tends to interfere with and burden the parent-child communication the minor voluntarily initiated with the custodial parent.

* * *

"* * * Indeed, 20 to 25% of minors seeking judicial authorization to proceed with an abortion without parental notification are accompanied to court by one parent, or at least have obtained the approval of one parent. In these cases the necessity either to notify the second parent despite the agreement of both the minor and the notified parent that such notification is undesirable, or to obtain a judicial waiver of the notification requirement, distracts the minor and her parent and disrupts their communication. Thus the need to notify the second parent or to make a burdensome court appearance actively interferes with the parent-child communication voluntarily initiated by the child, communication assertedly at the heart of the State's purpose in requiring notification of both parents. In these cases, requiring notification of both parents affirmatively discourages parent-child communication." * * *

V

Three separate but related interests—the interest in the welfare of the pregnant minor, the interest of the parents, and the interest of the family unit—are relevant to our consideration of the constitutionality of the 48-hour waiting period and the two-parent notification requirement.

The State has a strong and legitimate interest in the welfare of its young citizens, whose immaturity, inexperience, and lack of judgment may sometimes impair their ability to exercise their rights wisely. * * * That interest, which justifies state-imposed requirements that a minor obtain his or her parent's consent before undergoing an operation, marrying, or entering military service, * * * extends also to the minor's decision to terminate her pregnancy. Although the Court has held that parents may not exercise "an absolute and possibly arbitrary, veto" over that decision, *Danforth,* 428 U.S., at 74, it has never challenged a State's reasonable judgment that the decision should be made after notification to and consultation with a parent. * * *

Parents have an interest in controlling the education and upbringing of their children but that interest is "a counterpart of the responsibilities they have assumed." * * * The fact of biological parentage generally offers a person only "an opportunity * * * to develop a relationship with his offspring." * * * But the demonstration of commitment to the child through the assumption of personal, financial, or custodial responsibility may give the natural parent a stake in the relationship with the child rising to the level of a liberty interest. See *Stanley v. Illinois,* * * *; *Lehr,* * * *; *Michael H. v. Gerald D.,* * * * (White, J., dissenting); cf. *Caban,* * * * n. 14. But see *Michael H.,* * * * (plurality opinion).

While the State has a legitimate interest in the creation and dissolution of the marriage contract, * * * the family has a privacy interest in the upbringing and education of children and the intimacies of the marital relationship which is protected by the Constitution against undue state interference. * * * The family may assign one parent to guide the children's education and the other to look after their health. "The statist notion that governmental power should supersede parental authority in *all* cases because *some* parents abuse and neglect children is repugnant to American tradition." *Parham,* * * *. We have long held that there exists a "private realm of family life which the state cannot enter." *Prince v. Massachusetts,* * * *. Thus, when the government intrudes on choices concerning the arrangement of the household, this Court has carefully examined the "governmental interests advanced and the extent to which they are served by the challenged regulation." * * *

A natural parent who has demonstrated sufficient commitment to his or her children is thereafter entitled to raise the children free from undue state interference. * * *

VI

We think it is clear that a requirement that a minor wait 48 hours after notifying a single parent of her intention to get an abortion would reasonably further the legitimate state interest in ensuring that the minor's decision is knowing and intelligent. We have held that when a parent or another person has assumed "primary responsibility" for a minor's well-being, the State may properly enact "laws designed to aid discharge of that responsibility." *Ginsberg v. New York,* 390 U.S. 629, 639 (1968). To the extent that subdivision 2 of the Minnesota statute requires notification of only one parent, it does just that. The brief waiting period provides the parent the opportunity to consult with his or her spouse and a family physician, and it permits the parent to inquire into the competency of the doctor performing the abortion, discuss the religious or moral implications of the abortion decision, and provide the daughter needed guidance and counsel in evaluating the impact of the decision on her future. See *Zbaraz v. Hartigan,* 763 F.2d 1532, 1552 (CA7 1985), (COFFEY, J., dissenting), aff'd by an equally divided Court, 484 U.S. 171 (1987).

The 48-hour delay imposes only a minimal burden on the right of the minor to decide whether or not to terminate her pregnancy. Although the District Court found that scheduling factors, weather, and the minor's school and work commitments may combine, in many cases, to create a delay of a week or longer between the initiation of notification and the abortion, * * * there is no evidence that the 48-hour period itself is unreasonable or longer than appropriate for adequate consultation between parent and child. The statute does not impose any period of delay once the parents or a court, acting *in loco parentis,* express their agreement that the minor is mature or that the procedure would be in her best interest. Indeed, as the Court of Appeals noted and the record reveals,[34] the 48-hour waiting period may run concurrently with the time necessary to make an appointment for the procedure, thus, resulting in little or no delay.[35]

---

34. The record contains the telephone training manual of one clinic which contemplates that notification will be made on the date the patient contacts the clinic to arrange an abortion so that the appointment can be scheduled for a few days later. Since that clinic typically has a 1- to 2-day backlog, * * * the statutory waiting period creates little delay.

35. *Akron v. Akron Center for Reproductive Health, Inc.,* * * * upon which the plaintiffs rely, is not to the contrary. There we invalidated a provision that required that mature women, capable of consenting to an abortion, wait 24 hours after giving consent before undergoing an abortion. The only legitimate state interest asserted was that the "woman's decision be informed." * * * We decided that "if a woman, after appropriate counseling, is prepared to give her written informed consent and proceed with the abortion, a State may not demand that she delay the effectuation of that decision." * * * By contrast, in this case, the State asserts a legitimate interest in protecting minor women from their own immaturity. As we explain in the text, the right of the minor to make an informed decision to terminate her pregnancy is not defeated by the 48-hour waiting period. It is significant that the statute does not impose a waiting period if a substitute *competent* decisionmaker—a parent or court—gives affirmative consent to the abortion.

VII

It is equally clear that the requirement that *both* parents be notified, whether or not both wish to be notified or have assumed responsibility for the upbringing of the child, does not reasonably further any legitimate state interest. The usual justification for a parental consent or notifiation provision is that it supports the authority of a parent who is presumed to act in the minor's best interest and thereby assures that the minor's decision to terminate her pregnancy is knowing, intelligent, and deliberate. To the extent that such an interest is legitimate, it would be fully served by a requirement that the minor notify one parent who can then seek the counsel of his or her mate or any other party, when such advice and support is deemed necessary to help the child make a difficult decision. In the ideal family setting, of course, notice to either parent would normally constitute notice to both. A statute requiring two-parent notification would not further any state interest in those instances. In many families, however, the parent notified by the child would not notify the other parent. In those cases the State has no legitimate interest in questioning one parent's judgment that notice to the other parent would not assist the minor or in presuming that the parent who has assumed parental duties is incompetent to make decisions regarding the health and welfare of the child.

Not only does two-parent notification fail to serve any state interest with respect to functioning families, it disserves the state interest in protecting and assisting the minor with respect to dysfunctional families. The record reveals that in the thousands of dysfunctional families affected by this statute, the two-parent notice requirement proved positively harmful to the minor and her family. The testimony at trial established that this requirement, ostensibly designed for the benefit of the minor, resulted in major trauma to the child, and often to a parent as well. In some cases, the parents were divorced and the second parent did not have custody or otherwise participate in the child's upbringing. * * * In these circumstances, the privacy of the parent and child was violated, even when they suffered no other physical or psychological harm. In other instances, however, the second parent had either deserted or abused the child, * * * had died under tragic circumstances, * * * or was not notified because of the considered judgment that notification would inflict unnecessary stress on a parent who was ill.[36] * * * In these circumstances, the statute was not

---

36. The most common reason for not notifying the second parent was that that parent was a child or spouse-batterer, * * * and notification would have provoked further abuse. For example, Judge Allen Oleisky, whose familiarity with the Minnesota statute is based on his having heard over 1,000 petitions from minors, * * * testified that battering is a frequent crime in Minnesota, that parents seek an exemption from the notification requirement because they have been battered or are afraid of assault, and that notification of the father would "set the whole thing off again in some cases." * * * That testimony is confirmed by the uncontradicted testimony of one of plaintiffs' experts that notice of a daughter's pregnancy "would absolutely enrage [a batterer]. It would be much like show-

merely ineffectual in achieving the State's goals but actually counterproductive. The focus on notifying the second parent distracted both the parent and minor from the minor's imminent abortion decision.

The State does not rely primarily on the best interests of the minor in defending this statute. Rather, it argues that, in the ideal family, the minor should make her decision only after consultation with both parents who should naturally be concerned with the child's welfare and that the State has an interest in protecting the independent right of the parents "to determine and strive for what they believe to be best for their children." * * * Neither of these reasons can justify the two-parent notification requirement. The second parent may well have an interest in the minor's abortion decision, making full communication among all members of a family desirable in some cases, but such communication may not be decreed by the State. The State has no more interest in requiring all family members to talk with one another than it has in requiring certain of them to live together. In *Moore v. East Cleveland,* * * * we invalidated a zoning ordinance which "slic[ed] deeply into the family itself," * * * permitting the city to "standardiz[e] its children—and its adults—by forcing all to live in certain narrowly defined family patterns." * * * Although the ordinance was supported by state interests other than the state interest in substituting its conception of family life for the family's own view, the ordinance's relation to those state interests was too "tenuous" to satisfy constitutional standards. By implication, a state interest in standardizing its children and adults, making the "private realm of family life" conform to some state-designed ideal, is not a legitimate state interest at all. See also *Meyer v. Nebraska,* * * * (right to establish a home and bring up children may not be interfered with by legislative action which is without "reasonable relation to some purpose within the competency of the State to effect").

Nor can any state interest in protecting a parent's interest in shaping a child's values and lifestyle overcome the liberty interests of a minor acting with the consent of a single parent or court. See *Bellotti II,* * * *; *Bellotti I,* * * *; *Planned Parenthood of Central Missouri v. Danforth,* * * *. In *Danforth,* the majority identified the only state interest in requiring parental consent as that in "the safeguarding of the family unit and of parental authority" and held that that state interest was insufficient to support the requirement that mature minors receive parental consent. The Court summarily concluded that "[a]ny independent interest the parent may have in the termination of the minor daughter's pregnancy is no more weighty than the right of privacy of the competent minor mature enough to have become pregnant." * * * It follows that the combined force of the separate

ing a red cape to a bull. That kind of information just plays right into his worst fears and his most vulnerable spots. The sexual jealousy, his dislike of his daughter going out with anybody else, would make him very angry and would probably create severe abuse as well as long term communication difficulties." * * * (Testimony of Lenore Walker).

interest of one parent and the minor's privacy interest must outweigh the separate interest of the second parent.

In *Bellotti I* and *Bellotti II,* we also identified the difference between parental interests and the child's best interest. Although the District Court invalidated the Massachusetts statute there under review on the grounds that it permitted a parent or the court, acting *in loco parentis,* to refuse consent based on the parent's own interests, the state Attorney General argued that the parental right consisted " 'exclusively of the right to assess independently, for their minor child, what will serve that child's best interest.' " * * * Because we believed that the Attorney General's interpretation "would avoid or substantially modify the federal constitutional challenge," * * * we ordered the District Court to certify the state-law question to the Supreme Judicial Court of Massachusetts. * * * On review in this Court for the second time, after the Supreme Judicial Court stated unambiguously that the "good cause" standard required the judge to grant consent to an abortion found to be in the minor's best interest, * * * we confirmed that such a construction satisfied "some of the concerns" about the statute's constitutionality, * * * and thereby avoided "much of what was objectionable in the statute successfully challenged in *Danforth.*" * * * Indeed, the constitutional defects that Justice Powell identified in the statute—its failure to allow a minor who is found to be mature and fully competent to make the abortion decision independently and its requirement of parental consultation even when an abortion without notification would be in the minor's best interests—are predicated on the assumption that the justification for any rule requiring parental involvement in the abortion decision rests entirely on the best interests of the child. * * *[37]

Unsurprisingly, the Minnesota two-parent notification requirement is an oddity among state and federal consent provisions governing the health, welfare, and education of children. A minor desiring to enlist in the armed services or the Reserve Officers' Training Corps (ROTC) need only obtain the consent of "his parent or guardian." * * * The consent of "*a* parent or guardian" is also sufficient to obtain a passport for foreign travel from the United States Department of State, * * * and to participate as a subject in most forms of medical research. * * * In virtually every State, the consent of one parent is enough to obtain a driver's license or operator's permit. The same may be said with respect to the decision to submit to any medical or surgical procedure other than an abortion. Indeed, the only other Minnesota statute that the State has identified which requires two-parent consent is that authorizing the minor to change his name. * * * These

---

37. Justice Kennedy recognizes that parental rights are coupled with parental responsibilities, * * * and that "a State [may] legislate on the premise that parents, as a general rule, are interested in their children's welfare and will act in accord with it," * * *. That, of course, is precisely our point. What the State may not do is legislate on the generalized assumptions that a parent in an intact family will not act in his or her child's best interests and will fail to involve the other parent in the child's upbringing when that involvement is appropriate.

statutes provide testimony to the unreasonableness of the Minnesota two-parent notification requirement and to the ease with which the State can adopt less burdensome means to protect the minor's welfare. Cf. *Clark v. Jeter,* 486 U.S. 456, 464 (1988); *Turner v. Safley,* 482 U.S. 78, 98 (1987). We therefore hold that this requirement violates the Constitution.

VIII

The Court holds that the constitutional objection to the two-parent notice requirement is removed by the judicial bypass option provided in subdivision 6 of the Minnesota statute. I respectfully dissent from that holding.

A majority of the Court has previously held that a statute requiring one parent's consent to a minor's abortion will be upheld if the State provides an " 'alternate procedure whereby a pregnant minor may demonstrate that she is sufficiently mature to make the abortion decision herself or that, despite her immaturity, an abortion would be in her best interests.' " *Planned Parenthood Assn. of Kansas City, Mo., Inc. v. Ashcroft,* * * * (opinion of Powell, J.); * * * (opinion of O'Connor, J.). Indeed, in *Bellotti II,* four Members of the Court expressed the same opinion about a statute requiring the consent of both parents. * * * Neither of those precedents should control our decision today.

In *Bellotti II,* eight Members of the Court joined the judgment holding the Massachusetts statute unconstitutional. Thus, the Court did not *hold* that the judicial bypass set forth in that statute was valid; it held just the opposite. Moreover, the discussion of the minimum requirements for a valid judicial bypass in Justice Powell's opinion was joined by only four Members of the Court. Indeed, neither the arguments of the parties, nor any of the opinions in the case, considered the significant difference between a statute requiring the involvement of *both* parents in the abortion decision and a statute that merely requires the involvement of one. Thus, the doctrine of *stare decisis* does not require that the standards articulated in Justice Powell's opinion be applied to a statute that mandates the involvement of both parents.

Unlike *Bellotti II,* the judgment in *Ashcroft* sustained the constitutionality of the statute containing a judicial bypass as an alternative to the requirement of *one* parent's consent to a minor's abortion. The distinctions between notice and consent and between notification of both parents rather than just one arguably constitute a sufficient response to an argument resting on *stare decisis.* Further analysis is necessary, however, because, at least on the surface, the consent requirement would appear to be more onerous than a requirement of mere notice.

The significance of the distinction between a statute requiring the consent of one parent and a statute requiring notice to both parents must be tested by the relationship of the respective requirements to legitimate state interests. We have concluded that the State has a strong and legitimate interest in providing a pregnant minor with the advice and support of a parent during the decisional period. A general rule requiring the minor to obtain the consent of one parent reasonably furthers that interest. An exception from the general rule is necessary to protect the minor from an arbitrary veto that is motivated by the separate concerns of the parent rather than the best interest of the child. * * * But the need for an exception does not undermine the conclusion that the general rule is perfectly reasonable—just as a rule requiring the consent of either parent for any other medical procedure would surely be reasonable if an exception were made for those emergencies in which, for example, a parent might deny life saving treatment to a child on religious grounds. * * *

For reasons already set forth at length, a rule requiring consent or notification of both parents is not reasonably related to the state interest in giving the pregnant minor the benefit of parental advice. The State has not called our attention to, nor am I aware of, any other medical situation in Minnesota or elsewhere in which the provision of treatment for a child has been conditioned on notice to, or consent by, both parents rather than just one. Indeed, the fact that one-parent consent is the virtually uniform rule for any other activity which affects the minor's health, safety or welfare emphasizes the aberrant quality of the two-parent notice requirement.

A judicial bypass that is designed to handle exceptions from a reasonable general rule, and thereby preserve the constitutionality of that rule, is quite different from a requirement that a minor—or a minor and one of her parents—must apply to a court for permission to avoid the application of a rule that is not reasonably related to legitimate state goals. A requirement that a minor acting with the consent of *both* parents apply to a court for permission to effectuate her decision clearly would constitute an unjustified official interference with the privacy of the minor and her family. The requirement that the bypass procedure must be invoked when the minor and one parent agree that the other parent should not be notified represents an equally unjustified governmental intrusion into the family's decisional process. When the parents are living together and have joint custody over the child, the State has no legitimate interest in the communication between father and mother about the child. "[W]here the parents are divorced, the minor and/or custodial parent, and not a court, is in the best position to determine whether notifying the non-custodial parent would be in the child's best interests." * * * As the Court of Appeals panel originally concluded, the "minor and custodial parent, . . . by virtue of their major interest and superior position, should alone have the opportunity to decide to whom, if anyone, notice of the minor's abortion decision should be given." * * * I agree with that conclusion.

* * *

The judgment of the Court of Appeals in its entirety is affirmed. *It is so ordered.*

JUSTICE O'CONNOR, concurring in part and concurring in the judgment in part.

I

I join all but Parts III and VIII of JUSTICE STEVENS' opinion. While I agree with some of the central points made in Part III, I cannot join the broader discussion. I agree that the Court has characterized "[a] woman's decision to beget or to bear a child [as] a component of her liberty that is protected by the Due Process Clause of the Fourteenth Amendment to the Constitution." * * * See, *e.g., Carey v. Population Services International,* * * *; *Griswold v. Connecticut,* * * * (White, J., concurring in judgment). This Court extended that liberty interest to minors in *Bellotti v. Baird,* * * * (*Bellotti II*), and *Planned Parenthood of Central Missouri v. Danforth,* * * * albeit with some important limitations: "[P]arental notice and consent are qualifications that typically may be imposed by the State on a minor's right to make important decisions. As immature minors often lack the ability to make fully informed choices that take account of both immediate and long-range consequences, a State reasonably may determine that parental consultation often is desirable and in the best interest of the minor." *Bellotti II,* * * *; see also *H.L. v. Matheson,* * * * (Stevens, J., concurring in judgment); cf. *Thompson v. Oklahoma,* 487 U.S. 815, 835 (1988) ("Inexperience, less education, and less intelligence make the teenager less able to evaluate the consequences of his or her conduct while at the same time he or she is much more apt to be motivated by mere emotion or peer pressure than is an adult"); *Stanford v. Kentucky* 492 U.S. ___, ___ (1989) (BRENNAN, J., dissenting) (slip op., at 13) ("[M]inors are treated differently from adults in our laws, which reflects the simple truth derived from communal experience, that juveniles as a class have not the level of maturation and responsibility that we presume in adults and consider desirable for full participation in the rights and duties of modern life").

It has been my understanding in this area that "[i]f the particular regulation does not 'unduly burde[n]' the fundamental right, * * * then our evaluation of that regulation is limited to our determination that the regulation rationally relates to a legitimate state purpose." *Akron v. Akron Center for Reproductive Health, Inc.,* 462 U.S. 416, 453 (1983) (O'Connor, J., dissenting); see also *Webster v. Reproductive Health Services,* 492 U.S. ___, ___ (1989) (O'Connor, J., concurring in part and concurring in judgment) (slip op., at 9). It is with that understanding that I agree with Justice Stevens' statement that the "statute cannot be sustained if the obstacles it imposes are not reasonably related to legitimate state interests. Cf. *Turner v. Safley,* 482 U.S., at 97; *Carey v. Population Services International,* 431 U.S., at 704 (opinion of Powell, J.); *Doe v. Bolton,* 410 U.S. 179, 194–195, 199 (1973)." * * *

I agree with Justice Stevens that Minnesota has offered no sufficient justification for its interference with the family's decisionmaking processes created by subdivision 2—two-parent notification. Subdivision 2 is the most stringent notification statute in the country. See *ante,* at * * * n. 5. The only other state that defines the generic term "parents," see, *e.g.,* Tenn.Code Ann. § 36–1–201, Art. III (6) (Supp. 1989) (adoption statute) (" 'Parents' means either the singular or plural of the word 'parent' "); * * * as "both parents" is Arkansas, and that statute provides for numerous exceptions to the two-parent notification requirement and permits bypassing notification where notification would not be in the best interests of the minor. See Ark.Code §§ 20–16–802, 20–16–804, 20–16–808 (Supp.1989).

The Minnesota exception to notification for minors who are victims of neglect or abuse is, in reality, a means of notifying the parents. As Justice Stevens points out, * * * to avail herself of the neglect or abuse exception, the minor must report the abuse. A report requires the welfare agency to immediately "conduct an assessment." Minn. Stat. § 626.556(10)(a) (1988). If the agency interviews the victim, it must notify the parent of the fact of the interview; if the parent is the subject of an investigation, he has a right of access to the record of the investigation. §§ 626.556(10)(c); 626.556(11); see also Tr. of Oral Arg. 19 ("[I]t turns out that the reporting statute in Minnesota requires that after it's reported to the welfare department, the welfare department has to do an assessment and tell the parents about the assessment. This could all be done in a time frame even before the abortion occurs"). The combination of the abused minor's reluctance to report sexual or physical abuse, see *ante,* at * * * n. 26, with the likelihood that invoking the abuse exception for the purpose of avoiding notice will result in notice, makes the abuse exception less than effectual.

Minnesota's two-parent notice requirement is all the more unreasonable when one considers that only half of the minors in the State of Minnesota reside with both biological parents. * * * A third live with only one parent. * * * Given its broad sweep and its failure to serve the purposes asserted by the State in too many cases, I join the Court's striking of subdivision 2.

II

In a series of cases, this Court has explicitly approved judicial bypass as a means of tailoring a parental consent provision so as to avoid unduly burdening the minor's limited right to obtain an abortion. See *Bellotti v. Baird,* * * *; *Planned Parenthood of Central Missouri v. Danforth,* * * *; *Bellotti II,* * * *. In *Danforth,* the Court stated that the

> "primary constitutional deficiency lies in [the notification statute's] imposition of an absolute limitation on the minor's right to obtain an abortion. . . . [A] materially different constitutional issue would be presented under a provision requiring parental consent or consultation in most cases but providing for prompt (i) judicial resolution of any

disagreement between the parent and the minor, or (ii) judicial determination that the minor is mature enough to give an informed consent without parental concurrence or that abortion in any event is in the minor's best interest. Such a provision would not impose parental approval as an absolute condition upon the minor's right but would assure in most instances consultation between the parent and child."

* * *

Subdivision 6 passes constitutional muster because the interference with the internal operation of the family required by subdivision 2 simply does not exist where the minor can avoid notifying one or both parents by use of the bypass procedure.

JUSTICE MARSHALL, with whom JUSTICE BRENNAN and JUSTICE BLACKMUN join, concurring in part, concurring in the judgment in part, and dissenting in part.

I concur in Parts I, II, IV, and VII of JUSTICE STEVENS' opinion for the Court in No. 88–1309.[1] Although I do not believe that the Constitution permits a State to require a minor to notify or consult with a parent before obtaining an abortion, * * * I am in substantial agreement with the remainder of the reasoning in Part V of the Court's opinion. For the reasons stated by Justice Stevens, * * * Minnesota's two-parent notification requirement is not even reasonably related to a legitimate state interest. Therefore, that requirement surely would not pass the strict scrutiny applicable to restrictions on a woman's fundamental right to have an abortion.

I dissent from the judgment of the Court in No. 89–1125, however, that the judicial bypass option renders the parental notification and 48-hour delay requirements constitutional. See * * * (opinion of O'CONNOR, J.); * * * (opinion of KENNEDY, J.). The bypass procedure cannot save those requirements because the bypass itself is unconstitutional both on its face and as applied. At the very least, this scheme substantially burdens a woman's right to privacy without advancing a compelling state interest. More significantly, in some instances it usurps a young woman's control over her own body by giving either a parent or a court the power effectively to veto her decision to have an abortion.

I

This Court has consistently held since *Roe v. Wade,* * * * that the constitutional right of privacy "is broad enough to encompass a woman's decision whether or not to terminate her pregnancy." * * * We have also repeatedly stated that "[a] woman's right to make that choice freely is fundamental." *Thornburgh v. American College of Obstetricians and Gynecologists,* * * *. Accord *Akron v. Akron Center for Reproductive Health, Inc.,* * * *; *Roe,* * * *. As we

---

1. I concur in Part VII on the understanding that the opinion does not dispute that a minor's liberty interest alone outweighs the interest of the second parent in shaping a child's values and lifestyles, regardless of the interest of the first parent. * * *

reiterated in *American College of Obstetricians and Gynecologists, supra,* "Few decisions are more personal and intimate, more properly private, or more basic to individual dignity and autonomy, than a woman's decision—with the guidance of her physician and within the limits specified in *Roe*—whether to end her pregnancy." * * * Accordingly, we have subjected state laws limiting that right to the most exacting scrutiny, requiring a State to show that such a law is narrowly drawn to serve a compelling interest. *Roe,* * * *; *Akron Center for Reproductive Health,* * * *. Only such strict judicial scrutiny is sufficiently protective of a woman's right to make the intensely personal decision whether to terminate her pregnancy.

Roe remains the law of the land. See *Webster v. Reproductive Health Services,* 492 U.S. ___, ___ (1989) (plurality opinion); *id.,* at ___ (O'Connor, J., concurring in part and concurring in judgment); *id.,* at ___ (BLACKMUN, J., concurring in part and dissenting in part). Indeed, today's decision reaffirms the vitality of *Roe,* as five Justices have voted to strike down a state law restricting a woman's right to have an abortion. Accordingly, to be constitutional, state restrictions on abortion must meet the rigorous test set forth above.

II

I strongly disagree with the Court's conclusion that the State may constitutionally force a minor woman either to notify both parents (or in some cases only one parent) and then wait 48 hours before proceeding with an abortion, or disclose her intimate affairs to a judge and ask that he grant her permission to have an abortion. * * * First, the parental notification and delay requirements significantly restrict a young woman's right to reproductive choice. I base my conclusion not on my intuition about the needs and attitudes of young women, but on a sizable and impressive collection of empirical data documenting the effects of parental notification statutes and of delaying an abortion. Second, the burdensome restrictions are not narrowly tailored to serve any compelling state interest. Finally, for the reasons discussed in Part III, *infra,* the judicial bypass procedure does not save the notice and delay requirements.

A

Neither the scope of a woman's privacy right nor the magnitude of a law's burden is diminished because a woman is a minor. * * * Rather, a woman's minority status affects only the nature of the State's interests. Although the Court considers the burdens that the two-parent notification requirement imposes on a minor woman's exercise of her right to privacy, * * * it fails to recognize that forced notification of only one parent also significantly burdens a young woman's right to have an abortion, * * *.

A substantial proportion of pregnant minors voluntarily consult with a parent regardless of the existence of a notification requirement. * * * For these women, the notification requirement by itself does not impose a significant burden. But for those young women who would choose not to inform their parents, the burden is evident: the notification requirement destroys their right to avoid disclosure of a deeply personal matter. * * *

A notification requirement can also have severe physical and psychological effects on a young woman. First, forced notification of one parent, like forced notification of both parents, can be extremely traumatic for a young woman, depending on the nature of her relationship with her parents. * * * The disclosure of a daughter's intention to have an abortion often leads to a family crisis, characterized by severe parental anger and rejection. * * * The impact of any notification requirement is especially devastating for minors who live in fear of physical, psychological, or sexual abuse. * * * Certainly, child abuse is not limited to families with two parents.

Second, the prospect of having to notify a parent causes many young women to delay their abortions, thereby increasing the health risks of the procedure. * * *

In addition, a notification requirement compels many minors seeking an abortion to travel to a State without such a requirement to avoid notifying a parent. * * * Other women may resort to the horrors of self-abortion or illegal abortion rather than tell a parent. * * * [3] Still others would forgo an abortion entirely and carry the fetus to term, * * * subjecting themselves to the much greater health risks of pregnancy and childbirth and to the physical, psychological, and financial hardships of unwanted motherhood. * * * Clearly, then, requiring notification of one parent significantly burdens a young woman's right to terminate her pregnancy.

B

The 48-hour delay *after* notification further aggravates the harm caused by the *pre*-notification delay that may flow from a minor's fear of notifying a parent. Moreover, the 48-hour delay burdens the rights of all minors, including those who would voluntarily consult with one or both parents.[4] Justice Stevens' assertion that the 48-hour delay "imposes only a minimal burden," * * * ignores the increased health risks and costs that this delay entails. The District Court specifically found as a matter of fact that "[d]elay of any length in performing an abortion increases the statistical risk of mortality and morbidity." * * * Even a brief delay can have a particularly detrimental impact

---

3. Dr. Jane Hodgson testified before the District Court that one 14-year-old patient, in order to keep her pregnancy private, tried to induce an abortion with the help of her friends by inserting a metallic object into her vagina, thereby tearing her body, scarring her cervix, and causing bleeding. When that attempt failed to induce an abortion, the patient, then four or five months pregnant, finally went to an abortion clinic. Because of the damage to the patient's cervix, doctors had to perform a hysterotomy, meaning that that woman must have a Cesarean section to deliver a child in the future.

4. As Justice Stevens notes, * * * the 48-hour delay does not apply if a parent or court consents to the abortion.

if it pushes the abortion into the second trimester, when the operation is substantially more risky and costly. * * *

C

Because the parental notification and delay requirements burden a young woman's right freely to decide whether to terminate her pregnancy, the State must show that these requirements are justified by a compelling state interest and are closely tailored to further that interest. The main purpose of the notification requirement is to "protect the well-being of minors by encouraging minors to discuss with their parents the decision whether to terminate their pregnancies." * * * The 48-hour delay, in turn, is designed to provide parents with adequate time to consult with their daughters. * * * As Justice Stevens states, such consultation is intended to ensure that the minor's decision is "knowing and intelligent." * * * I need not determine whether the State's interest ultimately outweighs young women's privacy interests, however, because the strictures here are not closely tailored to further the State's asserted goal.

For the many young women who would voluntarily consult with a parent before having an abortion, * * * the notification and delay requirements are superfluous, and so do not advance the State's interest. The requirements affect only those women who would not otherwise notify a parent. But compelled notification is unlikely to result in productive consultation in families in which a daughter does not feel comfortable consulting her parents about intimate or sexual matters. * * * Moreover, in those families with a history of child abuse, a pregnant minor forced to notify a parent is more likely to be greeted by physical assault or psychological harassment than open and caring conversation about her predicament. * * * Forced notification in such situations would amount to punishing the daughter for the lack of a stable and communicative family environment, when the blame for that situation lies principally, if not entirely, with the parents. Parental notification in the less-than-ideal family, therefore, would not lead to an informed decision by the minor.

The State also claims that the statute serves the interest of protecting parents' independent right "to shape the[ir] child[ren]'s values and life style[s]" and "to determine and strive for what they believe to be best for their children." * * * If this is so, the statute is surely underinclusive, as it does not require parental notification where the minor seeks medical treatment for pregnancy, venereal disease, or alcohol and other drug abuse. See Minn.Stat. § 144.343(1) (1988). Are we to believe that Minnesota parents have no interest in their children's well-being in these other contexts?

In any event, parents' right to direct their children's upbringing is a right *against* state interference with family matters. * * * Yet, ironically, the State's requirements here affirmatively interfere in family life by trying to force families to conform to the State's archetype of the ideal family. * * * It is a strange constitutional alchemy that would transform a limitation on state power into a justification for governmental intrusion into family interactions. * * *

Even if the State's interest is construed as merely the *facilitation* of the exercise of parental authority, the notification and delay requirements are not narrowly drawn. Parental authority is not limitless. Certainly, where parental involvement threatens to harm the child, the parent's authority must yield. * * * Yet the notification and delay requirements facilitate the exercise of parental authority even where it may physically or psychologically harm the child. * * *

Furthermore, the exercise of parental authority in some instances will take the form of obstructing the minor's decision to have an abortion. A parent who objects to the abortion, once notified, can exert strong pressure on the minor—in the form of stern disapproval, withdrawal of financial support, or physical or emotional abuse—to block her from getting an abortion. * * * In such circumstances, the notification requirement becomes, in effect, a consent requirement. As discussed below, * * * the State may not permit any person, including a parent, to veto a woman's decision to terminate her pregnancy. Because the notification and delay requirements effectively give parents the opportunity to exercise an unconstitutional veto in some situations, those requirements are not narrowly tailored to the State's interest in facilitating *legitimate* exercises of parental authority.

III

The parental notification and 48-hour delay requirements, then, do not satisfy the strict scrutiny applicable to laws restricting a woman's constitutional right to have an abortion. The judicial bypass procedure cannot salvage those requirements because that procedure itself is unconstitutional.

A

The State argues that the bypass procedure saves the notification and delay requirements because it provides an alternative way to obtain a legal abortion for minors who would be harmed by those requirements. This Court has upheld a one-parent consent requirement where the State provided an alternative judicial procedure " 'whereby a pregnant minor [could] demonstrate that she [was] sufficiently mature to make the abortion decision herself or that, despite her immaturity, an abortion would be in her best interests.' " *Planned Parenthood Assn. of Kansas City, Inc. v. Ashcroft,* * * * (opinion of Powell, J.) (quoting *Akron Center for Reproductive Health,* * * *).

I continue to believe, however, that a judicial bypass procedure of this sort is itself unconstitutional because it effectively gives a judge "an absolute veto over the decision of the physician and his patient." * * * No person may veto *any* minor's decision, made in consultation with her physician, to terminate her pregnancy. An "immature" minor has no less right to make decisions regarding her own body than a mature adult.

* * *

The constitutional defects in any provision allowing someone to veto a woman's abortion decision are exacerbated by the vagueness of the standards contained in this statute. The statute gives no guidance on how a judge is to determine whether a minor is sufficiently "mature" and "capable" to make the decision on her own. * * * The statute similarly is silent as to how a judge is to determine whether an abortion without parental notification would serve an immature minor's "best interests." * * * Is the judge expected to know more about the woman's medical needs or psychological makeup than her doctor? Should he consider the woman's financial and emotional status to determine the quality of life the woman and her future child would enjoy in this world? Neither the record nor the Court answers such questions. As Justice Stevens wrote in *Bellotti II,* the best interest standard "provides little real guidance to the judge, and his decision must necessarily reflect personal and societal values and mores whose enforcement upon the minor—particularly when contrary to her own informed and reasonable decision—is fundamentally at odds with privacy interests underlying the constitutional protection afforded to her decision." * * * It is difficult to conceive of any reason, aside from a judge's personal opposition to abortion, that would justify a finding that an immature woman's best interests would be served by forcing her to endure pregnancy and childbirth against her will.

B

Even if I did not believe that a judicial bypass procedure was facially unconstitutional, the experience of Minnesota's procedure in operation demonstrates that the bypass provision before us cannot save the parental notification and delay requirements. This Court has addressed judicial bypass procedures only in the context of facial challenges. * * * The Court has never considered the actual burdens a particular bypass provision imposes on a woman's right to choose an abortion. Such consideration establishes that, even if judges authorized every abortion sought by petitioning minors, Minnesota's judicial bypass is far too burdensome to remedy an otherwise unconstitutional statute.

* * *

Yet, despite the substantial burdens imposed by these proceedings, the bypass is, in effect, a "rubber stamp," * * *; only an extremely small number of petitions are denied, * * *. * * * The large number of women who undergo the bypass process do not receive any sort of counseling from the court—which is not surprising, given the court's limited role and lack of expertise in that area. The bypass process itself thus cannot serve the state interest of promoting informed decisionmaking by all minors. If the State truly were concerned about ensuring that all minors consult with a knowledgeable and caring adult, it would provide for some form of counseling rather than for a judicial procedure in which a judge merely gives or withholds his consent.

Thus, regardless of one's view of the facial validity of a bypass procedure, Minnesota's procedure in practice imposes an excessive burden on young women's right to choose an abortion. * * * The Court's holding that the burdensome bypass procedure saves the State's burdensome notification and delay requirements thus strikes me as the equivalent of saying that two wrongs make a right. I cannot accept such a novel judicial calculus.

IV

A majority of the Court today strikes down an unreasonable and vastly overbroad requirement that a pregnant minor notify both her parents of her decision to obtain an abortion. With that decision I agree. At the same time, though, a different majority holds that a State may require a young woman to notify one or even both parents and then wait 48 hours before having an abortion, as long as the State provides a judicial bypass procedure. From that decision I vehemently dissent. This scheme forces a young woman in an already dire situation to choose between two fundamentally unacceptable alternatives: notifying a possibly dictatorial or even abusive parent and justifying her profoundly personal decision in an intimidating judicial proceeding to a black-robed stranger. For such a woman, this dilemma is more likely to result in trauma and pain than in an informed and voluntary decision.

JUSTICE SCALIA, concurring in the judgment in part and dissenting in part.

As I understand the various opinions today: One Justice holds that two-parent notification is unconstitutional (at least in the present circumstances) without judicial bypass, but constitutional with bypass, * * * (O'Connor, J., concurring in part and concurring in judgment); four Justices would hold that two-parent notification is constitutional with or without bypass, * * * (KENNEDY, J., concurring in judgment in part and dissenting in part); four Justices would hold that two-parent notification is unconstitutional with or without bypass, though the four apply two different standards, * * * (opinion of STEVENS, J.), * * * (MARSHALL, J., concurring in part and dissenting in part); six Justices hold that one-parent notification with bypass is constitutional, though for two different sets of reasons, *Ohio v. Akron Center for Reproductive Health,* * * * (Stevens, J., concurring in judgment); and three Justices would hold that one-parent notification with bypass is unconstitutional, * * * (BLACKMUN, J., dissenting). One will search in vain the document we are supposed to be construing for text that provides the basis for the argument over these distinctions; and will find in our society's tradition regarding abortion no hint that the distinctions are constitutionally relevant, much less any indication how a constitutional argument about them ought to be resolved. The random and unpredictable results of our consequently unchanneled individual views make it increasingly evident, Term after Term, that the tools for this job are not to be found in the lawyer's—and hence not in the judge's—work-box. I continue to dissent from this enterprise of devising an Abortion Code, and from the illusion that we have authority to do so.

JUSTICE KENNEDY, with whom THE CHIEF JUSTICE, JUSTICE WHITE, and JUSTICE SCALIA join, concurring in the judgment in part and dissenting in part.

" 'There can be little doubt that the State furthers a constitutionally permissible end by encouraging an unmarried pregnant minor to seek the help and advice of her parents in making the very important decision whether or not to bear a child. That is a grave decision, and a girl of tender years, under emotional stress, may be ill-equipped to make it without mature advice and emotional support.' " *Bellotti v. Baird (Bellotti II),* * * *. Today, the Court holds that a statute requiring a minor to notify both parents that she plans to have an abortion is not a permissible means of furthering the interest described with such specificity in *Bellotti II*. This conclusion, which no doubt will come as a surprise to most parents, is incompatible with our constitutional tradition and any acceptable notion of judicial review of legislative enactments. I dissent from the portion of the Court's judgment affirming the Court of Appeals' conclusion that Minnesota's two-parent notice statute is unconstitutional.

The Minnesota statute also provides, however, that if the two-parent notice requirement is invalidated, the same notice requirement is effective unless the pregnant minor obtains a court order permitting the abortion to proceed. * * * The Court of Appeals sustained this portion of the statute, in effect a two-parent notice requirement with a judicial bypass. Five Members of the Court, the four who join this opinion and Justice O'Connor, agree with the Court of Appeals' decision on this aspect of the statute. As announced by Justice Stevens, who dissents from this part of the Court's decision, the Court of Appeals' judgment on this portion of the statute is therefore affirmed.

* * *

II

The State identifies two interests served by the law. The first is the State's interest in the welfare of pregnant minors. The second is the State's interest in acknowledging and promoting the role of parents in the care and upbringing of their children. Justice Stevens, writing for two Members of the Court, acknowledges the legitimacy of the first interest, but decides that the second interest is somehow illegitimate, at least as to whichever parent a minor chooses not to notify. I cannot agree that the Constitution prevents a State from keeping both parents informed of the medical condition or medical treatment of their child under the terms and conditions of this statute.

The welfare of the child has always been the central concern of laws with regard to minors. The law does not give to children many rights given to adults, and provides, in general, that children can exercise the rights they do have only through and with parental consent. * * * Age is a rough but fair approximation of maturity and judgment, and a State has an interest in seeing that a child, when confronted with serious decisions such as whether or not to abort a pregnancy, has the assistance of her parents in making the choice. If anything is settled by our previous cases dealing with parental notification and consent laws, it is this point. * * *

Protection of the right of each parent to participate in the upbringing of her or his own children is a further discrete interest that the State recognizes by the statute. The common law historically has given recognition to the right of parents, not merely to be notified of their children's actions, but to speak and act on their behalf. Absent a showing of neglect or abuse, a father "possessed the paramount right to the custody and control of his minor children, and to superintend their education and nurture." * * * In this century, the common law of most States has abandoned the idea that parental rights are vested solely in fathers, with mothers being viewed merely as agents of their husbands, * * *; it is now the case that each parent has parental rights and parental responsibilities. * * * Limitations have emerged on the prerogatives of parents to act contrary to the best interests of the child with respect to matters such as compulsory schooling and child labor. As a general matter, however, it remains "cardinal with us that the custody, care and nurture of the child reside first in the parents, whose primary function and freedom include preparation for obligations the state can neither supply nor hinder." * * *

A State pursues a legitimate end under the Constitution when it attempts to foster and preserve the parent-child relation by giving all parents the opportunity to participate in the care and nurture of their children. * * *

The Court's descriptions of the State's interests in this case are caricatures, both of the law and of our most revered institutions. The Court labels these interests as ones in "standardizing its children and adults," and in ensuring that each family, to the extent possible, "conform to some state-designed ideal." * * * Minnesota asserts no such purpose, by explicit statement or by any permissible inference. All that Minnesota asserts is an interest in seeing that parents know about a vital decision facing their child. That interest is a valid one without regard to whether the child is living with either one or both parents, or to the attachment between the minor's parents. How the family unit responds to such notice is, for the most part, beyond the State's control. The State would no doubt prefer that all parents, after being notified under the statute, would contact their daughters and assist them in making their decisions with the child's best interests at heart; but it has not, contrary to the Court's intimation, "decreed" communication, nor could it. What the State can do is make the communication possible by at least informing parents of their daughter's intentions.

Minnesota has done no more than act upon the common-sense proposition that, in assisting their daughter in deciding whether to have an abortion, parents can best fulfill their roles if they have the same information about their own child's medical condition and medical choices as the child's doctor does; and that to deny parents this knowledge is to risk, or perpetuate, estrangement or alienation from the child when she is in the greatest need of parental guidance and support. The Court does the State, and our constitutional tradition, sad disservice by impugning the legitimacy of these elemental objectives.

Given the societal interest that underlies parental notice and consent laws, it comes as no surprise that most States have enacted statutes requiring that, in general, a physician must notify or obtain the consent of at least one of her parents or legal guardian before performing an abortion on a minor. * * * Whether these statutes are more or less restrictive than the Minnesota statute is not the issue, although I pause to note that because the Court's decision today turns upon its perception that the law's requirements, despite its exceptions are the most "stringent" in the country, * * * (O'CONNOR, J., concurring in part and concurring in judgment), the Court's decision has no import for the validity of these other statutes. What is important is that Minnesota is not alone in acknowledging the vitality of these governmental interests and adopting laws that, in the legislature's judgment, are best suited to serving them while protecting the minor's welfare.

On a more general level, the current trend among state legislatures is to enact joint custody laws making it the norm for divorced or separated parents to share the legal responsibility and authority for making decisions concerning their children's care, education, religion, and medical treatment. * * * Under Minnesota law, for example, there exists a presumption in divorce proceedings that joint custody, if requested by either or both parents is in the best interests of the child. See Minn.Stat. § 518.17(2) (Supp.1989). Even if joint custody is not awarded, Minnesota law provides that each parent, unless the court specifically directs otherwise to protect the welfare of a parent or the child, "has the right of access to, and to receive copies of, school, medical, dental, religious training, and other important records and information about the minor children"; the responsibility to "keep the other party informed as to the name and address of the school of attendance of the minor children"; the responsibility to "notify the other party of [an accident or serious illness of a minor child], and the name of the health care provider and the place of treatment"; and "the right to reasonable access and telephone contact with the minor children." Minn.Stat. § 518.17(3) (1988). Minnesota's two-parent notification law does no more than apply these general principles to the specific case of abortion.

* * *

III

At least two Members of the Court concede, as they must, that a State has a legitimate interest in the welfare of the pregnant minor and that, in furtherance of this interest, the State may require the minor to notify, and consult with, one of her parents. See * * * (opinion of Stevens, J.); cf. * * * (MARSHALL, J., concurring in part, concurring in judgment in part, and dissenting in part). The Court nonetheless holds the Minnesota statute unconstitutional because it requires the minor to notify not one parent, but both parents, a requirement that the Court says bears no reasonable relation to the minor's welfare. * * * The Court also concludes that Minnesota does not have a legitimate interest in facilitating the participation of both parents in the care and upbringing of their children. Given the substantial protection that minors have under Minnesota law generally, and under the statute in question, the judicial bypass provisions of the law are not necessary to its validity. The two-parent notification law enacted by Minnesota is, in my view, valid without the judicial bypass provision of subdivision 6.

A

We have been over much of this ground before. It is beyond dispute that in many families, whether the parents are living together or apart, notice to both parents serves the interests of the parents and the minor, and that the State can legislate with this fact in mind. In *H.L. v. Matheson*, * * * we considered the constitutionality of a statute which required a physician, before performing an abortion on a minor, to " '[n]otify, if possible, the [minor's] *parents* or guardian.' " * * * We held that the statute, as applied to unmarried, dependent, and immature minors, "plainly serves important state interests, is narrowly drawn to protect only those interests, and does not violate any guarantees of the Constitution." * * * Our holding was made with knowledge of the contentions, supported by citations to medical and sociological literature, that are proffered again today for the proposition that notification imposes burdens on minors. * * * We nonetheless rejected arguments that a requirement of parental notification was the equivalent of a requirement of parental consent, * * *; that the statute was unconstitutional because it required notification only as to abortions, and not as to other medical procedures, * * *; and that the statute was unconstitutional because it might deter some minors from seeking abortions, * * *.

Our decision was based upon the well-accepted premise that we must defer to a reasonable judgment by the state legislature when it determines what is sound public policy. Justice Stevens' opinion concurring in the Court's judgment relied upon an explicit statement of this principle. Concluding that the Utah statute requiring notification of both parents was valid as to all unmarried minors, both mature and immature, Justice Stevens reasoned that the State's interest in ensuring that a young woman considering an abortion receive appropriate consultation was "plainly sufficient to support a state legislature's determination that such appropriate consultation should include parental advice." * * * The Court today departs from this rule. It now suggests that a general requirement that both parents be notified is unconstitutional because of its own conclusion that the law is unnecessary when notice produces favorable results, * * * and irrational in all of the instances when it produces unfavorable results, * * *. In *Matheson,* Justice Stevens rejected these same arguments as insufficient to establish that the Utah statute was unconstitutional:

> "Of course, a conclusion that the Utah statute is invalid would not prevent young pregnant women from voluntarily seeking the advice of their parents prior to making the abortion decision. But the State may legitimately decide that such consultation should be made more probable by ensuring that parents are informed of their daughter's decision[.]
>
> * * * * * * * * *
>
> "Utah's interest in its parental-notice statute is not diminished by the fact that there can be no guarantee that meaningful parent-child communication will actually occur. Good-faith compliance with the statute's requirements would tend to facilitate communication between daughters and parents regarding the abortion decision. *The possibility that some parents will not react with compassion and understanding upon being informed of their daughter's predicament or that, even if they are receptive, they will incorrectly advise her, does not undercut the legitimacy of the State's attempt to establish a procedure that will enhance the probability that a pregnant young woman exercise as wisely as possible her right to make the abortion decision."* * * * (Stevens, J., concurring in judgment) (emphasis added).

Justice Stevens' reasoning was correct then and it remains correct today.

B

In applying the standards established in our prior decisions to the case at hand, "we must keep in mind that when we are concerned with extremely sensitive issues, such as the one involved here, 'the appropriate forum for their resolution in a democracy is the legislature. We should not forget that "legislatures are ultimate guardians of the liberties and welfare of the people in quite as great a degree as the courts." * * *' *Maher* * * *." The Minnesota Legislature, like the legislatures of many States, has found it necessary to address the issue of parental notice in its statutory laws. In my view it has acted in a permissible manner.

All must acknowledge that it was reasonable for the legislature to conclude that in most cases notice to both parents will work to the minor's benefit. * * * This is true not only in what the Court calls the "ideal family setting," where both parents and the minor live under one roof, but also where the minor no longer lives with both parents. The Court does not deny that many absent parents maintain significant ties with their children, and seek to participate in their lives, to guide, to teach, and to care for them. It is beyond dispute that these attachments, in cases not involving mistreatment or abuse, are essential to the minor's well-being, and that parental notice is supportive of this kind of family tie. Although it may be true that notice to one parent will often result in notice to both, the State need not rely upon the decision of one parent to notify the other, particularly where both parents maintain ties with their daughter but not with each other, and when both parents share responsibilities and duties with respect to the child.

* * *

The Minnesota statute in fact contains exceptions to ensure that the statutory notice requirement does not apply if it proves a serious threat to the minor's health or safety. * * * I cannot believe that these exceptions are too narrow to eliminate from the statute's coverage those instances in which notice would place the minor in danger of parental violence or other conduct that is a real threat to the physical or mental health of the child.

* * *

* * * Like all laws of general application, the Minnesota statute cannot produce perfect results in every situation to which it applies; but the State is under no obligation to enact perfect laws. The statute before us, including the 48-hour waiting period, which is necessary to enable notified parents to consult with their daughter or their daughter's physician, if they so wish, and results in little or no delay, represents a permissible, reasoned attempt to preserve the parents' role in a minor's decision to have an abortion without placing any absolute obstacles before a minor who is determined to elect an abortion for her own interest as she sees it. Section 144.343, without the judicial bypass provision of subdivision 6, is constitutional. I would reverse the contrary judgment of the Court of Appeals.

IV

Because a majority of the Court holds that the two-parent notice requirement contained in subdivision 2 is unconstitutional, it is necessary for the Court to consider whether the same notice requirement is constitutional if the minor has the option of obtaining a court order permitting the abortion to proceed in lieu of the required notice. Minn. Stat. § 144.343(6) (1988). Assuming, as I am bound to do for this part of the analysis, that the notice provisions standing alone are invalid, I conclude that the two-parent notice requirement with the judicial bypass alternative is constitutional.

The Court concludes that Minnesota's two-parent notice law without a judicial bypass is unconstitutional because of the possibility that, in some cases, the rule would not work to the benefit of minors or their parents. If one were to attempt to design a statute that would address the Court's concerns, one would do precisely what Minnesota has done in § 144.343(6): create a judicial mechanism to identify, and exempt from the strictures of the law those cases in which the minor is mature or in which notification of the minor's parents is not in the minor's best interests. The bypass procedure comports in all respects with our precedents. * * *

In providing for the bypass, Minnesota has done nothing other than attempt to fit its legislation into the framework that we have supplied in our previous cases. The simple fact is that our decision in *Bellotti II* stands for the proposition that a two-parent consent law is constitutional if it provides for a sufficient judicial bypass alternative, and it requires us to sustain the statute before us here. In *Bellotti II*, the Court considered the constitutionality of a statute which required a physician to obtain, in most circumstances, the consent of both of a minor's parents before performing an abortion on the minor. * * * Although eight Members of the Court concluded that the statute was unconstitutional, five indicated that they would uphold a two-parent consent statute with an adequate judicial bypass.

* * * In sum, five Members of the Court in *Bellotti II* found, either by express statement or by implication, that it was permissible under the Constitution for a State to require the consent of two parents, as long as it provides a consent substitute in the form of an adequate judicial bypass procedure.

I cannot accept Justice Stevens' suggestion today that the plurality, in announcing these rules, did not "consider" the fact that it was doing so in the context of a two-parent consent requirement, * * *. The statute was explicit in its command that both parents consent to the abortion. * * * The plurality indicated that it was aware of this fact, * * * and the dissent drew a specific contrast between the two-parent consent requirement then before the Court and the one-parent consent requirement before the Court in *Danforth*. See * * * (STEVENS, J., concurring in judgment). Aware of all of these circumstances, the plurality stated the controlling principles with specific reference to laws requiring the consent of "one or both" parents. * * * The plurality's considered reasoning, coupled with the dissenting views of Justice White, was intended to set forth the dispositive principles of law for deciding the constitutionality of parental consent laws. The Court has relied upon these principles in deciding the constitutionality of laws requiring notice or the consent of one parent, see *Akron v. Akron Center for Reproductive Health,* 462 U.S., at 439–442 (consent); *Ohio v. Akron Center for Reproductive Health,* ___ U.S. ___, ___– (1990) (notice). As *Bellotti II* dealt with the far more demanding requirement of two-parent consent, and approved of such a requirement when coupled with a judicial bypass alternative, I must conclude that these same principles validate a two-parent notice requirement when coupled with a judicial bypass alternative.

A second precedent that compels the conclusion that a two-parent notice law with a judicial bypass alternative is constitutional is our decision in *Matheson*. There we held that a two-parent notice statute without a bypass was constitutional as applied to immature minors whose best interests would be served by notice. Like the statute before the Court in *Matheson*, the Minnesota statute, as amended by subdivision 6, requires a physician to notify the parents of those immature minors whose best interests will be served by the communication.

If a two-parent notification law may be constitutional as applied to immature minors whose best interests are served by the law, but not as applied to minors who are mature or whose best interests are not so served, a judicial bypass is an expeditious and efficient means by which to separate the applications of the law which are constitutional from those which are not. Justice Stevens' characterization of the judicial bypass procedure discussed in our past cases as a necessary "exception" to a "reasonable general rule," such as a one-parent consent requirement, * * * is far off the mark. If a judicial bypass is mandated by the Constitution at all, it must be because a general consent rule is unreasonable in at least some of its applications, and the bypass is necessary to save the statute. * * * No reason can be given for refusing to apply a similar analysis to the less demanding case of a notice statute. It follows that a similar result should obtain: a law that requires notice to one or both parents is constitutional with a bypass. I thus concur in that portion of the judgment announced, but not agreed with, by Justice Stevens which affirms the Court of Appeals' conclusion that § 144.343(6) is constitutional.

V

In this case, the Court rejects a legislature's judgment that parents should at least be aware of their daughter's intention to seek an abortion, even if the State does not empower the parents to control the child's decision. That judgment is rejected although it rests upon a tradition of a parental role in the care and upbringing of children that is as old as civilization itself. Our precedents do not permit this result.

It is true that for all too many young women the prospect of two parents, perhaps even one parent, sustaining her with support that is compassionate and committed is an illusion. Statistics on drug and alcohol abuse by parents and documentations of child neglect and mistreatment are but fragments of the evidence showing the tragic reality that becomes day-to-day life for thousands of minors. But the Court errs in serious degree when it commands its own solution to the cruel consequences of individual misconduct, parental failure, and social ills. The legislative authority is entitled to attempt to meet these wrongs by taking reasonable measures to recognize and promote the primacy of the family tie, a concept which this Court now seems intent on declaring a constitutional irrelevance.

Notes on Webster and Hodgson

1. Public concern over the *Webster* decision was intense. A record number—78—*amicus curiae* briefs were filed with the Court: 31 supported appellees while 47 supported appellants. In addition to this formal advice from its "friends," public demonstrations on both sides of the issue were held in Washington and the individual Justices received an avalanche of mail from the public at large. Is it appropriate for either lawyers or the public to lobby the Court concerning its interpretation of the Constitution? See Kolbert, The *Webster Amicus Curiae* Briefs: Perspectives on the Abortion Controversy and the Role of the Supreme Court—Introduction: Did the *Amici* Effort Make a Difference?, 15 Am.J.L. & Med. 153 (1989).

2. What, exactly, does *Webster* hold? Can you count five votes for abandoning the trimester framework that forms the cornerstone of *Roe v. Wade?* Has Justice O'Connor abandoned her earlier critique in *Akron* that the *Roe* framework "is clearly on a collision course with itself?" (Quoted in the casebook at p. 456). As Justice Blackmun points out in footnote 9 of his opinion, the scientific basis for that critique was attacked by several of the *amici* briefs. Note, however, that Justice O'Connor indicated in *Webster* that she continues to consider the *Roe* trimester framework "problematic." What arguments remain viable after *Webster?* See generally, Colloquy, Webster v. Reproductive Health Services, 138 U.Pa.L.Rev. 83–177 (1989).

3. What is the impact of *Webster* on the validity of the 1988 regulations to Title X of the Public Health Service Act, 42 U.S.C.A. §§ 300 to 300a–41? Title X authorizes the Secretary of Health and Human Services to make federal grants to public and private nonprofit entities to establish and operate family planning projects. Section 1008 of the Act states that "None of the funds appropriated under this subchapter shall be used in programs where abortion is a method of family planning." Title X funds serve an estimated 14.5 million women and typically are granted to clinics operated by public health departments, public hospitals, and community agencies such as Planned Parenthood. Section 1008 was enacted in 1970; from 1971 until 1988, the Agency interpreted its ban on abortion as a method of family planning to prohibit the use of Title X funds to perform or subsidize the performance of abortions, while permitting and later requiring Title X projects to provide information about abortions to pregnant women and to offer referrals to abortion providers. The 1988 regulations marked a sharp departure from the former administrative practice. They expressly prohibit nondirective abortion counseling or referral and require financial and physical separation of federally and nonfederally funded activities conducted by Title X grantees. In addition, Title X projects cannot lobby for pro-choice legislation, provide speakers to promote the availability of abortion, pay dues to groups that advocate abortion, or develop and disseminate materials to promote abortion.

The First and Second Circuits are in disagreement over the impact of *Webster* on the Title X regulations. Prior to *Webster,* the First Circuit had affirmed a judgment enjoining the enforcement or application of the Title X regulations. Massachusetts v. Bowen, 679 F.Supp. 137 (D.Mass.1988), affirmed sub. nom. Massachusetts v. Secretary of Health and Human

Services, 873 F.2d 1528 (1st Cir.1989), opinion withdrawn; rehearing granted. Judge Bownes held that the regulations were not beyond the Secretary's authority, but that they impermissibly infringed upon the pregnant woman's range of choice guaranteed by *Roe*. Re-examining this position on rehearing en banc, Judge Bownes concluded that "*Webster* did not change the legal landscape upon which the panel opinion was based," going on to hold the regulations unconstitutional because they "pose a significant obstacle to a Title X client's decision to terminate her pregnancy by curtailing her ability to receive counseling on abortion from the physician responsible for her medical care." Massachusetts v. Secretary of Health and Human Services, 899 F.2d 53 (1st Cir.1990) (en banc). The Second Circuit disagrees. Judge Winter believes that the Missouri prohibition against the provision of abortion services in public facilities upheld in *Webster* was "a prohibition substantially greater in impact than the regulations challenged in the instant matter." Accordingly, he concluded that the regulations were constitutional. New York v. Sullivan, 889 F.2d 401, 411–412 (2d Cir.1989). Judge Kearse dissented, arguing that:

> By prohibiting the delivery of abortion information and prohibiting communication even as to where such information can be obtained, the present regulations deny a woman her constitutionally protected right to choose. She cannot make an informed choice between two options when she cannot obtain information as to one of them.

Id., at 417 (dissenting opinion). Who has it right? The Supreme Court has granted certiorari in *Sullivan*: Rust v. Sullivan, ___ U.S. ___, 110 S.Ct. 2559, 109 L.Ed.2d 742 (1990); New York v. Sullivan, ___ U.S. ___, 110 S.Ct. 2559, 109 L.Ed.2d 742 (1990). How and why should the Court resolve this conflict?

4. A significant matter left unresolved by *Webster* is whether a prohibition on abortion counseling and referral in publicly funded family planning clinics violates the First Amendment. The issue was raised by a section of the Missouri statute forbidding public employees from "encouraging or counseling a woman to have an abortion not necessary to save her life" in the course of their employment at public facilities. Missouri chose not to appeal from the invalidation of this provision, and the appellees withdrew their challenge to the related restriction on the use of public funds for this purpose, which Missouri did appeal. Accordingly, the Court treated the funding controversy as moot. 492 U.S. at ___, 109 S.Ct. at 3053–54, 106 L.Ed.2d at 431–32.

The First and Second Circuits disagree about this matter as well. The First Circuit believes that the Title X regulations "fall squarely on the unconstitutional side of the line" drawn in Regan v. Taxation with Representation of Washington, 461 U.S. 540, 103 S.Ct. 1997, 76 L.Ed.2d 129 (1983), a case upholding IRS sections prohibiting the use of tax deductible funds for lobbying purposes but noting that its holding did not protect Congressional attempts to suppress "dangerous" ideas. *Massachusetts v. Secretary of Health and Human Services,* supra Note 3, at 75. The Second Circuit, by contrast, read *Regan* to extend the doctrine that the government need not subsidize the exercise of fundamental rights to speech rights. *State of New York v. Sullivan,* supra Note 3, at 412. Once again, Judge

Kearse dissented. In her view, "the regulations facially discriminate on the basis of viewpoint and control the content of the grantee's permitted speech." Id., at 416 (dissenting opinion).

Andrew McCarthy persuasively argues that the traditional distinction between the government's permissible refusal to subsidize the exercise of a constitutional right and its impermissible imposition of a penalty on the exercise of that right is not adequate to the task of addressing the issue posed by the Title X regulations. Instead, he proposes an alternative approach that "would focus on the one issue crucial to the constitutionality of any conditional benefit: is the government indirectly suppressing the exercise of a constitutional right that it could not proscribe directly?" McCarthy, The Prohibition on Abortion Counseling and Referral in Federally–Funded Family Planning Clinics, 77 Calif.L.Rev. 1181, 1200 (1989). He concludes that:

> * * * the regulatory scheme fails in part because its means (total denial) are too broad, not because its end (promoting childbirth) is illegitimate. If it would be unconstitutional to remove a woman from the welfare rolls because she had an abortion, or because she gave a speech against the government, it should be unconstitutional to remove a clinic from the title X rolls because it facilitates abortions, or because it advances pro-choice positions in its lobbying.

Id., at 1209. Do you agree with this analysis? Is it likely to prove acceptable to a majority of the United States Supreme Court? See also Benshoof, The Chastity Act: Government Manipulation of Abortion Information and the First Amendment, 101 Harv.L.Rev. 1916 (1988); Appleton, More Thoughts on the Physician's Constitutional Role in Abortion and Related Choices, 66 Wash.U.L.Q. 499 (1988).

5. In view of Justice O'Connor's statement in *Webster* that "[w]hen the constitutional invalidity of a State's abortion statute actually turns on the constitutional validity of *Roe v. Wade,* there will be time enough to reexamine *Roe* ", antiabortion activists have worked to secure the enactment of such a statute. The National Right to Life Committee prepared a bill designed to appeal to Justice O'Connor's presumed unwillingness to impose criminal penalties on women who undergo abortions. Accordingly, the Committee's bill would impose civil fines of up to $10,000 on physicians who perform procedures not authorized by their bill, and would open the physicians to suits for damages brought by the father of the fetus and others. The bill would permit abortion only for rapes reported within seven days; incest if the victim was under 18 and reported the crime prior to the abortion; "profound" fetal deformity; and in cases where the physician finds the woman's physical health (not her mental health) to be threatened by continuance of the pregnancy. After failing to secure the bill's passage in several states, including Utah and Alabama, the Committee successfully lobbied it through the Idaho legislature on March 22, 1990. The New York Times, March 22, 1990, at A1, col. 4; id., March 23, 1990, at A8, col. 1. Reacting swiftly, President Molly Yard of the National Organization for Women called for a nationwide boycott of Idaho potatoes. Countering this move, President Beverly LaHaye of the Concerned Women for America urged supporters of the bill to increase their purchase of

Idaho's leading cash crop. State Senator Mark Ricks, a potato farmer who opposes abortion, was reported as commenting, "I had no idea these kinds of repercussions would result. I think it's unjust and narrow-minded." The New York Times, March 30, 1990, at A8, col. 1. Governor Cecil D. Andrus, a long-time opponent of abortion, ultimately vetoed the bill: in his veto message, the Governor commented that, "The bill is drawn so narrowly that it would punitively and without compassion further harm an Idaho woman who may find herself in the horrible, unthinkable position of confronting a pregnancy that resulted from rape or incest." The New York Times, March 31, 1990, at A1, col. 1. In political terms, that's no small potatoes.

The test case may originate in Guam. Territorial Governor Joseph Ada signed a bill on March 19, 1990 that prohibits abortion except where the mother's life is in danger. The bill also provides for a voter referendum in November to decide whether the law should be retained. A class of pregnant women, medical providers, and others have challenged the law on constitutional grounds. San Francisco Chronicle, March 24, 1990, at A3, col. 4.

6. The open confrontation in *Webster* between Justice Scalia and the dissenters, and his disdain for the plurality's unwillingness to end the Supreme Court's participation in the abortion debate has given new urgency to the struggle for Justice O'Connor's deciding vote. The political nature of the abortion question is evident in the state legislatures, see *supra* Note 5, but it is also being revealed in the writings of legal scholars. See, e.g., Estrich & Sullivan, Abortion Politics: Writing For An Audience Of One, 138 U.Pa.L.Rev. 119 (1989); Olsen, The Supreme Court 1988 Term, Comment: Unraveling Compromise, 103 Harv.L.Rev. 105 (1989); Loewy, Observation: Why *Roe v. Wade* Should Be Overruled, 67 No.Car.L.Rev. 939 (1989); Glendon, A World Without *Roe,* The New Republic, February 20, 1989, at 19.

7. *Hodgson* is the first case in which Justice O'Connor has voted to strike down a state regulation of abortion. What, if anything, does her concurring opinion tell you about how she might vote in a case reconsidering *Roe v. Wade*?

8. What is the present status of state laws restricting abortion deemed unconstitutional after *Roe* that might pass muster after *Webster*? Must they be re-enacted in order to be enforced? A notewriter thinks not. See Note, The Phenomenon of Antique Laws: Can a State Revive Old Abortion Laws in a New Era?, 58 George Washington L.Rev. 111 (1989). Just to be on the safe side, Connecticut recently repealed its pre-Roe criminal abortion laws and granted women a right to choose whether to continue a pregnancy under certain circumstances. See New York Times, April 28, 1990, at A1, col. 3.

9. Even if the United States Supreme Court decides to overrule *Roe,* that will not end legal abortion in states like California where a woman's right to choose whether to give birth is protected independent of federal law by the state constitution. See, e.g., Pressman, The Battle Over Abortion: What Happens After Roe v. Wade, 9 California Lawyer 56, 60 (1989) (quoting ACLU attorney Margaret C. Crosby as saying "[T]he day after the

Webster decision, whatever it says, abortion will still be a fundamental right in California"). See also Crosby, New Frontiers: Individual Rights Under the California Constitution, 17 Hastings Con. L. Q. 81, 100–103 (1989).

10. What do you think stimulated the Minnesota legislature to require notification of both parents of a pregnant minor of her intention to procure an abortion? Why do you suppose the Minnesota Attorney General declined to rely on a supposed legislative motivation to deter minors from having abortions? Would such a motivation, if proven at trial, be sufficient to undercut the statute's constitutionality? How do you evaluate Justice Marshall's argument that all notification statutes are invalid? Are you persuaded by Justice Kennedy's analogy to joint custody laws as a means of justifying the two parent requirement? Do you agree that the judicial bypass procedure validates the two parent notification requirement?

11. In a companion case to *Hodgson*, the Court upheld an Ohio statute that required notice to one of the pregnant minor's parents, coupled with a judicial bypass procedure. In Ohio v. Akron Center for Reproductive Health, ___ U.S. ___, 110 S.Ct. ___, ___ L.Ed.2d ___ (1990), Justice Kennedy, writing for himself and five other members of the Court, held that the Ohio bypass procedure satisfied the requirements set out in the plurality opinion in *Bellotti II*. Justice Stevens, concurring, pointed out that appellees had challenged the Ohio statute only on its face, and stated that he was unwilling to invalidate the statute before its provisions had been implemented and the significance of its restrictions evaluated in light of its administration. The three dissenters, Justices Blackmun, Brennan and Marshall, characterized the Ohio procedure as "a tortuous maze" deliberately designed to place a "pattern of obstacles in the path of the pregnant minor seeking to exercise her constitutional right to terminate a pregnancy." Id., ___ U.S. at ___, 110 S.Ct. at ___, ___ L.Ed.2d at ___. The Court left open the question whether the Fourteenth Amendment requires notice statutes to contain bypass procedures. In *Hodgson*, three members of the *Akron Center* majority—the Chief Justice and Justices Kennedy and Scalia—voted to uphold a two parent notification statute without a bypass procedure. Do you consider a bypass procedure constitutionally mandated?

Page 476. Add new Note 11:

11. In the supercharged political atmosphere surrounding the abortion controversy, both sides have resorted to imaginative strategies in support of their causes. Some anti-abortion activists have chosen to block the entrances to abortion clinics, hoping to prevent pregnant women from having abortions. Pro-abortion supporters have been generally successful in enjoining such activity, see, e.g., New York State N.O.W. v. Terry, 886 F.2d 1339 (2d Cir.1989), certiorari denied ___ U.S. ___, 110 S.Ct. 2206, 109 L.Ed.2d 532 (1990) (upholding permanent injunction against First Amendment claims), but not so successful in challenging the tax-exempt status of the Catholic Church, see In re United States Catholic Conference, 885 F.2d 1020 (2d Cir.1989), certiorari denied ___ U.S. ___, 110 S.Ct. 1946, 109 L.Ed. 2d 309 (1990). A suit for damages brought by antiabortion protesters against arresting officers did not survive a motion for summary judgment,

see Radich v. Goode, 886 F.2d 1391 (3rd Cir.1989). A women's health center in Philadelphia was successful in obtaining a civil RICO judgment for damages against aggressive antiabortion protestors who invaded the center and destroyed property, see Northeast Women's Center v. McMonagle, 868 F.2d 1342 (3d Cir.1989), certiorari denied ___ U.S. ___, 110 S.Ct. 261, 107 L.Ed.2d 210 (1989) (Justice White voted to grant certiorari), rehearing denied ___ U.S. ___, 110 S.Ct. 1515, 108 L.Ed.2d 651 (1990).

Chapter III

WOMEN AND EMPLOYMENT

A. TITLE VII OF THE CIVIL RIGHTS ACT OF 1964

1. THE STATUTORY DEFINITION OF SEX DISCRIMINATION IN EMPLOYMENT

a. *Coverage: What Is Sex Discrimination?*

Page 489. Add to Note 2:

See also Dowd, Work and Family: The Gender Paradox and the Limitations of Discrimination Analysis in Restructuring the Workplace, 24 Harv. Civ.Rts.Civ.Lib.L.Rev. 79 (1989).

Page 509. Add to end of Note 4:

Change citation to Florida v. Long, 487 U.S. 223, 108 S.Ct. 2354, 101 L.Ed. 2d 206 (1988), rehearing denied 487 U.S. 1263, 109 S.Ct. 25, 101 L.Ed.2d 975 (1988).

Page 521. Add to Note 6:

See also International Union, UAW v. Johnson Controls, Inc., 886 F.2d 871 (7th Cir.1989), cert. granted ___ U.S. ___, 110 S.Ct. 1522, 108 L.Ed.2d 762 (1990), set out at p. 132, infra.

Page 541. Add to end of Note 6:

See Comment, The Meaning of "Sex" in Title VII: Is Favoring an Employee Lover a Violation of the Act?, 83 Nw.U.L.Rev. 612, 657–64 (1989), proposing that plaintiffs like Mable King and the male therapists in *DeCintio* should be able to make out a prima facie case of sex discrimination, provided they are able to prove that the person hired or promoted was substantially less qualified than they. Do you agree?

Page 543. Add to Note 8:

Edgar Anderson, dismissed by Hewlett–Packard as personnel manager of its Cleveland office, sued the employer for breach of contract and promissory estoppel. Hewlett–Packard claimed that Anderson had been fired for gross misconduct, namely, the sexual harassment of women employees working under his supervision. District Judge Ann Aldrich found for the employer and dismissed Anderson's complaint, noting sharply that:

> It is clear to the Court that Anderson's constant sexual remarks, innuendos, insinuations and suggestions made life completely unbearable for the women working for him, as did the childish punishments he inflicted upon them when they would not accede to his demands.
>
> * * *
>
> It should be clear to corporate America, by now, that the law does not tolerate the type of behavior Anderson exhibited. The termination of employees who behave as Anderson did is justified and lawful. In fact, the only troublesome part of this case is that it took H–P as long as it did to fire Anderson. * * *

Anderson v. Hewlett–Packard, 694 F.Supp. 1294, 1303–04 (N.D.Ohio 1988). It is clear, however, that not everyone in "corporate America" has gotten the message. See, e.g., Jones v. Wesco Investments, Inc., 846 F.2d 1154 (8th Cir.1988), a sexual harassment case in which Senior Judge Bright affirmed a judgment for the plaintiff based on a showing of "repeated sexual advances, request for sexual favors, and other verbal or physical contact of a sexual nature" on the part of the President of the Company, Benjamin B. Rose. Noting that "any other result would have been a miscarriage of justice," Judge Bright quoted the following passage from defendant's brief, adding that the argument "accords neither with the facts nor the law in the present case":

> Any argument in this type of case on this issue is bound to sound sexist, but it is important to point out that one of the traditional places where man meets woman is at the work place. Such meetings often result in dating, blossom into love, and eventually into marriage. Not always are both parties in this cycle unmarried. If civil liability is implanted on an employer for its employees natural interaction between the genders, either the collapse of our commercial system or the end of the human race can be foreseen. No employer could safely employ both males and females, and the number of marriages with children will be substantially decreased. There should be nothing wrong with a man, even a supervisor, telling a female that she looks nice. Nor can there be anything wrong with a man, even a supervisor, asking a female our of [sic] a date. In doing so the man should not have to gamble civil liability upon her "yes" response. Where is the line between these instances and those held to be actionable in *Meritor* * * *?

Id., at 1156–57 & n. 6. On second thought, maybe it's legal America that hasn't gotten the message. See generally Comment, The Harms of Asking: Towards a Comprehensive Treatment of Sexual Harassment, 55 U.Chi.L. Rev. 328 (1988).

b. Scope: What Does Non-discrimination Entail?

Page 566. Add new Note 7:

What impact, if any, does *Cal Fed* have on the exclusion of fertile women from toxic workplaces? See the discussion of this question in the *Notes* on *Johnson Controls* at p. 159, infra.

Text Note

Ensuring Non-discrimination

Page 572. Add before Note 1:

Feminist writers continue to explore the practical and theoretical dimensions of equality and difference. See, e.g., D. Rhode, Justice and Gender 274–321 (1990); Symposium, Feminism in the Law: Theory, Practice and Criticism, 1989 University of Chicago Legal Forum; Symposium, Voices of Experience: New Responses to Gender Discourse, 24 Harv.Civ.Rts.Civ.Lib. L.Rev. 1–172 (1989); West, Jurisprudence and Gender, 55 U.Chi.L.Rev. 1 (1988); Becker, Prince Charming: Abstract Equality, 1987 Supreme Court Review 201 (1988); Brown, Parmet & Barmann, The Failure of Gender Equality: An Essay in Constitutional Dissonance, 36 Buf.L.Rev. 573 (1987). Some writers are beginning to examine feminist methodology in its own right. See, e.g., Katharine T. Bartlett, Feminist Legal Methods, 103 Harv. L.Rev. 829 (1990); Rhode, Feminist Critical Theories, 42 Stan.L.Rev. 617 (1990); Cain, Feminist Jurisprudence: Grounding The Theories, 4 Berkeley Wom.L.J. 191 (1989–90); Matsuda, When The First Quail Calls: Multiple Consciousness as Jurisprudential Method, 11 Wom.Rts.L.Rptr. 7 (1989). A distinctive minority voice is emerging that focuses on the confluence of race and sex in feminist legal theory. See, e.g., Harris, Race and Essentialism in Feminist Legal Theory, 42 Stan.L.Rev. 581 (1990); Crenshaw, Demarginalizing the Intersection of Race and Sex: A Black Feminist Critique of Antidiscrimination Doctrine, Feminist Theory and Antiracist Politics, 1989 U.Chi.Leg.F. 139; Scales-Trent, Black Women and the Constitution: Finding Our Place, Asserting Our Rights, 42 Harv.Civ.Rts.Civ. Lib.L.Rev. 9 (1989); Matsuda, Looking To The Bottom: Critical Legal Studies and Reparations, 22 Harv.Civ.Rts.Civ.Lib.L.Rev. 323 (1987).

Page 574. Add to Footnote 53:

See, denouncing the criticism of Rosenberg's testimony as a violation of her academic freedom while criticizing Kessler-Harris's testimony for its "obvious exaggeration" and dismissing the EEOC's trial strategy in *Sears* as "bewilderingly wrongheaded," Haskel & Levinson, Academic Freedom and Expert Witnessing: Historians and the *Sears* case, 66 Tex.L.Rev. 1629, 1635, 1638 (1988). The piece is followed by a response from Kessler-Harris and a reply from the authors: see Kessler-Harris, Response, 67 Tex.L.Rev. 429 (1988); Haskell & Levinson, Reply, 67 Tex.L.Rev. 1951 (1989).

2. THE EVIDENTIARY FRAMEWORK FOR TITLE VII LITIGATION

a. *Proving Discrimination: The Prima Facie Case*

i. *Disparate Impact*

Page 584–86. Delete discussion of Ninth Circuit opinion in *Wards Cove*.

Page 592. Add *Wards Cove* before *Notes on* McDonnell Douglas:

WARDS COVE PACKING CO., INC. v. ATONIO
Supreme Court of the United States, 1989.
490 U.S. ___, 109 S.Ct. 2115, 104 L.Ed.2d 733.

JUSTICE WHITE delivered the opinion of the Court.

Title VII of the Civil Rights Act of 1964 * * * makes it an unfair employment practice for an employer to discriminate against any individual with respect to hiring or the terms and condition of employment because of such individual's race, color, religion, sex, or national origin; or to limit, segregate or classify his employees in ways that would adversely affect any employee because of the employee's race, color, religion, sex, or national origin. *Griggs v. Duke Power Co.* * * * construed Title VII to proscribe "not only overt discrimination but also practices that are fair in form but discriminatory in practice." Under this basis for liability, which is known as the "disparate impact" theory and which is involved in this case, a facially neutral employment practice may be deemed violative of Title VII without evidence of the employer's subjective intent to discriminate that is required in a "disparate treatment" case.

I

The claims before us are disparate-impact claims, involving the employment practices of petitioners, two companies that operate salmon canneries in remote and widely separated areas of Alaska. The canneries operate only during the salmon runs in the summer months. They are inoperative and vacant for the rest of the year. In May or June of each year, a few weeks before the salmon runs begin, workers arrive and prepare the equipment and facilities for the canning operation. Most of these workers possess a variety of skills. When salmon runs are about to begin, the workers who will operate the cannery lines arrive, remain as long as there are fish to can, and then depart. The canneries are then closed down, winterized, and left vacant until the next spring. During the off season, the companies employ only a small number of individuals at their headquarters in Seattle and Astoria, Oregon, plus some employees at the winter shipyard in Seattle.

The length and size of salmon runs vary from year to year and hence the number of employees needed at each cannery also varies. Estimates are made as early in the winter as possible; the necessary employees are hired, and when the time comes, they are transported to the canneries. Salmon must be processed soon after they are caught, and the work during the canning season is therefore intense.[2] For this reason, and because the canneries are located in remote regions, all workers are housed at the canneries and have their meals in company-owned mess halls.

Jobs at the canneries are of two general types: "cannery jobs" on the cannery line, which are unskilled positions; and "noncannery jobs," which fall into a variety of classifications. Most noncannery jobs are classified as skilled positions.[3] Cannery jobs are filled predominantly by nonwhites, Filipinos and Alaska Natives. The Filipinos are hired through and dispatched by Local 37 of the International Longshoremen Workers Union pursuant to a hiring hall agreement with the Local. The Alaska Natives primarily reside in villages near the remote cannery locations. Noncannery jobs are filled with predominantly white workers, who are hired during the winter months from the companies' offices in Washington and Oregon. Virtually all of the noncannery jobs pay more than cannery positions. The predominantly white noncannery workers and the predominantly nonwhite cannery employees live in separate dormitories and eat in separate mess halls.

In 1974, respondents, a class of nonwhite cannery workers who were (or had been) employed at the canneries, brought this Title VII action against petitioners. Respondents alleged that a variety of petitioners' hiring/promotion practices—*e.g.*, nepotism, a rehire preference, a lack of objective hiring criteria, separate hiring channels, a practice of not promoting from within—were responsible for the racial stratification of the work force, and had denied them and other nonwhites employment as noncannery workers on the basis of race. Respondents also complained of petitioners' racially segregated housing and dining facilities. All of respondents' claims were advanced under both the disparate-treatment and disparate-impact theories of Title VII liability.

The District Court held a bench trial, after which it * * * rejected all of respondents' disparate-treatment claims. It also rejected the disparate-impact challenges involving the subjective employment criteria used by petitioners to fill these noncannery positions, on the ground that those criteria were not subject to attack under a disparate-impact theory. * * * Petitioner's "objective" employment practices (*e.g.*, an English language requirement, alleged nepotism in hiring,

---

2. "Independent fishermen catch the salmon and turn them over to company-owned boats called 'tenders,' which transport the fish from the fishing grounds to the canneries. Once at the cannery, the fish are eviscerated, the eggs pulled, and they are cleaned. Then, operating at a rate of approximately four cans per second, the salmon are filled into cans. Next, the canned salmon are cooked under precise time-temperature requirement established by the FDA, and the cans are inspected to ensure that proper seals are maintained on the top, bottom and sides." * * *

3. The noncannery jobs were described as follows by the Court of Appeals: "Machinists and engineers are hired to maintain the smooth and continuous operation of the canning equipment. Quality control personnel conduct the FDA-required inspections and recordkeeping. Tenders are staffed with a crew necessary to operate the vessel. A variety of support personnel are employed to operate the entire cannery community, including, for example, cooks, carpenters, store-keepers, bookkeepers, beach gangs for dock yard labor and construction, etc." * * *

failure to post noncannery openings, the rehire preference, etc.) were found to be subject to challenge under the disparate-impact theory, but these claims were rejected for failure of proof. Judgment was entered for petitioners.

On appeal, * * * the Court of Appeals held—as this Court subsequently ruled in *Watson v. Fort Worth Bank & Trust*, 487 U.S. ___, 108 S.Ct. 2777, 101 L.Ed.2d 827 (1988)—that disparate-impact analysis could be applied to subjective hiring practices. * * * The Ninth Circuit also concluded that in such a case, "[o]nce the plaintiff class has shown disparate-impact caused by specific, identifiable employment practices or criteria, the burden shifts to the employer," * * * to "prov[e the] business necessity" of the challenged practice. * * * Because the en banc holding on subjective employment practices reversed the District Court's contrary ruling, the en banc Court of Appeals remanded the case to a panel for further proceedings.

* * * Neither the en banc court nor the panel disturbed the District Court's rejection of the disparate-treatment claims.[4]

Petitioners sought review of the Court of Appeals' decision in this Court, challenging it on several grounds. Because some of the issues raised by the decision below were matters on which this Court was evenly divided in *Watson v. Fort Worth Bank & Trust Co.*, * * * we granted certiorari, * * * for the purpose of addressing these disputed questions of the proper application of Title VII's disparate-impact theory of liability.

II

In holding that respondents had made out a prima facie case of disparate impact, the court of appeals relied solely on respondents' statistics showing a high percentage of nonwhite workers in the cannery jobs and a low percentage of such workers in the noncannery positions. Although statistical proof can alone make out a prima facie case, see *Teamsters v. United States*, * * * *Hazelwood School Dist. v.*

---

4. The fact that neither the District Court, nor the Ninth Circuit *en banc*, nor the subsequent Court of Appeals panel ruled for respondents on their disparate treatment claims—*i.e.*, their allegations of intentional racial discrimination—warrants particular attention in light of the dissents' comment that the canneries "bear an unsettling resemblance to aspects of a plantation economy." * * * (Stevens, J., dissenting); * * * (Blackmun, J., dissenting).

Whatever the "resemblance," the unanimous view of the lower courts in this litigation has been that respondents did not prove that the canneries practice intentional racial discrimination. Consequently, Justice Blackmun's hyperbolic allegation that our decision in this case indicates that this Court no longer "believes that race discrimination * * * against non-whites * * * is a problem in our society," * * * is inapt. Of course, it is unfortunately true that race discrimination exists in our country. That does not mean, however, that it exists at the canneries—or more precisely, that it has been proven to exist at the canneries.

Indeed, Justice Stevens concedes that respondents did not press before us the legal theories under which the aspects of cannery life that he finds to most resemble a "plantation economy" might be unlawful. * * * Thus, the question here is not whether we "approve" of petitioners' employment practices or the society that exists at the canneries, but rather, whether respondents have properly established that these practices violate Title VII.

United States, * * * the Court of Appeals' ruling here misapprehends our precedents and the purposes of Title VII, and we therefore reverse.

"There can be no doubt," as there was when a similar mistaken analysis had been undertaken by the courts below in *Hazelwood,* * * * "that the * * * comparison * * * fundamentally misconceived the role of statistics in employment discrimination cases." The "proper comparison [is] between the racial composition of [the at-issue jobs] and the racial composition of the qualified * * * population in the relevant labor market." * * * It is such a comparison—between the racial composition of the qualified persons in the labor market and the persons holding at-issue jobs—that generally forms the proper basis for the initial inquiry in a disparate impact case. Alternatively, in cases where such labor market statistics will be difficult if not impossible to ascertain, we have recognized that certain other statistics—such as measures indicating the racial composition of "otherwise-qualified applicants" for at-issue jobs—are equally probative for this purpose. See, *e.g., New York City Transit Authority v. Beazer,* * * *.[6]

It is clear to us that the Court of Appeals' acceptance of the comparison between the racial composition of the cannery work force and that of the noncannery work force, as probative of a prima facie case of disparate impact in the selection of the latter group of workers, was flawed for several reasons. Most obviously, with respect to the skilled noncannery jobs at issue here, the cannery work force in no way reflected "the pool of *qualified* job applicants" or the "*qualified* population in the labor force." Measuring alleged discrimination in the selection of accountants, managers, boat captains, electricians, doctors, and engineers—and the long list of other "skilled" noncannery positions found to exist by the District Court, * * *—by comparing the number of nonwhites occupying these jobs to the number of nonwhites filling cannery worker positions is nonsensical. If the absence of minorities holding such skilled positions is due to a dearth of qualified nonwhite applicants (for reasons that are not petitioners' fault),[7] petitioners' selection methods or employment practices cannot be said to have had a "disparate impact" on nonwhites.

One example illustrates why this must be so. Respondents' own statistics concerning the noncannery work force at one of the canneries at issue here indicate that approximately 17% of the new hires for medical jobs, and 15% of the new hires for officer worker positions, were nonwhite. * * * If it were the case that less than 15–17% of the applicants for these jobs were nonwhite and that nonwhites made

---

6. In fact, where "figures for the general population might * * * accurately reflect the pool of qualified job applicants," cf. *Teamsters v. United States,* * * * we have even permitted plaintiffs to rest their prima facie cases on such statistics as well. See, e.g., *Dothard v. Rawlinson,* * * *.

7. Obviously, the analysis would be different if it were found that the dearth of qualified nonwhite applicants was due to practices on petitioner's part which—expressly or implicitly—deterred minority group members from applying for noncannery positions. See, *e.g., Teamsters v. United States,* * * *.

up a lower percentage of the relevant qualified labor market, it is hard to see how respondents, without more, cf. *Connecticut v. Teal*, * * * would have made out a prima facie case of disparate impact. Yet, under the Court of Appeals' theory, simply because nonwhites comprise 52% of the cannery workers at the cannery in question, * * * respondents would be successful in establishing a prima facie case of racial discrimination under Title VII.

Such a result cannot be squared with our cases or with the goals behind the statute. The Court of Appeals' theory, at the very least, would mean that any employer who had a segment of his work force that was—for some reason—racially imbalanced, could be haled into court and forced to engage in the expensive and time-consuming task of defending the "business necessity" of the methods used to select the other members of his work force. The only practicable option for many employers will be to adopt racial quotas, insuring that no portion of his work force deviates in racial composition from the other portions thereof; this is a result that Congress expressly rejected in drafting Title VII. See 42 U.S.C. § 2000e–2(j); see also *Watson v. Fort Worth Bank & Trust Co.*, * * * at n. 2, * * * (opinion of O'Connor, J.). The Court of Appeals' theory would "leave the employer little choice * * * but to engage in a subjective quota system of employment selection. This, of course, is far from the intent of Title VII." *Albemarle Paper Co. v. Moody*, * * * (BLACKMUN, J., concurring in judgment).

The Court of Appeals also erred with respect to the unskilled noncannery positions. Racial imbalance in one segment of an employer's work force does not, without more, establish a prima facie case of disparate impact with respect to the selection of workers for the employer's other positions, even where workers for the different positions may have somewhat fungible skills (as is arguably the case for cannery and unskilled noncannery workers). As long as there are no barriers or practices deterring qualified nonwhites from applying for noncannery positions, see *supra*, n. 6, if the percentage of selected applicants who are nonwhite is not significantly less than the percentage of qualified applicants who are nonwhite, the employer's selection mechanism probably does not operate with a disparate impact on minorities.[8] Where this is the case, the percentage of nonwhite workers found in other positions in the employer's labor force is irrelevant to the question of a prima facie statistical case of disparate impact. As noted above, a contrary ruling on this point would almost inexorably

---

8. We qualify this conclusion—observing that it is only "probable" that there has been no disparate impact on minorities in such circumstances—because bottom-line racial balance is not a defense under Title VII. See *Connecticut v. Teal*, 457 U.S. 440, 102 S.Ct. 2525, 73 L.Ed.2d 130 (1982). Thus, even if petitioners could show that the percentage of selected applicants who are nonwhite is not significantly less than the percentage of qualified applicants who are nonwhite, respondents would still have a case under Title VII, if they could prove that some particular hiring practice has a disparate impact on minorities, notwithstanding the bottom-line racial balance in petitioners' workforce. * * *

lead to the use of numerical quotas in the workplace, a result that Congress and this Court have rejected repeatedly in the past.

Moreover, isolating the cannery workers as the potential "labor force" for unskilled noncannery positions is at once both too broad and too narrow in its focus. Too broad because the vast majority of these cannery workers did not seek jobs in unskilled noncannery positions; there is no showing that many of them would have done so even if none of the arguably "deterring" practices existed. Thus, the pool of cannery workers cannot be used as a surrogate for the class of qualified job applicants because it contains many persons who have not (and would not) be noncannery job applicants. Conversely, if respondents propose to use the cannery workers for comparison purposes because they represent the "qualified labor population" generally, the group is too narrow because there are obviously many qualified persons in the labor market for noncannery jobs who are not cannery workers.

The peculiar facts of this case further illustrate why a comparison between the percentage of nonwhite cannery workers and nonwhite noncannery workers is an improper basis for making out a claim of disparate impact. Here, the District Court found that nonwhites were "overrepresent[ed]" among cannery workers because petitioners had contracted with a predominantly nonwhite union (Local 37) to fill these positions. * * * As a result, if petitioners (for some permissible reason) ceased using Local 37 as its hiring channel for cannery positions, it appears (according to the District Court's findings) that the racial stratification between the cannery and noncannery workers might diminish to statistical insignificance. Under the Court of Appeals' approach, therefore, it is possible that *with no change whatsoever* in their hiring practices for noncannery workers—the jobs at-issue in this lawsuit—petitioners could make respondents' prima facie case of disparate impact "disappear." But *if* there would be no prima facie case of disparate impact in the selection of noncannery workers absent petitioners' use of Local 37 to hire cannery workers, surely the petitioners' reliance on the union to fill the cannery jobs not at-issue here (and its resulting "overrepresentation" of nonwhites in those positions) does not—standing alone—make out a prima facie case of disparate impact. Yet it is precisely such an ironic result that the Court of Appeals reached below.

Consequently, we reverse the Court of Appeals' ruling that a comparison between the percentage of cannery workers who are nonwhite and the percentage of noncannery workers who are nonwhite makes out a prima facie case of disparate impact. Of course, this leaves unresolved whether the record made in the District Court will support a conclusion that a prima facie case of disparate impact has been established on some basis other than the racial disparity between cannery and noncannery workers. This is an issue that the Court of Appeals or the District Court should address in the first instance.

III

Since the statistical disparity relied on by the Court of Appeals did not suffice to make out a prima facie case, any inquiry by us into whether the specific challenged employment practices of petitioners caused that disparity is pretermitted, as is any inquiry into whether the disparate impact that any employment practice may have had was justified by business considerations.[9] Because we remand for further proceedings, however, on whether a prima facie case of disparate impact has been made in defensible fashion in this case, we address two other challenges petitioners have made to the decision of the Court of Appeals.

A

First is the question of causation in a disparate-impact case. The law in this respect was correctly stated by Justice O'Connor's opinion last Term in *Watson v. Fort Worth Bank & Trust*, * * *:

> "[W]e note that the plaintiff's burden in establishing a prima facie case goes beyond the need to show that there are statistical disparities in the employer's work force. The plaintiff must begin by identifying the specific employment practice that is challenged * * *. Especially in cases where an employer combines subjective criteria with the use of more rigid standardized rules or tests, the plaintiff is in our view responsible for isolating and identifying the specific employment practices that are allegedly responsible for any observed statistical disparities."

* * *

Indeed, even the Court of Appeals—whose decision petitioners assault on this score—noted that "it is * * * essential that the practices identified by the cannery workers be linked causally with the demonstrated adverse impact." * * * Notwithstanding the Court of Appeals' apparent adherence to the proper inquiry, petitioners contend that that court erred by permitting respondents to make out their case by offering "only [one] set of cumulative comparative statistics as evidence of the disparate impact of each and all of [petitioners' hiring] practices."

Our disparate-impact cases have always focused on the impact of *particular* hiring practices on employment opportunities for minorities. Just as an employer cannot escape liability under Title VII by demonstrating that, "at the bottom line," his work force is racially balanced

---

9. As we understand the opinions below, the specific employment practices were challenged only insofar as they were claimed to have been responsible for the overall disparity between the number of minority cannery and noncannery workers. The Court of Appeals did not purport to hold that any specified employment practice produced its own disparate impact that was actionable under Title VII. This is not to say that a specific practice, such as nepotism, if it were proved to exist, could not itself be subject to challenge if it had a disparate impact on minorities. Nor is it to say that segregated dormitories and eating facilities in the work-place may not be challenged under 42 U.S.C. § 2000e–2(a)(2) without showing a disparate impact on hiring or promotion.

(where particular hiring practices may operate to deprive minorities of employment opportunities), see *Connecticut v. Teal,* * * * a Title VII plaintiff does not make out a case of disparate impact simply by showing that, "at the bottom line," there is racial *imbalance* in the work force. As a general matter, a plaintiff must demonstrate that it is the application of a specific or particular employment practice that has created the disparate impact under attack. Such a showing is an integral part of the plaintiff's prima facie case in a disparate-impact suit under Title VII.

Here, respondents have alleged that several "objective" employment practices (*e.g.,* nepotism, separate hiring channels, rehire preferences), as well as the use of "subjective decision making" to select noncannery workers, have had a disparate impact on nonwhites. Respondents base this claim on statistics that allegedly show a disproportionately low percentage of nonwhites in the at-issue positions. However, even if on remand respondents can show that nonwhites are underrepresented in the at-issue jobs in a manner that is acceptable under the standards set forth in Part II, *supra,* this alone will *not* suffice to make out a prima facie case of disparate impact. Respondents will also have to demonstrate that the disparity they complain of is the result of one or more of the employment practices that they are attacking here, specifically showing that each challenged practice has a significantly disparate impact on employment opportunities for whites and nonwhites. To hold otherwise would result in employers being potentially liable for "the myriad of innocent causes that may lead to statistical imbalances in the composition of their work forces." *Watson v. Fort Worth Bank & Trust,* * * *

Some will complain that this specific causation requirement is unduly burdensome on Title VII plaintiffs. But liberal civil discovery rules give plaintiffs broad access to employers' records in an effort to document their claims. Also, employers falling within the scope of the Uniform Guidelines on Employee Selection Procedures, 29 CFR § 1607.1 *et seq.* (1988), are required to "maintain * * * records or other information which will disclose the impact which its tests and other selection procedures have upon employment opportunities of persons by identifiable race, sex, or ethnic group[s.]" See § 1607.4(A). This includes records concerning "the individual components of the selection process" where there is a significant disparity in the selection rates of whites and nonwhites. See § 1607.4(C). Plaintiffs as a general matter will have the benefit of these tools to meet their burden of showing a causal link between challenged employment practices and racial imbalances in the work force; respondents presumably took full advantage of these opportunities to build their case before the trial in the District Court was held.[10]

10. Of course, petitioners' obligation to collect or retain any of these data may be limited by the Guidelines themselves. See 29 CFR § 1602.14(b) (1988) (exempting "seasonal" jobs from certain record-keeping requirements).

Consequently, on remand, the courts below are instructed to require, as part of respondents' prima facie case, a demonstration that specific elements of the petitioners' hiring process have a significantly disparate impact on nonwhites.

B

If, on remand, respondents meet the proof burdens outlined above, and establish a prima facie case of disparate impact with respect to any of petitioners' employment practices, the case will shift to any business justification petitioners offer for their use of these practices. This phase of the disparate-impact case contains two components: first, a consideration of the justifications an employer offers for his use of these practices; and second, the availability of alternate practices to achieve the same business ends, with less racial impact. See, *e.g.*, *Albemarle Paper Co. v. Moody,* * * *. We consider these two components in turn.

(1)

Though we have phrased the query differently in different cases, it is generally well-established that at the justification stage of such a disparate impact case, the dispositive issue is whether a challenged practice serves, in a significant way, the legitimate employment goals of the employer. * * * The touchstone of this inquiry is a reasoned review of the employer's justification for his use of the challenged practice. A mere insubstantial justification in this regard will not suffice, because such a low standard of review would permit discrimination to be practiced through the use of spurious, seemingly neutral employment practices. At the same time, though, there is no requirement that the challenged practice be "essential" or "indispensable" to the employer's business for it to pass muster: this degree of scrutiny would be almost impossible for most employers to meet, and would result in a host of evils we have identified above.

In this phase, the employer carries the burden of producing evidence of a business justification for his employment practice. The burden of persuasion, however, remains with the disparate-impact plaintiff. To the extent that the Ninth Circuit held otherwise in its en banc decision in this case, * * * or in the panel's decision on remand, * * *—suggesting that the persuasion burden should shift to the petitioners once the respondents established a prima facie case of disparate impact—its decisions were erroneous. "[T]he ultimate burden of proving that discrimination against a protected group has been caused by a specific employment practice remains with the plaintiff *at all times.*" *Watson,* * * * (O'Connor, J.) (emphasis added). This rule conforms with the usual method for allocating persuasion and production burdens in the federal courts, see Fed.Rule.Evid. 301, and more specifically, it conforms to the rule in disparate-treatment cases that the plaintiff bears the burden of disproving an employer's assertion that the adverse employment action or practice was based solely on a legitimate neutral consideration. See *Texas Dept. of Community Affairs v. Burdine,* * * *. We acknowledge that some of our earlier decisions can be read as suggesting otherwise. See *Watson,* * * * (BLACKMUN, J., concurring). But to the extent that those cases speak of an employers' "burden of proof" with respect to a legitimate business justification defense, see, *e.g., Dothard v. Rawlinson,* * * * they should have been understood to mean an employer's production—but not persuasion—burden. Cf., *e.g., NLRB v. Transportation Management Corp.,* * * *. The persuasion burden here must remain with the plaintiff, for it is he who must prove that it was "because of such individual's race, color," etc., that he was denied a desired employment opportunity. See 42 U.S.C. § 2000e–2(a).

(2)

Finally, if on remand the case reaches this point, and respondents cannot persuade the trier of fact on the question of petitioners' business necessity defense, respondents may still be able to prevail. To do so, respondents will have to persuade the factfinder that "other tests or selection devices, without a similarly undesirable racial effect, would also serve the employer's legitimate [hiring] interest[s];" by so demonstrating, respondents would prove that "[petitioners were] using [their] tests merely as a 'pretext' for discrimination." *Albemarle Paper Co.,* * * *; see also *Watson,* * * *. If respondents, having established a prima facie case, come forward with alternatives to petitioners' hiring practices that reduce the racially-disparate impact of practices currently being used, and petitioners refuse to adopt these alternatives, such a refusal would belie a claim by petitioners that their incumbent practices are being employed for nondiscriminatory reasons.

Of course, any alternative practices which respondents offer up in this respect must be equally effective as petitioners' chosen hiring procedures in achieving petitioners' legitimate employment goals. Moreover, "[f]actors such as the cost or other burdens of proposed alternative selection devices are relevant in determining whether they would be equally as effective as the challenged practice in serving the employer's legitimate business goals." *Watson,* * * * (O'Connor, J.). "Courts are generally less competent than employers to restructure business practices," *Furnco Construction Corp. v. Waters,* * * *; consequently, the judiciary should proceed with care before mandating that an employer must adopt a plaintiff's alternate selection or hiring practice in response to a Title VII suit.

IV

For the reasons given above, the judgment of the Court of Appeals is reversed, and the case is remanded for further proceedings consistent with this opinion.

It is so ordered.

Justice STEVENS, with whom Justice BRENNAN, Justice MARSHALL, and Justice BLACKMUN join, dissenting.

Fully 18 years ago, this Court unanimously held that Title VII of the Civil Rights Act of 1964 prohibits employment practices that have discriminatory effects as well as those that are intended to discriminate. *Griggs v. Duke Power Co.,* * * *. Federal courts and agencies consistently have enforced that interpretation, thus promoting our national goal of eliminating barriers that define economic opportunity not by aptitude and ability but by race, color, national origin, and other traits that are easily identified but utterly irrelevant to one's qualification for a particular job. Regrettably, the Court retreats from these efforts in its review of an interlocutory judgment respecting the "peculiar facts" of this lawsuit.[3] Turning a blind eye to the meaning and purpose of Title VII, the majority's opinion perfunctorily rejects a longstanding rule of law and underestimates the probative value of evidence of a racially stratified work force.[4] I cannot join this latest sojourn into judicial activism.

I

I would have thought it superfluous to recount at this late date the development of our Title VII jurisprudence, but the majority's facile treatment of settled law necessitates such a primer. This Court initially considered the meaning of Title VII in *Griggs v. Duke Power Co.,* * * * in which a class of utility company employees challenged the conditioning of entry into higher paying jobs upon a high school education or passage of two written tests. Despite evidence that "these

---

3. The majority purports to reverse the Court of Appeals but in fact directs the District Court to make additional findings, some of which had already been ordered by the Court of Appeals. * * * Furthermore, nearly half the majority's opinion is devoted to two questions not fairly raised at this point: "the question of causation in a disparate impact case," and the nature of the employer's defense. Because I perceive no urgency to decide "these disputed questions," at an interlocutory stage of such a factually complicated case, I believe the Court should have denied certiorari and allowed the District Court to make the additional findings directed by the Court of Appeals.

4. Respondents comprise a class of present and former employees of petitioners, two Alaskan salmon canning companies. The class members, described by the parties as "nonwhite," include persons of Samoan, Chinese, Filipino, Japanese, and Alaska Native descent, all but one of whom are United States citizens. * * * Fifteen years ago they commenced this suit, alleging that petitioners engage in hiring, job assignment, housing, and messing practices that segregate nonwhites from whites, in violation of Title VII. Evidence included this response in 1971 by a foreman to a college student's inquiry about cannery employment:

" 'We are not in a position to take many young fellows to our Bristol Bay canneries as they do not have the background for our type of employees. Our cannery labor is either Eskimo or Filipino and we do not have the facilities to mix others with these groups.' "

Some characteristics of the Alaska salmon industry described in this litigation—in particular, the segregation of housing and dining facilities and the stratification of jobs along racial and ethnic lines—bear an unsettling resemblance to aspects of a plantation economy. See generally 'Plantation, Town, and County, Essays on the Local History of American Slave Society 163–334 (E. Miller & E. Genovese eds. 1974). Indeed the maintenance of inferior, segregated facilities for housing and feeding nonwhite employees, * * * strikes me as a form of discrimination that, although it does not necessarily fit neatly into a disparate impact or disparate treatment mold, nonetheless violates Title VII. See generally Brief for National Association for the Advancement of Colored People as *Amicus Curiae*. Respondents, however, do not press this theory before us.

two requirements operated to render ineligible a markedly disproportionate number of Negroes," the Court of Appeals had held that because there was no showing of an intent to discriminate on account of race, there was no Title VII violation. Chief Justice Burger's landmark opinion established that an employer may violate the statute even when acting in complete good faith without any invidious intent. * * *

The opinion in *Griggs* made it clear that a neutral practice that operates to exclude minorities is nevertheless lawful if it serves a valid business purpose. "The touchstone is business necessity," the Court stressed. Because "Congress directed the thrust of the Act to the *consequences* of employment practices, not simply the motivation[,] * * * Congress has placed on the employer the burden of showing that any given requirement must have a manifest relationship to the employment in question." (emphasis in original). Congress has declined to act—as the Court now sees fit—to limit the reach of this "disparate impact" theory; * * * indeed it has extended its application.[9] This approval lends added force to the *Griggs* holding.

The *Griggs* framework, with its focus on ostensibly neutral qualification standards, proved inapposite for analyzing an individual employee's claim, brought under § 703(a)(1), that an employer intentionally discriminated on account of race. The means for determining intent absent direct evidence was outlined in *McDonnell Douglas Corp. v. Green,* * * * and *Texas Dept. of Community Affairs v. Burdine,* * * * two opinions written by Justice Powell for unanimous Courts. In such a "disparate treatment" case, * * * the plaintiff's initial burden, which is "not onerous," * * * is to establish "a prima facie case of racial discrimination," * * * that is, to create a presumption of unlawful discrimination by "eliminat[ing] the most common nondiscriminatory reasons for the plaintiff's rejection." * * * "The burden then must shift to the employer to articulate some legitimate, nondiscriminatory reason for the employee's rejection." * * * Finally, because "Title VII does not * * * permit [the employer] to use [the employee's] conduct as a pretext for the sort of discrimination prohibited by § 703(a)(1)," the employee "must be given a full and fair opportunity to demonstrate by competent evidence that the presumptively valid reasons for his rejection were in fact a coverup for a racially discriminatory decision." * * * While the burdens of producing evidence thus shift, the "ultimate burden of persuading the trier of fact that the defendant intentionally discriminated against the plaintiff remains at all times with the plaintiff." * * *

9. Voting Rights Act Amendments of 1982, * * *. Legislative reports leading to 1972 amendments to Title VII also evince support for disparate impact analysis. * * * Moreover, the theory is employed to enforce fair housing and age discrimination statutes. See Note, Business Necessity in Title VIII: Importing an Employment Discrimination Doctrine into the Fair Housing Act, 54 Ford.L.Rev. 563 (1986); Note, Disparate Impact Analysis and the Age Discrimination in Employment Act, 68 Minn.L.Rev. 1038 (1984).

Decisions of this Court and other federal courts repeatedly have recognized that while the employer's burden in a disparate treatment case is simply one of coming forward with evidence of legitimate business purpose, its burden in a disparate impact case is proof of an affirmative defense of business necessity. Although the majority's opinion blurs that distinction, thoughtful reflection on common-law pleading principles clarifies the fundamental differences between the two types of "burdens of proof." In the ordinary civil trial, the plaintiff bears the burden of persuading the trier of fact that the defendant has harmed her. * * * The defendant may undercut plaintiff's efforts both by confronting plaintiff's evidence during her case in chief and by submitting countervailing evidence during its own case. But if the plaintiff proves the existence of the harmful act, the defendant can escape liability only by persuading the factfinder that the act was justified or excusable. * * * The plaintiff in turn may try to refute this affirmative defense. Although the burdens of producing evidence regarding the existence of harm or excuse thus shift between the plaintiff and the defendant, the burden of proving either proposition remains throughout on the party asserting it.

In a disparate treatment case there is no "discrimination" within the meaning of Title VII unless the employer intentionally treated the employee unfairly because of race. Therefore, the employee retains the burden of proving the existence of intent at all times. If there is direct evidence of intent, the employee may have little difficulty persuading the factfinder that discrimination has occurred. But in the likelier event that intent has to be established by inference, the employee may resort to the *McDonnell/Burdine* inquiry. In either instance, the employer may undermine the employee's evidence but has no independent burden of persuasion.

In contrast, intent plays no role in the disparate impact inquiry. The question, rather, is whether an employment practice has a significant, adverse effect on an identifiable class of workers—regardless of the cause or motive for the practice. The employer may attempt to contradict the factual basis for this effect; that is, to prevent the employee from establishing a prima facie case. But when an employer is faced with sufficient proof of disparate impact, its only recourse is to justify the practice by explaining why it is necessary to the operation of business. Such a justification is a classic example of an affirmative defense.

Failing to explore the interplay between these distinct orders of proof, the Court announces that our frequent statements that the employer shoulders the burden of proof respecting business necessity "should have been understood to mean an employer's production—but not persuasion—burden." [18] Our opinions always have emphasized that

---

18. The majority's only basis for this proposition is the plurality opinion in *Watson v. Fort Worth Bank & Trust*, * * *, which in turn cites no authority. As Justice Blackmun explained in *Watson*, * * * (concurring in part and concurring in judgment), and as I have shown here, the assertion profoundly misapprehends

in a disparate impact case the employer's burden is weighty. "The touchstone," the Court said in *Griggs*, "is business necessity." * * * Later, we held that prison administrators had failed to "rebu[t] the prima facie case of discrimination by showing that the height and weight requirements are * * * essential to effective job performance," *Dothard v. Rawlinson*, * * *. I am thus astonished to read that the "touchstone of this inquiry is a reasoned review of the employer's justification for his use of the challenged practice * * *. [T]here is no requirement that the challenged practice be * * * 'essential,' * * * ". This casual—almost summary—rejection of the statutory construction that developed in the wake of *Griggs* is most disturbing. I have always believed that the *Griggs* opinion correctly reflected the intent of the Congress that enacted Title VII. Even if I were not so persuaded, I could not join a rejection of a consistent interpretation of a federal statute. Congress frequently revisits this statutory scheme and can readily correct our mistakes if we misread its meaning. * * *

Also troubling is the Court's apparent redefinition of the employees' burden of proof in a disparate impact case. No prima facie case will be made, it declares, unless the employees " 'isolat[e] and identif[y] the specific employment practices that are allegedly responsible for any observed statistical disparities.' " (quoting *Watson v. Fort Worth Bank & Trust*, * * * (plurality opinion)). This additional proof requirement is unwarranted. It is elementary that a plaintiff cannot recover upon proof of injury alone; rather, the plaintiff must connect the injury to an act of the defendant in order to establish prima facie that the defendant is liable. * * * Although the causal link must have substance, the act need not constitute the sole or primary cause of the harm. * * * Thus in a disparate impact case, proof of numerous questionable employment practices ought to fortify an employee's assertion that the practices caused racial disparities.[20] Ordinary principles of fairness require that Title VII actions be tried like "any lawsuit." * * * The changes the majority makes today, tipping the scales in favor of employers, are not faithful to those principles.

II

Petitioners seek reversal of the Court of Appeals and dismissal of this suit on the ground that respondents' statistical evidence failed to prove a prima facie case of discrimination. * * * The District Court concluded "there were 'significant disparities' " between the racial

the difference between disparate impact and disparate treatment claims.

The Court also makes passing reference to Federal Rule of Evidence 301. * * * That Rule pertains only to shifting of evidentiary burdens upon establishment of a presumption and has no bearing on the substantive burdens of proof. See Louisell §§ 65–70; Wright § 5122.

20. The Court discounts the difficulty its causality requirement presents for employees, reasoning that they may employ "liberal civil discovery rules" to obtain the employer's statistical personnel records. * * * Even assuming that this generally is true, it has no bearing in this litigation, since it is undisputed that petitioners did not preserve such records. * * *

composition of the cannery workers and the noncannery workers, but it "made no precise numerical findings" on this and other critical points. Given this dearth of findings and the Court's newly articulated preference for individualized proof of causation, it would be manifestly unfair to consider respondents' evidence in the aggregate and deem it insufficient. Thus the Court properly rejects petitioners' request for a final judgment and remands for further determination of the strength of respondents' prima facie case. Even at this juncture, however, I believe that respondents' evidence deserves greater credit than the majority allows.

* * *

Evidence that virtually all the employees in the major categories of at-issue jobs were white, whereas about two-thirds of the cannery workers were nonwhite,[25] may not by itself suffice to establish a prima facie case of discrimination. But such evidence of racial stratification puts the specific employment practices challenged by respondents into perspective. Petitioners recruit employees for at-issue jobs from outside the work force rather than from lower-paying, overwhelmingly nonwhite, cannery worker positions. Information about availability of at-issue positions is conducted by word of mouth; therefore, the maintenance of housing and mess halls that separate the largely white noncannery work force from the cannery workers, * * *, coupled with the tendency toward nepotistic hiring,[28] are obvious barriers to employment opportunities for nonwhites. Putting to one side the issue of business justifications, it would be quite wrong to conclude that these practices have no discriminatory consequence.[29] Thus I agree with the Court of Appeals, that when the District Court makes the additional findings prescribed today, it should treat the evidence of racial stratification in the work force as a significant element of respondents' prima facie case.

25. The Court points out that nonwhites are "overrepresented" among the cannery workers. * * * Such an imbalance will be true in any racially stratified work force; its significance becomes apparent only upon examination of the pattern of segregation within the work force. In the cannery industry nonwhites are concentrated in positions offering low wages and little opportunity for promotion. Absent any showing that the "underrepresentation" of whites in this stratum is the result of a barrier to access, the "overrepresentation" of nonwhites does not offend Title VII.

28. The District Court found but downplayed the fact that relatives of employees are given preferential consideration. * * * But "of 349 nepotistic hires in four upper-level departments during 1970–75, 332 were of whites, 17 of nonwhites," the Court of Appeals noted. "If nepotism exists, it is by definition a practice of giving preference to relatives, and where those doing the hiring are predominantly white, the practice necessarily has an adverse impact on nonwhites." * * *

29. The Court suggests that the discrepancy in economic opportunities for white and nonwhite workers does not amount to disparate impact within the meaning of Title VII unless respondents show that it is "petitioners' fault." * * * This statement distorts the disparate impact theory, in which the critical inquiry is whether an employer's practices *operate* to discriminate. *E.g., Griggs,* * * *. Whether the employer intended such discrimination is irrelevant.

III

The majority's opinion begins with recognition of the settled rule that "a facially neutral employment practice may be deemed violative of Title VII without evidence of the employer's subjective intent to discriminate that is required in a 'disparate treatment' case." * * * It then departs from the body of law engendered by this disparate impact theory, reformulating the order of proof and the weight of the parties' burdens. Why the Court undertakes these unwise changes in elementary and eminently fair rules is a mystery to me.

I respectfully dissent.

JUSTICE BLACKMUN, with whom JUSTICE BRENNAN and JUSTICE MARSHALL join, dissenting.

I fully concur in Justice Stevens' analysis of this case. Today a bare majority of the Court takes three major strides backwards in the battle against race discrimination. It reaches out to make last Term's plurality opinion in *Watson v. Fort Worth Bank & Trust,* * * * the law, thereby upsetting the longstanding distribution of burdens of proof in Title VII disparate-impact cases. It bars the use of internal workforce comparisons in the making of a prima facie case of discrimination, even where the structure of the industry in question renders any other statistical comparison meaningless. And it requires practice-by-practice statistical proof of causation, even where, as here, such proof would be impossible.

The harshness of these results is well demonstrated by the facts of this case. The salmon industry as described by this record takes us back to a kind of overt and institutionalized discrimination we have not dealt with in years: a total residential and work environment organized on principles of racial stratification and segregation, which, as Justice Stevens points out, resembles a plantation economy. * * * This industry long has been characterized by a taste for discrimination of the old-fashioned sort: a preference for hiring nonwhites to fill its lowest-level positions, on the condition that they stay there. The majority's legal rulings essentially immunize these practices from attack under a Title VII disparate-impact analysis.

Sadly, this comes as no surprise. One wonders whether the majority still believes that race discrimination—or, more accurately, race discrimination against non-whites—is a problem in our society, or even remembers that it ever was. Cf. *City of Richmond v. J.A. Croson Co.,* 488 U.S. 469, 109 S.Ct. 706, 102 L.Ed.2d 854 (1989).

Notes on Wards Cove

1. Commenting on *Watson,* a Harvard notewriter said:

[T]he Court's discussion of the evidentiary standards to be applied in such challenges blurred the Court's prior distinctions between disparate treatment and disparate impact, and threatened to increase the hurdles for plaintiffs bringing disparate impact challenges against objective as well as subjective hiring practices. The Court's general uneasiness about the proper evidentiary standards to be applied to Watson's claim on remand may indicate that the Court is reconsidering altogether the principles underlying disparate impact doctrine, as originally articulated in *Griggs* itself.

The Supreme Court, 1987 Term—Leading Cases, 102 Harv.L.Rev. 143, 309–10 (1988). Does *Wards Cove* vindicate this forecast? A different Harvard notewriter, while admitting that the Court had "stiffened the requirements for the use of disparate-impact analysis," nevertheless stoutly denied that "the *Wards Cove* decision eliminated the disparate-impact model introduced in *Griggs* ":

> The case does not * * * reach that far: title VII plaintiffs retain the weapon of disparate impact, although the Court has stripped it of some power. *Wards Cove,* rather, reshapes the disparate-impact law in accordance with a theory of equality based on equal treatment and color blindness, and thus resolves a great deal of the ambiguity present in *Griggs*. In addition, by adopting this theory of equal treatment as its guide, the Court shapes title VII doctrine in a manner more consistent with congressional intent, and reaffirms the validity of merit and ability as criteria in employment decisions.

The Supreme Court, 1988 Term—Leading Cases, 103 Harv.L.Rev. 137, 351, 356 (1989). Do you agree with this analysis?

2. The Fourth Circuit applied the "stiffened" *Wards Cove/Watson* disparate impact standard in Walls v. City of Petersburg, 895 F.2d 188 (4th Cir.1990) to affirm a summary judgment against Teyonda Walls on her Title VII claim. Walls, a black woman hired to administer the City's "Community Diversion Incentive Program," refused to answer certain questions included in a "background check" that was required for all CDI employees upon their transfer from the City Manager's Office to the City Police Department. The questions concerned whether any member of Walls's family had ever been arrested or convicted of a crime; whether she had ever had sexual relations with a person of her same sex; and required her to list all her previous marriages, all children born to her, and all debts outstanding against her or her spouse. Walls submitted statistical evidence showing that blacks are more likely to have "negative" responses to these questions than whites, and that they would be more likely than whites to be the subject of negative personnel reviews as a result of answering the questions. In sustaining the summary judgment, Chief Judge Ervin reasoned as follows:

> Under *Watson* and *Wards Cove Packing Co.,* absent proof of causation, Walls has failed to satisfy her *prima facie* burden. She bases her claim on the speculation that, had she filled out the form, she would have been subject to some form of adverse job action based on her answers and that, in general, blacks would be subject to such action disproportionately to whites based on a statistical analysis of their likely responses. This is completely speculative. She offers no evidence that anyone, black or white, has ever been terminated or otherwise adversely affected as a result of their answers to the ques-

tionnaire. Speculation as to the potential for disparate impact cannot serve as evidence of such impact itself.

Id., at 191. Where do you think the Petersburg Bureau of Police got the questions? Would *Walls* have been decided any differently before *Wards Cove?*

3. Senator Kennedy and Congressman Hawkins have introduced companion bills, S 2104 and HR 4000, known as The Civil Rights Act of 1990, to overturn *Wards Cove* and several other employment discrimination cases decided during the 1988 Term. Section 4 of the companion bills as amended May 9, 1990, would add a new subsection (k) to section 703 to read as follows:

(k) Proof of Unlawful Employment Practices in Disparate Impact Cases.

(1) An unlawful employment practice based on disparate impact is established under this section when—

(A) a complaining party demonstrates that an employment practice results in a disparate impact on the basis of race, color, religion, sex, or national origin, and the respondent fails to demonstrate by objective evidence that such practice is required by business necessity; or

(B) a complaining party demonstrates that a group of employment practices results in a disparate impact on the basis of race, color, religion, sex, or national origin, and the respondent fails to demonstrate by objective evidence that such group of employment practices is required by business necessity, except that—

(i) if a complaining party demonstrates that a group of employment practices results in a disparate impact, such party shall not be required to demonstrate which specific practice or practices within the group results in such disparate impact; and

(ii) if the respondent demonstrates that a specific employment practice within such group of employment practices does not contribute to the disparate impact, the respondent shall not be required to demonstrate that such practice is required by business necessity.

(2) A demonstration that an employment practice is required by business necessity may be used as a defense only against a claim under this subsection.

Supporters of this provision of the bill claim that it is necessary to restore the *Griggs* standard and to make clear that workers are not required to pinpoint specific practices that result in an adverse impact on women and minorities. Does the bill accomplish this goal? Does it go beyond *Griggs?*

b. Rebutting the Prima Facie Case: Some Defense Strategies

i. The BFOQ and Business Necessity Defenses in Sex Discrimination Cases

Page 600. Add before *Wilson*:

INTERNATIONAL UNION, UAW v. JOHNSON CONTROLS, INC.

United States Court of Appeals, Seventh Circuit, 1989.
886 F.2d 871, cert. granted ___ U.S. ___, 110 S.Ct. 1522,
108 L.Ed.2d 762 (1990).

COFFEY, CIRCUIT JUDGE.

Since 1982 Johnson Controls, Inc. * * * has maintained a fetal protection policy designed to prevent unborn children and their mothers from suffering the adverse effects of lead exposure. International Union, United Automobile, Aerospace and Agricultural Implement Workers of America, UAW * * *, several UAW local unions and a group of individual employees brought suit alleging that this policy violated Title VII, * * *. The district court granted summary judgment in favor of Johnson Controls and the plaintiffs appealed. * * * [A] majority of the members voted to hear the case before an *en banc* court and, following rehearing *en banc*, a majority of the court voted to affirm the decision of the district court.

I.

The Battery Division of Johnson Controls, Inc., was created upon Johnson Controls' 1978 purchase of Globe Union, Inc. * * * Globe Union was formed through the consolidation of two battery companies and had been in the battery business for almost fifty years before Johnson's purchase. Globe Union and Johnson Controls have maintained ongoing efforts to improve industrial safety through measures designed to minimize the risk lead poses to those directly involved in the manufacturing of batteries.

The steps that Globe Union and Johnson Controls have taken to regulate lead exposure have not been focused merely on complying with governmental safety regulations, but originate from their longstanding corporate concern for the danger lead poses to the health and welfare of their employees, their employees' families and the general public. During the period of the 1970's when OSHA's regulation of employee exposure to lead was virtually non-existent, Johnson Controls' predecessor, Globe Union, initiated a large number of innovative programs in an attempt to control and regulate industrial lead exposure. * * *

Globe Union, Johnson Controls' predecessor, established its first policy regarding fetal protection from lead exposure in 1977 as part of its comprehensive efforts to protect its employees from exposure to lead. * * * In its 1977 "Statement of Risks," Globe also observed that at that time scientific and medical evidence had not as yet conclusively established the risk lead exposure posed to the unborn. However, after noting possible risks the 1977 policy statement read:

> "We would have to say that it is, medically speaking, just good sense not to run that risk [lead exposure] if you want children and do not wish to expose the unborn child to risk, however small, and so recommend that you counsel with your family doctor and advise us of your wishes to transfer."

Johnson adopted its current fetal protection program in 1982 following its determination, based upon scientific research, that it was medically necessary to bar women from working in high lead exposure positions in the battery manufacturing division. The fetal protection policy applies to work environments in which any current employee has recorded a blood lead level exceeding 30 µg/dl during the preceding year or in which the work site has yielded an air sample during the past year containing a lead level in excess of 30 µg per cubic meter. The policy recites that women with childbearing capacity will neither be hired for nor allowed to transfer into those jobs in which lead levels are defined as excessive.[8] A grandfather clause in Johnson's fetal protection policy permits fertile women who were assigned to high lead exposure positions at the time of the adoption of the policy to remain in those job assignments if they are able to maintain blood lead levels below 30 µg/dl.[9] Those employees who are removed from positions because of excessive lead levels are transferred to another job in Johnson's employ without suffering either a loss of pay or benefits.

The major reason Johnson adopted its current fetal protection policy was the inability of the previous voluntary policy to achieve the desired purpose: protecting pregnant women and their unborn children from dangerous blood lead levels. Between 1979 and 1983, at least six Johnson Controls employees in high lead exposure positions became pregnant while maintaining blood lead levels in excess of 30 micrograms. In addition, at least one of the babies born to this group of employees later recorded an elevated blood lead level. * * *

In announcing its new, more defined policy, Johnson Controls emphasized its continuing interest in the protection of employees and

---

8. The fetal protection policy defines women of childbearing capacity as: "All women except those whose inability to bear children is medically documented."

9. Under the fetal protection policy an incumbent female employee with a blood lead level reading above 30 µg/dl is permitted a period of time to reduce her blood lead level to 30 µg/dl. If the blood lead level of a fertile female employee is in excess of 40 µg/dl, she is transferred at the earliest possible date. The record does not disclose the number, if any, of female employees who remain in high lead exposure positions or who were transferred as a result of the fetal protection policy.

R. Berkow, *The Merck Manual of Diagnosis and Therapy*, 1744–45 (14th ed.1987). Thus, even in ideal cases, there is normally some time lag between pregnancy's onset and diagnosis. In other cases, a mother's failure to perceive a pregnancy or a delay in receiving prompt medical care can result in a pregnancy diagnosis later in pregnancy. Under a policy requiring removal only on discovery of pregnancy, the unborn child would be subject to lead exposure throughout the period prior to diagnosis of pregnancy.

their families from occupational health hazards and was responding to the increased understanding of the risk of lead exposure that had developed in the five years since it established its former voluntary policy: * * *

Prior to adopting its updated fetal protection policy, Johnson seriously considered alternatives to the exclusion of women with childbearing capacity from high lead exposure positions, but after research and consultation with medical and scientific experts found itself unable to structure and implement any alternatives which would adequately protect the unborn child from the risks associated with excessive lead exposure. Johnson's experience demonstrated that the voluntary exclusion program was ineffective. To date neither Johnson nor any other battery manufacturer has been able to produce a lead free battery, or to utilize engineering research and technology to implement a system or procedure capable of reducing the lead exposure of its employees to acceptable levels for fertile women. Limitation of the fetal protection policy to women actually pregnant was found ineffective because there is the very definite possibility that lead exposure will occur between conception and the time the woman discovers her pregnancy. Such a limitation is further inadequate because reduction of blood lead levels following removal from a lead exposure area requires a significant length of time that frequently extends well into the pregnancy term. Limitation of the policy to women planning pregnancy also was not found to be a suitable alternative because of one of the exigencies of life, the frequency of unplanned or undetected pregnancies. Permitting fertile female employees to attempt to maintain a blood lead level below 30 µg/dl or utilizing the mean or median blood lead levels of current workers as a measure of whether a woman should be permitted in a position would also not effectively protect the unborn child. The reason these actions would be inadequate is that an employee's risk of high lead levels is usually greatest immediately after commencement of work in a high lead environment.

* * *

In altering its fetal protection policy to more effectively protect the unborn child and its mother, Johnson responded to the most recent medical evidence which established that lead exposure *in utero* presents a substantial health risk to the unborn child, as well as its female employees, and believed that Title VII would allow it to address this risk.

II.

Proper analysis of the Title VII issues this case presents requires a thorough understanding of the following fundamental question: Does lead pose a health risk to the offspring of Johnson's female employees? In considering the evidence in the record on this subject it is important to note that *both* the UAW and Johnson Controls agree on appeal that a *substantial* health hazard to the unborn child in the womb has been established. * * *

The record very clearly establishes that once lead is deposited in a mother's blood, it crosses the placenta and affects her unborn child. Because the fetus' blood system is nourished by the mother, the unborn child possesses approximately the same blood lead level as the mother. It is similarly undisputed that the unborn child "is medically judged to be at least as sensitive, and, indeed, is probably even more sensitive to lead than the young child." * * *

The chief reason why an unborn child's lead exposure is of such great concern is that it has been medically established that lead attacks the fetus' central nervous system and retards cognitive development. * * *

Unlike physical birth defects, such as those associated with thalidomide, lead's sometimes subtle damaging effects may not fully manifest themselves until the child is diagnosed as having learning problems in a school setting some five to six years after birth. * * *

Probably the worst aspect of lead's influence upon an unborn child's future intellectual development is that its effects have frequently been found to be irreversible. Further, the most recent research suggests that the unborn child may be affected at lead levels previously believed safe. * * *

Lead exposure can also pose other physical threats to the unborn child such as reduction of the infant's birth weight, premature delivery, and stillbirth. * * * Lead may also affect the other vital fetal organs including, but not limited to, the liver and kidneys.

The danger resulting from lead exposure cannot simply be avoided through removing a pregnant woman from lead exposure promptly after the discovery of pregnancy. Dr. Chisholm, a recognized expert in the research field of treatment and prevention of lead poisoning in young children, observed that "excluding only women who are actually pregnant from work areas where there are elevated blood lead levels would not sufficiently protect the health and safety of the unborn child." * * * This is true because *lead continues to exert an effect upon the mother and her unborn child for a significant period of time after she has been removed from lead exposure.* * * *

The overwhelming evidence in this record establishes that an unborn child's exposure to lead creates a substantial health risk involving a danger of permanent harm. This evidence clearly approaches a "general consensus within the scientific community," and certainly "suffices to show that within that community there is [a] considerable body of opinion that significant risk exists to the unborn child from exposure to lead." *Wright v. Olin Corp.*, 697 F.2d 1172, 1191 (4th Cir. 1982). Next we consider the proper legal standards to be applied when employees bring a Title VII sex discrimination action challenging an employer's response to this serious health risk.

III.

Having considered both the nature of the risk of harm that lead exposure presents to the unborn child and the mother and the policies Johnson implemented in response to this problem, we now turn to the question of the proper legal analysis to be applied to Johnson's fetal protection program under Title VII. The question presented is should we follow the lead of the Fourth Circuit, the Eleventh Circuit and the EEOC in determining that these policies can be justified with a "business necessity" defense or must we conclude that these policies may only be justified with a bona fide occupational qualification defense.

* * *

Two other federal courts of appeals and the Equal Employment Opportunity Commission have addressed the question of the defenses available to an employer under Title VII in a case challenging a fetal protection program. The first court of appeals to address this question was the Fourth Circuit in *Wright v. Olin Corp.*, 697 F.2d 1172 (4th Cir. 1982). That case involved a fetal protection program very similar to the one Johnson instituted, in that it forbade any fertile woman from working in a job which "'may require contact with and exposure to known or suspected abortifacient or teratogenic agents.'" * * * In considering which of several possible theories of claim and defense should apply in a Title VII analysis of a fetal protection policy, the Fourth Circuit observed:

> "We must start by conceding that the fact situation [the fetal protection policy] presents does not fit with absolute precision into any of the developed theories. It differs in some respects—either in its claim or defense elements—from each of the paradigmatic fact situations with which the different theories have been centrally concerned. This of course accounts for the conflict on the point between the parties.
>
> "That there would be such fact situations in Title VII litigation has always been recognized by the Supreme Court as it has developed and applied the different theories. *The Court has continually admonished, and indeed demonstrated in its own decisions, that these theories were not expected nor intended to operate with rigid precision with respect to the infinite variety of factual patterns that would emerge in Title VII litigation.* So has this court." * * *

The court applied the disparate impact/business necessity theory of claim and defense that normally is applied only in cases in which an employer's policy is "facially neutral." Even though the court recognized that the facial neutrality of a fetal protection policy "might be subject to logical dispute, the dispute would involve mere semantic quibbling having no relevance to the underlying principle that gave rise to this theory." * * * Because a fetal protection policy involves motivations and consequences most closely resembling a disparate impact case, the Fourth Circuit felt it should be analyzed under the disparate impact/business necessity theory. * * * The Fourth Circuit defined the business necessity defense in the context of a fetal protection policy as requiring a demonstration that "significant risks of harm to the unborn children of women workers from their exposure during pregnancy to toxic hazards in the workplace make necessary, for the safety of the unborn children, that fertile women workers, though not men workers, be appropriately restricted from exposure to those hazards * * *." * * * However, the Fourth Circuit permitted this evidentiary demonstration to be rebutted with proof that "there are 'acceptable alternative policies or practices which would better accomplish the business purpose * * * [or protect against the risk of harm], or accomplish it equally well with a lesser differential * * * impact [between women and men workers].' " 25

The Eleventh Circuit utilized a similar analysis in *Hayes v. Shelby Memorial Hospital*, 726 F.2d 1543 (11th Cir.1984) (Tuttle, J.). In *Hayes* a hospital terminated a pregnant woman's employment upon discovering her pregnancy. In *Hayes* the Court utilized the elements of the business necessity defense found in *Olin* to establish that the involved policy was not "facially discriminatory." The Eleventh Circuit stated: "In other words, the employer must show (1) that there is a substantial risk of harm to the fetus or potential offspring of women employees from the women's exposure, either during pregnancy or while fertile, to toxic hazards in the workplace and (2) that the hazard applies to fertile or pregnant women, but not to men." * * * The theory underlying the facial neutrality analysis utilized in *Hayes* is that a policy meeting the above criteria "is neutral in the sense that it effectively and equally protects the offspring of all employees." * * * If facial neutrality is established, the court proceeds to a disparate impact/business necessity analysis. * * * Under the Eleventh Circuit's analysis, if facial neutrality is not established, the employer must present a bona fide occupational qualification defense to justify its fetal protection policy.

The Eleventh Circuit went on to set out the disparate impact/ business necessity analysis it would apply in cases where facial neutrality was established. The court recognized that a fetal protection policy, even if "facially neutral," "clearly has a disproportionate impact on women since only they are affected by it." * * * However "the

---

25. *Id.* at 1191 (quoting *Robinson v. Lorillard Corp.*, 444 F.2d 791 (4th Cir.), cert. dismissed, 404 U.S. 1006, 92 S.Ct. 573, 30 L.Ed.2d 655 (1971)). Johnson Controls' primary interest in this case is protecting the development and health of female employees and their unborn children. In construing the business necessity defense the Fourth Circuit in *Olin* cogently observed:

"We do not think that a general basis for the 'business necessity' asserted here need be sought in other considerations than the general societal interest—reflected in many national laws imposing legal obligations upon business enterprises—and having those enterprises operate in ways protective of the health of workers and their families, consumers, and environmental neighbors.

For this reason it is irrelevant that, as claimants point out, the mere purpose to avoid potential liability and consequent economic loss may not suffice, standing alone, to establish a business necessity defense. *See Los Angeles Dept. of Water & Power v. Manhart,* * * *

Although costs from tort judgments are merely a secondary consideration, they are still an important and legitimate additional consideration for an employer when lead safety policies may very well affect the development of the child in its most critical stage in the mother's womb.

employer's business necessity defense applies automatically, just as the employee's prima facie case of disparate impact applies automatically. That is because to reach the disparate impact stage of analysis in a fetal protection case, the employer has *already* proved—to overcome the presumption of facial discrimination—that its policy is justified on a scientific basis and addresses a harm that does not affect men." * * * As in *Olin,* "the employer's business necessity defense may be rebutted by proof that there are acceptable alternative policies that would better accomplish the purposes of promoting fetal health, or that would accomplish the purpose with less adverse impact on one sex." * * *

Although *Olin* and *Hayes* present somewhat different analyses, both cases, in essence, determine that a business necessity defense in a fetal protection policy case requires (1) a demonstration of the existence of a substantial health risk to the unborn child, and (2) establishment that transmission of the hazard to the unborn child occurs only through women. Both cases also allow the employee to present evidence of less discriminatory alternatives equally capable of preventing the health hazard to the unborn.

On October 3, 1988, the Equal Employment Opportunity Commission, the agency responsible for the administration of Title VII, issued a *Policy Statement on Reproductive and Fetal Hazards Under Title VII* that, in substance, endorsed the approaches that the Fourth and Eleventh Circuits have taken to fetal protection cases. Equal Employment Opportunity Commission, *Policy Statement on Reproductive and Fetal Hazards Under Title VII* (October 3, 1988) (found in Fair Empl.Prac. Manual (BNA) 401:6013). * * * A fair reading of the EEOC's Policy Statement reflects that the EEOC thoroughly considered the various interests under Title VII and followed earlier judicial decisions only after concluding that these decisions properly implemented Title VII policies. The EEOC noted that fetal protection "*cases do not fit neatly into the traditional Title VII analytical framework and, therefore, must be regarded as a class unto themselves.*" * * * The EEOC then candidly recognized that fetal protection policies that "exclude only women constitute *per se* violations of the Act." * * * However, the EEOC went on to observe that

"[a]lthough the BFOQ defense is normally the only one available in cases of overt discrimination, *the Commission follows the lead of every court of appeals to have addressed the question [in determining] that the business necessity defense applies to these cases. While business necessity has traditionally been limited to disparate impact cases, there is an argument that in this narrow class of cases the defense should be flexibly applied.*"

* * * The EEOC concluded that:

"The issues [in a fetal protection policy case to which the business necessity defense is applicable] are (1) whether there exists a substantial risk of harm to employees' offspring through the exposure of employees to a reproductive hazard in the workplace; (2) whether the harm to employees' offspring takes place through the exposure of employees of one sex but not employees of the opposite sex; and (3) whether the employer's policy effectively eliminates the risk of fetal or reproductive harm. Even if these elements are proved, the policy will not withstand scrutiny [if] it is shown that there exists a reasonable alternative policy that will protect employees' offspring from fetal or reproductive harm and that has a less discriminatory impact on employees of the restricted sex. Thus, an employer's reproductive or fetal protection policy must be neutrally designed to protect all employees' offspring from hazards existing in the workplace. Where substantial evidence exists that the risk of harm to employees' offspring takes place only through the exposure of one sex to a hazard existing in the workplace, an employer may exclude from the workplace employees of that sex, but only to the extent necessary to protect employees' offspring from reproductive or fetal hazards." * * *

We agree with the Fourth Circuit, the Eleventh Circuit and the EEOC in their conclusion that a business necessity defense may be utilized in a fetal protection policy case. It is interesting to note that neither the text of Title VII nor Supreme Court pronouncements mandate a holding that all forms of facial discrimination are justifiable only with a bona fide occupational qualification defense. *See Olin,* 697 F.2d at 1186 n. 21 ("While the loose equation—overt discrimination/only B.F.O.Q. defense—is * * * properly descriptive of a paradigmatic litigation pattern, it is not an accurate statement of any inherent constraints in Title VII doctrine"). *See also Scherr v. Woodland School Community Consolidated District, No. 50,* 867 F.2d 974, 977–81 (7th Cir. 1988) (Permitting business necessity defense to be utilized under Pregnancy Discrimination Act).

We are convinced that the components of the business necessity defense the courts of appeals and the EEOC have utilized in fetal protection cases balance the interests of the employer, the employee and the unborn child in a manner consistent with Title VII. The requirement of a substantial health risk to the unborn child effectively distinguishes between the legitimate risk of harm to health and safety which Title VII permits employers to consider and the "[m]yths or purely habitual assumptions" that employers sometimes attempt to impermissibly utilize to support the exclusion of women from employment opportunities. Likewise, the requirement that the risk of harm to offspring be substantially confined to female employees means that a fetal protection policy applying only to women recognizes the basic physical fact of human reproduction, that only women are capable of bearing children. Finally, the employee's option of presenting less discriminatory alternatives to a fetal protection policy assures that these policies are only as restrictive as necessary to prevent the serious risk of harm to the unborn child. Accordingly, we agree with the Fourth Circuit, Eleventh Circuit and EEOC that the business necessity defense can be appropriately applied to fetal protection policy cases under Title VII. We now proceed to determine whether this defense can be utilized to sustain Johnson Controls' fetal protection policy.

IV.

In *Wards Cove Packing Co. v. Atonio,* * * * the Supreme Court recently described the general policies underlying the business necessity defense that we utilize in considering Johnson Controls' fetal protection policy: * * *

In *Wards Cove* the Court also clarified the proof burdens to be applied in addressing an employer's business necessity defense: * * *

The allocation of the burden of proof under substantive Title VII law outlined in *Wards Cove* plays a significant role in summary judgment proceedings of this nature. We have previously recognized that: "Summary judgment is properly entered in favor of a party when the opposing party is unable to make a showing sufficient to prove an essential element of a case on which the opposing party bears the burden of proof." * * * Thus, the question we must address is whether the UAW, which bears the burden of persuasion, has presented evidence sufficient to permit the district court to conclude that Johnson Controls' business necessity defense cannot be factually supported.

Our inquiry must be based on the underlying premise that the creation of a record adequate to meet legal challenges is the responsibility of the parties litigating the case. We may neither add nor subtract from the record; we must accept it as it is. Thus, "[w]hen confronted with a motion for summary judgment, a party who bears the burden of proof on a particular issue, may not rest on its pleadings, but must affirmatively demonstrate by specific factual allegations, that there is a *genuine* issue of material fact which requires trial." * * * We now turn to whether the UAW has established a genuine issue of material fact concerning any of the elements of the business necessity defense upon which it bears the burden of persuasion.

A. SUBSTANTIAL RISK OF HARM TO THE UNBORN CHILD

Both the UAW and Johnson Controls agree on appeal that the significant evidence of risks to the health of the fetus contained in the record establishes a *substantial* health risk to the unborn child. * * * In light of the parties' agreement on the question of substantial risk of harm to the unborn child, this issue is not before this court on appeal.

* * * Accordingly, we are convinced that there is no genuine issue of material fact with respect to this component of Johnson Controls' business necessity defense.[28]

---

28. There might be a suggestion that the unborn child would be harmed if his or her mother were deprived of insurance benefits or wages that could be utilized for prenatal care as a result of the application of Johnson Controls' fetal protection policy. This issue bears no relevance to Johnson Controls' employment practices for any female employees deprived of jobs in high lead environments under Johnson's fetal protection policy, instituted in 1982, and are transferred to other positions in Johnson Controls' employ without *any* loss of either wages or benefits.

B. EXPOSURE THROUGH A SINGLE SEX

The UAW's efforts in this case have primarily been devoted toward negating the second element of Johnson's business necessity defense, that the risk of transmission of potentially harmful lead exposure to unborn children is substantially confined to fertile female employees. On this issue, as with the question of substantial risk of harm to the unborn child, "it is not necessary to prove the existence of a general consensus on the [issue] within the qualified scientific community."

* * *

In this case Johnson Controls' experts, without exception, testified that a male worker's exposure to lead at levels within the 50 µg/dl maximum set forth in OSHA's current (1978) lead exposure guidelines did not pose a substantial risk of genetically transmitted harm from the male to the unborn child. Moreover, Johnson's experts took the position that because this data dealt exclusively with animals, the results of these studies were not scientifically established as being applicable to humans. In contrast, the UAW witnesses posited that animal studies had demonstrated that there was a possible risk of genetic damage to human offspring as a result of male lead exposure. The UAW witnesses attempt to bridge the wide chasm between the results of animal studies and a conclusion of genetic harm allegedly transmitted through the male human being with human studies merely establishing a correlation between male lead exposure and changes in sperm shape. It is interesting to note that the UAW has not presented any medical evidence in the record of any human study scientifically documenting genetic defects in human beings resulting from male lead exposure. It is this lack of convincing scientific data that the plaintiffs attempt to gloss over and cast aside in ignoring the differences between the effect of lead on the human and animal reproductive systems.

As noted previously, when the Title VII disparate impact/business necessity proof scheme is applied at the summary judgment phase of litigation, the UAW is required to present facts sufficient for the trier of fact to conclude that transmission of the significant risk of harm lead presents to the unborn child is not substantially confined to female employees. Unlike the recorded evidence of a substantial risk of harm resulting to an unborn child from exposure to lead through the mother's blood stream and placenta, the evidence of risk to the unborn child resulting from exposure of the father to the lead levels currently present in Johnson Controls' battery manufacturing factories is, at best, speculative and unconvincing. The UAW's animal research evidence does not present the type of solid scientific data necessary for a reasonable factfinder to reach a non-speculative conclusion that a father's exposure to lead presents the same danger to the unborn child as that resulting from a female employee's exposure to lead. The facts the UAW posits do not negate the conclusion that the harm lead exposure causes to the unborn child is "substantially confined to female employees." Accordingly, we are convinced that the UAW has failed to present facts sufficient to carry its burden of demonstrating the absence of the second element of Johnson Controls' business necessity defense, application of the risk of transmitting lead exposure to unborn children only through females.

This recognition of the physical differences between the human sexes creates a distinction between men and women that accords with our previous recognition that Title VII permits distinctions based upon the real sex-based differences between men and women, especially those related to child birth. * * * Because scientific data available as of this date reflects that the risk of transmission of harm to unborn children is confined to fertile female employees, the sex-based distinction present in Johnson Controls' fetal protection policy is based upon real physical differences between men and women relating to childbearing capacity and is consistent with Title VII.

C. ADEQUATE BUT LESS DISCRIMINATORY ALTERNATIVES

We are cognizant of the fact that Johnson's fetal protection policy might very well not have been sustainable had the UAW presented facts and reasoning sufficient for the trier of fact to conclude that "there are 'acceptable alternative policies or practices which would better accomplish the business purpose * * * [of protecting against the risk of harm], or accomplish equally well with a lesser differential * * * impact [between women and men workers].'" *Olin,* * * *.

As an initial matter, we must determine whether the UAW has preserved this issue for appeal. The UAW's brief explicitly admits that "the plaintiffs did not respond to the defendant's allegations that it had considered a number of alternatives [to its fetal protection policy]," UAW Brief at 37 n. 14, and fails to present any of its own alternatives. * * * The UAW's failure to specifically articulate a less discriminatory alternative argument in the manner required in Federal Rule of Appellate Procedure 28(a)(4) means that it has failed to adequately present this issue to this court.

Even were we to conclude that the UAW had preserved this issue for appeal, we would be constrained to hold that the UAW failed to present facts sufficient for a trier of fact to conclude that less discriminatory alternatives would equally effectively achieve an employer's legitimate purpose of protecting unborn children from the substantial risk of harm lead exposure creates. * * *

* * * *Wards Cove* makes clear (1) that the UAW bears the burden of presenting specific economically and technologically feasible alternatives to Johnson Controls' fetal protection policy; (2) that if the UAW presents such alternatives, the UAW also bears the burden of demonstrating that its proposed alternative policy is "*equally* effective [as Johnson Controls' fetal protection policy] in achieving [Johnson's] legitimate employment goals," * * *; and (3) that this inquiry is to be undertaken with the recognition that " '[f]actors such as the cost or other burdens of proposed alternative selection devices are relevant in

determining whether they would be equally as effective as the challenged practices in serving the employer's legitimate business goals,'" * * * and that "'[c]ourts are generally less competent than employers to restructure business practices' * * *". * * * In our case the inquiry is terminated at the first stage. The UAW, in its briefs and argument, has failed to present even one specific alternative to Johnson's fetal protection policy, much less a demonstration of how any particular economically and technologically feasible alternative would effectively achieve Johnson's purpose of preventing the risk of fetal harm associated with the exposure to lead of fertile female employees.

The record also demonstrates that viable alternatives to the fetal protection program were not presented to the court that would equally effectively further Johnson's legitimate interests. As detailed in Section I, *supra*, Johnson Controls itself considered various possible less discriminatory alternatives prior to its adoption of the current fetal protection policy in 1982. In considering these alternatives, Johnson realized that lead could not be eliminated as a battery component. Furthermore, technically and economically feasible alternatives in the manufacturing process are incapable of reducing lead exposure to acceptable levels for pregnant women. Limitation of the exclusion from high lead positions to women actually pregnant or planning pregnancy was inadequate because lead exposure frequently takes place during the time period before the woman or her doctor determine her pregnancy. In addition, reduction of blood lead levels following removal of a pregnant female employee from lead exposure requires a significant period of time that can extend well into the pregnancy term. Although the Supreme Court has noted that "there is no requirement that the challenged practice be 'essential' or 'indispensable' to the employer's business for it to pass muster" under the business necessity defense, Johnson's policy could well have met this exacting standard.

Finally, in resolving this issue we must act with an awareness of the Supreme Court's warnings that "'[c]ourts are generally less competent than employers to restructure business practices,'" and that "the judiciary should proceed with care before mandating that an employer must adopt a plaintiff's [proposed alternative employment policy] in response to a Title VII suit." In light of these policies, the UAW has not met its evidentiary burden at the summary judgment phase of presenting facts from which a trier of fact could determine that an alternative policy would be equally as effective as Johnson Controls' fetal protection policy in preventing risk of harm to unborn children from lead exposure.

V.

Having just held that the business necessity defense shields an employer from liability for sex discrimination under Title VII in a fetal protection policy involving the type of facts present herein, we are also convinced that Johnson Controls' fetal protection policy could be upheld under the bona fide occupational qualification defense.

* * *

In the context of the Pregnancy Discrimination Act, application of the bona fide occupational qualification defense requires a court to consider the special concerns which pregnancy poses. A proposed BFOQ relating to capacity for pregnancy (or actual pregnancy) will exclude fewer employees than a BFOQ excluding all women. The court must also consider the physical changes caused by pregnancy, i.e., the presence of the unborn child, in determining whether the employee's continuance in a particular employment assignment will endanger the health of her unborn child. These concerns are in many ways quite similar to those a court should address in a business necessity defense analysis. * * *

Sitting *en banc*, this court recently considered the bona fide occupational qualification defense in *Torres v. Wisconsin Dept. of Health & Social Services,* 859 F.2d 1523 (7th Cir.1988) (en banc). At issue in *Torres* was the question of whether the Wisconsin Department of Health and Social Services could pursue its legitimate goal in furthering prisoner rehabilitation through a policy excluding men from nineteen of twenty-seven guard positions in the living and hygiene areas of an exclusively women's prison institution. * * *

* * *

Torres' conclusion that Congress intended the bona fide occupational qualification defense as a recognition of the real differences between men and women accords with Congress' approach in both Title VII and other contexts concerning matters involving distinctions based upon realistic physical differences between men and women. * * *

Torres bears particular relevance to our discussion of the description of Johnson Controls' business. At a broad level, Johnson's business, insofar as relevant to this case, is the manufacture of batteries. Johnson's business is "unique" because it requires the use of lead, an extremely toxic substance that has been scientifically established to pose very serious dangers to young children and, in particular, to the offspring of female employees. In order to respond to the problems accompanying its unique battery manufacturing operation, Johnson Controls has properly made it part of its business to attempt to manufacture batteries in as safe a manner as possible. This safety interest is every bit as critical to the mission of Johnson's battery manufacturing business as rehabilitation of prisoners is to the mission of the prison facility at issue in *Torres*. Furthermore, like the prison in *Torres,* Johnson has found it necessary to "innovate" to achieve its essential goal of manufacturing batteries safely through the adoption of a fetal protection policy that would address the health/safety problems related to its female employees significantly more effectively than the alternative policies it had considered. * * *

Having established that industrial safety (preventing hazards to health) is legitimately part of the "essence" of the "business" of a battery manufacturer, as it is of any manufacturing enterprise, the next inquiry under *Torres* is whether Johnson Controls' fetal protection policy is "directly related" to industrial safety. See *Torres*, 859 F.2d at 1530. Certainly a policy is directly related to industrial safety when it protects unborn children from a substantial risk of devastating and permanent impairment or loss of intellectual ability or injury to vital organs resulting from exposure to a toxic industrial chemical.

As in *Torres*, "[t]he more difficult question is whether the proposed BFOQ [is] 'reasonably necessary' to furthering the objective of [industrial safety]." * * * In "unique" businesses, like the living areas of the women's prison in *Torres* or Johnson Controls' battery manufacturing operation, where an employer adopts an employment policy designed to address a difficult societal problem, *Torres* requires that courts reviewing such a determination under Title VII give some deference to the employer's decisions. * * *

In resolving the question of whether Johnson Controls' BFOQ is reasonably necessary to industrial safety, we recognize that Title VII establishes the general propositions that a determination of whether a proposed BFOQ is "reasonably necessary" to furthering the objective of industrial safety requires that Johnson Controls " 'had reasonable cause to believe, that is, a factual basis for believing that all or substantially all [women capable of pregnancy] would be unable to perform safely and efficiently the duties of the job involved,' " *Dothard v. Rawlinson,* * * * (quoting *Weeks v. Southern Bell Telephone & Telegraph Co.,* 408 F.2d 228, 235 (5th Cir.1969)), and that "[i]n the *usual case,* the argument that a particular job is too dangerous for *women* may appropriately be met by the rejoinder that it is the purpose of Title VII to allow the *individual woman* to make that choice for *herself."* * * * *It is important to remember, however, that while Dothard established these propositions as general rules, the Supreme Court determined that Dothard was an unusual case justifying a departure from this general maxim.* The Court stated: "More is at stake in this case, however, than an individual woman's decision to weigh and accept the risks of employment in a 'contact' position in a maximum security male prison." * * * The Court concluded that a bona fide occupational qualification excluding women from such positions was justified because a woman's sex could create a risk of sexual assaults which would undermine prison security. * * *

Similarly, "[m]ore is at stake in this case * * * than an individual woman's decision to weigh and accept the risks of employment." * * * A female's decision to work in a high lead exposure job risks the intellectual and physical development of the baby she may carry. The status of women in America has changed both in the family and in the economic system. Since they have become a force in the workplace as well as in the home because of their desire to better the family's station in life, it would not be improbable that a female employee might somehow rationally discount this clear risk in her hope and belief that her infant would not be adversely affected from lead exposure. The unborn child has no opportunity to avoid this grave danger, but bears the definite risk of suffering permanent consequences. This situation is much like that involved in blood transfusion cases. There courts have held that individuals may choose for themselves whether to refuse to personally acquiesce in a blood transfusion that had been established as medically necessary, but that parents may not always rely upon parental rights or religious liberty rights to similarly refuse to consent to such a medically necessary transfusion for their minor children. The risks to the unborn child from lead are also shared by society in the form of government financed programs to train or maintain a handicapped child in non-institutional or institutional environments and to provide the child with the training necessary to overcome the mental and physical harm attributable to lead exposure. Thus, since "more is at stake" than the individual woman's decision to risk her own safety, *Dothard* supports, rather than bars, a conclusion that an employer's fetal protection policy constitutes a bona fide occupational qualification. In such circumstances, "given the reasonable objectives of the employer, the very womanhood * * * of the employee undermines * * * her capacity to perform a job satisfactorily." *Torres,* * * * (citing *Dothard,* * * *).

Against this substantive background, we hold that Johnson has carried its burden of demonstrating that its fetal protection plan is reasonably necessary to further industrial safety, a matter we have determined to be part of the essence of Johnson Controls' business. Initially, there can be no doubt that the exclusion of women who are actually pregnant from positions involving high levels of lead exposure sets forth a bona fide occupational qualification. As established in section II, *supra,* there is clear and unrefuted evidence in the record of a substantial and irreversible risk to the unborn child's mental development from lead exposure in the womb. This danger is "hardly a '[m]yth or purely habitual assumption.'" *Torres,* * * *. The convincing scientific evidence of this risk and the very serious consequences of this danger combine to make this health risk quite different from the concerns in *Muller v. Oregon,* 208 U.S. 412, 421–22, 28 S.Ct. 324, 326–27, 52 L.Ed. 551 (1908), which we would currently characterize as stereotypical rather than real. * * *

We are also of the opinion that Johnson Controls' well reasoned and scientifically documented decision to apply this policy to all fertile women employed in high lead exposure positions constitutes a bona fide occupational qualification. The evidence presented concerning the lingering effects of lead in a woman's body, combined with the magnitude of medical difficulties in detecting and diagnosing early pregnancy, lead us to agree with Johnson Controls that there exists a reasonable basis in fact to conclude that an extension of this policy to all fertile women is proper and reasonably necessary to further the industrial safety concern of preventing the unborn child's exposure to lead.

Based upon the current status of research into lead's hazardous effects, we also agree that Johnson Controls has demonstrated to our satisfaction that exclusion of fertile women from positions in any area of its battery plant in which an employee has reported a blood lead level in excess of 30 µg/dl or where an air lead measurement has been in excess of 30 is reasonably necessary to the industrial safety-based concern of protecting the unborn child from lead exposure. At the time Johnson Controls adopted its policy, the 30 µg/dl lead exposure level coincided with the Centers for Disease Control's determination of acceptable blood lead levels for children. *See* n. 7, *supra*. However, it is becoming increasingly clear that the 30 µg/dl lead exposure level once believed to be safe for unborn children is no longer medically accepted as risk free. As mentioned previously, the Centers for Disease Control, in 1985, based upon "current knowledge concerning screening, diagnosis, treatment, followup, and environmental intervention for children with elevated blood levels," revised the level of elevated lead exposure from 30 to 25 µg/dl and suggested that an unborn child's blood lead level remain below 25 µg/dl. As also noted previously, recent lead studies suggest that harm may be present at levels even lower than those earlier believed to be safe. Thus, lead absorption levels such as those mandated by OSHA, which were thought to have been sufficiently protective of the unborn child when they were enacted over ten years ago, are now considered insufficient. * * *

The analysis that we have conducted under the bona fide occupational qualification standards of Title VII is analogous to the approach the Supreme Court took in the First Amendment context in *Sable Communications v. F.C.C.*, ___ U.S. ___, 109 S.Ct. 2829, 106 L.Ed.2d 93 (1989). There the Supreme Court dealt with the question of whether Congress' ban on "dial-a-porn" services was narrowly tailored to serve a compelling governmental interest "in protecting the physical and psychological well-being of minors," very similar to Johnson's interest in protecting the health of the unborn through the female employee. In the constitutional context, as in the bona fide occupational qualification context, when an entity attempts to further this type of interest it must be accomplished with " 'narrowly drawn regulations designed to serve those interests without unnecessarily interfering with First Amendment freedoms,' " or, in this case, Title VII rights. The Court went on to apply this analysis in considering the same type of question at issue in this case, whether the current status of technology requires a "total ban" or whether there are alternatives which would less comprehensively restrict the involved rights while still effectively furthering the relevant institutional interests. The Court determined that Congress' enactment was improper based upon its conclusion that "the congressional record contains no legislative findings that would justify us in concluding that there is no constitutionally acceptable less restrictive means, short of a total ban, to achieve the Government's interest in protecting minors." *Sable,* * * *. In contrast to the government in *Sable,* as noted above, Johnson Controls researched, innovated and spent at least $15 million in lead control policies and has been unable to devise a policy other than the exclusion of fertile women from high lead exposure positions that would be capable of adequately serving Johnson's legitimate interest in protecting the health of the unborn. There has been no convincing exposition in the record of any suitable alternative or of scientific, medical or technical evidence supporting the efficacy of such an alternative. We believe that in a bona fide occupational qualification case, as in a business necessity case, we are constrained by the maxim that: "'Courts are generally less competent than employers to restructure business practices,' *Furnco Construction Corp. v. Waters,* 438 U.S. 567, 578, 98 S.Ct. 2943, 2950, 57 L.Ed.2d 957 (1978); consequently, the judiciary should proceed with care before mandating that an employer must adopt [an alternative employment practice] in response to a Title VII suit." *Wards Cove,* * * *. Accordingly, the absence of economically and technologically feasible alternatives to Johnson Controls' fetal protection policy also supports a bona fide occupational qualification determination.

There is a reasonable basis in fact, grounded in medical and scientific research data, for concluding that Johnson Controls has met its burden of establishing that the fetal protection policy is reasonably necessary to industrial safety.[43] Thus, the fetal protection policy should be recognized as establishing a bona fide occupational qualification protecting the policy against claims of sex discrimination.

VI.

A business necessity defense should be applied to a challenge to a fetal protection policy under Title VII. Johnson Controls has produced facts which would demonstrate the availability of such a defense and the UAW has failed to carry its burden of persuasion through exposition of facts necessary to present a genuine issue of material fact with respect to the absence of such a defense. Even if the bona fide occupational qualification defense is applied to this matter, Johnson Controls has demonstrated that its fetal protection policy is reasonably necessary to industrial safety. Thus, the district court's entry of summary judgment in favor of Johnson Controls is

Affirmed.

CUDAHY, CIRCUIT JUDGE, dissenting:

---

43. Judge Easterbrook suggests that "by one estimate 20 million industrial jobs could be closed to women," if "the majority is right," "for many substances in addition to lead pose fetal risks." * * * This assertion is based upon the following language in Bureau of National Affairs' Special Report, *Pregnancy and Employment* p. 57 (1987): "One government source estimates that 15 million to 20 million jobs in the United States expose workers to chemicals that *may* cause reproductive injury." (Emphasis supplied). This speculative statement, taken at its face value, merely suggests a possibility of reproductive injury from unidentified and undefined toxic substances. Before our decision could be applied to any of these unidentified substances, obviously they would have to be subjected to the myriad tests and research that have conclusively established the grave risk from lead substances. Thus, an employer presenting a business necessity or bona fide occupational qualification defense would have to establish that the substance had undergone the same rigid testing and research. In addition, if ever a lead-free battery were developed, the problems in this case would fall by the wayside. We hope that this is achieved tomorrow.

I respectfully dissent from the majority opinion. I would be pleased to join almost all of Judge Easterbrook's eloquent dissent except for its disposition of the case. Here I join Judge Posner's equally cogent statement, which adopts the BFOQ standard but advocates remand for a full trial on that basis. It may (and should) be difficult to establish a BFOQ here but I would afford the defendant an opportunity to try.[1] I agree with Judge Easterbrook that this "is likely the most important sex-discrimination case in any court since 1964 * * *" and its painful complexities are manifestly unsuited for summary judgment. In any event, the BFOQ defense is clearly the only one the statute allows in this disparate treatment case. It is unfortunate that the majority gives a new life of sorts to the result-oriented gimmickery of *Wright v. Olson Corp.*, * * *.

It is a matter of some interest that, of the twelve federal judges to have considered this case to date, none has been female. This may be quite significant because this case, like other controversies of great potential consequence, demands, in addition to command of the disembodied rules, some insight into social reality. What is the situation of the pregnant woman, unemployed or working for the minimum wage and unprotected by health insurance, in relation to her pregnant sister, exposed to an indeterminate lead risk but well-fed, housed and doctored? Whose fetus is at greater risk? Whose decision is this to make? We, who are unfortunately all male, must address these and other equally complex questions through the clumsy vehicle of litigation. At least let it be complete litigation focusing on the right standard.

POSNER, CIRCUIT JUDGE, dissenting.

Johnson Controls refuses to employ any woman to make batteries unless she presents medical evidence of sterility. Today this court holds the refusal lawful under Title VII. A reader of the majority opinion might be excused for thinking that the case had been fully tried—and before this court—rather than decided by a district judge on

---

1. On this issue, I disagree with Judge Easterbrook's conclusion that the BFOQ standard could *never* be satisfied in a case such as this. As Judge Posner's dissent suggests, the BFOQ defense need not be narrowly limited to matters of worker productivity, product quality and occupational safety. The employer may permissibly consider the possible risks to (even potential) third parties in the normal course of business decisionmaking. However, the employer must demonstrate "a factual basis for believing that all or substantially all women would be unable to perform safely [i.e., without inordinate risk to third parties, including fetuses] and efficiently the duties of the job involved." *Weeks v. Southern Bell Tel. & Tel. Co.*, 408 F.2d 228, 235 (5th Cir.1969). As Judge Easterbrook notes in discussing the disposition of this case under the *Wright–Hayes* standard, substantial factual questions remain concerning whether occupational exposure to lead presents a substantial risk to the fetus, whether this risk is transmitted only through the pregnant woman and whether less restrictive alternatives would adequately safeguard the employer's interest in fetal health and safety. So long as it is understood that the burden to prove these matters rests on the employer, and that this burden may not be met by unsubstantiated hypotheses or claims of scientific uncertainty, *see Torres v. Wisconsin Dep't of Health & Social Servs.*, 859 F.2d 1523, 1533–34 (7th Cir.1988) (en banc) (Cudahy, J., dissenting), I am comfortable with allowing the employer at least the opportunity to attempt to meet this demanding standard.

a motion for summary judgment. I think it a mistake to suppose that we can decide this case once and for all on so meager a record. It is a mistake whether we affirm, on the ground that the evidence of danger to the fetus of a woman working in an environment dense with airborne lead, combined with evidence of the difficulty of reducing the amount of lead any further, conclusively establishes the lawfulness of Johnson Controls' policy; or reverse, with directions to enter judgment for the plaintiffs, on the ground that Title VII outlaws all fetal protection policies because all bear more heavily on female than on male workers.

Title VII forbids an employer deliberately to exclude a worker from a particular job because of the worker's sex unless sex is a "bona fide occupational qualification reasonably necessary to the normal operation of that particular business or enterprise." * * * This defense is central to the appeal and we should attend carefully to its scope and meaning. It is written narrowly and has been read narrowly. See, e.g., *Dothard v. Rawlinson,* * * *; *Torres v. Wisconsin Dept. of Health & Social Services,* * * *. There is no useful legislative history concerning the defense, and—no doubt because the prohibition of sex discrimination was added to Title VII at the last minute—no reference at all to the application of the defense to sex discrimination. A narrow reading is, nevertheless, inevitable. A broad reading would gut the statute. For it is unlikely that most employment discrimination in the private sector is irrational. Few private employers discriminate without having some reason for doing so; competition tends to drive from the market firms that behave irrationally. See Becker, The Economics of Discrimination (2d ed. 1971). If the defense of bona fide occupational qualification were broadly construed—for example, to excuse all sex discrimination that the employer could show was cost-justified—very little sex discrimination in employment, as well as very little employment discrimination based on religion or national origin (forms of discrimination that, like sex discrimination but unlike discrimination based on race or color, are also excused if a bona fide occupational qualification is established), would be forbidden. Title VII's reach would be shortened drastically.

Two courts of appeals faced with challenges under Title VII to fetal protection policies have concluded that such policies can never satisfy the stringent requirements of the occupational qualification defense. See *Wright v. Olin Corp.,* * * *; *Hayes v. Shelby Memorial Hospital,* * * *. But this conclusion, rather than resulting in instant victory for the plaintiffs, led those courts to stitch a new defense expressly for fetal protection cases. * * * I do not think judges must or should ratify absurd results by sticking doggedly to the plain meaning of statutory language.

But we do not need to bite this bullet here, because the wording of the occupational qualification provision is not so cramped that it has to be stretched to bring (some) fetal protection policies within its scope.

* * * Nor is a defensible way of stretching it to recast what is plainly a disparate treatment case—that is, a case of intentional discrimination against a protected group—as a disparate impact case, and then invoke the recent decision in which the Supreme Court expanded the "business necessity" defense. See *Wards Cove Packing Co. v. Atonio,* * * *. This legerdemain is as unnecessary as it is questionable. "[R]easonably necessary," one of the key terms of the occupational qualification defense, means more than just reasonable but less than absolutely necessary. On the way to concluding that the defense is unavailable in fetal protection cases the court in *Wright* misquoted the provision by leaving out the word "reasonably," * * * and the misquotation is faithfully repeated in *Hayes,* * * *. The other key words of the defense, "*normal* operation" (emphasis added), should dispel concern that consideration of all interests other than the employer's interest in selling a quality product at the lowest possible price is precluded. It is possible to make batteries without considering the possible consequences for people who might be injured in the manufacturing process, just as it would be possible to make batteries with slave laborers, but neither mode of operation would be normal. To confine the occupational qualification defense to concerns with price and product quality would deny a defense to Johnson Controls even if the company excluded only pregnant women, as distinct from all women who might become pregnant, from making batteries. I do not understand the plaintiffs to be arguing that Title VII requires Johnson Controls to permit women known to be pregnant to continue working in an atmosphere dense with lead. If on the other hand a fetal protection policy that excludes women from a given job classification cannot be said to be reasonably necessary to the employer's normal operation, I do not see why we should *want* to save it from condemnation under Title VII.

I have described what I conceive to be the scope of the bona fide occupational qualification defense, and its application to sex discrimination, as of the original enactment of Title VII. I must now consider the bearing of the Pregnancy Discrimination Act of 1982, * * *. [T]he amendment shows that the present case really is a disparate treatment case, that is, a case of intentional discrimination that can be excused only if the defendant establishes a bona fide occupational qualification; the amendment makes fertile women, the group that Johnson Controls deliberately excluded from a job classification, a group protected by Title VII. The amendment also helps us understand that the occupational qualification defense could not be merely a cost justification or reasonable relation defense, for if it were, the amendment would be ineffectual. Any employer can prove that it costs *something* to make an accommodation for pregnant or potentially pregnant workers and therefore that it is rational not to make the accommodation. But we already knew the defense was a narrow one.

The defense is applicable to this case and although it is of limited scope it is not the proverbial eye of a needle. In particular, the "normal operation" of a business encompasses ethical, legal, and business concerns about the effects of an employer's activities on third parties. An employer might be validly concerned on a variety of grounds both practical and ethical with the hazards of his workplace to the children of his employees. A pregnant employee exposed to heavy concentrations of lead in the air may absorb the lead into her bloodstream and from there transmit it to her fetus through the placenta, causing, years later, mental retardation or other injury to the child. The parties agree that there is a solid medical basis for concern with fetal injury from airborne lead in the concentration found in battery plants, and this concern could in turn cause the employer to worry about being sued by injured children of his employees. Such a suit would not be preempted by workers' compensation law, because the plaintiff would not be the worker. The employer would therefore be exposed to full common law damages, punitive as well as compensatory. The mother's own negligence—for if she had been clearly warned of the hazard, but voluntarily became pregnant anyway and continued to work making batteries, she would be acting negligently with regard to the fetus—would not be imputed to the child and therefore would not reduce the employer's liability. * * * It would merely make the mother a joint tortfeasor with the employer. Moreover, she might not be negligent; the pregnancy might be involuntary, and lead can injure the fetus before the mother knows she is pregnant.

* * *

We should not dismiss the concern over tort liability as a narrow, selfish "bottom line" concern irrelevant to the purposes of Title VII. The potential cost of tort liability to Johnson Controls is an approximation of the potential cost to the children who have suffered prenatal injury from the airborne lead absorbed into their mothers' bloodstreams. That is a social cost that Title VII does not require a company to ignore. At some point it may become large enough to affect the company's normal method of operation and supply the ground for a bona fide occupational qualification of infertility.

A related point is that an employer might have moral qualms about endangering children or might fear the effect on his public relations. The ethical concern cannot be wholly dismissed, as could an ethical conviction that a woman's place is in the home. We know from the controversy over abortion that many people are passionately protective of fetal welfare, and they cannot all be expected—perhaps they cannot be required—to park their passions at the company gate. That "strong [state] interest in protecting the potential life of the fetus" of which the Supreme Court spoke in *Maher v. Roe,* 432 U.S. 464, 478, 97 S.Ct. 2376, 2385, 53 L.Ed.2d 484 (1977), and other cases is not a judicial invention; it is the product of a groundswell of powerful emotion by a significant part of the community, and is only indirectly, although possibly substantially, in conflict with women's workplace aspirations. Granted, in *Doe v. First National Bank,* 865 F.2d 864, 873 (7th Cir. 1989), we assumed that the Pregnancy Discrimination Act forbids an employer to fire a woman for having an abortion, and although the point had not been argued our assumption may well have been correct. * * * If so, the result is to place a limitation on an employer's effort to protect fetal life. But the Pregnancy Discrimination Act affects only the prima facie case of sex discrimination. The defenses are untouched. No defense of bona fide occupational qualification was pleaded in *Doe*.

If the hazard to the fetus from airborne lead in the mother's workplace is sufficiently great, if the amount of lead in the environment cannot be reduced without discontinuing the production of batteries, and if experience demonstrates that some women will become pregnant even after being clearly warned of the hazards to which the fetus would be exposed (there are many careless pregnancies, as is shown by the frequency of abortion and of illegitimate birth), I can find nothing in the text of the statute, or in its history or purpose, to prevent an employer from defending his refusal to allow fertile women to work in jobs in which they are exposed to dangerous concentrations of airborne lead on the ground that such refusal is reasonably necessary to the normal (civilized, humane, prudent, ethical) operation of his particular business. It is a matter of degree, and this we cannot assess on a summary judgment record. Of course the acceptance of the defense might be a hardship for those women who, though fertile, would not become pregnant. But hardship for the plaintiff is a possibility whenever a defense is sustained. It is no more than a possibility here, as we shall see.

Let us not be deceived by superficial historical analogies or facile invocations of "paternalistic." It is true that laws discriminating against women were once defended on the basis of a compelling social interest in protecting their fitness to bear and raise children, see, e.g., *Muller v. Oregon,* * * * that this ground may have masked a desire to prevent women from competing with men for jobs (in any event this may have been the effect, see Landes, *The Effect of State Maximum Hours Laws on the Employment of Women in 1920,* 88 J.Pol.Econ. 476 (1980)), and that many modern American women resent the suggestion that women have a special responsibility for perpetuating the human race. But we do not have a discriminatory *law* here. A law that commands all employers in a given line of business to treat women specially cannot be equated to a decision by a firm in a competitive market to treat them specially, if only because in the latter case other firms are free to follow a different course. There is also a difference between protecting women against themselves as well as protecting children, and protecting an employer and his employees' unborn children. A paternalistic measure is one that protects a person against himself, and insofar as Johnson Controls was motivated in adopting its fetal protection policy by concern with tort liability or adverse public relations, it was acting to protect its own interests. A fetus, moreover, is a different person (or proto-person) from its mother, and not all pregnant women fully internalize the welfare of their fetus, infant, or child. There are plenty of selfish and irresponsible parents, not all of whom are male. A fetal protection policy is less paternalistic than a maximum-hours law.

I conclude that Title VII even as amended by the Pregnancy Discrimination Act does not outlaw all fetal protection policies. Whether a particular policy is lawful is a question of fact, and since the burden of proof is on the defendant it will be the rare case where the lawfulness of such a policy can be decided on the defendant's motion for summary judgment. This is not that rare case. * * *

* * *

Even on the limited record before us, however, it is clear that the defendant's fetal protection policy is excessively cautious in two regards: first in presuming that any woman under the age of 70 is fertile, and second in excluding a presumptively fertile woman from any job from which she might ultimately be promoted into battery making, even if her present job does not expose her to lead. * * *

The issue of the legality of fetal protection is as novel and difficult as it is contentious and the most sensible way to approach it at this early stage is on a case-by-case basis, involving careful examination of the facts as developed by the full adversary process of a trial. * * *

* * * We should be as hesitant to endanger the health of children by condemning all fetal protection policies as we should be hesitant to endanger the jobs of women by placing our imprimatur on such policies. We should vacate the district court's judgment and remand for further proceedings to enable the compilation of an adequate evidentiary record.

EASTERBROOK, CIRCUIT JUDGE, with whom FLAUM, CIRCUIT JUDGE, joins, dissenting.

Whether employers should restrain adults from engaging in acts hazardous to their children is an ethical, medical, economic, and political problem of great complexity. But this is a statutory case, and we must implement the law rather than give our own answer. Johnson's policy is sex discrimination, forbidden unless sex is a "bona fide occupational qualification"—which it is not.

I

Title VII of the Civil Rights Act of 1964 forbids employers "to discriminate against any individual * * * because of such individual's * * * sex", * * * unless sex is a "bona fide occupational qualification reasonably necessary to the normal operation of that particular business or enterprise", * * *. Both the district court and the majority believe that the fetal protection policy may be lawful despite the absence of a BFOQ.

A

Johnson uses sex as a ground of decision. The fetal protection policy applies to all women and no men. It is not written without reference to gender, having an unwelcome side effect. Cf. *Personnel*

Administrator of Massachusetts v. Feeney, * * *. Differences between the sexes are its stated rationale. Only women transmit lead to children during pregnancy. Because a few women become pregnant with elevated levels of lead in the blood (in four years, eight out of an unknown number), Johnson excludes all women from the danger zone. This treats an employee not as an individual but as a woman. A plan using sex as a criterion and justified by arguments referring to sex is "discriminat[ion] * * * because of * * * sex". *Los Angeles Department of Water & Power v. Manhart,* * * *.

* * * [The PDA] makes distinctions based on women's ability to bear children sex discrimination. It also has a built-in BFOQ standard: unless pregnant employees differ from others "in their ability or inability to work", they must be treated "the same" as other employees "for all employment-related purposes". Although located in a definitional provision, the language after the semicolon is substantive and governs Johnson's plan.

Wright v. Olin Corp., * * * took a different view. *Wright* observed that a policy using sex as a ground of decision may cause women no more injury than a policy neutral with regard to sex, yet having a disparate impact. A policy designed to promote the health of offspring of both sexes is neutral in objective. A sex-neutral policy is judged under an approach more lenient than the BFOQ standard. Believing that a fetal protection policy rests on strong justifications, *Wright* treated the policy as sex-neutral so that it could sustain a rule functionally identical to Johnson's. * * *

* * * In other words, this *must* be a disparate impact case because an employer couldn't win it as a disparate treatment case. If the rigors of the BFOQ suggest the need for a fresh approach, that is a job for another branch. * * *

* * *

When the employer engages in sex, race or age discrimination in an effort to protect customers or members of the public, courts regularly see this as disparate treatment, for which a BFOQ is essential. * * * There is no reason why things should be different when fetuses, rather than adult bystanders, are the object of the employer's protection.

* * * Here, too, there is disparate treatment. Fetal protection policies therefore may be justified, if at all, as BFOQs.

* * *

B

The statute allows an employer to show that consideration of sex is "reasonably necessary to the normal operation of that particular business". * * *

Johnson defends its fetal protection policy on the basis of concern for the welfare of the next generation, an objective unrelated to its ability to make batteries (§ 2000e–2(e)(1) speaks of the "operation of the business") or to any woman's "ability or inability to work" (the standard of the PDA). Johnson allowed women to work until 1982, without ill effects on its business; for all we know (the record is silent), other firms in the same business employ women in the kinds of jobs from which Johnson excludes them. The majority does not mention the PDA, which, added to the BFOQ rule, puts out of bounds the justifications Johnson offers.

* * * No legal or ethical principle compels or allows Johnson to assume that women are less able than men to make intelligent decisions about the welfare of the next generation, that the interests of the next generation always trump the interests of living women, and that the only acceptable level of risk is zero. "[T]he purpose of Title VII is to allow the individual woman to make that choice for herself." *Dothard*, * * *.

Although some women may become pregnant, and a subset of their children might suffer, Johnson cannot exclude all fertile women from its labor force on their account. Most women in an industrial labor force do not become pregnant; most of these will have blood lead levels under 30 μg/dl (only about ⅓ of the employees exposed to lead at Johnson's plants have higher levels); most of those who become pregnant with levels exceeding 30 μg/dl will bear normal children (Johnson reports no birth defects or other abnormalities in the eight pregnancies among its employees). Concerns about a tiny minority of women cannot set the standard by which all are judged. * * *

To meet the "all or almost all" requirement, Johnson relies on an elaboration of the BFOQ for age discrimination offered in customer-safety cases: if all persons over a certain age are unsafe pilots (drivers, police officers, etc.), *or* if it is impossible to tell which of the older employees is unsafe, then age may be a BFOQ for employment. * * * The genesis of the "impossible to tell" branch of the BFOQ in age cases is that an unsafe employee can't do the job the employer demands. It is word play to say that "the job" at Johnson is to make batteries without risk to fetuses in the same way "the job" at Western Air Lines is to fly planes without crashing. When an employer genuinely can't tell which employees are unfit, *and* when unfitness *for work* is a serious problem, it may use a proxy that otherwise would be off limits. Johnson is not using sex to avert harm to customers. To repeat the statutory language: sex is a BFOQ when its use is "reasonably necessary to the normal operation of [the employer's] particular business" (the BFOQ rule), and employers must treat men and pregnant women equally with respect to their "ability or inability to work" (the PDA). Risk to fetuses falls outside these rules.

Johnson might be concerned about cost. It could have argued that the only alternative to the fetal protection policy is a much cleaner workplace, so that no employee's blood lead level exceeds 30 μg/dl, which would be prohibitively expensive and lead it to close the business. Johnson does not make that argument, so the majority properly does not decide whether it would be a BFOQ. Another potential cost comes from tort law. Perhaps Johnson anticipated litigation filed by children injured by lead. The firm does not make this argument either, and so far as I know no child has recovered a judgment on account of parents' occupational exposure to lead. * * * Anyway, the prospect of tort judgments means only that female employees' average cost to Johnson exceeds that of male employees. Title VII requires employers to deal with individual employees rather than with group averages. No firm could exclude women from its work force by saying that higher costs of pensions and health care made them too costly. If these costs do not establish a BFOQ, could not establish it even in principle, how may the prospect of tort judgments do so? Title VII applies even when—*especially* when—discrimination is rational as the employer sees things.

All of this is not to say where wisdom lies. * * * No one can treat lightly the possibility of injury to future children, who cannot protect themselves or participate in the decisions that will govern their lives. Trying to find the "right" accommodation would rob many a person of sleep—for rigorous implementation of fetal protection policies could close more than 20 million jobs to women,[7] while failure to do anything causes injury to unknown numbers. Under the PDA neither the employer nor the court is authorized to essay an answer to this social puzzle. The disparate treatment—BFOQ approach governs, and it resolves today's dispute. Title VII gives parents the power to make occupational decisions affecting their families. A legislative forum is available to those who believe that such decisions should be made elsewhere.

II

Having adopted the *Wright–Hayes* approach, we still should not affirm the district court's judgment. *Hayes* opined that a fetal protection policy applicable only to women violates Title VII

> unless the employer shows (1) that a substantial risk of harm exists and (2) that the risk is borne only by members of one sex; and (3) the employee fails to show that there are acceptable alternative policies that would have a lesser impact on the affected sex.

* * * At the time *Wright* and *Hayes* were decided, and when the EEOC issued its policy statement, courts believed that "business necessity" in a disparate impact case is a *defense*. "Business necessity" and "BFOQ" were not so distinct. We know from *Wards Cove Packing Co. v. Atonio,* * * * however, that the plaintiff bears the burden of persuasion on all questions in every disparate impact case, as the majority today emphasizes. So the *Wright–Hayes* standard has been

---

7. Fifteen to twenty million jobs is the estimate of the Bureau of National Affairs in *Pregnancy and Employment* 57 (1987), limited to injury caused by chemicals. Cases such as *Hayes* and *Zuniga* show that many additional women are affected by restrictions placed on other jobs, such as the x-ray technician jobs that exposed embryos to radiation. Concern about emissions from computers and their terminals has led to proposals that could restrict access even to traditional office jobs.

watered down. The court's "adoption" of *Wright, Hayes,* and the EEOC's policy statement is thus in practice more favorable to employers than the Fourth and Eleventh Circuits (and the EEOC) anticipated their approach would be. The plaintiff won in *Hayes;* she would lose under the majority's approach.

Even on the majority's un-demanding standard, however, there are material disputes. * * *

* * *

III

The *Wright–Hayes* standard is the wrong one. Johnson needed to, and did not, establish that sex is a BFOQ for employment at its battery plants. Yet even given the majority's decision to adopt the *Wright–Hayes* standard, the plaintiffs are entitled to a trial. Seven judges of this court have analyzed the conflicting medical evidence and reached their own conclusions about its significance, conclusions at variance with those drawn by the American Public Health Association and the Occupational Safety and Health Administration from the same kind of evidence. Judges may be astute students of medical findings, but the presence of thoughtful persons on the other side suggests caution—and at all events appellate judges should not be resolving scientific disputes.

This is the most important sex-discrimination case this circuit has ever decided. It is likely the most important sex-discrimination case in any court since 1964, when Congress enacted Title VII. If the majority is right, then by one estimate 20 million industrial jobs could be closed to women, for many substances in addition to lead pose fetal risks. See note 7 above. Whether that would happen is of course a separate question; legal entitlements need not translate to action. But the law would allow employers to consign more women to "women's work" while reserving better-paying but more hazardous jobs for men. Title VII was designed to eliminate rather than perpetuate such matching of sexes to jobs.

Title VII requires employers to evaluate applicants and employees as individuals rather than as members of a group defined by sex. The statute has its costs; prenatal injuries are among these. Appeals to the "flexibility" with which the Supreme Court has allocated burdens of proof and persuasion get us nowhere. No amount of "flexibility" justifies sex discrimination without a BFOQ, unless by "flexibility" we mean a prerogative to disregard the statute when it requires decisions antithetical to our beliefs. Although my colleagues refer to many constitutional cases, such as *Rostker v. Goldberg,* * * * for the proposition that sex discrimination sometimes is permissible, cases showing that Congress *may* authorize sex-based decisions hardly shows that in this instance it *did.* Title VII forbids rather than requires resort to sex as a basis of decision.

Risk to the next generation is incident to all activity, starting with getting out of bed. (Staying in bed all day has its own hazards.) To insist on zero risk, which the court says Johnson may do, is to exclude women from the industrial jobs that have been a male preserve. By all means let society bend its energies to improving the prospects of those who come after us. Demanding zero risk produces not progress but paralysis. Defining tolerable risk, and seeking to reduce that limit, is more useful—but it is a job for Congress or OSHA in conjunction with medical and other sciences. Laudable though its objective be, Johnson may not reach its goal at the expense of women.

Notes on Johnson Controls

1. Is *Johnson Controls* a disparate treatment or a disparate impact case? After *Wards Cove,* supra p. 114, does the distinction have any practical relevance as far as plaintiff's burden of proof is concerned? On the question whether the BFOQ defense is the only one properly available, do you agree with the majority, Judge Posner, or Judge Easterbrook? What is the relevance to the existence of a BFOQ defense of a substantial risk of harm to the fetus? Does that risk impair the capacity of a fertile woman who chooses to work in the battery division to do her job?

2. A California appellate court has come to the opposite conclusion under state law about the validity of Johnson's fetal protection policy. In Johnson Controls, Inc. v. California Fair Employment and Housing Comm'n, 218 Cal.App.3d 517, 267 Cal.Rptr. 158 (1990), rehearing denied, 218 Cal.App.3d 1492e (1990), petition for review denied, California Supreme Court Minutes (May 17, 1990), real party in interest Queen Elizabeth Foster applied for work at Johnson's Globe Automotive Battery Plant in Fullerton, California. She was rejected because she declined to show medical evidence of infertility. She filed a complaint with the Commission, which found that the employer's refusal to hire Foster constituted unlawful sex discrimination under California law and was not justified by proof of a BFOQ defense. It also found that the business necessity defense was available only to excuse a facially neutral practice having only an incidental adverse affect on women. On review, the Court of Appeals sustained the Commission's order and declined to follow the Eighth Circuit decision in *Johnson Controls.* The Court noted that the decision "has been recently reviewed and sharply criticized by the federal Equal Employment Opportunity Commission in the policy guidance rules issued by that administrative body" going on to point out that the Commission concluded that "Commission field offices should not rely on the Johnson Controls decision as guidance for processing 'fetal hazards' charges." Id., 218 Cal.App.3d at 547, 267 Cal.Rptr. at 174–75. If the California Supreme Court grants a hearing and agrees with the Court of Appeals on the interpretation of state law, and if the United States Supreme Court affirms the Eighth Circuit in its interpretation of Title VII, which holding will control the fetal hazards policy in Johnson Controls' California plants? Will a question of federal preemption arise? Or does *Cal Fed,* set forth in the Casebook at p. 549, provide a way to permit different federal-state outcomes in this context? The United States Supreme Court has recently held that state and federal courts have concurrent jurisdiction in Title VII cases. See Yellow Freight System, Inc. v. Donnelly, 494 U.S. ___, 110 S.Ct. 1566, 108 L.Ed.2d 834

(1990). What would have happened in *Johnson Controls* if both claims—that under California state law and that under Title VII—had been brought in the California state court?

3. What position should those who are concerned with equality for working women take concerning fetal protection policies? Does *Cal Fed*, set out in the Casebook at p. 549, provide a foundation for framing employer policies or state legislation that will enable women "to have families without losing their jobs"—or risking damage to their future children? Professor Furnish believes it does. See Furnish, Beyond Protection: Relevant Difference and Equality in the Toxic Work Environment, 21 U.C. Davis L.Rev. 1 (1987).

4. How and why do you think the United States Supreme Court will decide *Johnson Controls*? How should the case be decided? Section 5(a)–(1) of the proposed Civil Rights Act of 1990, discussed at p. 131, supra, would add the following language to section 703 of Title VII: "Except as otherwise provided in this title, an unlawful employment practice is established when the complaining party demonstrates that race, color, religion, sex, or national origin was a motivating factor for any employment practice, even though such practice was also motivated by other factors." Would this provision make it impossible, as a practical matter, for an employer who grudgingly hired women in non-traditional positions to fire them for incompetence? Section 5(b) sharply limits the remedies available for violations of 5(a)–(1). It would add the following italicized language to the end of present section 706(g) of Title VII dealing with Enforcement Provisions:

> (g) If the court finds that the respondent has intentionally engaged in an unlawful employment practice charged in the complaint, the court may enjoin the respondent from engaging in such unlawful employment practice, and order such affirmative action as may be appropriate, which may include, but is not limited to, reinstatement or hiring of employees, with or without back pay (payable by the employer, employment agency, or labor organization, as the case may be, responsible for the unlawful employment practice), or any other equitable relief as the court deems appropriate. Back pay liability shall not accrue from a date more than two years prior to the filing of a charge with the Commission. Interim earnings or amounts earnable with reasonable diligence by the person or persons discriminated against shall operate to reduce the back pay otherwise allowable. No order of the court shall require the admission or reinstatement of an individual as an employee, or the payment to him of any back pay, if such individual was refused admission, suspended, or expelled, or was refused employment or advancement or was suspended or discharged for any reason other than discrimination on account of race, color, religion, sex, or national origin or in violation of section 2000e–3(a) of this title, *or, in a case where a violation is established under section 703(1), if the respondent establishes that it would have taken the same action in the absence of any discrimination.*

Does this amendment to 706(g) take away what the amendment to 703(1) gave to plaintiffs? Or does it merely place the burden of proof on employers to show that the challenged action would have occurred absent discrimination?

Page 618. Add to Note 10:

The Ninth Circuit affirmed Judge Patel's order confirming the consent decree, holding that it passed muster both when measured against "some level of elevated scrutiny" required by the Equal Protection clause and the showing of "manifest imbalance" required for voluntary race-based affirmative action plans under Title VII. See Davis v. City and County of San Francisco, 890 F.2d 1438, 1445–48 (Equal Protection), 1448–49 (Title VII) (9th Cir.1989).

Page 622. Add to end of Note 10:

The Supreme Court's decision in *Johnson Controls* should resolve this question. Which way do you think it should come out?

ii. Articulating Legitimate and Nondiscriminatory Reasons

Page 629. Add to end of Note 2:

What is the impact of *Wards Cove* on *Burdine*? Is *Uncle Ben's*, cited in the Casebook at the top of page 631, still good law?

Page 635. Add to end of Note 7:

Professor Kimberle Crenshaw has criticized antidiscrimination doctrine for its failure to take account of the "intersectionality" that represents the experience of Black women. She argues that

> Black women are sometimes excluded from feminist theory and antiracist policy discourse because both are predicated on a discrete set of expectations that often does not accurately reflect the interaction of race and gender. These problems cannot be solved simply by including Black women within an already established analytical structure. Because the intersectional experience is greater than the sum of racism and sexism, any analysis that does not take intersectionality into account cannot sufficiently address the particular manner in which Black women are subordinated. Thus, for feminist theory and antiracist policy discourse to embrace the experiences and concerns of Black women, the entire framework that has been used as a basis for translating "women's experience" or "the Black experience" into concrete policy demands must be rethought and recast.

Crenshaw, Demarginalizing the Intersection of Race and Sex: A Black Feminist Critique of Antidiscrimination Doctrine, Feminist Theory and Antiracist Politics, 1989 U.Chi.L.F. 139, 140 (1989). Applying this critique to the question of compound discrimination claims brought by Black women, Crenshaw argues that the consequence of rejecting such claims is that "the employment experiences of white women obscured the distinct discrimination that Black women experienced." Id., at 148 (discussing Degraffenreid v. General Motors, 413 F.Supp. 142 (E.D.Mo.1976) affirmed in part on other grounds, reversed in part, and remanded, 558 F.2d 480 (8th Cir. 1977)). She also criticizes Moore v. Hughes Helicopter, 708 F.2d 475 (9th Cir.1983) for its failure to certify a Black woman as a class representative in a case challenging sex discrimination against all women, pointing out that the court's action "left Moore with the task of supporting her race and sex discrimination claims with statistical evidence of discrimination against Black females alone." Id., at 145. Crenshaw recognizes that critics might respond that she is trying to have the argument both ways by insisting that Black women are harmed both by being treated differently than other protected groups and by being treated the same as they are. Id., at 148–49. She responds, "The point is that Black women can experience discrimination in any number of ways and that the contradiction arises from our assumptions that their claims of exclusion must be unidirectional." Id., at 149.

Does Crenshaw's critique mean that *Jefferies* is right? A Notewriter argues that the "sex plus" rationale offered in *Jefferies* and limited in *Judge* to only one "plus" factor is inadequate to redress the multi-factored discrimination often experienced by women of color. She believes that both *Jeffries* and *Judge* should be rejected in favor of a "category-plus" approach that would recognize Black women as a single class for Title VII purposes, and would permit "plus" factors to be added that are not themselves protected categories under the statute. A "category plus" case might then be a claim that a Black woman or another woman of color was discriminated against because she is married, has children, or speaks with an accent. Note, Conceptualizing Black Women's Employment Experiences, 98 Yale L.J. 1457 (1989). Does this approach expand Title VII beyond the intent of Congress?

c. *The Plaintiff's Ultimate Burden of Persuasion*

Page 640. Add to Note 3:

What do you make of Justice Kennedy's references to footnote 2 of the *Aikens* opinion in his dissenting opinion (joined by the Chief Justice and Justice Scalia) in *Hopkins,* infra at p. 190?

Page 642. Add new Note 5:

5. *Aikens* made clear that plaintiff had the ultimate burden of persuasion in disparate treatment cases. After *Wards Cove,* the plaintiff bears the ultimate burden of persuasion in disparate impact cases as well. What impact will this clarification have on future Title VII litigation?

3. TITLE VII AND "UPPER LEVEL" JOBS

Page 651. Delete the D.C. Circuit's opinion and substitute the Supreme Court's opinion in *Hopkins***:**

PRICE WATERHOUSE v. HOPKINS
Supreme Court of the United States, 1989.
490 U.S. ___, 109 S.Ct. 1775, 104 L.Ed.2d 268.

JUSTICE BRENNAN announced the judgment of the Court and delivered an opinion, in which JUSTICE MARSHALL, JUSTICE BLACKMUN, and JUSTICE STEVENS join.

Ann Hopkins was a senior manager in an office of Price Waterhouse when she was proposed for partnership in 1982. She was neither offered nor denied admission to the partnership; instead, her candidacy was held for reconsideration the following year. When the partners in her office later refused to repropose her for partnership, she sued Price Waterhouse under Title VII, * * * charging that the firm had discriminated against her on the basis of sex in its decisions regarding partnership. Judge Gesell in the District Court for the District of Columbia ruled in her favor on the question of liability, * * * and the Court of Appeals for the District of Columbia Circuit affirmed. * * * We granted certiorari to resolve a conflict among the Courts of Appeals concerning the respective burdens of proof of a defendant and plaintiff in a suit under Title VII when it has been shown that an employment decision resulted from a mixture of legitimate and illegitimate motives. * * *

I

At Price Waterhouse, a nationwide professional accounting partnership, a senior manager becomes a candidate for partnership when the partners in her local office submit her name as a candidate. All of the other partners in the firm are then invited to submit written comments on each candidate—either on a "long" or a "short" form, depending on the partner's degree of exposure to the candidate. Not every partner in the firm submits comments on every candidate. After reviewing the comments and interviewing the partners who submitted them, the firm's Admissions Committee makes a recommendation to the Policy Board. This recommendation will be either that the firm accept the candidate for partnership, put her application on "hold," or deny her the promotion outright. The Policy Board then decides whether to submit the candidate's name to the entire partnership for a vote, to "hold" her candidacy, or to reject her. The recommendation of the Admissions Committee, and the decision of the Policy Board, are not controlled by fixed guidelines: a certain number of positive comments from partners will not guarantee a candidate's admission to the partnership, nor will a specific quantity of negative comments necessarily defeat her application. Price Waterhouse places no limit on the number of persons whom it will admit to the partnership in any given year.

Ann Hopkins had worked at Price Waterhouse's Office of Government Services in Washington, D.C., for five years when the partners in that office proposed her as a candidate for partnership. Of the 662 partners at the firm at that time, 7 were women. Of the 88 persons proposed for partnership that year, only 1—Hopkins—was a woman. Forty-seven of these candidates were admitted to the partnership, 21 were rejected, and 20—including Hopkins—were "held" for reconsideration the following year.[1] Thirteen of the 32 partners who had submit-

---

1. Before the time for reconsideration came, two of the partners in Hopkins' office withdrew their support for her, and the office informed her that she would not be reconsidered for partnership. Hopkins then resigned. Price Waterhouse does not challenge the Court of Appeals' conclusion that the refusal to repropose her for partnership amounted to a constructive discharge. That court remanded the case to

ted comments on Hopkins supported her bid for partnership. Three partners recommended that her candidacy be placed on hold, eight stated that they did not have an informed opinion about her, and eight recommended that she be denied partnership.

In a jointly prepared statement supporting her candidacy, the partners in Hopkins' office showcased her successful 2-year effort to secure a $25 million contract with the Department of State, labeling it "an outstanding performance" and one that Hopkins carried out "virtually at the partner level." * * * Despite Price Waterhouse's attempt at trial to minimize her contribution to this project, Judge Gesell specifically found that Hopkins had "played a key role in Price Waterhouse's successful effort to win a multi-million dollar contract with the Department of State." * * * Indeed, he went on, "[n]one of the other partnership candidates at Price Waterhouse that year had a comparable record in terms of successfully securing major contracts for the partnership." * * *

The partners in Hopkins' office praised her character as well as her accomplishments, describing her in their joint statement as "an outstanding professional" who had a "deft touch," a "strong character, independence and integrity." * * * Clients appear to have agreed with these assessments. At trial, one official from the State Department described her as "extremely competent, intelligent," "strong and forthright, very productive, energetic and creative." * * * Another high-ranking official praised Hopkins' decisiveness, broadmindedness, and "intellectual clarity"; she was, in his words, "a stimulating conversationalist." * * * Evaluations such as these led Judge Gesell to conclude that Hopkins "had no difficulty dealing with clients and her clients appear to have been very pleased with her work" and that she "was generally viewed as a highly competent project leader who worked long hours, pushed vigorously to meet deadlines and demanded much from the multidisciplinary staffs with which she worked." * * *

On too many occasions, however, Hopkins' aggressiveness apparently spilled over into abrasiveness. Staff members seem to have borne the brunt of Hopkins' brusqueness. Long before her bid for partnership, partners evaluating her work had counseled her to improve her relations with staff members. Although later evaluations indicate an improvement, Hopkins' perceived shortcomings in this important area eventually doomed her bid for partnership. Virtually all of the partners' negative remarks about Hopkins—even those of partners supporting her—had to do with her "interpersonal skills." Both "[s]upporters and opponents of her candidacy," stressed Judge Gesell, "indicated that

the District Court for further proceedings to determine appropriate relief, and those proceedings have been stayed pending our decision. * * * We are concerned today only with Price Waterhouse's decision to place Hopkins' candidacy on hold. Decisions pertaining to advancement to partnership are, of course, subject to challenge under Title VII. *Hishon v. King & Spalding*, 467 U.S. 69, 104 S.Ct. 2229, 81 L.Ed.2d 59 (1984).

she was sometimes overly aggressive, unduly harsh, difficult to work with and impatient with staff." * * *

There were clear signs, though, that some of the partners reacted negatively to Hopkins' personality because she was a woman. One partner described her as "macho"; * * * another suggested that she "overcompensated for being a woman"; * * * a third advised her to take "a course at charm school". * * * Several partners criticized her use of profanity; in response, one partner suggested that those partners objected to her swearing only "because it[']s a lady using foul language." * * * Another supporter explained that Hopkins "ha[d] matured from a tough-talking somewhat masculine hardnosed mgr to an authoritative, formidable, but much more appealing lady ptr candidate." * * * But it was the man who, as Judge Gesell found, bore responsibility for explaining to Hopkins the reasons for the Policy Board's decision to place her candidacy on hold who delivered the *coup de grace:* in order to improve her chances for partnership, Thomas Beyer advised, Hopkins should "walk more femininely, talk more femininely, dress more femininely, wear make-up, have her hair styled, and wear jewelry." * * *

Dr. Susan Fiske, a social psychologist and Associate Professor of Psychology at Carnegie–Mellon University, testified at trial that the partnership selection process at Price Waterhouse was likely influenced by sex stereotyping. Her testimony focused not only on the overtly sex-based comments of partners but also on gender-neutral remarks, made by partners who knew Hopkins only slightly, that were intensely critical of her. One partner, for example, baldly stated that Hopkins was "universally disliked" by staff, * * * and another described her as "consistently annoying and irritating"; * * * yet these were people who had had very little contact with Hopkins. According to Fiske, Hopkins' uniqueness (as the only woman in the pool of candidates) and the subjectivity of the evaluations made it likely that sharply critical remarks such as these were the product of sex stereotyping—although Fiske admitted that she could not say with certainty whether any particular comment was the result of stereotyping. Fiske based her opinion on a review of the submitted comments, explaining that it was commonly accepted practice for social psychologists to reach this kind of conclusion without having met any of the people involved in the decisionmaking process.

In previous years, other female candidates for partnership also had been evaluated in sex-based terms. As a general matter, Judge Gesell concluded, "[c]andidates were viewed favorably if partners believed they maintained their femin[in]ity while becoming effective professional managers"; in this environment, "[t]o be identified as a 'women's lib[b]er' was regarded as [a] negative comment." * * * In fact, the judge found that in previous years "[o]ne partner repeatedly commented that he could not consider any woman seriously as a partnership candidate and believed that women were not even capable of functioning as senior managers—yet the firm took no action to discourage his comments and recorded his vote in the overall summary of the evaluations." * * *

Judge Gesell found that Price Waterhouse legitimately emphasized interpersonal skills in its partnership decisions, and also found that the firm had not fabricated its complaints about Hopkins' interpersonal skills as a pretext for discrimination. Moreover, he concluded, the firm did not give decisive emphasis to such traits only because Hopkins was a woman; although there were male candidates who lacked these skills but who were admitted to partnership, the judge found that these candidates possessed other, positive traits that Hopkins lacked.

The judge went on to decide, however, that some of the partners' remarks about Hopkins stemmed from an impermissibly cabined view of the proper behavior of women, and that Price Waterhouse had done nothing to disavow reliance on such comments. He held that Price Waterhouse had unlawfully discriminated against Hopkins on the basis of sex by consciously giving credence and effect to partners' comments that resulted from sex stereotyping. Noting that Price Waterhouse could avoid equitable relief by proving by clear and convincing evidence that it would have placed Hopkins' candidacy on hold even absent this discrimination, the judge decided that the firm had not carried this heavy burden.

The Court of Appeals affirmed the District Court's ultimate conclusion, but departed from its analysis in one particular: it held that even if a plaintiff proves that discrimination played a role in an employment decision, the defendant will not be found liable if it proves, by clear and convincing evidence, that it would have made the same decision in the absence of discrimination. * * * Under this approach, an employer is not deemed to have violated Title VII if it proves that it would have made the same decision in the absence of an impermissible motive, whereas under the District Court's approach, the employer's proof in that respect only avoids equitable relief. We decide today that the Court of Appeals had the better approach, but that both courts erred in requiring the employer to make its proof by clear and convincing evidence.

II

The specification of the standard of causation under Title VII is a decision about the kind of conduct that violates that statute. According to Price Waterhouse, an employer violates Title VII only if it gives decisive consideration to an employee's gender, race, national origin, or religion in making a decision that affects that employee. On Price Waterhouse's theory, even if a plaintiff shows that her gender played a part in an employment decision, it is still her burden to show that the decision would have been different if the employer had not discriminated. In Hopkins' view, on the other hand, an employer violates the statute whenever it allows one of these attributes to play any part in an employment decision. Once a plaintiff shows that this occurred, according to Hopkins, the employer's proof that it would have made the same decision in the absence of discrimination can serve to limit equitable relief but not to avoid a finding of liability. We conclude that, as often happens, the truth lies somewhere in-between.

A

In passing Title VII, Congress made the simple but momentous announcement that sex, race, religion, and national origin are not relevant to the selection, evaluation, or compensation of employees.[3] Yet, the statute does not purport to limit the other qualities and characteristics that employers *may* take into account in making employment decisions. The converse, therefore, of "for cause" legislation, Title VII eliminates certain bases for distinguishing among employees while otherwise preserving employers' freedom of choice. This balance between employee rights and employer prerogatives turns out to be decisive in the case before us.

Congress' intent to forbid employers to take gender into account in making employment decisions appears on the face of the statute. In now-familiar language, the statute forbids an employer to "fail or refuse to hire or to discharge any individual, or otherwise to discriminate with respect to his compensation, terms, conditions, or privileges of employment," or to "limit, segregate, or classify his employees or applicants for employment in any way which would deprive or tend to deprive any individual of employment opportunities or otherwise adversely affect his status as an employee, *because of* such individual's * * * sex." * * * We take these words to mean that gender must be irrelevant to employment decisions. To construe the words "because of" as colloquial shorthand for "but-for causation," as does Price Waterhouse, is to misunderstand them.[6]

But-for causation is a hypothetical construct. In determining whether a particular factor was a but-for cause of a given event, we begin by assuming that that factor was present at the time of the event, and then ask whether, even if that factor had been absent, the event nevertheless would have transpired in the same way. The present, active tense of the operative verbs of § 703(a)(1) ("to fail or refuse"), in contrast, turns our attention to the actual moment of the event in question, the adverse employment decision. The critical inquiry, the one commanded by the words of § 703(a)(1), is whether gender was a

---

3. We disregard, for purposes of this discussion, the special context of affirmative action.

6. We made passing reference to a similar question in *McDonald v. Santa Fe Trail Transportation Co.,* 427 U.S. 273, 282, n. 10, 96 S.Ct. 2574, 2580, n. 10, 49 L.Ed.2d 493 (1976), where we stated that when a Title VII plaintiff seeks to show that an employer's explanation for a challenged employment decision is pretextual, "no more is required to be shown than that race was a 'but for' cause." This passage, however, does not suggest that the plaintiff *must* show but-for cause; it indicates only that if she does so, she prevails. More important, *McDonald* dealt with the question whether the employer's stated reason for its decision was *the* reason for its action; unlike the case before us today, therefore, *McDonald* did not involve mixed motives. This difference is decisive in distinguishing this case from those involving "pretext." * * *

factor in the employment decision *at the moment it was made*. Moreover, since we know that the words "because of" do not mean "*solely because of*," [7] we also know that Title VII meant to condemn even those decisions based on a mixture of legitimate and illegitimate considerations. When, therefore, an employer considers both gender and legitimate factors at the time of making a decision, that decision was "because of" sex and the other, legitimate considerations—even if we may say later, in the context of litigation, that the decision would have been the same if gender had not been taken into account.

To attribute this meaning to the words "because of" does not, as the dissent asserts, * * * divest them of causal significance. A simple example illustrates the point. Suppose two physical forces act upon and move an object, and suppose that either force acting alone would have moved the object. As the dissent would have it, *neither* physical force was a "cause" of the motion unless we can show that but for one or both of them, the object would not have moved; to use the dissent's terminology, both forces were simply "in the air" unless we can identify at least one of them as a but-for cause of the object's movement. * * * Events that are causally overdetermined, in other words, may not have any "cause" at all. This cannot be so.

We need not leave our common-sense at the doorstep when we interpret a statute. It is difficult for us to imagine that, in the simple words "because of," Congress meant to obligate a plaintiff to identify the precise causal role played by legitimate and illegitimate motivations in the employment decision she challenges. We conclude, instead, that Congress meant to obligate her to prove that the employer relied upon sex-based considerations in coming to its decision.

Our interpretation of the words "because of" also is supported by the fact that Title VII does identify one circumstance in which an employer may take gender into account in making an employment decision, namely, when gender is a "bona fide occupational qualification [(BFOQ)] reasonably necessary to the normal operation of th[e] particular business or enterprise." * * * The only plausible inference to draw from this provision is that, in all other circumstances, a person's gender may not be considered in making decisions that affect her. Indeed, Title VII even forbids employers to make gender an indirect stumbling block to employment opportunities. An employer may not, we have held, condition employment opportunities on the satisfaction of facially neutral tests or qualifications that have a disproportionate, adverse impact on members of protected groups when those tests or qualifications are not required for performance of the job. See *Watson v. Fort Worth Bank & Trust*, * * *; *Griggs v. Duke Power Co.*, * * *.

7. Congress specifically rejected an amendment that would have placed the word "solely" in front of the words "because of." 110 Cong.Rec. 2728, 13837 (1964).

To say that an employer may not take gender into account is not, however, the end of the matter, for that describes only one aspect of Title VII. The other important aspect of the statute is its preservation of an employer's remaining freedom of choice. We conclude that the preservation of this freedom means that an employer shall not be liable if it can prove that, even if it had not taken gender into account, it would have come to the same decision regarding a particular person. The statute's maintenance of employer prerogatives is evident from the statute itself and from its history, both in Congress and in this Court.

To begin with, the existence of the BFOQ exception shows Congress' unwillingness to require employers to change the very nature of their operations in response to the statute. And our emphasis on "business necessity" in disparate-impact cases, see *Watson* and *Griggs*, and on "legitimate, nondiscriminatory reason[s]" in disparate-treatment cases, see *McDonnell Douglas Corp. v. Green*, * * *; *Texas Dept. of Community Affairs v. Burdine*, * * * results from our awareness of Title VII's balance between employee rights and employer prerogatives. In *McDonnell Douglas*, we described as follows Title VII's goal to eradicate discrimination while preserving workplace efficiency: "The broad, overriding interest, shared by employer, employee, and consumer, is efficient and trustworthy workmanship assured through fair and racially neutral employment and personnel decisions. In the implementation of such decisions, it is abundantly clear that Title VII tolerates no racial discrimination, subtle or otherwise." * * *

When an employer ignored the attributes enumerated in the statute, Congress hoped, it naturally would focus on the qualifications of the applicant or employee. The intent to drive employers to focus on qualifications rather than on race, religion, sex, or national origin is the theme of a good deal of the statute's legislative history. * * *

* * * The central point is this: while an employer may not take gender into account in making an employment decision (except in those very narrow circumstances in which gender is a BFOQ), it is free to decide against a woman for other reasons. We think these principles require that, once a plaintiff in a Title VII case shows that gender played a motivating part in an employment decision, the defendant may avoid a finding of liability [10] only by proving that it would have

10. Hopkins argues that once she made this showing, she was entitled to a finding that Price Waterhouse had discriminated against her on the basis of sex; as a consequence, she says, the partnership's proof could only limit the relief she received. She relies on Title VII's § 706(g), which permits a court to award affirmative relief when it finds that an employer "has intentionally engaged in or is intentionally engaging in an unlawful employment practice," and yet forbids a court to order reinstatement of, or backpay to, "an individual * * * if such individual was refused * * * employment or advancement or was suspended or discharged *for any reason other than* discrimination on account of race, color, religion, sex, or national origin." 42 U.S.C. § 2000e–5(g) (emphasis added). We do not take this provision to mean that a court inevitably can find a violation of the statute without having considered whether the employment decision would have been the same absent the impermissible motive. That would be to interpret § 706(g)—a provision defining *remedies*—to influence the substantive commands of the statute. We think that

made the same decision even if it had not allowed gender to play such a role. This balance of burdens is the direct result of Title VII's balance of rights.

Our holding casts no shadow on *Burdine,* in which we decided that, even after a plaintiff has made out a prima facie case of discrimination under Title VII, the burden of persuasion does not shift to the employer to show that its stated legitimate reason for the employment decision was the true reason. * * * We stress, first, that neither court below shifted the burden of persuasion to Price Waterhouse on this question, and in fact, the District Court found that Hopkins had not shown that the firm's stated reason for its decision was pretextual. * * * Moreover, since we hold that the plaintiff retains the burden of persuasion on the issue whether gender played a part in the employment decision, the situation before us is not the one of "shifting burdens" that we addressed in *Burdine.* Instead, the employer's burden is most appropriately deemed an affirmative defense: the plaintiff must persuade the factfinder on one point, and then the employer, if it wishes to prevail, must persuade it on another. See *NLRB v. Transportation Management Corp.,* 462 U.S. 393, 400, 103 S.Ct. 2469, 2473, 76 L.Ed.2d 667 (1983).[11]

this provision merely limits courts' authority to award affirmative relief in those circumstances in which a violation of the statute is not dependent upon the effect of the employer's discriminatory practices on a particular employee, as in pattern-or-practice suits and class actions. "The crucial difference between an individual's claim of discrimination and a class action alleging a general pattern or practice of discrimination is manifest. The inquiry regarding an individual's claim is the reason for a particular employment decision, while 'at the liability stage of a pattern-or-practice trial the focus often will not be on individual hiring decisions, but on a pattern of discriminatory decisionmaking.'" *Cooper v. Federal Reserve Bank of Richmond,* 467 U.S. 867, 876, 104 S.Ct. 2794, 2799–2800, 81 L.Ed.2d 718 (1984), quoting *Teamsters v. United States,* 431 U.S. 324, 360, n. 46, 97 S.Ct. 1843, 1867, n. 46, 52 L.Ed.2d 396 (1977).

Without explicitly mentioning this portion of § 706(g), we have in the past held that Title VII does not authorize affirmative relief for individuals as to whom, the employer shows, the existence of systemic discrimination had no effect. See *Franks v. Bowman Transportation Co.,* 424 U.S. 747, 772, 96 S.Ct. 1251, 1268, 47 L.Ed.2d 444 (1976); *Teamsters v. United States,* 431 U.S. 324, 367–371, 97 S.Ct. 1843, 1870–1873, 52 L.Ed.2d 396 (1977); *East Texas Motor Freight System, Inc. v. Rodriguez,* 431 U.S. 395, 404, n. 9, 97 S.Ct. 1891, 1897, n. 9, 52 L.Ed.2d 453 (1977). These decisions suggest that the proper focus of § 706(g) is on claims of systemic discrimination, not on charges of individual discrimination. Cf. *NLRB v. Transportation Management Corp.,* 462 U.S. 393, 103 S.Ct. 2469, 76 L.Ed.2d 667 (1983) (upholding the National Labor Relations Board's identical interpretation of § 10(c) of the National Labor Relations Act, 29 U.S.C. § 160(c), which contains language almost identical to § 706(g)).

11. Given that both the plaintiff and defendant bear a burden of proof in cases such as this one, it is surprising that the dissent insists that our approach requires the employer to bear "the ultimate burden of proof." It is, moreover, perfectly consistent to say *both* that gender was a factor in a particular decision when it was made *and* that, when the situation is viewed hypothetically and after the fact, the same decision would have been made even in the absence of discrimination. Thus, we do not see the "internal inconsistency" in our opinion that the dissent perceives. Finally, where liability is imposed because an employer is unable to prove that it would have made the same decision even if it had not discriminated, this is not an imposition of liability "where sex made no difference to the outcome." In our adversary system, where a party has the burden of proving a particular assertion and where that party is unable to meet its burden, we assume that that assertion is inaccurate. Thus,

Price Waterhouse's claim that the employer does not bear any burden of proof (if it bears one at all) until the plaintiff has shown "substantial evidence that Price Waterhouse's explanation for failing to promote Hopkins was not the 'true reason' for its action" * * * merely restates its argument that the plaintiff in a mixed-motives case must squeeze her proof into *Burdine's* framework. Where a decision was the product of a mixture of legitimate and illegitimate motives, however, it simply makes no sense to ask whether the legitimate reason was "*the* 'true reason'" * * * for the decision—which is the question asked by *Burdine*. See *Transportation Management, supra,* * * *.[12] Oblivious to this last point, the dissent would insist that *Burdine's* framework perform work that it was never intended to perform. It would require a plaintiff who challenges an adverse employment decision in which both legitimate and illegitimate considerations played a part to pretend that the decision, in fact, stemmed from a single source—for the premise of *Burdine* is that *either* a legitimate *or* an illegitimate set of considerations led to the challenged decision. To say that *Burdine's* evidentiary scheme will not help us decide a case admittedly involving *both* kinds of considerations is not to cast aspersions on the utility of that scheme in the circumstances for which it was designed.

B

In deciding as we do today, we do not traverse new ground. We have in the past confronted Title VII cases in which an employer has used an illegitimate criterion to distinguish among employees, and have held that it is the employer's burden to justify decisions resulting from that practice. When an employer has asserted that gender is a bona fide occupational qualification within the meaning of § 703(e), for example, we have assumed that it is the employer who must show why it must use gender as a criterion in employment. See *Dothard v. Rawlinson,* * * *. In a related context, although the Equal Pay Act expressly permits employers to pay different wages to women where

where an employer is unable to prove its claim that it would have made the same decision in the absence of discrimination, we are entitled to conclude that gender *did* make a difference to the outcome.

12. Nothing in this opinion should be taken to suggest that a case must be correctly labeled as either a "pretext" case or a "mixed motives" case from the beginning in the District Court; indeed, we expect that plaintiffs often will allege, in the alternative, that their cases are both. Discovery often will be necessary before the plaintiff can know whether both legitimate and illegitimate considerations played a part in the decision against her. At some point in the proceedings, of course, the District Court must decide whether a particular case involves mixed motives. If the plaintiff fails to satisfy the factfinder that it is more likely than not that a forbidden characteristic played a part in the employment decision, then she may prevail only if she proves, following *Burdine,* that the employer's stated reason for its decision is pretextual. The dissent need not worry that this evidentiary scheme, if used during a jury trial, will be so impossibly confused and complex as it imagines. Juries long have decided cases in which defendants raise affirmative defenses. The dissent fails, moreover, to explain why the evidentiary scheme that we endorsed over ten years ago in *Mt. Healthy* has not proved unworkable in that context but would be hopelessly complicated in a case brought under federal antidiscrimination statutes.

disparate pay is the result of a "factor other than sex," see 29 U.S.C. § 206(d)(1), we have decided that it is the employer, not the employee, who must prove that the actual disparity is not sex-linked. See *Corning Glass Works v. Brennan,* * * *. As these examples demonstrate, our assumption always has been that if an employer allows gender to affect its decisionmaking process, then it must carry the burden of justifying its ultimate decision. We have not in the past required women whose gender has proved relevant to an employment decision to establish the negative proposition that they would not have been subject to that decision had they been men, and we do not do so today.

We have reached a similar conclusion in other contexts where the law announces that a certain characteristic is irrelevant to the allocation of burdens and benefits. In *Mt. Healthy City School Dist. Board of Education v. Doyle,* 429 U.S. 274, 97 S.Ct. 568, 50 L.Ed.2d 471 (1977), the plaintiff claimed that he had been discharged as a public school teacher for exercising his free-speech rights under the First Amendment. Because we did not wish to "place an employee in a better position as a result of the exercise of constitutionally protected conduct than he would have occupied had he done nothing," we concluded that such an employee "ought not to be able, by engaging in such conduct, to prevent his employer from assessing his performance record and reaching a decision not to rehire on the basis of that record." We therefore held that once the plaintiff had shown that his constitutionally protected speech was a "substantial" or "motivating factor" in the adverse treatment of him by his employer, the employer was obligated to prove "by a preponderance of the evidence that it would have reached the same decision as to [the plaintiff] even in the absence of the protected conduct." A court that finds for a plaintiff under this standard has effectively concluded that an illegitimate motive was a "but-for" cause of the employment decision. * * *

In *Transportation Management,* we upheld the NLRB's interpretation of § 10(c) of the National Labor Relations Act, which forbids a court to order affirmative relief for discriminatory conduct against a union member "if such individual was suspended or discharged for cause." * * * The Board had decided that this provision meant that once an employee had shown that his suspension or discharge was based in part on hostility to unions, it was up to the employer to prove by a preponderance of the evidence that it would have made the same decision in the absence of this impermissible motive. In such a situation, we emphasized, "[t]he employer is a wrongdoer; he has acted out of a motive that is declared illegitimate by the statute. It is fair that he bear the risk that the influence of legal and illegal motives cannot be separated, because he knowingly created the risk and because the risk was created not by innocent activity but by his own wrongdoing." * * *

We have, in short, been here before. Each time, we have concluded that the plaintiff who shows that an impermissible motive played a motivating part in an adverse employment decision has thereby placed upon the defendant the burden to show that it would have made the same decision in the absence of the unlawful motive. Our decision today treads this well-worn path.

C

In saying that gender played a motivating part in an employment decision, we mean that, if we asked the employer at the moment of the decision what its reasons were and if we received a truthful response, one of those reasons would be that the applicant or employee was a woman.[13] In the specific context of sex stereotyping, an employer who acts on the basis of a belief that a woman cannot be aggressive, or that she must not be, has acted on the basis of gender.

Although the parties do not overtly dispute this last proposition, the placement by Price Waterhouse of "sex stereotyping" in quotation marks throughout its brief seems to us an insinuation either that such stereotyping was not present in this case or that it lacks legal relevance. We reject both possibilities. As to the existence of sex stereotyping in this case, we are not inclined to quarrel with the District Court's conclusion that a number of the partners' comments showed sex stereotyping at work. * * * As for the legal relevance of sex stereotyping, we are beyond the day when an employer could evaluate employees by assuming or insisting that they matched the stereotype associated with their group, for " '[i]n forbidding employers to discriminate against individuals because of their sex, Congress intended to strike at the entire spectrum of disparate treatment of men and women resulting from sex stereotypes.' " *Los Angeles Dept. of Water & Power v. Manhart*, * * * quoting *Sprogis v. United Air Lines, Inc.*, * * *. An employer who objects to aggressiveness in women but whose positions require this trait places women in an intolerable and impermissible Catch–22: out of a job if they behave aggressively and out of a job if they don't. Title VII lifts women out of this bind.

Remarks at work that are based on sex stereotypes do not inevitably prove that gender played a part in a particular employment decision. The plaintiff must show that the employer actually relied on her gender in making its decision. In making this showing, stereotyped remarks can certainly be *evidence* that gender played a part. In any event, the stereotyping in this case did not simply consist of stray remarks. On the contrary, Hopkins proved that Price Waterhouse

13. After comparing this description of the plaintiff's proof to that offered by the concurring opinion, * * * we do not understand why the concurrence suggests that they are meaningfully different from each other * * *. Nor do we see how the inquiry that we have described is "hypothetical," * * *. It seeks to determine the content of the entire set of reasons for a decision, rather than shaving off one reason in an attempt to determine what the decision would have been in the absence of that consideration. The inquiry that we describe thus strikes us as a distinctly non-hypothetical one.

invited partners to submit comments; that some of the comments stemmed from sex stereotypes; that an important part of the Policy Board's decision on Hopkins was an assessment of the submitted comments; and that Price Waterhouse in no way disclaimed reliance on the sex-linked evaluations. This is not, as Price Waterhouse suggests, "discrimination in the air"; rather, it is, as Hopkins puts it, "discrimination brought to ground and visited upon" an employee. By focusing on Hopkins' specific proof, however, we do not suggest a limitation on the possible ways of proving that stereotyping played a motivating role in an employment decision, and we refrain from deciding here which specific facts, "standing alone," would or would not establish a plaintiff's case, since such a decision is unnecessary in this case. *But see post,* (JUSTICE O'CONNOR, concurring in judgment).

As to the employer's proof, in most cases, the employer should be able to present some objective evidence as to its probable decision in the absence of an impermissible motive.[14] Moreover, proving "that the same decision would have been justified * * * is not the same as proving that the same decision would have been made." * * * An employer may not, in other words, prevail in a mixed-motives case by offering a legitimate and sufficient reason for its decision if that reason did not motivate it at the time of the decision. Finally, an employer may not meet its burden in such a case by merely showing that at the time of the decision it was motivated only in part by a legitimate reason. The very premise of a mixed-motives case is that a legitimate reason was present, and indeed, in this case, Price Waterhouse already has made this showing by convincing Judge Gesell that Hopkins' interpersonal problems were a legitimate concern. The employer instead must show that its legitimate reason, standing alone, would have induced it to make the same decision.

III

The courts below held that an employer who has allowed a discriminatory impulse to play a motivating part in an employment decision must prove by clear and convincing evidence that it would have made the same decision in the absence of discrimination. We are persuaded that the better rule is that the employer must make this showing by a preponderance of the evidence.

Conventional rules of civil litigation generally apply in Title VII cases, * * * and one of these rules is that parties to civil litigation need only prove their case by a preponderance of the evidence. * * * Exceptions to this standard are uncommon, and in fact are ordinarily recognized only when the government seeks to take unusual coercive action—action more dramatic than entering an award of money damages or other conventional relief—against an individual. * * * Only

---

14. Justice White's suggestion, that the employer's own testimony as to the probable decision in the absence of discrimination is due special credence where the court has, contrary to the employer's testimony, found that an illegitimate factor played a part in the decision, is baffling.

rarely have we required clear and convincing proof where the action defended against seeks only conventional relief, * * * and we find it significant that in such cases it was the defendant rather than the plaintiff who sought the elevated standard of proof—suggesting that this standard ordinarily serves as a shield rather than, as Hopkins seeks to use it, as a sword.

* * *

Although Price Waterhouse does not concretely tell us how its proof was preponderant even if it was not clear and convincing, this general claim is implicit in its request for the less stringent standard. Since the lower courts required Price Waterhouse to make its proof by clear and convincing evidence, they did not determine whether Price Waterhouse had proved by *a preponderance of the evidence* that it would have placed Hopkins' candidacy on hold even if it had not permitted sex-linked evaluations to play a part in the decisionmaking process. Thus, we shall remand this case so that that determination can be made.

IV

The District Court found that sex stereotyping "was permitted to play a part" in the evaluation of Hopkins as a candidate for partnership. * * * Price Waterhouse disputes both that stereotyping occurred and that it played any part in the decision to place Hopkins' candidacy on hold. In the firm's view, in other words, the District Court's factual conclusions are clearly erroneous. We do not agree.

In finding that some of the partners' comments reflected sex stereotyping, the District Court relied in part on Dr. Fiske's expert testimony. Without directly impugning Dr. Fiske's credentials or qualifications, Price Waterhouse insinuates that a social psychologist is unable to identify sex stereotyping in evaluations without investigating whether those evaluations have a basis in reality. This argument comes too late. At trial, counsel for Price Waterhouse twice assured the court that he did not question Dr. Fiske's expertise * * * and failed to challenge the legitimacy of her discipline. Without contradiction from Price Waterhouse, Fiske testified that she discerned sex stereotyping in the partners' evaluations of Hopkins and she further explained that it was part of her business to identify stereotyping in written documents. * * * We are not inclined to accept petitioner's belated and unsubstantiated characterization of Dr. Fiske's testimony as "gossamer evidence" * * * based only on "intuitive hunches" * * * and of her detection of sex stereotyping as "intuitively divined" * * *. Nor are we disposed to adopt the dissent's dismissive attitude toward Dr. Fiske's field of study and toward her own professional integrity, * * *.

Indeed, we are tempted to say that Dr. Fiske's expert testimony was merely icing on Hopkins' cake. It takes no special training to discern sex stereotyping in a description of an aggressive female employee as requiring "a course at charm school." Nor, turning to

Thomas Beyer's memorable advice to Hopkins, does it require expertise in psychology to know that, if an employee's flawed "interpersonal skills" can be corrected by a soft-hued suit or a new shade of lipstick, perhaps it is the employee's sex and not her interpersonal skills that has drawn the criticism.[15]

Price Waterhouse also charges that Hopkins produced no evidence that sex stereotyping played a role in the decision to place her candidacy on hold. As we have stressed, however, Hopkins showed that the partnership solicited evaluations from all of the firm's partners; that it generally relied very heavily on such evaluations in making its decision; that some of the partners' comments were the product of stereotyping; and that the firm in no way disclaimed reliance on those particular comments, either in Hopkins' case or in the past. Certainly a plausible—and, one might say, inevitable—conclusion to draw from this set of circumstances is that the Policy Board in making its decision did in fact take into account all of the partners' comments, including the comments that were motivated by stereotypical notions about women's proper deportment.[16]

* * *

Nor is the finding that sex stereotyping played a part in the Policy Board's decision undermined by the fact that many of the suspect comments were made by supporters rather than detractors of Hopkins. A negative comment, even when made in the context of a generally favorable review, nevertheless may influence the decisionmaker to think less highly of the candidate; the Policy Board, in fact, did not simply tally the "yes's" and "no's" regarding a candidate, but carefully reviewed the content of the submitted comments. The additional suggestion that the comments were made by "persons outside the decisionmaking chain" * * *—and therefore could not have harmed Hopkins—simply ignores the critical role that partners' comments played in the Policy Board's partnership decisions.

Price Waterhouse appears to think that we cannot affirm the factual findings of the trial court without deciding that, instead of being overbearing and aggressive and curt, Hopkins is in fact kind and considerate and patient. If this is indeed its impression, petitioner misunderstands the theory on which Hopkins prevailed. The District Judge acknowledged that Hopkins' conduct justified complaints about

15. We reject the claim, advanced by Price Waterhouse here and by the dissenting judge below, that the District Court clearly erred in finding that Beyer was "responsible for telling [Hopkins] what problems the Policy Board had identified with her candidacy." * * * This conclusion was reasonable in light of the testimony at trial of a member of both the Policy Board and the Admissions Committee, who stated that he had "no doubt" that Beyer would discuss with Hopkins the reasons for placing her candidacy on hold and that Beyer "knew exactly where the problems were" regarding Hopkins.

16. We do not understand the dissenters' dissatisfaction with the District Judge's statements regarding the failure of Price Waterhouse to "sensitize" partners to the dangers of sexism. * * * Made in the context of determining that Price Waterhouse had not disclaimed reliance on sex-based evaluations, and following the judge's description of the firm's history of condoning such evaluations, the judge's remarks seem to us justified.

her behavior as a senior manager. But he also concluded that the reactions of at least some of the partners were reactions to her as a *woman* manager. Where an evaluation is based on a subjective assessment of a person's strengths and weaknesses, it is simply not true that each evaluator will focus on, or even mention, the same weaknesses. Thus, even if we knew that Hopkins had "personality problems," this would not tell us that the partners who cast their evaluations of Hopkins in sex-based terms would have criticized her as sharply (or criticized her at all) if she had been a man. It is not our job to review the evidence and decide that the negative reactions to Hopkins were based on reality; our perception of Hopkins' character is irrelevant. We sit not to determine whether Ms. Hopkins is nice, but to decide whether the partners reacted negatively to her personality because she is a woman.

V

We hold that when a plaintiff in a Title VII case proves that her gender played a motivating part in an employment decision, the defendant may avoid a finding of liability only by proving by a preponderance of the evidence that it would have made the same decision even if it had not taken the plaintiff's gender into account. Because the courts below erred by deciding that the defendant must make this proof by clear and convincing evidence, we reverse the Court of Appeals' judgment against Price Waterhouse on liability and remand the case to that court for further proceedings.

It is so ordered.

JUSTICE WHITE, concurring in the judgment.

In my view, to determine the proper approach to causation in this case, we need look only to the Court's opinion in *Mt. Healthy City School District Bd. of Ed. v. Doyle*, * * *.

It is not necessary to get into semantic discussions on whether the *Mt. Healthy* approach is "but for" causation in another guise or creates an affirmative defense on the part of the employer to see its clear application to the issues before us in this case. As in *Mt. Healthy,* the District Court found that the employer was motivated by both legitimate and illegitimate factors. And here, as in *Mt. Healthy,* and as the Court now holds, Hopkins was not required to prove that the illegitimate factor was the only, principal, or true reason for the petitioner's action. Rather, as Justice O'Connor states, her burden was to show that the unlawful motive was a *substantial* factor in the adverse employment action. The District Court, as its opinion was construed by the Court of Appeals, so found, * * * and I agree that the finding was supported by the record. The burden of persuasion then should have shifted to Price Waterhouse to prove "by a preponderance of the evidence that it would have reached the same decision * * * in the absence of" the unlawful motive. * * *

I agree with Justice Brennan that applying this approach to causation in Title VII cases is not a departure from and does not require modification of the Court's holdings in * * * *Burdine* and *McDonnell Douglas* * * *. The Court has made clear that "mixed motive" cases, such as the present one, are different from pretext cases such as *McDonnell Douglas* and *Burdine*. In pretext cases, "the issue is whether either illegal or legal motives, but not both, were the 'true' motives behind the decision." * * * In mixed motive cases, however, there is no one "true" motive behind the decision. Instead, the decision is a result of multiple factors, at least one of which is legitimate. It can hardly be said that our decision in this case is a departure from cases that are "inapposite." I also disagree with the dissent's assertion that this approach to causation is inconsistent with our statement in *Burdine* that "[t]he ultimate burden of persuading the trier of fact that the defendant intentionally discriminated against the plaintiff remains at all times with the plaintiff." * * * As we indicated in *Transportation Management Corp.*, the showing required by *Mt. Healthy* does not improperly shift from the plaintiff the ultimate burden of persuasion on whether the defendant intentionally discriminated against him or her. * * *

Because the Court of Appeals required Price Waterhouse to prove by clear and convincing evidence that it would have reached the same employment decision in the absence of the improper motive, rather than merely requiring proof by a preponderance of the evidence as in *Mt. Healthy,* I concur in the judgment reversing this case in part and remanding. With respect to the employer's burden, however, the plurality seems to require, at least in most cases, that the employer submit objective evidence that the same result would have occurred absent the unlawful motivation. * * * In my view, however, there is no special requirement that the employer carry its burden by objective evidence. In a mixed motive case, where the legitimate motive found would have been ample grounds for the action taken, and the employer credibly testifies that the action would have been taken for the legitimate reasons alone, this should be ample proof. This would even more plainly be the case where the employer denies any illegitimate motive in the first place but the court finds that illegitimate, as well as legitimate, factors motivated the adverse action.**

JUSTICE O'CONNOR, concurring in the judgment.

I agree with the plurality that on the facts presented in this case, the burden of persuasion should shift to the employer to demonstrate by a preponderance of the evidence that it would have reached the same decision concerning Ann Hopkins' candidacy absent consideration of her gender. I further agree that this burden shift is properly part of the liability phase of the litigation. I thus concur in the judgment of

---

** I agree with the plurality that if the employer carries this burden, there has been no violation of Title VII.

the Court. My disagreement stems from the plurality's conclusions concerning the substantive requirement of causation under the statute and its broad statements regarding the applicability of the allocation of the burden of proof applied in this case. The evidentiary rule the Court adopts today should be viewed as a supplement to the careful framework established by our unanimous decisions in *McDonnell Douglas Corp.* * * * and *Burdine,* * * * for use in cases such as this one where the employer has created uncertainty as to causation by knowingly giving substantial weight to an impermissible criterion. I write separately to explain why I believe such a departure from the *McDonnell Douglas* standard is justified in the circumstances presented by this and like cases, and to express my views as to when and how the strong medicine of requiring the employer to bear the burden of persuasion on the issue of causation should be administered.

I

* * * The legislative history of Title VII bears out what its plain language suggests: a substantive violation of the statute only occurs when consideration of an illegitimate criterion is the "but-for" cause of an adverse employment action. The legislative history makes it clear that Congress was attempting to eradicate discriminatory actions in the employment setting, not mere discriminatory thoughts. Critics of the bill that became Title VII labeled it a "thought control bill," and argued that it created a "punishable crime that does not require an illegal external act as a basis for judgment." * * * Senator Case, whose views the plurality finds so persuasive elsewhere, responded:

> "The man must do or fail to do something in regard to employment. There must be some specific external act, more than a mental act. Only if he does the act because of the grounds stated in the bill would there be any legal consequences."

Thus, I disagree with the plurality's dictum that the words "because of" do not mean "but-for" causation; manifestly they do. * * * We should not, and need not, deviate from that policy today. The question for decision in this case is what allocation of the burden of persuasion on the issue of causation best conforms with the intent of Congress and the purposes behind Title VII.

* * *

Like the common law of torts, the statutory employment "tort" created by Title VII has two basic purposes. The first is to deter conduct which has been identified as contrary to public policy and harmful to society as a whole. As we have noted in the past, the award of backpay to a Title VII plaintiff provides "the spur or catalyst which causes employers and unions to self-examine and to self-evaluate their employment practices and to endeavor to eliminate, so far as possible, the last vestiges" of discrimination in employment. * * * The second goal of Title VII is "to make persons whole for injuries suffered on account of unlawful employment discrimination." * * *

Both these goals are reflected in the elements of a disparate treatment action. There is no doubt that Congress considered reliance on gender or race in making employment decisions an evil in itself. * * * Reliance on such factors is exactly what the threat of Title VII liability was meant to deter. While the main concern of the statute was with employment opportunity, Congress was certainly not blind to the stigmatic harm which comes from being evaluated by a process which treats one as an inferior by reason of one's race or sex. * * * At the same time, Congress clearly conditioned legal liability on a determination that the consideration of an illegitimate factor *caused* a tangible employment injury of some kind.

Where an individual disparate treatment plaintiff has shown by a preponderance of the evidence that an illegitimate criterion was a *substantial* factor in an adverse employment decision, the deterrent purpose of the statute has clearly been triggered. More importantly, as an evidentiary matter, a reasonable factfinder could conclude that absent further explanation, the employer's discriminatory motivation "caused" the employment decision. The employer has not yet been shown to be a violator, but neither is it entitled to the same presumption of good faith concerning its employment decisions which is accorded employers facing only circumstantial evidence of discrimination. Both the policies behind the statute, and the evidentiary principles developed in the analogous area of causation in the law of torts, suggest that at this point the employer may be required to convince the factfinder that, despite the smoke, there is no fire.

We have given recognition to these principles in our cases which have discussed the "remedial phase" of class action disparate treatment cases. Once the class has established that discrimination against a protected group was essentially the employer's "standard practice," there has been harm to the group and injunctive relief is appropriate. But as to the individual members of the class, the liability phase of the litigation is not complete. * * * Because the class has already demonstrated that, as a rule, illegitimate factors were considered in the employer's decisions, the burden shifts to the employer "to demonstrate that the individual applicant was denied an employment opportunity for legitimate reasons." *Teamsters v. United States,* * * *.

The individual members of a class action treatment case stand in much the same position as Ann Hopkins here. There has been a strong showing that the employer has done exactly what Title VII forbids, but the connection between the employer's illegitimate motivation and any injury to the individual plaintiff is unclear. At this point calling upon the employer to show that despite consideration of illegitimate factors the individual plaintiff would not have been hired or promoted in any event hardly seems "unfair" or contrary to the substantive command of the statute. In fact, an individual plaintiff who has shown that an illegitimate factor played a substantial role in the decision in her case has proved *more* than the class member in a *Teamsters* type action.

The latter receives the benefit of a burden shift to the defendant based on the *likelihood* that an illegitimate criterion was a factor in the individual employment decision.

* * *

II

The dissent's summary of our individual disparate treatment cases to date is fair and accurate, and amply demonstrates that the rule we adopt today is at least a change in direction from some of our prior precedents. * * * We have indeed emphasized in the past that in an individual disparate treatment action the plaintiff bears the burden of persuasion throughout the litigation. Nor have we confined the word "pretext" to the narrow definition which the plurality attempts to pin on it today. * * * *McDonnell Douglas* and *Burdine* clearly contemplated that a disparate treatment plaintiff could show that the employer's proffered explanation for an event was not "the true reason" either because it *never* motivated the employer in its employment decisions or because it did not do so in a particular case. *McDonnell Douglas* and *Burdine* assumed that the plaintiff would bear the burden of persuasion as to both these attacks, and we clearly depart from that framework today. Such a departure requires justification, and its outlines should be carefully drawn.

First, *McDonnell Douglas* itself dealt with a situation where the plaintiff presented no direct evidence that the employer had relied on a forbidden factor under Title VII in making an employment decision. The prima facie case established there was not difficult to prove, and was based only on the statistical probability that when a number of potential causes for an employment decision are eliminated an inference arises that an illegitimate factor was in fact the motivation behind the decision. * * * In the face of this inferential proof, the employer's burden was deemed to be only one of production; the employer must articulate a legitimate reason for the adverse employment action. * * * The plaintiff must then be given an "opportunity to demonstrate by competent evidence that the presumptively valid reasons for his rejection were in fact a coverup for a racially discriminatory decision." * * * As the discussion of *Teamsters* and *Arlington Heights* indicates, I do not think that the employer is entitled to the same presumption of good faith where there is direct evidence that it has placed substantial reliance on factors whose consideration is forbidden by Title VII.

The only individual treatment case cited by the dissent which involved the kind of direct evidence of discriminatory animus with which we are confronted here is *United States Postal Service Bd. of Governors v. Aikens,* 460 U.S. 711, 713–714, n. 2, 103 S.Ct. 1478, 1481, n. 2, 75 L.Ed.2d 403 (1983). The question presented to the Court in that case involved only a challenge to the elements of the prima facie case under *McDonnell Douglas* and *Burdine,* see Pet. for Cert. in *United States Postal Service Bd. of Governors v. Aiken,* O.T.1981, No. 1044, and the question we confront today was neither briefed nor argued to the Court. As should be apparent, the entire purpose of the *McDonnell Douglas* prima facie case is to compensate for the fact that direct evidence of intentional discrimination is hard to come by. That the employer's burden in rebutting such an inferential case of discrimination is only one of production does not mean that the scales should be weighted in the same manner where there *is* direct evidence of intentional discrimination. * * *

Second, the facts of this case, and a growing number like it decided by the Courts of Appeals, convince me that the evidentiary standard I propose is necessary to make real the promise of *McDonnell Douglas* that "[i]n the implementation of [employment] decisions, it is abundantly clear that Title VII tolerates no * * * discrimination, subtle or otherwise." * * * In this case, the District Court found that a number of the evaluations of Ann Hopkins submitted by partners in the firm overtly referred to her failure to conform to certain gender stereotypes as a factor militating against her election to the partnership. * * * The District Court further found that these evaluations were given "great weight" by the decisionmakers at Price Waterhouse. * * * In addition, the District Court found that the partner responsible for informing Hopkins of the factors which caused her candidacy to be placed on hold, indicated that her "professional" problems would be solved if she would "walk more femininely, talk more femininely, wear make-up, have her hair styled, and wear jewelry." * * * As the Court of Appeals characterized it, Ann Hopkins proved that Price Waterhouse "permitt[ed] stereotypical attitudes towards women to play a significant, though unquantifiable, role in its decision not to invite her to become a partner." * * *

At this point Ann Hopkins had taken her proof as far as it could go. She had proved discriminatory input into the decisional process, and had proved that participants in the process considered her failure to conform to the stereotypes credited by a number of the decisionmakers had been a substantial factor in the decision. It is as if Ann Hopkins were sitting in the hall outside the room where partnership decisions were being made. As the partners filed in to consider her candidacy, she heard several of them make sexist remarks in discussing her suitability for partnership. As the decisionmakers exited the room, she was *told* by one of those privy to the decisionmaking process that her gender was a major reason for the rejection of her partnership bid. If, as we noted in *Teamsters,* "[p]resumptions shifting the burden of proof are often created to reflect judicial evaluations of probabilities and to conform with a party's superior access to the proof," * * * one would be hard pressed to think of a situation where it would be more appropriate to require the defendant to show that its decision would have been justified by wholly legitimate concerns.

Moreover, there is mounting evidence in the decisions of the lower courts that respondent here is not alone in her inability to pinpoint discrimination as the precise cause of her injury, despite having shown that it played a significant role in the decisional process. Many of these courts, which deal with the evidentiary issues in Title VII cases on a regular basis, have concluded that placing the risk of nonpersuasion on the defendant in a situation where uncertainty as to causation has been created by its consideration of an illegitimate criterion makes sense as a rule of evidence and furthers the substantive command of Title VII. * * * Particularly in the context of the professional world, where decisions are often made by collegial bodies on the basis of largely subjective criteria, requiring the plaintiff to prove that *any* one factor was the definitive cause of the decisionmakers' action may be tantamount to declaring Title VII inapplicable to such decisions. See, *e.g., Fields v. Clark University,* 817 F.2d 931, 935–937 (CA1 1987) (where plaintiff produced "strong evidence" that sexist attitudes infected faculty tenure decision burden properly shifted to defendant to show that it would have reached the same decision absent discrimination); *Thompkins v. Morris Brown College,* 752 F.2d 558, 563 (CA11 1985) (direct evidence of discriminatory animus in decision to discharge college professor shifted burden of persuasion to defendant).

Finally, I am convinced that a rule shifting the burden to the defendant where the plaintiff has shown that an illegitimate criterion was a "substantial factor" in the employment decision will not conflict with other congressional policies embodied in Title VII. Title VII expressly provides that an employer need not give preferential treatment to employees or applicants of any race, color, religion, sex, or national origin in order to maintain a work force in balance with the general population. * * * The interpretive memorandum, whose authoritative force is noted by the plurality, * * * specifically provides: "There is no requirement in title VII that an employer maintain a racial balance in his work force. On the contrary, any deliberate attempt to maintain a racial balance, whatever such a balance may be, would involve a violation of title VII because maintaining such a balance would require an employer to hire or refuse to hire on the basis of race." * * *

Last Term, in *Watson* * * * the Court unanimously concluded that the disparate impact analysis first enunciated in *Griggs* * * * should be extended to subjective or discretionary selection processes. At the same time a plurality of the Court indicated concern that the focus on bare statistics in the disparate impact setting could force employers to adopt "inappropriate prophylactic measures" in violation of § 2000e–2(j). The plurality went on to emphasize that in a disparate impact case, the plaintiff may not simply point to a statistical disparity in the employer's work force. Instead, the plaintiff must identify a particular employment practice and "must offer statistical evidence of a kind and degree sufficient to show that the practice in question has caused the exclusion of applicants for jobs or promotions because of their membership in a protected group." * * * The plurality indicated that "the ultimate burden of proving that discrimination against a protected group has been caused by a specific employment practice remains with the plaintiff at all times." * * *

I believe there are significant differences between shifting the burden of persuasion to the employer in a case resting purely on statistical proof as in the disparate impact setting and shifting the burden of persuasion in a case like this one, where an employee has demonstrated by direct evidence that an illegitimate factor played a substantial role in a particular employment decision. First, the explicit consideration of race, color, religion, sex, or national origin in making employment decisions "was the most obvious evil Congress had in mind when it enacted Title VII." *Teamsters,* * * *. While the prima facie case under *McDonnell Douglas* and the statistical showing of imbalance involved in an impact case may both be indicators of discrimination or its "functional equivalent," they are not, in and of themselves, the evils Congress sought to eradicate from the employment setting. Second, shifting the burden of persuasion to the employer in a situation like this one creates no incentive to preferential treatment in violation of § 2000e–2(j). To avoid bearing the burden of justifying its decision, the employer need not seek racial or sexual balance in its work force; rather, all it need do is avoid substantial reliance on forbidden criteria in making its employment decisions.

While the danger of forcing employers to engage in unwarranted preferential treatment is thus less dramatic in this setting than in the situation the Court faced in *Watson,* it is far from wholly illusory. Based on its misreading of the words "because of" in the statute, * * * the plurality appears to conclude that if a decisional process is "tainted" by awareness of sex or race in any way, the employer has violated the statute, and Title VII thus *commands* that the burden shift to the employer to justify its decision. * * * The plurality thus effectively reads the causation requirement out of the statute, and then replaces it with an "affirmative defense." * * *

In my view, in order to justify shifting the burden on the issue of causation to the defendant, a disparate treatment plaintiff must show by direct evidence that an illegitimate criterion was a substantial factor in the decision. * * * Requiring that the plaintiff demonstrate that an illegitimate factor played a substantial role in the employment decision identifies those employment situations where the deterrent purpose of Title VII is most clearly implicated. As an evidentiary matter, where a plaintiff has made this type of strong showing of illicit motivation, the factfinder is entitled to presume that the employer's discriminatory animus made a difference to the outcome, absent proof to the contrary from the employer. Where a disparate treatment plaintiff has made such a showing, the burden then rests with the employer to convince the trier of fact that it is more likely than not that the decision would have been the same absent consideration of the illegitimate factor. The employer need not isolate the sole cause for the decision, rather it must demonstrate that with the illegitimate factor removed from the calculus, sufficient business reasons would have induced it to take the same employment action. This evidentiary scheme essentially requires the employer to place the employee in the same position he or she would have occupied absent discrimination. Cf. *Mt. Healthy* * * *. If the employer fails to carry this burden, the factfinder is justified in concluding that the decision was made "because of" consideration of the illegitimate factor and the substantive standard for liability under the statute is satisfied.

Thus, stray remarks in the workplace, while perhaps probative of sexual harassment, see *Meritor Savings Bank v. Vinson,* * * * cannot justify requiring the employer to prove that its hiring or promotion decisions were based on legitimate criteria. Nor can statements by nondecisionmakers, or statements by decisionmakers unrelated to the decisional process itself suffice to satisfy the plaintiff's burden in this regard. In addition, in my view testimony such as Dr. Fiske's in this case, standing alone, would not justify shifting the burden of persuasion to the employer. Race and gender always "play a role" in an employment decision in the benign sense that these are human characteristics of which decisionmakers are aware and may comment on in a perfectly neutral and nondiscriminatory fashion. For example, in the context of this case, a mere reference to "a lady candidate" might show that gender "played a role" in the decision, but by no means could support a rational factfinder's inference that the decision was made "because of" sex. What is required is what Ann Hopkins showed here: direct evidence that decisionmakers placed substantial negative reliance on an illegitimate criterion in reaching their decision.

It should be obvious that the threshold standard I would adopt for shifting the burden of persuasion to the defendant differs substantially from that proposed by the plurality, the plurality's suggestion to the contrary notwithstanding. See *ante,* at * * * n. 13. The plurality proceeds from the premise that the words "because of" in the statute do not embody any causal requirement at all. Under my approach, the plaintiff must produce evidence sufficient to show that an illegitimate criterion was a substantial factor in the particular employment decision such that a reasonable factfinder could draw an inference that the decision was made "because of" the plaintiff's protected status. Only then would the burden of proof shift to the defendant to prove that the decision would have been justified by other, wholly legitimate considerations. See also *ante,* * * * (WHITE, J., concurring in judgment).

In sum, because of the concerns outlined above, and because I believe that the deterrent purpose of Title VII is disserved by a rule which places the burden of proof on plaintiffs on the issue of causation in all circumstances, I would retain but supplement the framework we established in *McDonnell Douglas* and subsequent cases. The structure of the presentation of evidence in an individual treatment case should conform to the general outlines we established in *McDonnell Douglas* and *Burdine.* First, the plaintiff must establish the *McDonnell Douglas* prima facie case by showing membership in a protected group, qualification for the job, rejection for the position, and that after rejection the employer continued to seek applicants of complainant's general qualifications. * * * The plaintiff should also present any direct evidence of discriminatory animus in the decisional process. The defendant should then present its case, including its evidence as to legitimate, nondiscriminatory reasons for the employment decision. As the dissent notes, under this framework, the employer "has every incentive to convince the trier of fact that the decision was lawful." * * * Once all the evidence has been received, the court should determine whether the *McDonnell Douglas* or *Price Waterhouse* framework properly applies to the evidence before it. If the plaintiff has failed to satisfy the *Price Waterhouse* threshold, the case should be decided under the principles enunciated in *McDonnell Douglas* and *Burdine,* with the plaintiff bearing the burden of persuasion on the ultimate issue whether the employment action was taken because of discrimination. In my view, such a system is both fair and workable and it calibrates the evidentiary requirements demanded of the parties to the goals behind the statute itself.

I agree with the dissent, see *post,* at * * * n. 4, that the evidentiary framework I propose should be available to all disparate treatment plaintiffs where an illegitimate consideration played a substantial role in an adverse employment decision. The Court's allocation of the burden of proof in *Johnson v. Transportation Agency,* * * * rested squarely on "the analytical framework set forth in *McDonnell Douglas,*" * * * which we alter today. It would be odd to say the least if the evidentiary rules applicable to Title VII actions were themselves dependent on the gender or the skin color of the litigants.

In this case, I agree with the plurality that petitioner should be called upon to show that the outcome would have been the same if respondent's professional merit had been its only concern. On remand, the District Court should determine whether Price Waterhouse has shown by a preponderance of the evidence that if gender had not been part of the process, its employment decision concerning Ann Hopkins would nonetheless have been the same.

JUSTICE KENNEDY, with whom the CHIEF JUSTICE and JUSTICE SCALIA join, dissenting.

Today the Court manipulates existing and complex rules for employment discrimination cases in a way certain to result in confusion. Continued adherence to the evidentiary scheme established in *McDonnell Douglas* and *Burdine* is a wiser course than creation of more disarray in an area of the law already difficult for the bench and bar, and so I must dissent.

* * *

I

The plurality describes this as a case about the standard of *causation* under Title VII, but I respectfully suggest that the description is misleading. Much of the plurality's rhetoric is spent denouncing a "but-for" standard of causation. The theory of Title VII liability the plurality adopts, however, essentially incorporates the but-for standard. The importance of today's decision is not the standard of causation it employs, but its shift to the defendant of the burden of proof. The plurality's causation analysis is misdirected, for it is clear that, whoever bears the burden of proof on the issue, Title VII liability requires a finding of but-for causation. See also *ante,* * * * (opinion of O'Connor, J.); *ante,* * * * (opinion of White, J.).

* * *

By any normal understanding, the phrase "because of" conveys the idea that the motive in question made a difference to the outcome. We use the words this way in everyday speech. * * * Congress could not have chosen a clearer way to indicate that proof of liability under Title VII requires a showing that race, color, religion, sex, or national origin caused the decision at issue.

* * *

What we term "but-for" cause is the least rigorous standard that is consistent with the approach to causation our precedents describe. If a motive is not a but-for cause of an event, then by definition it did not make a difference to the outcome. The event would have occurred just the same without it. Common law approaches to causation often require proof of but-for cause as a starting point toward proof of legal cause. The law may require more than but-for cause, for instance proximate cause, before imposing liability. Any standard less than but-for, however, simply represents a decision to impose liability without causation. As Dean Prosser puts it, "[a]n act or omission is not regarded as a cause of an event if the particular event would have occurred without it." W. Keeton, D. Dobbs, R. Keeton, & D. Owen, Prosser and Keeton on Law of Torts 265 (5th ed. 1984).

One of the principal reasons the plurality decision may sow confusion is that it claims Title VII liability is unrelated to but-for causation, yet it adopts a but-for standard once it has placed the burden of proof as to causation upon the employer. This approach conflates the question whether causation must be shown with the question of how it is to be shown. Because the plurality's theory of Title VII causation is ultimately consistent with a but-for standard, it might be said that my disagreement with the plurality's comments on but-for cause is simply academic. See *ante,* * * * (opinion of White, J.). But since those comments seem to influence the decision, I turn now to that part of the plurality's analysis.

The plurality begins by noting the quite unremarkable fact that Title VII is written in the present tense. * * * This observation, however, tells us nothing of particular relevance to Title VII or the cause of action it creates. I am unaware of any federal prohibitory statute that is written in the past tense. Every liability determination, including the novel one constructed by the plurality, necessarily is concerned with the examination of a past event.[1] The plurality's analysis of verb tense serves only to divert attention from the causation requirement that is made part of the statute by the "because of" phrase. That phrase, I respectfully submit, embodies a rather simple concept that the plurality labors to ignore.[2]

We are told next that but-for cause is not required, since the words "because of" do not mean "*solely* because of." * * * No one contends, however, that sex must be the sole cause of a decision before there is a Title VII violation. This is a separate question from whether consideration of sex must be *a* cause of the decision. Under the accepted approach to causation that I have discussed, sex is a cause for the employment decision whenever, either by itself or in combination with other factors, it made a difference to the decision. Discrimination need not be the sole cause in order for liability to arise, but merely a necessary element of the set of factors that caused the decision, *i.e.*, a but-for cause. * * * The plurality seems to say that since we know the words "because of" do not mean "solely because of," they must not mean "because of" at all. This does not follow, as a matter of either semantics or logic.

The plurality's reliance on the "bona fide occupational qualification" (BFOQ) provisions of Title VII, is particularly inapt. The BFOQ provisions allow an employer, in certain cases, to make an employment decision of which it is conceded that sex is the cause. That sex may be the legitimate cause of an employment decision where gender is a BFOQ is consistent with the opposite command that a decision caused by sex in any other case justifies the imposition of Title VII liability. This principle does not support, however, the novel assertion that a violation has occurred where sex made no difference to the outcome.

The most confusing aspect of the plurality's analysis of causation and liability is its internal inconsistency. The plurality begins by saying: "When * * * an employer considers both gender and legitimate factors at the time of making a decision, that decision was 'because of' sex and the other, legitimate considerations—even if we

---

1. The plurality's description of its own standard is both hypothetical and retrospective. The inquiry seeks to determine whether "if we asked the employer at the moment of decision what its reasons were and if we received a truthful response, one of those reasons would be that the applicant or employee was a woman."

2. The plurality's discussion of overdetermined causes only highlights the error of its insistence that but-for is not the substantive standard of causation under Title VII. The opinion discusses the situation where two physical forces move an object, and either force acting alone would have moved the object. Translated to the context of Title VII, this situation would arise where an employer took an adverse action in reliance both on sex and on legitimate reasons, and *either* the illegitimate or the legitimate reason standing alone would have produced the action. If this state of affairs is proved to the factfinder, there will be no liability under the plurality's own test, for the same decision would have been made had the illegitimate reason never been considered.

may say later, in the context of litigation, that the decision would have been the same if gender had not been taken into account." Yet it goes on to state that "an employer shall not be liable if it can prove that, even if it had not taken gender into account, it would have come to the same decision."

Given the language of the statute, these statements cannot both be true. Title VII unambiguously states that an employer who makes decisions "because of" sex has violated the statute. The plurality's first statement therefore appears to indicate that an employer who considers illegitimate reasons when making a decision is a violator. But the opinion then tells us that the employer who shows that the same decision would have been made absent consideration of sex is *not* a violator. If the second statement is to be reconciled with the language of Title VII, it must be that a decision that would have been the same absent consideration of sex was not made "because of" sex. In other words, there is no violation of the statute absent but-for causation. The plurality's description of the "same decision" test it adopts supports this view. The opinion states that "[a] court that finds for a plaintiff under this standard has effectively concluded that an illegitimate motive was a 'but-for' cause of the employment decision," * * * and that this "is not an imposition of liability 'where sex made no difference to the outcome,' * * *."

The plurality attempts to reconcile its internal inconsistency on the causation issue by describing the employer's showing as an "affirmative defense." This is nothing more than a label, and one not found in the language or legislative history of Title VII. Section 703(a)(1) is the statutory basis of the cause of action, and the Court is obligated to explain how its disparate treatment decisions are consistent with the terms of § 703(a)(1), not with general themes of legislative history or with other parts of the statute that are plainly inapposite. While the test ultimately adopted by the plurality may not be inconsistent with the terms of § 703(a)(1), * * * the same cannot be said of the plurality's reasoning with respect to causation. As Justice O'Connor describes it, the plurality "reads the causation requirement out of the statute, and then replaces it with an 'affirmative defense.'" * * * Labels aside, the import of today's decision is not that Title VII liability can arise without but-for causation, but that in certain cases it is not the plaintiff who must prove the presence of causation, but the defendant who must prove its absence.

II

We established the order of proof for individual Title VII disparate treatment cases in *McDonnell Douglas* * * * and reaffirmed this allocation in * * * *Burdine.* * * * I would adhere to this established evidentiary framework, which provides the appropriate standard for this and other individual disparate treatment cases. Today's creation of a new set of rules for "mixed-motive" cases is not mandated by the statute itself. The Court's attempt at refinement provides limited practical benefits at the cost of confusion and complexity, with the attendent risk that the trier of fact will misapprehend the controlling legal principles and reach an incorrect decision.

* * *

Our opinions make plain that *Burdine* applies to all individual disparate treatment cases, whether the plaintiff offers direct proof that discrimination motivated the employer's actions or chooses the indirect method of showing that the employer's proffered justification is false, that is to say, a pretext. * * * The plurality is mistaken in suggesting that the plaintiff in a so-called "mixed motives" case will be disadvantaged by having to "squeeze her proof into *Burdine's* framework." * * * *Burdine* compels the employer to come forward with its explanation of the decision and permits the plaintiff to offer evidence under either of the logical methods for proof of discrimination. This is hardly a framework that confines the plaintiff; still less is it a justification for saying that the ultimate burden of proof must be on the employer in a mixed motives case. *Burdine* provides an orderly and adequate way to place both inferential and direct proof before the factfinder for a determination whether intentional discrimination has caused the employment decision. Regardless of the character of the evidence presented, we have consistently held that the ultimate burden "remains at all times with the plaintiff." * * *

Aikens illustrates the point. There, the evidence showed that the plaintiff, a black man, was far more qualified than any of the white applicants promoted ahead of him. More important, the testimony showed that "the person responsible for the promotion decisions at issue had made numerous derogatory comments about blacks in general and Aikens in particular." 460 U.S., at 713–714, n. 2, 103 S.Ct., at 1481, n. 2. Yet the Court in *Aikens* reiterated that the case was to be tried under the proof scheme of *Burdine*. JUSTICE BRENNAN and JUSTICE BLACKMUN concurred to stress that the plaintiff could prevail under the *Burdine* scheme in either of two ways, one of which was directly to persuade the court that the employment decision was motivated by discrimination. * * * *Aikens* leaves no doubt that the so-called "pretext" framework of *Burdine* has been considered to provide a flexible means of addressing all individual disparate treatment claims.

Downplaying the novelty of its opinion, the plurality claims to have followed a "well-worn path" from our prior cases. The path may be well-worn, but it is in the wrong forest. The plurality again relies on Title VII's BFOQ provisions, under which an employer bears the burden of justifying the use of a sex-based employment qualification. See *Dothard v. Rawlinson,* * * *. In the BFOQ context this is a sensible, indeed necessary, allocation of the burden, for there by definition sex is the but-for cause of the employment decision and the only question remaining is how the employer can justify it. * * *

Closer analogies to the plurality's new approach are found in *Mt. Healthy Board of Education* * * * and *NRLB v. Transportation*

Management Corp., * * * but these cases were decided in different contexts. *Mt. Healthy* was a First Amendment case involving the firing of a teacher, and *Transportation Management* involved review of the NLRB's interpretation of the National Labor Relations Act. The *Transportation Management* decision was based on the deference that the Court traditionally accords NLRB interpretations of the statutes it administers. Neither case therefore tells us why the established *Burdine* framework should not continue to govern the order of proof under Title VII.

In contrast to the plurality, Justice O'Connor acknowledges that the approach adopted today is a "departure from the *McDonnell Douglas* standard." * * * Although her reasons for supporting this departure are not without force, they are not dispositive. As Justice O'Connor states, the most that can be said with respect to the Title VII itself is that "nothing in the language, history, or purpose of Title VII *prohibits* adoption" of the new approach. * * * Justice O'Connor also relies on analogies from the common law of torts, other types of Title VII litigation, and our equal protection cases. These analogies demonstrate that shifts in the burden of proof are not unprecedented in the law of torts or employment discrimination. Nonetheless, I believe continued adherence to the *Burdine* framework is more consistent with the statutory mandate. Congress' manifest concern with preventing imposition of liability in cases where discriminatory animus did not actually cause an adverse action, see *ante,* * * * (opinion of O'Connor, J.), suggests to me that an affirmative showing of causation should be required. And the most relevant portion of the legislative history supports just this view. * * * The limited benefits that are likely to be produced by today's innovation come at the sacrifice of clarity and practical application.

The potential benefits of the new approach, in my view, are overstated. First, the Court makes clear that the *Price Waterhouse* scheme is applicable only in those cases where the plaintiff has produced direct and substantial proof that an impermissible motive was relied upon in making the decision at issue. The burden shift properly will be found to apply in only a limited number of employment discrimination cases. The application of the new scheme, furthermore, will make a difference only in a smaller subset of cases. The practical importance of the burden of proof is the "risk of nonpersuasion," and the new system will make a difference only where the evidence is so evenly balanced that the factfinder cannot say that either side's explanation of the case is "more likely" true. This category will not include cases in which the allocation of the burden of proof will be dispositive because of a complete lack of evidence on the causation issue, cf. *Summers v. Tice,* 33 Cal.2d 80, 199 P.2d 1 (1948) (allocation of burden dispositive because no evidence of which of two negligently fired shots hit plaintiff). Rather, *Price Waterhouse* will apply only to cases in which there is substantial evidence of reliance on an impermissible motive, as well as evidence from the employer that legitimate reasons supported its action.

Although the *Price Waterhouse* system is not for every case, almost every plaintiff is certain to ask for a *Price Waterhouse* instruction, perhaps on the basis of "stray remarks" or other evidence of discriminatory animus. Trial and appellate courts will therefore be saddled with the task of developing standards for determining when to apply the burden shift. One of their new tasks will be the generation of a jurisprudence of the meaning of "substantial factor." Courts will also be required to make the often subtle and difficult distinction between "direct" and "indirect" or "circumstantial" evidence. Lower courts long have had difficulty applying *McDonnell Douglas* and *Burdine*. Addition of a second burden-shifting mechanism, the application of which itself depends on assessment of credibility and a determination whether evidence is sufficiently direct and substantial, is not likely to lend clarity to the process. The presence of an existing burden-shifting mechanism distinguishes the individual disparate treatment case from the tort, class action discrimination, and equal protection cases on which Justice O'Connor relies. The distinction makes Justice White's assertions that one "need look only to" *Mt. Healthy* and *Transportation Management* to resolve this case, and that our Title VII cases in this area are "inapposite," * * * at best hard to understand.

* * *

I do not believe the minor refinement in Title VII procedures accomplished by today's holding can justify the difficulties that will accompany it. Rather, I "remain confident that the *McDonnell Douglas* framework permits the plaintiff meriting relief to demonstrate intertional discrimination." * * * Although the employer does not bear the burden of persuasion under *Burdine*, it must offer clear and reasonably specific reasons for the contested decision, and has every incentive to persuade the trier of fact that the decision was lawful. * * * Further, the suggestion that the employer should bear the burden of persuasion due to superior access to evidence has little force in the Title VII context, where the liberal discovery rules available to all litigants are supplemented by EEOC investigatory files. * * * In sum, the *Burdine* framework provides a "sensible, orderly way to evaluate the evidence in light of common experience as it bears on the critical question of discrimination," * * * and it should continue to govern the order of proof in Title VII disparate treatment cases.[4]

4. The plurality states that it disregards the special context of affirmative action. It is not clear that this is possible. Some courts have held that in a suit challenging an affirmative action plan, the question of the plan's validity need not be reached unless the plaintiff shows that the plan was a but-for cause of the adverse decision. See *McQuillen v. Wisconsin Education Association Council*, 830 F.2d 659, 665 (CA7 1987), cert. denied, 485 U.S. 914, 108 S.Ct. 1068, 99 L.Ed.2d 248 (1988). Presumably it will be easier for a plaintiff to show that consideration of race or sex pursuant to an affirmative action plan was a substantial factor in a decision, and the court will need to move on to the question of a plan's validity. Moreover, if the structure of the burdens of proof in Title VII suits is to be consistent, as might be expected given the identical statutory language involved, today's decision suggests

III

The ultimate question in every individual disparate treatment case is whether discrimination caused the particular decision at issue. Some of the plurality's comments with respect to the District Court's findings in this case, however, are potentially misleading. As the plurality notes, the District Court based its liability determination on expert evidence that some evaluations of respondent Hopkins were based on unconscious sex stereotypes,[5] and on the fact that Price Waterhouse failed to disclaim reliance on these comments when it conducted the partnership review. The District Court also based liability on Price Waterhouse's failure to "make partners sensitive to the dangers [of stereotyping], to discourage comments tainted by sexism, or to investigate comments to determine whether they were influenced by stereotypes." * * *

Although the District Court's version of Title VII liability is improper under any of today's opinions, I think it important to stress that Title VII creates no independent cause of action for sex stereotyping. Evidence of use by decisionmakers of sex stereotypes is, of course, quite relevant to the question of discriminatory intent. The ultimate question, however, is whether discrimination caused the plaintiff's harm. Our cases do not support the suggestion that failure to "disclaim reliance" on stereotypical comments itself violates Title VII. Neither do they support creation of a "duty to sensitize." As the dissenting judge in the Court of Appeals observed, acceptance of such theories would turn Title VII "from a prohibition of discriminatory conduct into an engine for rooting out sexist thoughts." * * *

Employment discrimination claims require factfinders to make difficult and sensitive decisions. Sometimes this may mean that no finding of discrimination is justified even though a qualified employee is passed over by a less than admirable employer. In other cases, Title VII's protections properly extend to plaintiffs who are by no means model employees. As Justice Brennan notes, * * * courts do not sit to determine whether litigants are nice. In this case, Hopkins plainly

---

that plaintiffs should no longer bear the burden of showing that affirmative action plans are illegal. See *Johnson v. Transportation Agency,* 480 U.S. 616, 626–627, 107 S.Ct. 1442, 1449, 94 L.Ed.2d 615 (1987).

5. The plaintiff who engages the services of Dr. Susan Fiske should have no trouble showing that sex discrimination played a part in any decision. Price Waterhouse chose not to object to Fiske's testimony, and at this late stage we are constrained to accept it, but I think the plurality's enthusiasm for Fiske's conclusions unwarranted. Fiske purported to discern stereotyping in comments that were gender neutral—*e.g.,* "overbearing and abrasive"—without any knowledge of the comments' basis in reality and without having met the speaker or subject. "To an expert of Dr. Fiske's qualifications, it seems plain that no woman could *be* overbearing, arrogant, or abrasive: any observations to that effect would necessarily be discounted as the product of stereotyping. If analysis like this is to prevail in federal courts, no employer can base any adverse action as to a woman on such attributes." 263 U.S.App.D.C. 321, 825 F.2d 458, 477 (1987) (Williams, J., dissenting). Today's opinions cannot be read as requiring factfinders to credit testimony based on this type of analysis. See also *ante,* * * * (opinion of O'Connor, J.).

presented a strong case both of her own professional qualifications and of the presence of discrimination in Price Waterhouse's partnership process. Had the District Court found on this record that sex discrimination caused the adverse decision, I doubt it would have been reversible error. Cf. *Aikens,* 460 U.S., at 714, n. 2, 103 S.Ct., at 1481, n. 2. That decision was for the finder of fact, however, and the District Court made plain that sex discrimination was not a but-for cause of the decision to place Hopkin's partnership candidacy on hold. Attempts to evade tough decisions by erecting novel theories of liability or multitiered systems of shifting burdens are misguided.

IV

The language of Title VII and our well-considered precedents require this plaintiff to establish that the decision to place her candidacy on hold was made "because of" sex. Here the District Court found that the "comments of the individual partners and the expert evidence of Dr. Fiske do not prove an intentional discriminatory motive or purpose," * * * and that "[b]ecause plaintiff has considerable problems dealing with staff and peers, the Court cannot say that she would have been elected to partnership if the Policy Board's decision had not been tainted by sexually based evaluations," * * *. Hopkins thus failed to meet the requisite standard of proof after a full trial. I would remand the case for entry of judgment in favor of Price Waterhouse.

Notes on Hopkins

1. What, exactly, distinguishes a "mixed motive" case from a disparate treatment case? Compare the views of the plurality and Justice O'Connor on this point. Why does Justice Kennedy resist the recognition of a category of mixed motive cases under Title VII?

2. What impact, if any, did the Court's subsequent decision in *Wards Cove,* set out supra at p. 114, have on *Hopkins?* Is *Hopkins* the only example of a Title VII case in which the employer bears the ultimate burden of persuasion on liability? What support does Justice Kennedy draw from *Aikens,* set out in the Casebook at p. 635? Does Justice O'Connor successfully rebut the use of *Aikens?*

3. Does the Court adopt the view that sex stereotyping *per se* constitutes a violation of Title VII? If not, what weight do the individual Justices give to that concept? Do you agree with Justice O'Connor that a "mere reference" to Ann Hopkins as "a lady candidate" is insufficient to support a finding that the decision not to make her a partner was made "because of sex"? Would the Price Waterhouse partners have spoken of a "male candidate"? See generally, Radford, Sex Stereotyping and the Promotion of Women to Positions of Power, 41 Hastings L.J. 471 (1990).

4. Price Waterhouse's success in obtaining a lower standard of proof did not secure ultimate victory for its cause. On remand, Judge Gesell announced that he was not persuaded that non-discriminatory factors alone justified the hold decision:

Although the Supreme Court's decision lowered the standard of proof, it did not shift the burden of proof. Price Waterhouse, having permitted discriminatory comments to be weighed in the hold decision when appraising Ms. Hopkins, was required to separate the good from the bad. As Justice Brennan's plurality opinion states, where the proof shows that the employer acted with an illegitimate motive, " '[i]t is fair that he bear the risk that the inference of illegal and legal motives cannot be separated, because he knowingly created the risk and because the risk was created not by innocent activity but by his own wrongdoing.' " * * * Price Waterhouse had the burden to prove something; it had to persuade the Court. This it has failed to do.

Hopkins v. Price Waterhouse, ___ F.Supp. ___, ___ (D.D.C.1990) (Slip opinion at 8.) In addition to back pay, Judge Gesell ordered Price Waterhouse to admit Ann Hopkins to partnership, effective July 1, 1990. This aspect of the case is discussed infra, at p. 206.

Page 681. Delete Note 6, and add *University of Pennsylvania v. EEOC*:

UNIVERSITY OF PENNSYLVANIA v. E.E.O.C.

Supreme Court of the United States, 1990.
493 U.S. ___, 110 S.Ct. 577, 107 L.Ed.2d 571.

JUSTICE BLACKMUN delivered the opinion of the Court.

In this case we are asked to decide whether a university enjoys a special privilege, grounded in either the common law or the First Amendment, against disclosure of peer review materials that are relevant to charges of racial or sexual discrimination in tenure decisions.

I

The University of Pennsylvania, petitioner here, is a private institution. It currently operates 12 schools, including the Wharton School of Business, which collectively enroll approximately 18,000 full-time students.

In 1985, the University denied tenure to Rosalie Tung, an associate professor on the Wharton faculty. Tung then filed a sworn charge of discrimination with respondent Equal Employment Opportunity Commission (EEOC or Commission). * * * As subsequently amended, the charge alleged that Tung was the victim of discrimination on the basis of race, sex, and national origin, in violation of § 703(a) of Title VII * * *.

In her charge, Tung stated that the Department Chairman had sexually harassed her and that, in her belief, after she insisted that their relationship remain professional, he had submitted a negative letter to the University's Personnel Committee which possessed ultimate responsibility for tenure decisions. She also alleged that her qualifications were "equal to or better than" those of five named male faculty members who had received more favorable treatment. Tung noted that the majority of the members of her Department had recommended her for tenure, and stated that she had been given no reason for the decision against her, but had discovered of her own efforts that the Personnel Committee had attempted to justify its decision "on the ground that the Wharton School is not interested in China-related research." * * * This explanation, Tung's charge alleged, was a pretext for discrimination: "simply their way of saying they do not want a Chinese–American, Oriental, woman in their school." * * *

The Commission undertook an investigation into Tung's charge, and requested a variety of relevant information from petitioner. When the University refused to provide certain of that information, the Commission's Acting District Director issued a subpoena seeking, among other things, Tung's tenure-review file and the tenure files of the five male faculty members identified in the charge. * * * Petitioner refused to produce a number of the tenure-file documents. It applied to the Commission for modification of the subpoena to exclude what it termed "confidential peer review information," specifically, (1) confidential letters written by Tung's evaluators; (2) the Department Chairman's letter of evaluation; (3) documents reflecting the internal deliberations of faculty committees considering applications for tenure, including the Department Evaluation Report summarizing the deliberations relating to Tung's application for tenure; and (4) comparable portions of the tenure-review files of the five males. The University urged the Commission to "adopt a balancing approach reflecting the constitutional and societal interest inherent in the peer review process" and to resort to "all feasible methods to minimize the intrusive effects of its investigations." * * *

The Commission denied the University's application. It concluded that the withheld documents were needed in order to determine the merit of Tung's charges. The Commission found: "There has not been enough data supplied in order for the Commission to determine whether there is reasonable cause to believe that the allegations of sex, race and national origin discrimination is true." * * * The Commission rejected petitioner's contention that a letter, which set forth the Personnel Committee's reasons for denying Tung tenure, was sufficient for disposition of the charge. "The Commission would fall short of its obligation" to investigate charges of discrimination, the EEOC's order stated, "if it stopped its investigation once [the employer] has * * * provided the reasons for its employment decisions, without verifying whether that reason is a pretext for discrimination." * * * The Commission also rejected petitioner's proposed balancing test, explaining that "such an approach in the instant case * * * would impair the Commission's ability to fully investigate this charge of discrimination." * * * The Commission indicated that enforcement proceedings might be necessary if a response was not forthcoming within 20 days. * * *

The University continued to withhold the tenure-review materials. The Commission then applied to the United States District Court for

ACT OF 1964   197

[sticky note:]
Ch 3 pp 642-650 ✓
Supp 162-205, 694-720
esp: Anderson p 642 ✓
Price Waterhouse v. Hopkins ✓
   Supp p 162
Univ PA v EEOC Supp p 195
Yellow Freight (Xerox)
Gunther p 694
Amer. Nurses p 704
Topics: Std of Review, Title VII,
upper level jobs, Procedural issues,
wage discrimination

...a for enforcement of its subpoena.
...ent order. * * *

...hird Circuit affirmed the enforce-
...² Relying upon its earlier opinion
...College, 775 F.2d 110 (1985), cert.
...8, 90 L.Ed.2d 729 (1986), the court
...y considerations and First Amend-
...om required the recognition of a
...of a balancing approach that would
...trate some particularized need, be-
...in peer review materials. Because
...nflict in approach with the Seventh
...sity of Notre Dame du Lac, 715 F.2d
...importance of the issue, we granted
...-disclosure question. * * *

I

...mission, the District Court, and the
...raises here essentially two claims.
...lified common-law privilege against
...ew materials. Second, it asserts a
First Amendment right of "academic freedom" against wholesale disclosure of the contested documents. With respect to each of the two
claims, the remedy petitioner seeks is the same: a requirement of a
judicial finding of particularized necessity of access, beyond a showing
of mere relevance, before peer review materials are disclosed to the
Commission.

A

Petitioner's common-law privilege claim is grounded in Federal
Rule of Evidence 501. This provides in relevant part:

"Except as otherwise required by the Constitution * * * or
provided by Act of Congress or in rules prescribed by the Supreme
Court * * *, the privilege of a witness * * * shall be governed by
the principles of the common law as they may be interpreted by the
courts of the United States in the light of reason and experience."

The University asks us to invoke this provision to fashion a new
privilege that it claims is necessary to protect the integrity of the peer
review process, which in turn is central to the proper functioning of
many colleges and universities. These institutions are special, observes
petitioner, because they function as "centers of learning, innovation
and discovery." * * *

* * *

2. The Court of Appeals did not rule on the question whether the Commission's subpoena permits petitioner to engage in any redaction of the disputed records before producing them, because the District Court had not fully considered that issue. The Third Circuit therefore ordered that the case be remanded for further consideration of possible redaction. See 850 F.2d, at 982.

[W]e cannot accept the University's invitation to create a new privilege against the disclosure of peer review materials. We begin by noting that Congress, in extending Title VII to educational institutions and in providing for broad EEOC subpoena powers, did not see fit to create a privilege for peer review documents.

When Title VII was enacted originally in 1964, it exempted an "educational institution with respect to the employment of individuals to perform work connected with the educational activities of such institution." * * * Eight years later, Congress eliminated that specific exemption by enacting § 3 of the Equal Employment Opportunity Act of 1972, 86 Stat. 103. This extension of Title VII was Congress' considered response to the widespread and compelling problem of invidious discrimination in educational institutions. The House Report focused specifically on discrimination in higher education, including the lack of access for women and minorities to higher ranking (*i.e.,* tenured) academic positions. * * * Significantly, opponents of the extension claimed that enforcement of Title VII would weaken institutions of higher education by interfering with decisions to hire and promote faculty members. Petitioner therefore cannot seriously contend that Congress was oblivious to concerns of academic autonomy when it abandoned the exemption for educational institutions.

The effect of the elimination of this exemption was to expose tenure determinations to the same enforcement procedures applicable to other employment decisions. * * *

* * *

On their face, § 2000e–8(a) and § 2000e–9 do not carve out any special privilege relating to peer review materials, despite the fact that Congress undoubtedly was aware, when it extended Title VII's coverage, of the potential burden that access to such material might create. Moreover, we have noted previously that when a court is asked to enforce a Commission subpoena, its responsibility is to "satisfy itself that the charge is valid and that the material requested is 'relevant' to the charge * * * and more generally to assess any contentions by the employer that the demand for information is too indefinite or has been made for an illegitimate purpose." It is not then to determine "whether the charge of discrimination is 'well founded' or 'verifiable.'" *EEOC v. Shell Oil Co.,* 466 U.S., at 72, n. 26, 104 S.Ct., at 1632, n. 26.

The University concedes that the information sought by the Commission in this case passes the relevance test set forth in *Shell Oil.* Tr. of Oral Arg. 6. Petitioner argues, nevertheless, that Title VII affirmatively grants courts the discretion to require more than relevance in order to protect tenure-review documents. Although petitioner recognizes that Title VII gives the Commission broad "power to *seek* access to all evidence that may be 'relevant to the charge under investigation,'" * * * it contends that Title VII's subpoena enforcement provisions do not give the Commission an unqualified right to *acquire* such evidence. * * * This interpretation simply cannot be reconciled with the plain language of the text of § 2000e–8(a), which states that the Commission "*shall * * * have* access" to "relevant" evidence (emphasis added). The provision can be read only as giving the Commission a right to obtain that evidence, not a mere license to seek it.

Although the text of the access provisions thus provides no privilege, Congress did address situations in which an employer may have an interest in the confidentiality of its records. The same § 2000e–8 which gives the Commission access to any evidence relevant to its investigation also makes it "unlawful for any officer or employee of the Commission to make public in any manner whatever any information obtained by the Commission pursuant to its authority under this section prior to the institution of any proceeding" under the Act. A violation of this provision subjects the employee to criminal penalties. * * * To be sure, the protection of confidentiality that § 2000–8(e) provides is less than complete.[5] But this, if anything, weakens petitioner's argument. Congress apparently considered the issue of confidentiality, and it provided a modicum of protection. Petitioner urges us to go further than Congress thought necessary to safeguard that value, that is, to strike the balance differently from the one Congress adopted. Petitioner, however, does not offer any persuasive justification for that suggestion.

We readily agree with petitioner that universities and colleges play significant roles in American society. Nor need we question, at this point, petitioner's assertion that confidentiality is important to the proper functioning of the peer review process under which many academic institutions operate. The costs that ensue from disclosure, however, constitute only one side of the balance. As Congress has recognized, the costs associated with racial and sexual discrimination in institutions of higher learning are very substantial. Few would deny that ferreting out this kind of invidious discrimination is a great if not compelling governmental interest. Often, as even petitioner seems to admit, * * * disclosure of peer review materials will be necessary in order for the Commission to determine whether illegal discrimination has taken place. Indeed, if there is a "smoking gun" to be found that demonstrates discrimination in tenure decisions, it is likely to be tucked away in peer review files. * * *

Moreover, we agree with the EEOC that the adoption of a requirement that the Commission demonstrate a "specific reason for disclosure," * * * beyond a showing of relevance, would place a substantial litigation-producing obstacle in the way of the Commission's efforts to investigate and remedy alleged discrimination. * * * A university faced with a disclosure request might well utilize the privilege in a way that frustrates the EEOC's mission. We are reluctant to "place a potent weapon in the hands of employers who have no interest in

---

5. The prohibition on Commission disclosure does not apply, for example, to the charging party. See *EEOC v. Associated Dry Goods Corp.*, 449 U.S. 590, 598–604, 101 S.Ct. 817, 822–825, 66 L.Ed.2d 762 (1981).

complying voluntarily with the Act, who wish instead to delay as long as possible investigations by the EEOC." * * *

Acceptance of petitioner's claim would also lead to a wave of similar privilege claims by other employers who play significant roles in furthering speech and learning in society. What of writers, publishers, musicians, lawyers? It surely is not unreasonable to believe, for example, that confidential peer reviews play an important part in partnership determinations at some law firms. We perceive no limiting principle in petitioner's argument. Accordingly, we stand behind the breakwater Congress has established: unless specifically provided otherwise in the statute, the EEOC may obtain "relevant" evidence. Congress has made the choice. If it dislikes the result, it of course may revise the statute.

Finally, we see nothing in our precedents that supports petitioner's claim. * * *

* * *

B

As noted above, petitioner characterizes its First Amendment claim as one of "academic freedom." Petitioner begins its argument by focusing our attention upon language in prior cases acknowledging the crucial role universities play in the dissemination of ideas in our society and recognizing "academic freedom" as a "special concern of the First Amendment." *Keyishian v. Board of Regents,* 385 U.S. 589, 603, 87 S.Ct. 675, 683, 17 L.Ed.2d 629 (1967). In that case the Court said: "Our Nation is deeply committed to safeguarding academic freedom, which is of transcendent value to all of us and not merely to the teachers concerned." See also *Adler v. Board of Education,* 342 U.S. 485, 511, 72 S.Ct. 380, 394, 96 L.Ed. 517 (1952) (academic freedom is central to "the pursuit of truth which the First Amendment is designed to protect" (dissenting opinion of Douglas, J.)). Petitioner places special reliance on Justice Frankfurter's opinion, concurring in the result, in *Sweezy v. New Hampshire,* 354 U.S. 234, 263, 77 S.Ct. 1203, 1218, 1 L.Ed.2d 1311 (1957), where the Justice recognized that one of "four essential freedoms" that a university possesses under the First Amendment is the right to "determine for itself on academic grounds *who may teach*" (emphasis added).

Petitioner contends that it exercises this right of determining "on academic grounds who may teach" through the process of awarding tenure. A tenure system, asserts petitioner, determines what the university will look like over time. "In making tenure decisions, therefore, a university is doing nothing less than shaping its own identity." * * *

Petitioner next maintains that the peer review process is the most important element in the effective operation of a tenure system. A properly functioning tenure system requires the faculty to obtain candid and detailed written evaluations of the candidate's scholarship, both from the candidate's peers at the university and from scholars at other institutions. These evaluations, says petitioner, traditionally have been provided with express or implied assurances of confidentiality. It is confidentiality that ensures candor and enables an institution to make its tenure decisions on the basis of valid academic criteria.

Building from these premises, petitioner claims that requiring the disclosure of peer review evaluations on a finding of mere relevance will undermine the existing process of awarding tenure, and therefore will result in a significant infringement of petitioner's First Amendment right of academic freedom. As more and more peer evaluations are disclosed to the EEOC and become public, a "chilling effect" on candid evaluations and discussions of candidates will result. And as the quality of peer review evaluations declines, tenure committees will no longer be able to rely on them. "This will work to the detriment of universities, as less qualified persons achieve tenure causing the quality of instruction and scholarship to decline." * * * Compelling disclosure of materials "also will result in divisiveness and tension, placing strain on faculty relations and impairing the free interchange of ideas that is a hallmark of academic freedom." * * * The prospect of these deleterious effects on American colleges and universities, concludes petitioner, compels recognition of a First Amendment privilege.

In our view, petitioner's reliance on the so-called academic freedom cases is somewhat misplaced. In those cases government was attempting to control or direct the *content* of the speech engaged in by the university or those affiliated with it. In *Sweezy,* for example, the Court invalidated the conviction of a person found in contempt for refusing to answer questions about the content of a lecture he had delivered at a state university. Similarly, in *Keyishian,* the Court invalidated a network of state laws that required public employees, including teachers at state universities, to make certifications with respect to their membership in the Communist Party. When, in those cases, the Court spoke of "academic freedom" and the right to determine on "academic grounds who may teach" the Court was speaking in reaction to content-based regulation. See *Sweezy v. New Hampshire,* 354 U.S., at 250, 77 S.Ct., at 1211 (plurality opinion discussing problems that result from imposition of a "strait jacket upon the intellectual leaders in our colleges and universities"); *Keyishian v. Board of Regents,* 385 U.S., at 603, 87 S.Ct., at 683 (discussing dangers that are present when a "pall of orthodoxy" is cast "over the classroom").

Fortunately, we need not define today the precise contours of any academic-freedom right against governmental attempts to influence the content of academic speech through the selection of faculty or by other means, because petitioner does not allege that the Commission's subpoenas are intended to or will in fact direct the content of university discourse toward or away from particular subjects or points of view. Instead, as noted above, petitioner claims that the "quality of instruction and scholarship [will] decline" as a result of the burden EEOC subpoenas place on the peer review process.

Also, the cases upon which petitioner places emphasis involved *direct* infringements on the asserted right to "determine for itself on academic grounds who may teach." In *Keyishian,* for example, government was attempting to *substitute* its teaching employment criteria for those already in place at the academic institutions, directly and completely usurping the discretion of each institution. In contrast, the EEOC subpoena at issue here effects no such usurpation. The Commission is not providing criteria that petitioner *must* use in selecting teachers. Nor is it preventing the University from using any criteria it may wish to use, except those—including race, sex, and national origin—that are proscribed under Title VII.[7] In keeping with Title VII's preservation of employers' remaining freedom of choice, see *Price Waterhouse v. Hopkins,* 490 U.S. ___, 109 S.Ct. 1775, 104 L.Ed.2d 268 (1989) (plurality opinion), courts have stressed the importance of avoiding second-guessing of legitimate academic judgments. This Court itself has cautioned that "judges * * * asked to review the substance of a genuinely academic decision * * * should show great respect for the faculty's professional judgment." *Regents of University of Michigan v. Ewing,* 474 U.S. 214, 225, 106 S.Ct. 507, 513, 88 L.Ed.2d 523 (1985). Nothing we say today should be understood as a retreat from this principle of respect for *legitimate* academic decisionmaking.

That the burden of which the University complains is neither content-based nor direct does not necessarily mean that petitioner has no valid First Amendment claim. Rather, it means only that petitioner's claim does not fit neatly within any right of academic freedom that could be derived from the cases on which petitioner relies. In essence, petitioner asks us to recognize an *expanded* right of academic freedom to protect confidential peer review materials from disclosure. Although we are sensitive to the effects that content-neutral government action may have on speech, see, *e.g., Heffron v. International Society for Krishna Consciousness, Inc.,* 452 U.S. 640, 647–648, 101 S.Ct. 2559, 2563–2564, 69 L.Ed.2d 298 (1981), and believe that burdens that are less than direct may sometimes pose First Amendment concerns, see, *e.g., NAACP v. Alabama ex rel. Patterson,* 357 U.S. 449, 78 S.Ct. 1163, 2 L.Ed.2d 1488 (1958), we think the First Amendment cannot be extended to embrace petitioner's claim.

First, by comparison with the cases in which we have found a cognizable First Amendment claim, the infringement the University complains of is extremely attenuated. To repeat, it argues that the First Amendment is infringed by disclosure of peer review materials because disclosure undermines the confidentiality which is central to the peer review process, and this in turn is central to the tenure process, which in turn is the means by which petitioner seeks to

---

7. Petitioner does not argue in this case that race, sex, and national origin constitute "academic grounds" for the purposes of its claimed First Amendment right to academic freedom. Cf. *Regents of the University of California v. Bakke,* 438 U.S. 265, 312–313, 98 S.Ct. 2733, 2759–2760, 57 L.Ed. 2d 750 (1978) (opinion of Powell, J.).

exercise its asserted academic-freedom right of choosing who will teach. To verbalize the claim is to recognize how distant the burden is from the asserted right.

Indeed, if the University's attenuated claim were accepted, many other generally applicable laws might also be said to infringe the First Amendment. In effect, petitioner says no more than that disclosure of peer review materials makes it more difficult to acquire information regarding the "academic grounds" on which petitioner wishes to base its tenure decisions. But many laws make the exercise of First Amendment rights more difficult. For example, a university cannot claim a First Amendment violation simply because it may be subject to taxation or other government regulation, even though such regulation might deprive the university of revenue it needs to bid for professors who are contemplating working for other academic institutions or in industry. We doubt that the peer review process is any more essential in effectuating the right to determine "who may teach" than is the availability of money. Cf. *Buckley v. Valeo,* 424 U.S. 1, 19, 96 S.Ct. 612, 634, 46 L.Ed.2d 659 (1976) (discussing how money is sometimes necessary to effectuate First Amendment rights).

In addition to being remote and attenuated, the injury to academic freedom claimed by petitioner is also speculative. As the EEOC points out, confidentiality is not the norm in all peer review systems. See, *e.g.*, G. Bednash, The Relationship Between Access and Selectivity in Tenure Review Outcomes (1989) (unpublished Ph.D. Dissertation, University of Maryland). Moreover, some disclosure of peer evaluations would take place even if petitioner's "special necessity" test were adopted. Thus, the "chilling effect" petitioner fears is at most only incrementally worsened by the absence of a privilege. Finally, we are not so ready as petitioner seems to be to assume the worst about those in the academic community. Although it is possible that some evaluators may become less candid as the possibility of disclosure increases, others may simply ground their evaluations in specific examples and illustrations in order to deflect potential claims of bias or unfairness. Not all academics will hesitate to stand up and be counted when they evaluate their peers.

* * *

Because we conclude that the EEOC subpoena process does not infringe any First Amendment right enjoyed by petitioner, the EEOC need not demonstrate any special justification to sustain the constitutionality of Title VII as applied to tenure peer review materials in general or to the subpoena involved in this case. Accordingly, we need not address the Commission's alternative argument that any infringement of petitioner's First Amendment rights is permissible because of the substantial relation between the Commission's request and the overriding and compelling state interest in eradicating invidious discrimination.[9]

9. We also do not consider the question, not passed upon by the Court of Appeals, whether the District Court's enforcement of the Commission's subpoena will allow petitioner to redact information from the

The judgment of the Court of Appeals is affirmed.

It is so ordered.

Notes on University of Pennsylvania v. EEOC

1. A notewriter, commenting on Namenwirth v. Board of Regents of the University of Wisconsin System, 769 F.2d 1235 (7th Cir.1985), certiorari denied 474 U.S. 1061, 106 S.Ct. 807, 88 L.Ed.2d 782 (1986), a case holding that an academic plaintiff had failed to prove that her tenure denial was based on sex discrimination, ventured the opinion that "[f]ifteen years of Title VII litigation seems to have had no great effect on the way academic institutions make their tenure decisions." Note, *Namenwirth v. Board of Regents of the University of Wisconsin System:* Proving Pretext in a Title VII Tenure Denial Case, 1987 Wis.L.Rev. 1041, 1059 (1987). Will the unanimous decision in *University of Pennsylvania* make it any easier for academic plaintiffs to win tenure cases?

2. In footnote 9, the Court reserved the question of whether plaintiff is entitled to nonredacted files. What kind of information do you imagine a University would like to be able to conceal from plaintiffs in Title VII tenure cases? The names of faculty members at other institutions who acted as "external reviewers" of plaintiff's scholarly or creative work? The identity of faculty members appointed to serve on internal *ad hoc* review committees charged with making recommendations concerning plaintiff's tenure? In a University with several levels of review, such as that described in *Lynn,* set out in the Casebook at p. 668, the precise level at which the negative recommendation or decision was made? Given the Court's approach to the First Amendment claim in *University of Pennsylvania,* which, if any, of these crucial bits of information can the university hope to conceal?

3. Did Justice Blackmun give a satisfactory rationale for the Court's rejection of the University of Pennsylvania's claim that, without assurances of confidentiality, reviewers would refuse to provide candid examinations of a tenure candidate's work, thus undercutting the academic quest for excellence? As you might expect, reaction to the decision by some University spokespersons expressed fear that the frankness of reviewers would be inhibited. Law Professor William Van Alstyne commented that, "To operate in a fishbowl is necessarily to inhibit candor." In his view, the EEOC should be required to prove sufficient cause before files are released. The Chronicle of Higher Education, Jan. 17, 1990, at A–1, A–17 at col. 1–2. Professor Michael Olivas, an expert in higher education law and author of *The Law and Higher Education: Cases and Materials on Colleges in Court* (Carolina Academic Press, Durham, No.Car.1989), was of the opinion that the case "should encourage the fair treatment of all individuals, encourage institutions to keep records more carefully, and help faculty members who were planning to pursue discrimination claims to prove their cases." Ibid. Others, however, believe that the decision will have no impact on tenure

contested materials before disclosing them.
See n. 2, *supra.*

decisions. The New York Times, January 10, 1990, at A16, col. 4. If the latter observers are correct, why did the University make such a fuss?

4. Rosalie Tung, the real party in interest in *University of Pennsylvania*, now holds a tenured professorship at the University of Wisconsin, Milwaukee, where she also acts as Director of the International Business Center. The Chronicle of Higher Education, Jan. 17, 1990, p. A1, at col. 4.

Text Note

Proving Discrimination: Title VII in Academe

Page 687. Add to text following Ford v. Nicks:

In Brown v. Trustees of Brown University, 891 F.2d 337 (1st Cir.1989), certiorari denied ___ U.S. ___, 110 S.Ct. 3217, ___ L.Ed.2d ___ (1990), the court affirmed an order requiring Brown University to award tenure to Julia Prewitt Brown as an Associate Professor of English after a finding that she had been denied tenure because of her sex in violation of Title VII. Judge Campbell agreed that courts should be "wary" of intruding into university tenure decisions, but pointed out that "[O]nce a university has been found to have impermissibly discriminated in making a tenure decision, as here, the University's prerogative to make tenure decisions must be subordinated to the goals embodied in Title VII." Id., at 359. He went on to hold that the award of tenure did not violate the University's First Amendment right to decide for itself who may teach, observing that "Academic freedom does not include the freedom to discriminate against tenure candidates on the basis of sex or other impermissible grounds." Id., at 360.

Page 690. Add to Footnote 32:

See also Professor Eleanor Swift's account of her experiences in waging a successful out-of-court tenure battle against the School of Law at the University of California, Berkeley: Swift, Becoming a Plaintiff, 4 Berkeley Wom.L.J. 245 (1989–90) (describing the essential but difficult transition from being a "tenure victim" to becoming a "discrimination plaintiff").

4. WAGE DISCRIMINATION

Page 716. Add to Note 5:

The United States Supreme Court overturned the Ninth Circuit's decision in *Wards Cove*. See this Supplement at p. 114, supra. Does that fact reinforce Judge Posner's view? See also California State Employees' Ass'n v. State of California, 724 F.Supp. 717 (N.D.Cal.1989), where Judge Marilyn Patel, acting under compulsion of the Ninth Circuit's requirement in AFSCME v. Washington, 770 F.2d 1401 (9th Cir.1985) that intentional discrimination be shown in disparate treatment cases involving wage discrimination, held that plaintiffs had failed to show that the defendant had intentionally discriminated against women state workers in the 1930s and that such discrimination carried over to present wage structures.

5. TITLE VII REMEDIES

a. Introductory Note

Page 721. Add before last paragraph:

The proposed Civil Rights Act of 1990, discussed supra at p. 131, would amend § 706(g) of Title VII to permit compensatory or punitive damages. Section 8 of the bill reads in part as follows:

> With respect to an unlawful employment practice (other than an unlawful employment practice established in accordance with section 703(k)—
>
> (A) compensatory damages may be awarded; and
>
> (B) if the respondent (other than a government, government agency, or a political subdivision) engaged in the unlawful employment practice with malice, or with reckless or callous indifference to the Federally protected rights of others, punitive damages may be awarded against such respondent;
>
> in addition to the relief authorized by the preceding sentences of this subsection, except that compensatory damages shall not include backpay or any interest thereon. If compensatory or punitive damages are sought with respect to a claim arising under this title, any party may demand a trial by jury.

Do you think this provision is likely to become law?

Page 722. Add to first paragraph:

The implementation of race-conscious relief, however, may be a lengthy and frustrating process for all concerned, including the federal judiciary. See United States v. City of Chicago, 894 F.2d 943, 948–49 (7th Cir. 1990) (concurring opinion of Judge Easterbrook).

Page 722. Add to third paragraph:

In Hopkins v. Price Waterhouse, ___ F.Supp. ___ (D.D.C.1990), Judge Gesell ordered that Ann Hopkins be admitted to partnership in the firm, despite his clear recognition that "Price Waterhouse plainly does not want her and would not voluntarily admit her." Id., at ___ (Slip opinion at 19.) In doing so, he reasoned in part that controlling law required that Title VII victims should be made "whole" as near as may be; that Price Waterhouse is a national firm with approximately 900 partners spread over some 90 offices nationwide; and that for non-accountant management consultant partners, such as Ann Hopkins would be, partnership is more like a promotion carrying increased pay and greater opportunity than a recognition of increased status within the firm. Id., at ___ (Slip opinion at 17–18.) For her part, Ann Hopkins declared herself "tough-minded" and ready to go back to Price Waterhouse's Washington office, where, she noted, many of the people who criticized her are no longer working. New York Times, May 19, 1990, at 7, col. 1.

Sec. A   CIVIL RIGHTS ACT OF 1964   207

Page 723. Add at end of Introductory Note:

MARTIN v. WILKS

Supreme Court of the United States, 1989.
490 U.S. ___, 109 S.Ct. 2180, 104 L.Ed.2d 835.

CHIEF JUSTICE REHNQUIST delivered the opinion of the court.

A group of white firefighters sued the City of Birmingham, Alabama (City) and the Jefferson County Personnel Board (Board) alleging that they were being denied promotions in favor of less qualified black firefighters. They claimed that the City and the Board were making promotion decisions on the basis of race in reliance on certain consent decrees, and that these decisions constituted impermissible racial discrimination in violation of the Constitution and federal statute. The District Court held that the white firefighters were precluded from challenging employment decisions taken pursuant to the decrees, even though these firefighters had not been parties to the proceedings in which the decrees were entered. We think this holding contravenes the general rule that a person cannot be deprived of his legal rights in a proceeding to which he is not a party.

The litigation in which the consent decrees were entered began in 1974, when the Ensley Branch of the NAACP and seven black individuals filed separate class-action complaints against the City and the Board. They alleged that both had engaged in racially discriminatory hiring and promotion practices in various public service jobs in violation of Title VII of the Civil Rights Act of 1964, 42 U.S.C. § 2000e *et seq.*, and other federal law. After a bench trial on some issues, but before judgment, the parties entered into two consent decrees, one between the black individuals and the City and the other between them and the Board. These proposed decrees set forth an extensive remedial scheme, including long-term and interim annual goals for the hiring of blacks as firefighters. The decrees also provided for goals for promotion of blacks within the department.

The District Court entered an order provisionally approving the decrees and directing publication of notice of the upcoming fairness hearings. * * * Notice of the hearings, with a reference to the general nature of the decrees, was published in two local newspapers. At that hearing, the Birmingham Firefighters Association (BFA) appeared and filed objections as *amicus curiae*. After the hearing, but before final approval of the decrees, the BFA and two of its members also moved to intervene on the ground that the decrees would adversely affect their rights. The District Court denied the motions as untimely and approved the decrees. * * * Seven white firefighters, all members of the BFA, then filed a complaint against the City and the Board seeking injunctive relief against enforcement of the decrees. The seven argued that the decrees would operate to illegally discriminate against them; the District Court denied relief. * * *

Both the denial of intervention and the denial of injunctive relief were affirmed on appeal. * * * The District Court had not abused its discretion in refusing to let the BFA intervene, thought the Eleventh Circuit, in part because the firefighters could "institut[e] an independent Title VII suit, asserting specific violations of their rights." * * * And, for the same reason, petitioners had not adequately shown the potential for irreparable harm from the operation of the decrees necessary to obtain injunctive relief. * * *

A new group of white firefighters, the *Wilks* respondents, then brought suit against the City and the Board in district court. They too alleged that, because of their race, they were being denied promotions in favor of less qualified blacks in violation of federal law. The Board and the City admitted to making race conscious employment decisions, but argued the decisions were unassailable because they were made pursuant to the consent decrees. A group of black individuals, the *Martin* petitioners, were allowed to intervene in their individual capacities to defend the decrees.

The defendants moved to dismiss the reverse discrimination cases as impermissible collateral attacks on the consent decrees. The District Court denied the motions, ruling that the decrees would provide a defense to claims of discrimination for employment decisions "mandated" by the decrees, leaving the principal issue for trial whether the challenged promotions were indeed required by the decrees. * * * After trial the District Court granted the motion to dismiss. * * * The court concluded that "if in fact the City was required to [make promotions of blacks] by the consent decree, then they would not be guilty of [illegal] racial discrimination" and that the defendants had "establish[ed] that the promotions of the black individuals * * * were in fact required by the terms of the consent decree." * * *

On appeal, the Eleventh Circuit reversed. * * *

We granted certiorari, * * * and now affirm the Eleventh Circuit's judgment. All agree that "[i]t is a principle of general application in anglo-American jurisprudence that one is not bound by a judgment *in personam* in a litigation in which he is not designated as a party or to which he has not been made a party by service of process." * * * This rule is part of our "deep-rooted historic tradition that everyone should have his own day in court." * * * A judgment or decree among parties to a lawsuit resolves issues as among them, but it does not conclude the rights of strangers to those proceedings.

Petitioners argue that, because respondents failed to timely intervene in the initial proceedings, their current challenge to actions taken under the consent decree constitutes an impermissible "collateral attack." They argue that respondents were aware that the underlying suit might affect them and if they chose to pass up an opportunity to intervene, they should not be permitted to later litigate the issues in a new action. The position has sufficient appeal to have commanded the approval of the great majority of the federal courts of appeals, but we agree with the contrary view expressed by the Court of Appeals for the Eleventh Circuit in this case.

We begin with the words of Justice Brandeis in *Chase National Bank v. Norwalk,* 291 U.S. 431, 54 S.Ct. 475, 78 L.Ed. 894 (1934):

> "The law does not impose upon any person absolutely entitled to a hearing the burden of voluntary intervention in a suit to which he is a stranger * * *. Unless duly summoned to appear in a legal proceeding, a person not a privy may rest assured that a judgment recovered therein will not affect his legal rights." * * *

While these words were written before the adoption of the Federal Rules of Civil Procedure, we think the Rules incorporate the same principle; a party seeking a judgment binding on another cannot obligate that person to intervene; he must be joined. * * * Against the background of permissive intervention set forth in *Chase National Bank,* the drafters cast Rule 24, governing intervention, in permissive terms. See Fed.Rule Civ.Proc. 24(a) (intervention as of right) ("[u]pon timely application anyone may be permitted to intervene"); Fed.Rule Civ.Proc. 24(b) (permissive intervention) ("[u]pon timely application anyone may be permitted to intervene"). They determined that the concern for finality and completeness of judgments would be "better [served] by mandatory joinder procedures." 18 Wright § 4452, p. 453. Accordingly, Rule 19(a) provides for mandatory joinder in circumstances where a judgment rendered in the absence of a person may "leave * * * persons already parties subject to a substantial risk of incurring * * * inconsistent obligations * * *." Rule 19(b) sets forth the factors to be considered by a court in deciding whether to allow an action to proceed in the absence of an interested party.

Joinder as a party, rather than knowledge of a lawsuit and an opportunity to intervene, is the method by which potential parties are subjected to the jurisdiction of the court and bound by a judgment or decree.[6] The parties to a lawsuit presumably know better than anyone else the nature and scope of relief sought in the action, and at whose expense such relief might be granted. It makes sense, therefore, to place on them a burden of bringing in additional parties where such a step is indicated, rather than placing on potential additional parties a duty to intervene when they acquire knowledge of the lawsuit. The linchpin of the "impermissible collateral attack" doctrine—the attribu-

---

6. The dissent argues on the one hand that respondents have not been "bound" by the decree but rather, that they are only suffering practical adverse affects from the consent decree. * * * On the other hand, the dissent characterizes respondents' suit not as an assertion of their own independent rights, but as a collateral attack on the consent decree which, it is said, can only proceed on very limited grounds. * * * Respondents in their suit have alleged that they are being racially discriminated against by their employer in violation of Title VII: either the fact that the disputed employment decisions are being made pursuant to a consent decree is a defense to respondents' Title VII claims or it is not. If it is a defense to challenges to employment practices which would otherwise violate Title VII, it is very difficult to see why respondents are not being "bound" by the decree.

tion of preclusive effect to a failure to intervene—is therefore quite inconsistent with Rule 19 and Rule 24.

* * *

Petitioners contend that a different result should be reached because the need to join affected parties will be burdensome and ultimately discouraging to civil rights litigation. Potential adverse claimants may be numerous and difficult to identify; if they are not joined, the possibility for inconsistent judgments exists. Judicial resources will be needlessly consumed in relitigation of the same question.

Even if we were wholly persuaded by these arguments as a matter of policy, acceptance of them would require a rewriting rather than an interpretation of the relevant Rules. But we are not persuaded that their acceptance would lead to a more satisfactory method of handling cases like this one. It must be remembered that the alternatives are a duty to intervene based on knowledge, on the one hand, and some form of joinder, as the Rules presently provide, on the other. No one can seriously contend that an employer might successfully defend against a Title VII claim by one group of employees on the ground that its actions were required by an earlier decree entered in a suit brought against it by another, if the later group did not have adequate notice or knowledge of the earlier suit.

The difficulties petitioners foresee in identifying those who could be adversely affected by a decree granting broad remedial relief are undoubtedly present, but they arise from the nature of the relief sought and not because of any choice between mandatory intervention and joinder. Rule 19's provisions for joining interested parties are designed to accomodate the sort of complexities that may arise from a decree affecting numerous people in various ways. We doubt that a mandatory intervention rule would be any less awkward. As mentioned, plaintiffs who seek the aid of the courts to alter existing employment policies, or the employer who might be subject to conflicting decrees, are best able to bear the burden of designating those who would be adversely affected if plaintiffs prevail; these parties will generally have a better understanding of the scope of likely relief than employees who are not named but might be affected. Petitioners' alternative does not eliminate the need for, or difficulty of, identifying persons who, because of their interests, should be included in a lawsuit. It merely shifts that responsibility to less able shoulders.

Nor do we think that the system of joinder called for by the Rules is likely to produce more relitigation of issues than the converse rule. The breadth of a lawsuit and concomitant relief may be at least partially shaped in advance through Rule 19 to avoid needless clashes with future litigation. And even under a regime of mandatory intervention, parties who did not have adequate knowledge of the suit would relitigate issues. Additional questions about the adequacy and timeliness of knowledge would inevitably crop up. We think that the system of joinder presently contemplated by the Rules best serves the many interests involved in the run of litigated cases, including cases like the present one.

Petitioners also urge that the congressional policy favoring voluntary settlement of employment discrimination claims, referred to in cases such as *Carson v. American Brands, Inc.,* 450 U.S. 79, 101 S.Ct. 993, 67 L.Ed.2d 59 (1981), also supports the "impermissible collateral attack" doctrine. But once again it is essential to note just what is meant by "voluntary settlement." A voluntary settlement in the form of a consent decree between one group of employees and their employer cannot possibly "settle," voluntarily or otherwise, the conflicting claims of another group of employees who do not join in the agreement. This is true even if the second group of employees is a party to the litigation:

> "[P]arties who choose to resolve litigation through settlement may not dispose of the claims of a third party * * * without that party's agreement. A court's approval of a consent decree between some of the parties therefore cannot dispose of the valid claims of nonconsenting intervenors." *Firefighters v. Cleveland,* 478 U.S. 501, 529, 106 S.Ct. 3063, 3079, 92 L.Ed.2d 405 (1986).

Insofar as the argument is bottomed on the idea that it may be easier to settle claims among a disparate group of affected persons if they are all before the Court, joinder bids fair to accomplish that result as well as a regime of mandatory intervention.

For the foregoing reasons we affirm the decision of the Court of Appeals for the Eleventh Circuit. That court remanded the case for trial of the reverse discrimination claims. *Birmingham Reverse Discrimination,* 833 F.2d, at 1500–1502. Petitioners point to language in the District Court's findings of fact and conclusions of law which suggests that respondents will not prevail on the merits. We agree with the view of the Court of Appeals, however, that the proceedings in the District Court may have been affected by the mistaken view that respondents' claims on the merits were barred to the extent they were inconsistent with the consent decree.

Affirmed.

JUSTICE STEVENS, with whom JUSTICE BRENNAN, JUSTICE MARSHALL, and JUSTICE BLACKMUN join, dissenting.

As a matter of law there is a vast difference between persons who are actual parties to litigation and persons who merely have the kind of interest that may as a practical matter be impaired by the outcome of a case. Persons in the first category have a right to participate in a trial and to appeal from an adverse judgment; depending on whether they win or lose, their legal rights may be enhanced or impaired. Persons in the latter category have a right to intervene in the action in a timely fashion, or they may be joined as parties against their will. But if they remain on the sidelines, they may be harmed as a practical matter even though their legal rights are unaffected. One of the disadvantages of sideline-sitting is that the bystander has no right to appeal from a judgment no matter how harmful it may be.

In this case the Court quite rightly concludes that the white firefighters who brought the second series of Title VII cases could not be deprived of their legal rights in the first series of cases because they had neither intervened nor been joined as parties. * * * The consent decrees obviously could not deprive them of any contractual rights, such as seniority, * * * or accrued vacation pay, * * * or of any other legal rights, such as the right to have their employer comply with federal statutes like Title VII, * * *. There is no reason, however, why the consent decrees might not produce changes in conditions at the white firefighters' place of employment that, as a practical matter, may have a serious effect on their opportunities for employment or promotion even though they are not bound by the decrees in any legal sense. The fact that one of the effects of a decree is to curtail the job opportunities of nonparties does not mean that the nonparties have been deprived of legal rights or that they have standing to appeal from that decree without becoming parties.

Persons who have no right to appeal from a final judgment—either because the time to appeal has elapsed or because they never became parties to the case—may nevertheless collaterally attack a judgment on certain narrow grounds. If the court had no jurisdiction over the subject matter, or if the judgment is the product of corruption, duress, fraud, collusion, or mistake, under limited circumstances it may be set aside in an appropriate collateral proceeding. * * * This rule not only applies to parties to the original action, but also allows interested third parties collaterally to attack judgments. In both civil and criminal cases, however, the grounds that may be invoked to support a collateral attack are much more limited than those that may be asserted as error on direct appeal. Thus, a person who can foresee that a lawsuit is likely to have a practical impact on his interests may pay a heavy price if he elects to sit on the sidelines instead of intervening and taking the risk that his legal rights will be impaired.

In this case there is no dispute about the fact that the respondents are not parties to the consent decrees. It follows as a matter of course that they are not bound by those decrees. Those judgments could not, and did not, deprive them of any legal rights. The judgments did, however, have a practical impact on respondents' opportunities for advancement in their profession. For that reason, respondents had standing to challenge the validity of the decrees, but the grounds that they may advance in support of a collateral challenge are much more limited than would be allowed if they were parties prosecuting a direct appeal.

* * * [T]his Court's opinion seems to assume that the District Court had interpreted its consent decrees in the earlier litigation as holding "that the white firefighters were precluded from challenging employment decisions taken pursuant to the decrees." * * * It is important, therefore, to make clear exactly what the District Court did hold and why its judgment should be affirmed.

I

The litigation in which the consent decrees were entered was a genuine adversary proceeding. * * *

* * * In any event, * * * it is absolutely clear that the court did not hold that respondents were bound by the decree. Nowhere in the District Court's lengthy findings of fact and conclusions of law is there a single word suggesting that respondents were bound by the consent decree or that the court intended to treat them as though they had been actual parties to that litigation and not merely as persons whose interests, as a practical matter, had been affected. Indeed, respondents, the Court of Appeals, and the majority opinion all fail to draw attention to any point in this case's long history at which the judge may have given the impression that any nonparty was legally bound by the consent decree.

II

Regardless of whether the white firefighters were parties to the decrees granting relief to their black co-workers, it would be quite wrong to assume that they could never collaterally attack such a decree. If a litigant has standing, he or she can always collaterally attack a judgment for certain narrowly defined defects. * * *

Hence, there is no basis for collaterally attacking the judgment as collusive, fraudulent, or transparently invalid. Moreover, respondents do not claim—nor has there been any showing of—mistake, duress, or lack of jurisdiction. Instead, respondents are left to argue that somewhat different relief would have been more appropriate than the relief that was actually granted. Although this sort of issue may provide the basis for a direct appeal, it cannot, and should not, serve to open the door to relitigation of a settled judgment.

III

The facts that respondents are not bound by the decree and that they have no basis for a collateral attack, moreover, do not compel the conclusion that the District Court should have treated the decree as nonexistent for purposes of respondents' discrimination suit. That the decree may not directly interfere with any of respondents' legal rights does not mean that it may not affect the factual setting in a way that negates respondents' claim. The fact that a criminal suspect is not a party to the issuance of a search warrant does not imply that the presence of a facially valid warrant may not be taken as evidence that the police acted in good faith. * * * Similarly, the fact that an employer is acting under court compulsion may be evidence that the employer is acting in good faith and without discriminatory intent. * * * Indeed, the threat of a contempt citation provides as good a reason to act as most, if not all, other business justifications.

After reviewing the evidence, the District Court found that the City had in fact acted under compulsion of the consent decree. * * *

Based on this finding, the court concluded that the City carried its burden of coming forward with a legitimate business reason for its promotion policy, and, accordingly, held that the promotion decisions were "not taken with the requisite discriminatory intent" necessary to make out a claim of disparate treatment under Title VII or the Equal Protection Clause. * * * For this reason, and not because it thought that respondents were legally bound by the consent decree, the court entered an order in favor of the City and defendant-intervenors.

* * *

In a case such as this, however, in which there has been no showing that the decree was collusive, fraudulent, transparently invalid, or entered without jurisdiction, it would be "unconscionable" to conclude that obedience to an order remedying a Title VII violation could subject a defendant to additional liability. * * * Rather, all of the reasons that support the Court's view that a police officer should not generally be held liable when he carries out the commands in a facially valid warrant apply with added force to city officials, or indeed to private employers, who obey the commands contained in a decree entered by a federal court. In fact, Equal Employment Opportunity Commission regulations concur in this assessment. They assert, "[t]he Commission interprets Title VII to mean that actions taken pursuant to the direction of a Court Order cannot give rise to liability under Title VII." * * * Assuming that the District Court's findings of fact were not clearly erroneous—which of course is a matter that is not before us—it seems perfectly clear that its judgment should have been affirmed. Any other conclusion would subject large employers who seek to comply with the law by remedying past discrimination to a never-ending stream of litigation and potential liability. It is unfathomable that either Title VII or the Equal Protection Clause demands such a counter-productive result.

IV

The predecessor to this litigation was brought to change a pattern of hiring and promotion practices that had discriminated against black citizens in Birmingham for decades. The white respondents in this case are not responsible for that history of discrimination, but they are nevertheless beneficiaries of the discriminatory practices that the litigation was designed to correct. Any remedy that seeks to create employment conditions that would have obtained if there had been no violations of law will necessarily have an adverse impact on whites, who must now share their job and promotion opportunities with blacks.[31] Just as white employees in the past were innocent benefi-

---

31. It is inevitable that nonminority employees or applicants will be less well off under an affirmative action plan than without it, no matter what form it takes. For example, even when an employer simply agrees to recruit minority job applicants more actively, white applicants suffer the "nebulous" harm of facing increased competition and the diminished likelihood of eventually being hired. See Schwarzchild, Public Law By Private Bargain: Title VII Consent Decrees and the Fairness of Negotiated Institutional Reform, 1984 Duke L.J. 887, 909–910.

ciaries of illegal discriminatory practices, so is it inevitable that some of the same white employees will be innocent victims who must share some of the burdens resulting from the redress of the past wrongs.

There is nothing unusual about the fact that litigation between adverse parties may, as a practical matter, seriously impair the interests of third persons who elect to sit on the sidelines. Indeed, in complex litigation this Court has squarely held that a sideline-sitter may be bound as firmly as an actual party if he had adequate notice and a fair opportunity to intervene and if the judicial interest in finality is sufficiently strong. * * *

There is no need, however, to go that far in order to agree with the District Court's eminently sensible view that compliance with the terms of a valid decree remedying violations of Title VII cannot itself violate that statute or the Equal Protection Clause.[32] The City of Birmingham, in entering into and complying with this decree, has made a substantial step toward the eradication of the long history of pervasive racial discrimination that has plagued its fire department. The District Court, after conducting a trial and carefully considering respondents' arguments, concluded that this effort is lawful and should go forward. Because respondents have thus already had their day in court and have failed to carry their burden, I would vacate the judgment of the Court of Appeals and remand for further proceedings consistent with this opinion.

Notes on Martin

1. Does *Martin* take away the practical value of consent decrees in Title VII cases? What potential adversaries would a Title VII class action plaintiff be required to join in order to prevent reopening of a consent decree?

2. In the wake of *Martin,* reverse discrimination suits challenging actions taken to implement consent decrees were filed around the country. For example, seven white firefighters have filed a suit asserting the unconstitutionality of personnel decisions taken by San Francisco to implement the consent decree upheld in Davis v. City and County of San Francisco, discussed at p. 161, supra. Van Pool v. City and County of San Francisco, No. C89–4304MHP (N.D.Cal.1989). Section 6 of the proposed Civil Rights Act of 1990, discussed at p. 131, supra, would repeal Martin v.

---

32. In professing difficulty in understanding why respondents are not "bound" by a decree that provides a defense to employment practices that would otherwise violate Title VII, see *ante,* at * * * n. 6, the Court uses the word "bound" in a sense that is different from that used earlier in its opinion. A judgment against an employer requiring it to institute a seniority system may provide the employer with a defense to employment practices that would otherwise violate Title VII. In the sense in which the word "bound" is used in the cases cited by the Court at pages 2184 and 2185 of its opinion, only the parties to the litigation would be "bound" by the judgment. But employees who first worked for the company 180 days after the litigation ended would be "bound" by the judgment in the sense that the Court uses when it responds to my argument. The cases on which the Court relies are entirely consistent with my position. Its facile use of the word "bound" should not be allowed to conceal the obvious flaws in its analysis.

Wilks by refusing to permit challenges to employment practices implementing litigated or consent judgments brought by a person "who, prior to the entry of such judgment or order had (i) notice from any source of the proposed judgment or order sufficient to apprise such person that such judgment or order might affect the interests of such person; and (ii) a reasonable opportunity to present objections to such judgment or order." In addition, a person who does not fit this description may be barred from such challenges if a court determines "that the interests of such person were adequately represented by another person who challenged such judgment or order prior to or after the entry of such judgment or order." Would either of these provisions prevent suit by the *Van Pool* plaintiffs?

b. *Voluntary Affirmative Action: Reverse Discrimination Under Title VII?*

Page 750. Add to Note 4:

For the first time, a majority of the United States Supreme Court held in City of Richmond v. J.A. Croson Co., 488 U.S. 469, 109 S.Ct. 706, 102 L.Ed. 2d 854 (1989) that voluntary affirmative action plans creating set-asides favoring minority business enterprises promulgated by states or their political subdivisions must be tested under the Equal Protection Clause by a strict scrutiny standard, rather than an intermediate standard. Only Chief Justice Rehnquist and Justice White joined Part II of Justice O'Connor's plurality opinion explaining why a strict scrutiny standard was appropriate to measure set-asides established by states and municipalities but not to test similar plans adopted by the United States Congress. Both Justices Kennedy and Scalia, however, separately indicated their agreement with the use of a strict scrutiny standard. Justice Kennedy would limit the standard to racial preferences, while Justice Scalia would apply it to all race-based governmental classification. Justice Marshall, joined in dissent by Justices Brennan and Blackmun, restated his belief that an intermediate standard was the appropriate vehicle for testing race-conscious classifications designed to further remedial goals. Professor Michel Rosenfeld argues that the "seeming order emerging from *Croson's* embrace of the strict scrutiny test" is achieved only by a process of "decontextualization" that leaves in place "the same turmoil and uncertainty that have previously thwarted the Court's efforts to overcome conflict and fragmentation." Rosenfeld, Decoding *Richmond:* Affirmative Action and the Elusive Meaning of Constitutional Equality, 87 Mich.L.Rev. 1729, 1732 (1989).

A 6–3 majority, including Justice Stevens, voted to invalidate the Richmond plan, which mandated a 30% set-aside favoring minority business enterprises in city-awarded construction contracts for businesses owned and controlled by "citizens of the United States who are Blacks, Spanish-speaking, Orientals, Indians, Eskimos, or Aleuts." *Croson* is discussed further in the *Notes on the Executive Order,* at p. 236, infra.

Page 750. Add to Note 5:

Professor Roy Brooks argues powerfully that the public policy of formal equal opportunity established in Brown v. Board of Education, 347 U.S. 483, 74 S.Ct. 686, 98 L.Ed. 873 (1954) has failed to cure the American race problem; he urges the current generation of civil rights scholars and policymakers to fashion a new approach, that will meet three conditions: come to grips with the existence of class stratification in Black society; avoid new forms of racial subordination; and be reconcilable with the existing liberal democratic state. See Brooks, Racial Subordination Through Formal Equal Opportunity, 25 San Diego L.Rev. 881 (1988).

Page 751. Add new Note 6:

6. In Metro Broadcasting, Inc. v. FCC, ___ U.S. ___, 110 S.Ct. ___, ___ L.Ed.2d ___ (1990), the Court applied an intermediate scrutiny standard to uphold two minority preference policies designed by the FCC to promote diversity of broadcast viewpoint. *Metro Broadcasting* is discussed in conjunction with *Croson* in the *Notes on the Executive Order*, at p. 238, infra.

B. CONSTITUTIONAL PROHIBITIONS AGAINST INTENTIONAL DISCRIMINATION IN EMPLOYMENT

Text Note

The Post Civil War Civil Rights Acts

Page 764. Substitute for Discussion of Section 1981:

PATTERSON v. McLEAN CREDIT UNION

Supreme Court of the United States, 1989.
491 U.S. ___, 109 S.Ct. 2363, 105 L.Ed.2d 132.

JUSTICE KENNEDY delivered the opinion of the Court.

In this case, we consider important issues respecting the meaning and coverage of one of our oldest civil rights statutes, 42 U.S.C. § 1981.

I

Petitioner Brenda Patterson, a black woman, was employed by respondent McLean Credit Union as a teller and a file coordinator, commencing in May 1972. In July 1982, she was laid off. After the termination, petitioner commenced this action in District Court. She alleged that respondent, in violation of 42 U.S.C. § 1981, had harassed her, failed to promote her to an intermediate accounting clerk position, and then discharged her, all because of her race. * * *

The District Court determined that a claim for racial harassment is not actionable under § 1981 and declined to submit that part of the case to the jury. * * *

* * *

We granted certiorari to decide whether petitioner's claim of racial harassment in her employment is actionable under § 1981, and whether the jury instruction given by the District Court on petitioner's § 1981 promotion claim was error. * * * After oral argument on these issues, we requested the parties to brief and argue an additional question:

"Whether or not the interpretation of 42 U.S.C. § 1981 adopted by this Court in *Runyon v. McCrary,* * * * should be reconsidered."
* * *

We now decline to overrule our decision in *Runyon v. McCrary,* * * * We hold further that racial harassment relating to the conditions of employment is not actionable under § 1981 because that provision does not apply to conduct which occurs after the formation of a contract and which does not interfere with the right to enforce established contract obligations. Finally, we hold that the District Court erred in instructing the jury regarding petitioner's burden in proving her discriminatory promotion claim.

II

In *Runyon,* the Court considered whether § 1981 prohibits private schools from excluding children who are qualified for admission, solely on the basis of race. We held that § 1981 did prohibit such conduct, noting that it was already well established in prior decisions that § 1981 "prohibits racial discrimination in the making and enforcement of private contracts." * * * The arguments about whether *Runyon* was decided correctly in light of the language and history of the statute were examined and discussed with great care in our decision. It was recognized at the time that a strong case could be made for the view that the statute does not reach private conduct, see 427 U.S., at 186, 96 S.Ct., at 2602 (Powell, J., concurring); *id.,* at 189, 96 S.Ct., at 2603–04 (STEVENS, J., concurring); *id.,* at 192, 96 S.Ct., at 2605 (WHITE, J., dissenting), but that view did not prevail. Some Members of this Court believe that *Runyon* was decided incorrectly, and others consider it correct on its own footing, but the question before us is whether it ought now to be overturned. We conclude after reargument that *Runyon* should not be overruled, and we now reaffirm that § 1981 prohibits racial discrimination in the making and enforcement of private contracts.

* * *

* * * We have said also that the burden borne by the party advocating the abandonment of an established precedent is greater where the Court is asked to overrule a point of statutory construction. Considerations of *stare decisis* have special force in the area of statutory interpretation, for here, unlike in the context of constitutional interpretation, the legislative power is implicated, and Congress remains free to alter what we have done. * * *

We conclude, upon direct consideration of the issue, that no special justification has been shown for overruling *Runyon.* In cases where statutory precedents have been overruled, the primary reason for the Court's shift in position has been the intervening development of the law, through either the growth of judicial doctrine or further action taken by Congress. Where such changes have removed or weakened the conceptual underpinnings from the prior decision, * * * or where the later law has rendered the decision irreconcilable with competing legal doctrines or policies, * * * the Court has not hesitated to overrule an earlier decision. Our decision in *Runyon* has not been undermined by subsequent changes or development in the law.

Another traditional justification for overruling a prior case is that a precedent may be a positive detriment to coherence and consistency in the law, either because of inherent confusion created by an unworkable decision, * * * or because the decision poses a direct obstacle to the realization of important objectives embodied in other laws, * * *. In this regard, we do not find *Runyon* to be unworkable or confusing. Respondent and various *amici* have urged that *Runyon's* interpretation of § 1981, as applied to contracts of employment, frustrates the objectives of Title VII. The argument is that a substantial overlap in coverage between the two statutes, given the considerable differences in their remedial schemes, undermines Congress' detailed efforts in Title VII to resolve disputes about racial discrimination in private employment through conciliation rather than litigation as an initial matter. After examining the point with care, however, we believe that a sound construction of the language of § 1981 yields an interpretation which does not frustrate the congressional objectives in Title VII to any significant degree. See Part III, *infra*.

Finally, it has sometimes been said that a precedent becomes more vulnerable as it becomes outdated and after being "'tested by experience, has been found to be inconsistent with the sense of justice or with the social welfare.'" *Runyon*, 427 U.S., at 191, 96 S.Ct., at 2604 (STEVENS, J., concurring), quoting B. Cardozo, The Nature of the Judicial Process 149 (1921). Whatever the effect of this consideration may be in statutory cases, it offers no support for overruling *Runyon*. In recent decades, state and federal legislation has been enacted to prohibit private racial discrimination in many aspects of our society. Whether *Runyon's* interpretation of § 1981 as prohibiting racial discrimination in the making and enforcement of private contracts is right or wrong as an original matter, it is certain that it is not inconsistent with the prevailing sense of justice in this country. To the contrary, *Runyon* is entirely consistent with our society's deep commitment to the eradication of discrimination based on a person's race or the color of his or her skin. * * *

We decline to overrule *Runyon* and acknowledge that its holding remains the governing law in this area.

III

Our conclusion that we should adhere to our decision in *Runyon* that § 1981 applies to private conduct is not enough to decide this case. We must decide also whether the conduct of which petitioner complains falls within one of the enumerated rights protected by § 1981.

A

* * * The most obvious feature of the provision is the restriction of its scope to forbidding discrimination in the "mak[ing] and en-

force[ment]" of contracts alone. Where an alleged act of discrimination does not involve the impairment of one of these specific rights, § 1981 provides no relief. Section 1981 cannot be construed as a general proscription of racial discrimination in all aspects of contract relations, for it expressly prohibits discrimination only in the making and enforcement of contracts. See also *Jones v. Alfred H. Mayer Co.*, 392 U.S. 409, 436, 88 S.Ct. 2186, 2201, 20 L.Ed.2d 1189 (1968) (§ 1982, the companion statute to § 1981, was designed "to prohibit all racial discrimination, whether or not under color of law, *with respect to the rights enumerated therein*") (emphasis added); *Georgia v. Rachel*, 384 U.S. 780, 791, 86 S.Ct. 1783, 1789, 16 L.Ed.2d 925 (1966) ("The legislative history of the 1866 Act clearly indicates that Congress intended to protect a limited category of rights").

By its plain terms, the relevant provision in § 1981 protects two rights: "the same right * * * to make * * * contracts" and "the same right * * * to * * * enforce contracts." The first of these protections extends only to the formation of a contract, but not to problems that may arise later from the conditions of continuing employment. The statute prohibits, when based on race, the refusal to enter into a contract with someone, as well as the offer to make a contract only on discriminatory terms. But the right to make contracts does not extend, as a matter of either logic or semantics, to conduct by the employer after the contract relation has been established, including breach of the terms of the contract or imposition of discriminatory working conditions. Such postformation conduct does not involve the right to make a contract, but rather implicates the performance of established contract obligations and the conditions of continuing employment, matters more naturally governed by state contract law and Title VII.

The second of these guarantees, "the same right * * * to * * * enforce contracts * * * as is enjoyed by white citizens," embraces protection of a legal process, and of a right of access to legal process, that will address and resolve contract-law claims without regard to race. In this respect, it prohibits discrimination that infects the legal process in ways that prevent one from enforcing contract rights, by reason of his or her race, and this is so whether this discrimination is attributed to a statute or simply to existing practices. It also covers wholly *private* efforts to impede access to the courts or obstruct nonjudicial methods of adjudicating disputes about the force of binding obligations, as well as discrimination by private entities, such as labor unions, in enforcing the terms of a contract. Following this principle and consistent with our holding in *Runyon* that § 1981 applies to private conduct, we have held that certain private entities such as labor unions, which bear explicit responsibilities to process grievances, press claims, and represent member in disputes over the terms of binding obligations that run from the employer to the employee, are subject to liability under § 1981 for racial discrimination in the enforcement of labor contracts. * * * The right to enforce contracts does not, however, extend beyond conduct by an employer which impairs an employee's ability to enforce through legal process his or her established contract rights. As Justice White put it with much force in *Runyon,* one cannot seriously "contend that the grant of the other rights enumerated in § 1981 [that is, other than the right to "make" contracts,] *i.e.,* the rights 'to sue, be parties, give evidence,' and '*enforce* contracts' accomplishes anything other than the removal of *legal* disabilities to sue, be a party, testify or enforce a contract. Indeed, it is impossible to give such language any other meaning." * * *

B

Applying these principles to the case before us, we agree with the Court of Appeals that petitioner's racial harassment claim is not actionable under § 1981. Petitioner has alleged that during her employment with respondent, she was subjected to various forms of racial harassment from her supervisor. As summarized by the Court of Appeals, petitioner testified that

"[her supervisor] periodically stared at her for several minutes at a time; that he gave her too many tasks, causing her to complain that she was under too much pressure; that among the tasks given her were sweeping and dusting, jobs not given to white employees. On one occasion, she testified, [her supervisor] told [her] that blacks are known to work slower than whites. According to [petitioner, her supervisor] also criticized her in staff meetings while not similarly criticizing white employees." * * *

Petitioner also alleges that she was passed over for promotion, not offered training for higher level jobs, and denied wage increases, all because of her race.

With the exception perhaps of her claim that respondent refused to promote her to a position as an accountant, see Part IV, *infra,* none of the conduct which petitioner alleges as part of the racial harassment against her involves either a refusal to make a contract with her or the impairment of her ability to enforce her established contract rights. Rather, the conduct which petitioner labels as actionable racial harassment is postformation conduct by the employer relating to the terms and conditions of continuing employment. * * *

This type of conduct, reprehensible though it be if true, is not actionable under § 1981, which covers only conduct at the initial formation of the contract and conduct which impairs the right to enforce contract obligations through legal process. Rather, such conduct is actionable under the more expansive reach of Title VII of the Civil Rights Act of 1964. The latter statute makes it unlawful for an employer to "discriminate against any individual with respect to his compensation, terms, conditions, or privileges of employment." 42 U.S.C. § 2000e–2(a)(1). Racial harassment in the course of employment is actionable under Title VII's prohibition against discrimination in the "terms, conditions, or privileges of employment." "[T]he [Equal Employment Opportunity Commission (EEOC)] has long recognized that harassment on the basis of race * * * is an unlawful employment practice in violation of § 703 of Title VII of the Civil Rights Act." See EEOC Compliance Manual § 615.7 (1982). While this Court has not yet had the opportunity to pass directly upon this interpretation of Title VII, the lower federal courts have uniformly upheld this view, and we implicitly have approved it in a recent decision concerning sexual harassment, *Meritor Savings Bank v. Vinson,* 477 U.S. 57, 65–66, 106 S.Ct. 2399, 2405–06, 91 L.Ed.2d 49 (1986). As we said in that case, "harassment [which is] sufficiently severe or pervasive 'to alter the conditions of [the victim's] employment and create an abusive working environment,'" *id.,* at 67, 106 S.Ct., at 2406, is actionable under Title VII because it "affects a 'term, condition, or privilege' of employment," *ibid.*

Interpreting § 1981 to cover postformation conduct unrelated to an employee's right to enforce her contract, such as incidents relating to the conditions of employment, is not only inconsistent with that statute's limitation to the making and enforcement of contracts, but would also undermine the detailed and well-crafted procedures for conciliation and resolution of Title VII claims. In Title VII, Congress set up an elaborate administrative procedure, implemented through the EEOC, that is designed to assist in the investigation of claims of racial discrimination in the workplace and to work towards the resolution of these claims through conciliation rather than litigation. See 42 U.S.C. § 2000e–5(b). Only after these procedures have been exhausted, and the plaintiff has obtained a "right to sue" letter from the EEOC, may she bring a Title VII action in court. See 42 U.S.C. § 2000e–5(f)(1). Section 1981, by contrast, provides no administrative review or opportunity for conciliation.

Where conduct is covered by both § 1981 and Title VII, the detailed procedures of Title VII are rendered a dead letter, as the plaintiff is free to pursue a claim by bringing suit under § 1981 without resort to those statutory prerequisites. We agree that, after *Runyon,* there is some necessary overlap between Title VII and § 1981, and that where the statutes do in fact overlap we are not at liberty "to infer any positive preference for one over the other." * * * We should be reluctant, however, to read an earlier statute broadly where the result is to circumvent the detailed remedial scheme constructed in a later statute. * * * That egregious racial harassment of employees is forbidden by a clearly applicable law (Title VII), moreover, should lessen the temptation for this Court to twist the interpretation of another statute (§ 1981) to cover the same conduct. In the particular case before us, we do not know for certain why petitioner chose to pursue only remedies under § 1981, and not under Title VII. * * * But in any event, the availability of the latter statute should deter us from a tortuous construction of the former statute to cover this type of claim.

By reading § 1981 not as a general proscription of racial discrimination in all aspects of contract relations, but as limited to the enumerated rights within its express protection, specifically the right to make and enforce contracts, we may preserve the integrity of Title VII's procedures without sacrificing any significant coverage of the civil rights laws.[4] Of course, some overlap will remain between the two statutes: specifically, a refusal to enter into an employment contract on the basis of race. Such a claim would be actionable under Title VII as a "refus[al] to hire" based on race, 42 U.S.C. § 2000e–2(a), and under § 1981 as an impairment of "the same right * * * to make * * * contracts * * * as * * * white citizens," 42 U.S.C. § 1981. But this is precisely where it would make sense for Congress to provide for the overlap. At this stage of the employee-employer relation Title VII's mediation and conciliation procedures would be of minimal effect, for there is not yet a relation to salvage.

* * *

IV

Petitioner's claim that respondent violated § 1981 by failing to promote her, because of race, to a position as an intermediate accounting clerk is a different matter. As a preliminary point, we note that the Court of Appeals distinguished between petitioner's claims of racial harassment and discriminatory promotion, stating that although the former did not give rise to a discrete § 1981 claim, "[c]laims of racially discriminatory * * * promotion go to the very existence and nature of the employment contract and thus fall easily within § 1981's protection." * * * We think that somewhat overstates the case. Consistent with what we have said in Part III, *supra*, the question whether a promotion claim is actionable under § 1981 depends upon whether the nature of the change in position was such that it involved the opportunity to enter into a new contract with the employer. If so, then the employer's refusal to enter the new contract is actionable under § 1981. In making this determination, a lower court should give a fair and natural reading to the statutory phrase "the same right * * * to make * * * contracts," and should not strain in an undue manner the language of § 1981. Only where the promotion rises to the level of an opportunity for a new and distinct relation between the employee and the employer is such a claim actionable under § 1981. Cf. *Hishon v. King & Spaulding*, 467 U.S. 69, 104 S.Ct. 2229, 81 L.Ed.2d 59 (1984) (refusal of law firm to accept associate into partnership) (Title VII). Because respondent has not argued at any stage that petitioner's

---

4. Unnecessary overlap between Title VII and § 1981 would also serve to upset the delicate balance between employee and employer rights struck by Title VII in other respects. For instance, a plaintiff in a Title VII action is limited to a recovery of backpay, whereas under § 1981 a plaintiff may be entitled to plenary compensatory damages, as well as punitive damages in an appropriate case. Both the employee and employer will be unlikely to agree to a conciliatory resolution of the dispute under Title VII if the employer can be found liable for much greater amounts under § 1981.

promotion claim is not cognizable under § 1981, we need not address the issue further here.

This brings us to the question of the District Court's jury instructions on petitioner's promotion claim. We think the District Court erred when it instructed the jury that petitioner had to prove that she was better qualified than the white employee who allegedly received the promotion. In order to prevail under § 1981, a plaintiff must prove purposeful discrimination. *General Building Contractors Assn., Inc. v. Pennsylvania,* 458 U.S. 375, 391, 102 S.Ct. 3141, 3150, 73 L.Ed.2d 835 (1982). We have developed, in analogous areas of civil rights law, a carefully designed framework of proof to determine, in the context of disparate treatment, the ultimate issue of whether the defendant intentionally discriminated against the plaintiff. See *Texas Dept. of Community Affairs v. Burdine,* 450 U.S. 248, 101 S.Ct. 1089, 67 L.Ed.2d 207 (1981); *McDonnell Douglas Corp. v. Green,* 411 U.S. 792, 93 S.Ct. 1817, 36 L.Ed.2d 668 (1973). We agree with the Court of Appeals that this scheme of proof, structured as a "sensible, orderly way to evaluate the evidence in light of common experience as it bears on the critical question of discrimination," *Furnco Construction Corp. v. Waters,* 438 U.S. 567, 577, 98 S.Ct. 2943, 2949–50, 57 L.Ed.2d 957 (1978), should apply to claims of racial discrimination under § 1981.

Although the Court of Appeals recognized that the *McDonnell Douglas/Burdine* scheme of proof should apply in § 1981 cases such as this one, it erred in describing petitioner's burden. Under our well-established framework, the plaintiff has the initial burden of proving, by the preponderance of the evidence, a prima facie case of discrimination. *Burdine,* * * *. The burden is not onerous. *Id.* * * * Here, petitioner need only prove by a preponderance of the evidence that she applied for and was qualified for an available position, that she was rejected, and that after she was rejected respondent either continued to seek applicants for the position, or, as is alleged here, filled the position with a white employee. * * * *McDonnell Douglas, supra.*[7]

Once the plaintiff establishes a prima facie case, an inference of discrimination arises. * * * In order to rebut this inference, the employer must present evidence that the plaintiff was rejected, or the other applicant was chosen, for a legitimate nondiscriminatory reason. * * * Here, respondent presented evidence that it gave the job to the white applicant because she was better qualified for the position, and therefore rebutted any presumption of discrimination that petitioner may have established. At this point, as our prior cases make clear,

---

7. Here, respondent argues that petitioner cannot make out a prima facie case on her promotion claim because she did not prove either that respondent was seeking applicants for the intermediate accounting clerk position or that the white employee named to fill that position in fact received a "promotion" from her prior job. Although we express no opinion on the merits of these claims, we do emphasize that in order to prove that she was denied the same right to make and enforce contracts as white citizens, petitioner must show, *inter alia,* that she was in fact denied an *available* position.

petitioner retains the final burden of persuading the jury of intentional discrimination. * * *

Although petitioner retains the ultimate burden of persuasion, our cases make clear that she must also have the opportunity to demonstrate that respondent's proffered reasons for its decision were not its true reasons. * * * In doing so, petitioner is not limited to presenting evidence of a certain type. This is where the District Court erred. The evidence which petitioner can present in an attempt to establish that respondent's stated reasons are pretextual may take a variety of forms. * * * Indeed, she might seek to demonstrate that respondent's claim to have promoted a better-qualified applicant was pretextual by showing that she was in fact better qualified than the person chosen for the position. The District Court erred, however, in instructing the jury that in order to succeed petitioner was *required* to make such a showing. There are certainly other ways in which petitioner could seek to prove that respondent's reasons were pretextual. Thus, for example, petitioner could seek to persuade the jury that respondent had not offered the true reason for its promotion decision by presenting evidence of respondent's past treatment of petitioner, including the instances of the racial harassment which she alleges and respondent's failure to train her for an accounting position. * * * While we do not intend to say this evidence necessarily would be sufficient to carry the day, it cannot be denied that it is one of the various ways in which petitioner might seek to prove intentional discrimination on the part of respondent. She may not be forced to pursue any particular means of demonstrating that respondent's stated reasons are pretextual. It was, therefore, error for the District Court to instruct the jury that petitioner could carry her burden of persuasion only by showing that she was in fact better qualified than the white applicant who got the job.

V

The law now reflects society's consensus that discrimination based on the color of one's skin is a profound wrong of tragic dimension. Neither our words nor our decisions should be interpreted as signaling one inch of retreat from Congress' policy to forbid discrimination in the private, as well as the public, sphere. Nevertheless, in the area of private discrimination, to which the ordinance of the Constitution does not directly extend, our role is limited to interpreting what Congress may do and has done. The statute before us, which is only one part of Congress' extensive civil rights legislation, does not cover the acts of harassment alleged here.

In sum, we affirm the Court of Appeals' dismissal of petitioner's racial harassment claim as not actionable under § 1981. The Court of Appeals erred, however, in holding that petitioner could succeed in her discriminatory promotion claim under § 1981 only by proving that she was better qualified for the position of intermediate accounting clerk than the white employee who in fact was promoted. The judgment of the Court of Appeals is therefore vacated insofar as it relates to petitioner's discriminatory promotion claim, and the case is remanded for further proceedings consistent with this opinion.

It is so ordered.

JUSTICE BRENNAN, with whom JUSTICE MARSHALL and JUSTICE BLACKMUN join, and with whom JUSTICE STEVENS joins as to Parts II–B, II–C, and III, concurring in the judgment in part and dissenting in part.

What the Court declines to snatch away with one hand, it takes with the other. Though the Court today reaffirms § 1981's applicability to private conduct, it simultaneously gives this landmark civil rights statute a needlessly cramped interpretation. The Court has to strain hard to justify this choice to confine § 1981 within the narrowest possible scope, selecting the most pinched reading of the phrase "same right to make a contract," ignoring powerful historical evidence about the Reconstruction Congress' concerns, and bolstering its parsimonious rendering by reference to a statute enacted nearly a century after § 1981, and plainly not intended to affect its reach. When it comes to deciding whether a civil rights statute should be construed to further our Nation's commitment to the eradication of racial discrimination, the Court adopts a formalistic method of interpretation antithetical to Congress' vision of a society in which contractual opportunities are equal. I dissent from the Court's holding that § 1981 does not encompass Patterson's racial harassment claim.

* * *

II

I turn now to the two issues on which certiorari was originally requested and granted in this case. The first of these is whether a plaintiff may state a cause of action under § 1981 based upon allegations that her employer harassed her because of her race. In my view, she may. The Court reaches a contrary conclusion by conducting an ahistorical analysis that ignores the circumstances and legislative history of § 1981. The Court reasons that Title VII or modern state contract law "more naturally gover[n]" harassment actions, * * *— nowhere acknowledging the anachronism attendant upon the implication that the Reconstruction Congress would have viewed state law, or a federal civil rights statute passed nearly a century later, as the primary bases for challenging private discrimination.

A

The legislative history of § 1981—to which the Court does not advert—makes clear that we must not take an overly narrow view of what it means to have the "same right * * * to make and enforce contracts" as white citizens. The very same legislative history that supports our interpretation of § 1981 in *Runyon* also demonstrates that the 39th Congress intended, in the employment context, to go beyond protecting the freedmen from refusals to contract for their labor and from discriminatory decisions to discharge them. Section 1 of the Civil

Rights Act was also designed to protect the freedmen from the imposition of working conditions that evidence an intent on the part of the employer not to contract on nondiscriminatory terms. * * * Congress realized that, in the former Confederate States, employers were attempting to "adher[e], as to the *treatment of the laborers,* as much as possible to the traditions of the old system, *even where the relations between employers and laborers had been fixed by contract.*" Report of C. Schurz, S.Exec.Doc. No. 2, 39th Cong., 1st Sess., p. 19 (1865) (emphasis added). These working conditions included the use of the whip as an incentive to work harder—the commonplace result of an entrenched attitude that "[y]ou cannot make the negro work without physical compulsion," *id.,* at 16—and the practice of handing out severe and unequal punishment for perceived transgressions. See *id.,* at 20 ("The habit [of corporal punishment] is so inveterate with a great many persons as to render, on the least provocation, the impulse to whip a negro almost irrestible"). Since such "acts of persecution" against *employed* freedmen, *ibid.,* were one of the 39th Congress' concerns in enacting the Civil Rights Act, it is clear that in granting the freedmen the "same right * * * to make and enforce contracts" as white citizens, Congress meant to encompass post-contractual conduct.

B

The Court holds that § 1981, insofar as it gives an equal right to make a contract, "covers only conduct at the initial formation of the contract." * * * This narrow interpretation is not, as the Court would have us believe, * * * the inevitable result of the statutory grant of an equal right "to make contracts." On the contrary, the language of § 1981 is quite naturally read as extending to cover postformation conduct that demonstrates that the contract was not really made on equal terms at all. It is indeed clear that the statutory language of § 1981 imposes some limit upon the type of harassment claims that are cognizable under § 1981, for the statute's prohibition is against discrimination in the making and enforcement of contracts; but the Court mistakes the nature of that limit. In my view, harassment is properly actionable under the language of § 1981 mandating that all persons "shall have the same right * * * to make * * * contracts * * * as is enjoyed by white citizens" if it demonstrates that the employer has in fact imposed discriminatory terms and hence has not allowed blacks to make a contract on an equal basis.

The question in a case in which an employee makes a § 1981 claim alleging racial harassment should be whether the acts constituting harassment were sufficiently severe or pervasive as effectively to belie any claim that the contract was entered into in a racially neutral manner. Where a black employee demonstrates that she has worked in conditions substantially different from those enjoyed by similarly situated white employees, and can show the necessary racial animus, a jury may infer that the black employee has not been afforded the same right to make an employment contract as white employees. Obviously, as respondent conceded at oral argument, * * * if an employer offers a black and a white applicant for employment the same written contract, but then tells the black employee that her working conditions will be much worse than those of the white hired for the same job because "there's a lot of harassment going on in this work place and you have to agree to that," it would have to be concluded that the white and black had not enjoyed an equal right to make a contract. I see no relevant distinction between that case and one in which the employer's different contractual expectations are unspoken, but become clear during the course of employment as the black employee is subjected to substantially harsher conditions than her white co-workers. In neither case can it be said that whites and blacks have had the same right to make an employment contract.[13] The Court's failure to consider such examples, and to explain the abundance of legislative history that confounds its claim that § 1981 unambiguously decrees the result it favors, underscore just how untenable is the Court's position.

Having reached its decision based upon a supposedly literal reading of § 1981, the Court goes on to suggest that its grudging interpretation of this civil rights statute has the benefit of not undermining Title VII. * * * It is unclear how the interpretation of § 1981 to reach pervasive postcontractual harassment could be thought in any way to undermine Congress' intentions as regards Title VII. Congress has rejected an amendment to Title VII that would have rendered § 1981 unavailable as a remedy for employment discrimination, and has explicitly stated that § 1981 "protects similar rights [to Title VII] but involves fewer technical prerequisites to the filing of an action," * * * that the Acts "provide alternative means to redress individual grievances," * * * and that an employee who is discriminated against "should be accorded every protection that the law has in its purview, and * * * the person should not be forced to seek his remedy in only one place," * * *. Evidently, Title VII and § 1981 provide independent remedies, and neither statute has a preferred status that is to guide interpretation of the other. The Court, indeed, is forced to concede this fact, admitting that where the statutes overlap "we are not at liberty 'to infer any positive preference for one over the other.'" * * * But the Court then goes on to say that the existence of Title VII "should lessen the temptation for this Court to twist the interpretation of [§ 1981] to cover the same conduct." * * * This, of course, brings us back to the question of what § 1981, properly interpreted, means. The Court's lengthy discussion of Title VII adds nothing to an understanding of that issue.

The Court's use of Title VII is not only question-begging; it is also misleading. Section 1981 is a statute of general application, extending

---

13. I observe too that a company's imposition of discriminatory working conditions on black employees will tend to deter other black persons from seeking employment. "[W]hen a person is deterred, because of his race, from even entering negotiations, his equal opportunity to contract is denied as effectively as if he were discouraged by an offer of less favorable terms." Comment, Developments in the Law—Section 1981, 15 Harv.Civ.Rights—Civ.Lib.L.Rev. 29, 101 (1980).

not just to employment contracts, but to *all* contracts. Thus we have held that it prohibits a private school from applying a racially discriminatory admissions policy, *Runyon,* and a community recreational facility from denying membership based on race, *Tillman.* The lower federal courts have found a broad variety of claims of contractual discrimination cognizable under § 1981. *E.g., Wyatt v. Security Inn Food & Beverage, Inc.,* 819 F.2d 69 (CA4 1987) (discriminatory application of hotel bar's policy of ejecting persons who do not order drinks); *Hall v. Bio–Medical Application, Inc.,* 671 F.2d 300 (CA8 1982) (medical facility's refusal to treat black person potentially cognizable under § 1981); *Hall v. Pennsylvania State Police,* 570 F.2d 86 (CA3 1978) (bank policy to offer its services on different terms dependent upon race); *Cody v. Union Electric,* 518 F.2d 978 (CA8 1975) (discrimination with regard to the amount of security deposit required to obtain service); *Howard Security Services, Inc. v. Johns Hopkins Hospital,* 516 F.Supp. 508 (Md.1981) (racially discriminatory award of contract to supply services); *Grier v. Specialized Skills, Inc.,* 326 F.Supp. 856 (WDNC 1971) (discrimination in admissions to barber school); *Scott v. Young,* 307 F.Supp. 1005 (ED Va.1969), aff'd, 421 F.2d 143 (CA4), cert. denied, 398 U.S. 929, 90 S.Ct. 1820, 26 L.Ed.2d 91 (1970) (discrimination in amusement park admissions policy). The Court, however, demonstrates no awareness at all that § 1981 is so much broader in scope than Title VII, instead focusing exclusively upon the claim that its cramped construction of § 1981 "preserve[s] the integrity of Title VII's procedures," * * * and avoids "[u]nnecessary overlap" that would "upset the delicate balance between employee and employer rights struck by Title VII," * * *. Rights as between an employer and employee simply are not involved in many § 1981 cases, and the Court's restrictive interpretation of § 1981, minimizing the overlap with Title VII, may also have the effect of restricting the availability of § 1981 as a remedy for discrimination in a host of contractual situations to which Title VII does not extend.

Even as regards their coverage of employment discrimination, § 1981 and Title VII are quite different. As we have previously noted, "the remedies available under Title VII and under § 1981, although related, and although directed to most of the same ends, are separate, distinct, and independent." * * * Perhaps most important, § 1981 is not limited in scope to employment discrimination by businesses with 15 or more employees, cf. 42 U.S.C. § 2000e(b), and hence may reach the nearly 15% of the workforce not covered by Title VII. See Eisenberg & Schwab, The Importance of Section 1981, 73 Cornell L.Rev. 596, 602 (1988). A § 1981 backpay award may also extend beyond the two-year limit of Title VII. * * * Moreover, a § 1981 plaintiff is not limited to recovering backpay: she may also obtain damages, including punitive damages in an appropriate case. * * * Other differences between the two statutes include the right to a jury trial under § 1981, but not Title VII; a different statute of limitations in § 1981 cases, * * * and the availability under Title VII, but not § 1981, of administrative machinery designed to provide assistance in investigation and conciliation, see *Johnson, supra,* 421 U.S., at 460, 95 S.Ct., at 1720. The fact that § 1981 provides a remedy for a type of racism that remains a serious social ill broader than that available under Title VII hardly provides a good reason to see it, as the Court seems to, as a disruptive blot on the legal landscape, a provision to be construed as narrowly as possible.

C

Applying the standards set forth above, I believe the evidence in this case brings petitioner's harassment claim firmly within the scope of § 1981. Petitioner testified at trial that during her 10 years at McLean she was subjected to racial slurs; given more work than white employees and assigned the most demeaning tasks; passed over for promotion, not informed of promotion opportunities, and not offered training for higher-level jobs; denied wage increases routinely given other employees; and singled out for scrutiny and criticism.

Robert Stevenson, the General Manager and later President of McLean, interviewed petitioner for a file clerk position in 1972. At that time he warned her that all those with whom she would be working were white women, and that they probably would not like working with a black. * * * In fact, however, petitioner testified that it was Stevenson and her supervisors who subjected her to racial harassment, rather than her co-workers. For example, petitioner testified that Stevenson told her on a number of occasions that "blacks are known to work slower than whites by nature," * * *, or, as he put it in one instance, that "some animals [are] faster than other animals." * * * Stevenson also repeatedly suggested that a white would be able to do petitioner's job better than she could. * * * [16]

Despite petitioner's stated desire to "move up and advance" at McLean to an accounting or secretarial position, * * * she testified that she was offered no training for a higher-level job during her entire tenure at the credit union. * * * White employees were offered training, * * * including a white employee at the same level as petitioner but with less seniority. That less senior white employee was eventually promoted to an intermediate accounting clerk position. * * * As with every other promotion opportunity that occurred, petitioner was never informed of the opening. * * * During the 10 years petitioner worked for McLean, white persons were repeatedly hired for more senior positions, without any notice of these job openings being posted, and without petitioner ever being informed of, let alone interviewed for, any of these opportunities. * * * Petitioner claimed to have received different treatment as to wage increases as

---

16. A former manager of data processing for McLean testified that when he recommended a black person for a position as a data processor, Stevenson criticized him, saying that he did not "need any more problems around here," that he would interview the person, but not hire him, and that he would then "search for additional people who are not black." * * *

well as promotion opportunities. Thus she testified that she had been denied a promised pay raise after her first six months at McLean, though white employees automatically received pay raises after six months. * * *

Petitioner testified at length about allegedly unequal work assignments given by Stevenson and her other supervisors, * * * and detailed the extent of her work assignments. * * * When petitioner complained about her workload, she was given no help with it. * * * In fact, she was given more work, and was told she always had the option of quitting. * * * Petitioner claimed that she was also given more demeaning tasks than white employees, and was the only clerical worker who was required to dust and to sweep. * * * She was also the only clerical worker whose tasks were not reassigned during a vacation. Whenever white employees went on vacation, their work was reassigned; but petitioner's work was allowed to accumulate for her return. * * *

Petitioner further claimed that Stevenson scrutinized her more closely and criticized her more severely than white employees. Stevenson, she testified, would repeatedly stare at her while she was working, although he would not do this to white employees. * * * Stevenson also made a point of criticizing the work of white employees in private, or discussing their mistakes at staff meetings without attributing the error to a particular individual. But he would chastise petitioner and the only other black employee publicly at staff meetings. * * *

The defense introduced evidence at trial contesting each of these assertions by petitioner. But given the extent and nature of the evidence produced by Patterson, and the importance of credibility determinations in assigning weight to that evidence, the jury may well have concluded that petitioner was subjected to such serious and extensive racial harassment as to have been denied the right to make an employment contract on the same basis as white employees of the credit union.

III

I agree that the District Court erred when it instructed the jury as to petitioner's burden in proving her claim that McLean violated § 1981 by failing to promote her, because she is black, to an intermediate accounting clerk position. * * *

* * *

I therefore agree that petitioner's promotion discrimination claim must be remanded because of the District Court's erroneous instruction as to petitioner's burden. It seems to me, however, that the Court of Appeals was correct when it said that promotion-discrimination claims are cognizable under § 1981 because they "go to the very existence and nature of the employment contract." * * * The Court's disagreement with this common-sense view, and its statement that "the question whether a promotion claim is actionable under § 1981 depends upon whether the nature of the change in position was such that it involved the opportunity to enter into a new contract with the employer," * * * display nicely how it seeks to eliminate with technicalities the protection § 1981 was intended to afford—to limit protection to the form of the contract entered into, and not to extend it, as Congress intended, to the substance of the contract as it is worked out in practice. Under the Court's view, the employer may deny any number of promotions solely on the basis of race, safe from a § 1981 suit, provided it is careful that promotions do not involve new contracts. It is admittedly difficult to see how a "promotion"—which would seem to imply different duties and employment terms—could be achieved without a new contract, and it may well be as a result that promotion claims will always be cognizable under § 1981. Nevertheless, the same criticisms I have made of the Court's decision regarding harassment claims apply here: proof that an employee was not promoted because she is black—while all around white peers are advanced—shows that the black employee has in substance been denied the opportunity to contract on the equal terms that § 1981 guarantees.

IV

In summary, I would hold that the Court of Appeals erred in deciding that petitioner's racial harassment claim is not cognizable under § 1981. It likewise erred in holding that petitioner could succeed in her promotion-discrimination claim only by proving that she was better qualified for the position of intermediate accounting clerk than the white employee who was in fact promoted.

JUSTICE STEVENS, concurring in the judgment in part and dissenting in part.

When I first confronted the task of interpreting § 1981, I was persuaded by Justice Cardozo's admonition that it is wise for the judge to " 'lay one's own course of bricks on the secure foundation of the courses laid by others who had gone before him.' " *Runyon v. McCrary,* 427 U.S. 160, 191, 96 S.Ct. 2586, 2604, 49 L.Ed.2d 415 (1976) (concurring opinion) (quoting B. Cardozo, The Nature of the Judicial Process 149 (1921)). The Court had already construed the statutory reference to the right "to make and enforce contracts" as a guarantee of equal opportunity, and not merely a guarantee of equal rights. Today the Court declines its own invitation to tear down that foundation and begin to build a different legal structure on its original text. I agree, of course, that *Runyon* should not be overruled. I am also persuaded, however, that the meaning that had already been given to "the same right * * * to make and enforce contracts" that "is enjoyed by white citizens"—the statutory foundation that was preserved in *Runyon*—encompasses an employee's right to protection from racial harassment by her employer.

In *Runyon* we held that § 1981 prohibits a private school from excluding qualified children because they are not white citizens. Just as a qualified nonwhite child has a statutory right to equal access to a private school, so does a nonwhite applicant for employment have a statutory right to enter into a personal service contract with a private employer on the same terms as a white citizen. If an employer should place special obstacles in the path of a black job applicant—perhaps by requiring her to confront an openly biased and hostile interviewer—the interference with the statutory right to make contracts to the same extent "as is enjoyed by white citizens" would be plain.

Similarly, if the white and the black applicants are offered the same terms of employment with just one exception—that the black employee would be required to work in dark, uncomfortable surroundings, whereas the white employee would be given a well-furnished, two-window office—the discrimination would be covered by the statute. In such a case, the Court would find discrimination in the making of the contract because the disparity surfaced before the contract was made. * * * Under the Court's understanding of the statute, the black applicant might recover on one of two theories: She might demonstrate that the employer intended to discourage her from taking the job—which is the equivalent of a "refusal to enter into a contract"—or she might show that the employer actually intended to enter a contract, but "only on discriminatory terms." * * * Under the second of these theories of recovery, however, it is difficult to discern why an employer who makes his intentions known has discriminated in the "making" of a contract, while the employer who conceals his discriminatory intent until after the applicant has accepted the job, only later to reveal that black employees are intentionally harassed and insulted, has not.

It is also difficult to discern why an employer who does not decide to treat black employees less favorably than white employees until after the contract of employment is first conceived is any less guilty of discriminating in the "making" of a contract. A contract is not just a piece of paper. Just as a single word is the skin of a living thought, so is a contract evidence of a vital, ongoing relationship between human beings. An at-will employee, such as petitioner, is not merely performing an existing contract; she is constantly remaking that contract. Whenever significant new duties are assigned to the employee—whether they better or worsen the relationship—the contract is amended and a new contract is made. Thus, if after the employment relationship is formed, the employer deliberately implements a policy of harassment of black employees, he has imposed a contractual term on them that is not the "same" as the contractual provisions that are "enjoyed by white citizens." Moreover, whether employed at-will or for a fixed term, employees typically strive to achieve a more rewarding relationship with their employers. By requiring black employees to work in a hostile environment, the employer has denied them the same opportunity for advancement that is available to white citizens. A deliberate policy of harassment of black employees who are competing with white citizens is, I submit, manifest discrimination in the making of contracts in the sense in which that concept was interpreted in *Runyon v. McCrary, supra*. I cannot believe that the decision in that case would have been different if the school had agreed to allow the black students to attend, but subjected them to segregated classes and other racial abuse.

Indeed, in *Goodman v. Lukens Steel Co.*, 482 U.S. 656, 107 S.Ct. 2617, 96 L.Ed.2d 572 (1987), we built further on the foundation laid in *Runyon*. We decided that a union's "toleration and tacit encouragement of racial harassment" violates § 1981. *Id.*, at 665, 107 S.Ct., at 2623. Although the Court now explains that the *Lukens* decision rested on the union's interference with its members' right to enforce their collective bargaining agreement, * * * when I joined that opinion I thought—and I still think—that the holding rested comfortably on the foundation identified in *Runyon*. In fact, in the section of the *Lukens* opinion discussing the substantive claim, the Court did not once use the term "enforce" or otherwise refer to that particular language in the statute. * * *

The Court's repeated emphasis on the literal language of § 1981 might be appropriate if it were building a new foundation, but it is not a satisfactory method of adding to the existing structure. In the name of logic and coherence, the Court today adds a course of bricks dramatically askew from "the secure foundation of the courses laid by others," replacing a sense of rational direction and purpose in the law with an aimless confinement to a narrow construction of what it means to "make" a contract.

For the foregoing reasons, and for those stated in Parts II(B) and II(C) of Justice Brennan's opinion, I respectfully dissent from the conclusion reached in Part III of the Court's opinion. I also agree with Justice Brennan's discussion of the promotion claim.

Notes on Patterson

1. What do you make of Justice Kennedy's interpretation of Section 1981? Is an employment contract limited to a simple agreement to hire or to promote a worker? Do you think Brenda Patterson would have consented to work under the conditions imposed on her by the Credit Union? What light does the enactment of Title VII in 1964 shed on your understanding of the Congressional purposes underlying the enactment of the original version of Section 1981 in 1866? What are the differences in coverage and remedies under Section 1981 and Title VII?

2. In footnote 6 of his opinion, Justice Kennedy brushed aside the objections offered by Justice Stevens, commenting that "[w]e believe the lower courts will have little difficulty applying the straightforward principles that we announce today." Patterson v. McLean Credit Union, 491 U.S. ___, ___ n. 6, 109 S.Ct. 2363, 2377 n. 6, 105 L.Ed.2d 132, 156 n. 6 (1989). But what appeared so "straightforward" to the Court has not been as obvious to the lower courts. For example, a lively dispute has developed over the question whether a racially-motivated discharge is subject to Section 1981. Compare Booth v. Terminix International, Inc., 722 F.Supp. 675 (D.Kan.1989) (Judge Saffels reiterates his earlier position taken in

Birdwhistle v. Kansas Power & Light Co., 723 F.Supp. 570 (D.Kan.1989) that since termination is directly related to contract enforcement, discharge claims survive *Patterson*) with Rivera v. AT & T Information Systems, Inc., 719 F.Supp. 962 (D.Colo.1989) (holding that "discriminatory discharge, like racial harassment amounting to a breach of contract, is post contract formation conduct" and thus not actionable under section 1981 after *Patterson*). See also Fowler v. McCrory Corporation, 727 F.Supp. 228, 234 (D.Md.1989) (white store manager who claimed constructive discharge because he refused to implement employer's racially discriminatory hiring policies can proceed under section 1981 despite *Patterson;* the court observed that although some plaintiffs may seek to evade *Patterson* by "artful pleading and manipulative interpretation of the Court's language," in this case, "Fowler alleges that he was wronged by misconduct, the deterrence of which lies at the very core of the civil rights laws, and his claim is fully cognizable under § 1981." Which of these two conflicting readings of the case is required by the Court's "straightforward" principles?

3. There appears to be general agreement between the Bush administration and the proponents of The Civil Rights Act of 1990, see p. 131, supra, that the Court's interpretation of section 1981 should be corrected by Congress. Section 12 of the Kennedy-Hawkins bill would add a new subsection (b) to section 1981, to read as follows: "For purposes of this section, the right to 'make and enforce contracts' shall include the making, performance, modification and termination of contracts, and the enjoyment of all benefits, privileges, terms and conditions of the contractual relationship." Deputy General Donald B. Ayer expects a similar proposal to be included in the Administration bill. See Biskupic, "A Bipartisan Hill Coalition Unveils Rights Measure," 48 CQ 392 (No. 6, Feb. 10, 1990).

Page 765. Add to end of discussion of Section 1983:

The Supreme Court held in Will v. Michigan Department of State Police, 490 U.S. ___, 109 S.Ct. 2304, 105 L.Ed.2d 45 (1989) that neither a state nor a state official acting in his or her official capacity may be sued for damages under § 1983 because neither is a "person" within the meaning of that statute. The majority claims that its analysis does not affect Monell v. New York City Department of Social Services, 436 U.S. 658, 98 S.Ct. 2018, 56 L.Ed.2d 611 (1978), cited in the Casebook at p. 765 n. 12. Do you agree? You might also want to consult Jett v. Dallas Independent School District, 491 U.S. ___, 109 S.Ct. 2702, 105 L.Ed.2d 598 (1989).

C. THE EQUAL PAY ACT OF 1963

Page 804. Add new Note 6:

6. Given the persistent wage gap between men and women, can an employer who hires a man and a woman for the same job description, setting their current salaries based in part on their wages in a prior job, escape Equal Pay Act liability if it turns out that the man is paid more than the woman? What about the validity of continuing to pay the higher salary earned by a male employee elsewhere to get him to transfer into a job where the women already working there are being paid a lower amount? Do the first "previous employer salary" cases raise the same

issues under the Equal Pay Act as the second "salary retention plan" cases do? Can the employer justify either practice as a "factor other than sex" under the Act? See Note, When Prior Pay Isn't Equal Pay: A Proposed Standard for the Identification of "Factors Other Than Sex" Under the Equal Pay Act, 89 Colum.L.Rev. 1085 (1989).

D. EXECUTIVE ORDER 11246

Notes on the Executive Order

Page 808. Add new Notes 4 and 5; renumber old Note 4 as Note 6:

4. A set-aside for minority business enterprises adopted by the City of Richmond and modeled on the Public Works Employment Act of 1977 upheld in *Fullilove* did not pass constitutional muster. A majority of the Court held in City of Richmond v. J.A. Croson Co., 488 U.S. 469, 109 S.Ct. 706, 102 L.Ed.2d 854 (1989) that a 30% set-aside favoring minority businesses owned and controlled by "Blacks, Spanish-speaking, Orientals, Indians, Eskimos, or Aleuts" impermissibly discriminated against other contractors on the basis of their race. In Part III–A of her opinion, which was joined only by Chief Justice Rehnquist and Justices White and Kennedy, Justice O'Connor noted that blacks composed approximately 50% of the Richmond City Council. Why is this fact relevant to an assessment of the plan's validity? See The Supreme Court—Leading Cases, 103 Harv.L.Rev. 137, 227 (1989), arguing that the plurality's focus on the racial composition of the Richmond City Council is "misleading" because "[d]ue to their monopoly on the attributes of wealth and power and their dominance at the state and national levels, whites simply do not require extraordinary protection from majoritarian politics at the local level." Do you agree with this analysis?

Speaking for the Court in Part III–B of her opinion, Justice O'Connor wrote:

> In sum, none of the evidence presented by the city points to any identified discrimination in the Richmond construction industry. We, therefore, hold that the city has failed to demonstrate a compelling interest in apportioning public contracting opportunities on the basis of race. To accept Richmond's claim that past societal discrimination alone can serve as the basis for rigid racial preferences would be to open the door to competing claims for "remedial relief" for every disadvantaged group. The dream of a Nation of equal citizens in a society where race is irrelevant to personal opportunity and achievement would be lost in a mosaic of shifting preferences based on inherently unmeasurable claims of past wrongs. "Courts would be asked to evaluate the extent of the prejudice and consequent harm suffered by various minority groups. Those whose societal injury is thought to exceed some arbitrary level of tolerability then would be entitled to preferential classifications * * *." *Bakke*, 438 U.S., at 296–297, 98 S.Ct., at 2751 (Powell, J.). We think such a result would be contrary to both the letter and spirit of a constitutional provision whose central command is equality.

The foregoing analysis applies only to the inclusion of blacks within the Richmond set-aside program. There is *absolutely no evidence* of past discrimination against Spanish-speaking, Oriental, Indian, Eskimo, or Aleut persons in any aspect of the Richmond construction industry. The District Court took judicial notice of the fact that the vast majority of "minority" persons in Richmond were black. * * * It may well be that Richmond has never had an Aleut or Eskimo citizen. The random inclusion of racial groups that, as a practical matter, may never have suffered from discrimination in the construction industry in Richmond, suggests that perhaps the city's purpose was not in fact to remedy past discrimination.

If a 30% set-aside was "narrowly tailored" to compensate black contractors for past discrimination, one may legitimately ask why they are forced to share this "remedial relief" with an Aleut citizen who moves to Richmond tomorrow? The gross overinclusiveness of Richmond's racial preference strongly impugns the city's claim of remedial motivation. See *Wygant,* 476 U.S., at 284, n. 13, 106 S.Ct., at 1852, n. 13 (haphazard inclusion of racial groups "further illustrates the undifferentiated nature of the plan"); see also Days 482 ("Such programs leave one with the sense that the racial and ethnic groups favored by the set-aside were added without attention to whether their inclusion was justified by evidence of past discrimination").

In dissent, Justice Marshall warned that:

A majority of this Court holds today, however, that the Equal Protection Clause of the Fourteenth Amendment blocks Richmond's initiative. The essence of the majority's position is that Richmond has failed to catalogue adequate findings to prove that past discrimination has impeded minorities from joining or participating fully in Richmond's construction contracting industry. I find deep irony in second-guessing Richmond's judgment on this point. As much as any municipality in the United States, Richmond knows what racial discrimination is; a century of decisions by this and other federal courts has richly documented the city's disgraceful history of public and private racial discrimination. In any event, the Richmond City Council has supported its determination that minorities have been wrongly excluded from local construction contracting. Its proof includes statistics showing that minority-owned businesses have received virtually no city contracting dollars and rarely if ever belonged to area trade associations; testimony by municipal officials that discrimination has been widespread in the local construction industry; and the same exhaustive and widely publicized federal studies relied on in *Fullilove,* studies which showed that pervasive discrimination in the Nation's tight-knit construction industry had operated to exclude minorities from public contracting. These are precisely the types of statistical and testimonial evidence which, until today, this Court had credited in cases approving of race-conscious measures designed to remedy past discrimination.

More fundamentally, today's decision marks a deliberate and giant step backward in this Court's affirmative action jurisprudence. Cynical of one municipality's attempt to redress the effects of past racial discrimination in a particular industry, the majority launches a grape-shot attack on race-conscious remedies in general. The majority's unnecessary pronouncements will inevitably discourage or prevent governmental entities, particularly States and localities, from acting to rectify the scourge of past discrimination. This is the harsh reality of the majority's decision, but it is not the Constitution's command.

In an effort to avert the wholesale dismantling of municipal affirmative action plans, Professor Laurence Tribe convened an unprecedented Constitutional Scholars' Conference on Affirmative Action at the African Meeting House in Boston on March 30, 1989. The resulting "Constitutional Scholars' Statement on Affirmative Action After *City of Richmond v. J.A. Croson Co.* was subsequently published in 98 Yale L.J. 1711 (1989). Its message, that the conclusion that "the Constitution forbids all such inclusive remedial measures, or requires that such measures be treated in exactly the same way as the invidious discrimination of the Nation's past" was in turn sharply disputed by former Solicitor General Charles Fried in "A Response to the Scholars' Statement," 99 Yale L.J. 155 (1989). See also the "Scholars' Reply to Professor Fried," 99 Yale L.J. 163 (1989). What do you suppose motivated the convening of the Conference?

Professor Devins places the affirmative action controversy in a political as well as a doctrinal context, concluding that "[t]he boundaries of permissible affirmative action remain uncertain" after *Croson*. See Devins, Essay: Affirmative Action After Reagan, 68 Tex.L.Rev. 353 (1989).

5. The Court reduced some of the uncertainty surrounding the boundaries of permissible affirmative action in its 5–4 decision in Metro Broadcasting, Inc. v. FCC, ___ U.S. ___, 110 S.Ct. ___, ___ L.Ed.2d ___ (1990). The case involved a constitutional challoenge to FCC policies designed to promote diversity in programming by increasing the number of broadcast license holders who are members of minority groups. Two FCC policies were at issue: the "distress sale" program, which, according to the agency's 1978 Policy Statement, permits

> licensees whose licenses have been designated for revocation hearing, or whose renewal applications have been designated for hearing on basic qualification issues ... to transfer or assign their licenses at a "distress sale" price to applicants with a significant minority ownership interest, assuming the proposed assignee or transferee meets our other qualifications.

The second FCC policy is that of granting qualitative enhancements to minority applicants for new licenses in comparative hearings. Both policies also contain sex preferences, but those preferences were not before the Court in *Metro Broadcasting*.

Justice Brennan aligned the legal problem in *Metro Broadcasting* with that presented in *Fullilove* rather than *Croson*, pointing out the "overriding significance" of the fact that the FCC's minority ownership programs had been "specifically approved—indeed, mandated—by Congress" and going on to "hold that benign race-conscious measures mandated by Congress—even if those measures are not 'remedial' in the sense of being designed to compensate victims of past governmental or societal discrimination—are constitutionally permissible to the extent that they serve important govern-

Sec. D   EXECUTIVE ORDER 11246   239

mental objectives within the power of Congress and are substantially related to achievement of those objectives." Id., ___ U.S. at ___, 110 S.Ct. at ___, ___ L.Ed.2d at ___. The Court limited *Croson* to minority set-aside programs adopted by a municipality, noting that the case does not control the level of scrutiny applied to a "benign racial classification employed by Congress." Id., ___ U.S. at ___, 110 S.Ct. at ___, ___ L.Ed.2d ___. Applying this newly-adopted intermediate level of scrutiny, the Court held that the FCC minority ownership policies served the important governmental objective of broadcast diversity, and that those policies are substantially related to the achievement of that objective. In announcing the Court's position on the latter point, Justice Brennan reaffirmed and expanded Justice Powell's approach to educational diversity in University of California Regents v. Bakke, 438 U.S. 265, 311–15, 98 S.Ct. 2733, 2759–61, 57 L.Ed.2d 750, 785–86 (1978) (opinion of Powell, J.), as follows:

C

The judgment that there is a link between expanded minority ownership and broadcast diversity does not rest on impermissible stereotyping. Congressional policy does not assume that in every case minority ownership and management will lead to more minority-oriented programming or to the expression of a discrete "minority viewpoint" on the airwaves. Neither does it pretend that all programming that appeals to minority audiences can be labeled "minority programming" or that programming that might be described as "minority" does not appeal to nonminorities. Rather, both Congress and the FCC maintain simply that expanded minority ownership of broadcast outlets will, in the aggregate, result in greater broadcast diversity. A broadcasting industry with representative minority participation will produce more variation and diversity than will one whose ownership is drawn from a single racially and ethnically homogeneous group. The predictive judgment about the overall result of minority entry into broadcasting is not a rigid assumption about how minority owners will behave in every case but rather is akin to Justice Powell's conclusion in *Bakke* that greater admission of minorities would contribute, on average, "to the 'robust exchange of ideas.'" * * * To be sure, there is no ironclad guarantee that each minority owner will contribute to diversity. But neither was there an assurance in *Bakke* that minority students would interact with nonminority students or that the particular minority students admitted would have typical or distinct "minority" viewpoints. See *id.*, * * * (opinion of Powell, J.) (noting only that educational excellence is "*widely believed* to be promoted by a diverse student body") (emphasis added); *id.*, * * * (" 'In the nature of things, it is hard to know how, and when, and even if, this informal "learning through diversity" actually occurs' ") (citation omitted).

Although all station owners are guided to some extent by market demand in their programming decisions, Congress and the Commission have determined that there may be important differences between the broadcasting practices of minority owners and those of their nonminority counterparts. This judgment—and the conclusion that there is a nexus between minority ownership and broadcasting diversity—is corroborated by a host of empirical evidence. * * *

Id., ___ U.S. at ___, 110 S.Ct. at ___, ___ L.Ed.2d at ___.

Justice Stevens, concurring, welcomed the Court's new approach to affirmative action:

> Today the Court squarely rejects the proposition that a governmental decision that rests on a racial classification is never permissible except as a remedy for a past wrong. * * * I endorse this focus on the future benefit, rather than the remedial justification, of such decisions.
>
> I remain convinced, of course, that racial or ethnic characteristics provide a relevant basis for disparate treatment only in extremely rare situations and that it is therefore "especially important that the reasons for any such classification be clearly identified and unquestionably legitimate." *Fullilove v. Klutznick,* * * * (dissenting opinion). The Court's opinion explains how both elements of that standard are satisfied. Specifically, the reason for the classification—the recognized interest in broadcast diversity—is clearly identified and does not imply any judgment concerning the abilities of owners of different races or the merits of different kinds of programming. Neither the favored nor the disfavored class is stigmatized in any way. In addition, the Court demonstrates that this case falls within the extremely narrow category of governmental decisions for which racial or ethnic heritage may provide a rational basis for differential treatment. The public interest in broadcast diversity—like the interest in an integrated police force, diversity in the composition of a public school faculty or diversity in the student body of a professional school—is in my view unquestionably legitimate.
>
> Therefore, I join both the opinion and the judgment of the Court.

Id., ___ U.S. at ___, 110 S.Ct. at ___, ___ L.Ed.2d at ___.

Justice O'Connor, joined in dissent by the Chief Justice and Justices Scalia and Kennedy, strongly protested the Court's "renewed toleration of racial classifications and [its] repudiation of our recent affirmation that the Constitution's equal protection guarantees extend equally to all citizens." Id., ___ U.S. at ___, 110 S.Ct. at ___, ___ L.Ed.2d at ___. Justices Kennedy and Scalia dissenting separately, scathingly compared the Court's opinion to the decision in Plessy v. Ferguson, 163 U.S. 537, 16 S.Ct. 1138, 41 L.Ed. 256 (1896), which they characterized as having upheld "a government-sponsored race-conscious measure" designed to serve "the governmental interest of increasing the riding pleasure of railroad passengers." Id., ___ U.S. at ___, 110 S.Ct. at ___, ___ L.Ed.2d at ___. They concluded by repeating Justice Harlan's warning:

> Though the racial composition of this Nation is far more diverse than the first Justice Harlan foresaw, his warning in dissent is now all the more apposite: "The destinies of the two races, in this country, are indissolubly linked together, and the interests of both require that the common government of all shall not permit the seeds of race hate to be planted under the sanction of law." *Plessy,* * * * (dissenting opin-

ion). Perhaps the Court can succeed in its assumed role of case-by-case arbiter of when it is desirable and benign for the Government to disfavor some citizens and favor others based on the color of their skin. Perhaps the tolerance and decency to which our people aspire will let the disfavored rise above hostility and the favored escape condescension. But history suggests much peril in this enterprise, and so the Constitution forbids us to undertake it. I regret that after a century of judicial opinions we interpret the Constitution to do no more than move us from "separate but equal" to "unequal but benign."

Id., ___ U.S. at ___, 110 S.Ct. at ___, ___ L.Ed.2d at ___.

Text Note

The Role of Unions in Employment Discrimination

Page 812. Add before last paragraph:

In Lorance v. AT & T Technologies, Inc., 490 U.S. ___, 109 S.Ct. 2261, 104 L.Ed.2d 961 (1989), women working as testers who had lost plantwide seniority as the result of a collective-bargaining agreement that changed the way seniority was calculated for workers who were promoted into tester jobs from hourly wage jobs challenged the agreement as discriminatory. The higher-paying tester jobs had traditionally been held by men; plaintiffs claimed that the collective-bargaining agreement was intended to protect those jobs for men by forcing women who sought promotion to give up their plantwide seniority for a period of five years after the promotion. Plaintiff Patricia Lorance had held her job as a tester for four years when she was demoted; plaintiffs Janice King and Carol Bueschen became testers several months after the restructured seniority system became effective on July 23, 1979. During an economic downswing in 1982, all three women were selected for demotion. Had the plantwide seniority system remained in effect, all would have been able to keep their jobs. Plaintiffs did not claim that restructured seniority system treats similarly situated workers differently, or that it was applied in an intentionally discriminatory manner. Rather, they claimed that the original agreement was the product of intentional sex discrimination, designed to protect the incumbent male testers.

The Supreme Court never reached the merits of the women's claim in *Lorence,* however, for it held instead that their claim was time-barred. Justice Scalia pointed out that:

> Under the collective-bargaining agreements in effect prior to 1979, each petitioner had earned the right to receive a favorable position in the hierarchy of seniority among testers (if and when she became a tester), and respondents eliminated those rights for reasons alleged to be discriminatory. Because this diminution in employment status occurred in 1979—well outside the period of limitations for a complaint filed with the EEOC in 1983—the Seventh Circuit was correct to find petitioners' claims time-barred under § 706(e).

When should plaintiffs have filed their challenge to the reconstituted seniority system? 300 days after its adoption, or in case of a complaint not previously filed with a state or local agency, 180 days. What were plaintiffs doing at that time? Patricia Lorance was working as a tester and accruing time on her five year period; Janice King and Carol Bueschen were still working as hourly wage employees. As Justice Marshall commented in dissent, none of these plaintiffs was given any "advance warning" that they might be harmed by the new seniority system at the time it was adopted: "For them, the majority holds, the limitations clock began running, and ran out, long before it was apparent that they would be demoted by AT & T's discriminatory system."

Section Seven of the proposed Civil Rights Act of 1990, see supra p. 131, would reverse *Lorance* by amending section 703(h) of Title VII to add a special provision for challenges to seniority systems contained in collective-bargaining agreements. The text reads as follows:

> Where a seniority system or seniority practice is part of a collective bargaining agreement and such system or practice was included in such agreement with the intent to discriminate on the basis of race, color, religion, sex, or national origin, the application of such system or practice during the period that such collective bargaining agreement is in effect shall be an unlawful employment practice.

In addition, the bill proposes to extend the 180 day filing period in section 706(e) to two years. Are these changes a good idea?

Chapter IV

EDUCATIONAL OPPORTUNITY

A. SEX SEGREGATION IN EDUCATIONAL INSTITUTIONS

1. ADMISSION BARRIERS: SINGLE–SEX AND SEX QUOTA SCHOOLS

Page 822. Add to Note 3:

The Justice Department has begun an investigation of The Citadel's policy of restricting admission to men. San Francisco Chronicle, March 12, 1990, p. A3, at col. 1. The Department had earlier filed suit against the Virginia Military Institute claiming that its male-only admission policy violates the 14th Amendment. The San Francisco Banner Daily Journal, March 5, 1990, p. 6, col. 1.

Text Note

Is There a Place for Women's Colleges?

Page 828. Add to text at footnote 7:

On May 3, 1990, The Board of Trustees of Mills College voted to admit men as undergraduates, beginning in 1991. Women students shaved their heads, shut down classes, and demonstrated in T-shirts reading "Better dead than co-ed." Chair Warren Hellman explained that "Mills needs at least 1,000 undergraduates in order to secure a strong future." Mills currently enrolls 777 women undergraduates; tuition is $17,000 per year. San Francisco Chronicle, May 4, 1990, at A1, col. 1.

The students' tactics were successful. On May 18, 1990, the Mills Trustees reversed their decision as faculty, alumnae, and staff dedicated themselves to resolve the school's financial problems by 1995. President Mary Metz, who had voted to admit men, declared, "A passion for women's education has made history." New York Times, May 19, 1990, at 1, col. 1. Metz herself, however, will not be available to lead the five-year effort at student recruitment and fund-raising necessary to translate the new decision into reality. On June 22, 1990, she resigned as President, effective immediately. New York Times, June 23, 1990, at 7, col. 4. See generally D. Rhode, Justice and Gender 288–98 (1989).

2. THE RIGHT TO EQUAL PLAY: SEX SEGREGATION IN ATHLETIC PROGRAMS

Page 835. Add to Note 1:

The Ninth Circuit adhered to its position in Clark v. Arizona Interscholastic Association, 886 F.2d 1191 (9th Cir.1989) (Clark II), an identical challenge to the AIA rule restricting interscholastic competition in volleyball to single-sex teams brought by Wade Clark, the younger brother of the named plaintiff in the class action suit considered in *Clark I*, Gregory Clark. Wade argued in part that because the social attitudes contributing to women's unequal participation in sports "may persist forever," the chosen remedy of excluding males from volleyball did not qualify as a narrowly drawn, constitutional affirmative action plan permissible under City of Richmond v. J.A. Croson Co., discussed supra at p. 236. The court rejected this argument on the ground that, as Clark conceded, female athletes within AIA's jurisdiction presently suffer the effects of past discrimination, and that the AIA's rule protecting them against being displaced is substantially related to the goal of redressing past discrimination. Is that sufficient under *Croson?* See also Rowley v. Board of Education of St. Vrain Valley School District, 863 F.2d 39 (10th Cir.1988), reversing a district court's preliminary injunction ordering that a male be allowed to try out for the girls' volleyball team, provided he did not displace any member of the Varsity team, on the ground that the court had used an equal protection standard more stringent than that approved in Craig v. Boren, set out in the Casebook at p. 30.

Page 836. Add to Note 2:

See also Croteau v. Fair, 686 F.Supp. 552 (E.D.Va.1988), dismissing Nancy Croteau's claim that she was not allowed to play on the varsity baseball team after passing the first cut because of her sex. Judge Ellis was not persuaded that Nancy was eliminated because of her sex: "[r]ather, the Court is convinced that plaintiff received a fair tryout and that the decision to cut her was made in good faith and for reasons unrelated to gender." The judge pointed out that plaintiff had no constitutional or statutory right to play baseball, only a right "to compete for such a position on equal terms and to be free from sex discrimination in state action." Did Nancy Croteau compete on equal terms?

B. LEGAL REMEDIES FOR SEX DISCRIMINATION IN EDUCATIONAL INSTITUTIONS

Page 854. Add new Note 3:

3. In Sharif by Salahuddin v. New York State Educ. Dept., 709 F.Supp. 345 (S.D.N.Y.1989), plaintiffs relied on Title IX and its implementing regulations as well as the Equal Protection Clause to challenge defendants' practice of using Scholastic Aptitude Test (SAT) scores as the sole basis for awarding Regents College Scholarships and Empire State Scholarships of Excellence to high school students. Plaintiffs did not allege intentional discrimination; rather, they argued that the practice had a

disparate impact on females. Plaintiffs presented the following showing of statistical impact:

3. STATISTICAL IMPACT ON MEN AND WOMEN STATEWIDE

Males have outscored females on the verbal portion of the SAT since 1972, with an average score differential of at least 10 points since 1981. Males have also consistently outscored females on the mathematics portion, with an average differential of at least 40 points since 1967. In 1988, for example, girls scored 56 points lower than boys on the test. The probability that these score differentials happened by chance is approximately about one in a billion and the probability that the result could consistently be so different is essentially zero. * * *

Statisticians have attempted to explain the score differentials between males and females by removing the effect of "neutral" variables, such as ethnicity, socioeducational status (parental education), high school classes, and proposed college major. However, under the most conservative studies presented in evidence, even after removing the effect of these factors, at least a 30 point combined differential remains unexplained.

As a result of the State's practice of basing scholarship awards solely upon SAT scores, males have consistently received substantially more scholarships than females. In 1987 for example, males were 47 percent of the scholarship competitors, but received 72 percent of the Empire State Scholarships and 57 percent of the Regents Scholarships. For Empire State Scholarships, these results represent 15.8 standard deviations from the mean; for Regents Scholarships, the difference represents 31.7 standard deviations. In other words, the probability that the Empire Scholarship results would occur by chance is less than one in a billion, and the probability of the Regents Scholarship results would occur by chance is even less.

Id., 709 F.Supp. at 355–56.

Judge Walker ruled that the Title IX claim could proceed without a showing of intentional discrimination, and granted a preliminary injunction based on plaintiff's showing of disparate impact. He also held that the challenged practice could not survive even the minimal scrutiny required by the rational relationship standard. Excerpts from his opinion follow.

2. LIKELIHOOD OF SUCCESS ON MERITS

a. Title IX

Plaintiffs invoke the protections provided by Title IX, which prohibits sex discrimination in federally-funded educational programs. Plaintiffs do not claim that defendants have intentionally discriminated against them based on their sex. Rather, they claim that defendants' practice of sole reliance upon SAT scores to award prestigious state scholarships disparately impacts female students. To this Court's knowledge, this is the first disparate impact case challenging educational testing practices under Title IX.

Neither the Supreme Court nor any court in the Second Circuit has determined whether intent must be shown in Title IX cases. This

Court, however, is not without substantial guidance. Recognizing that "Title IX was patterned after Title VI of the Civil Rights Act of 1964," Grove City College v. Bell, 465 U.S. 555, 566, 104 S.Ct. 1211, 1218, 79 L.Ed.2d 516 (1984), courts examining Title IX questions have looked to the substantial body of law developed under Title VI, 42 U.S.C. § 2000d, which prohibits race discrimination in federally-funded programs, and Title VII, 42 U.S.C. § 2000e, which prohibits discrimination in employment. See, e.g., Mabry v. State Board of Community Colleges and Occupational Education, 813 F.2d 311, 317 (10th Cir.), cert. denied, 484 U.S. 849, 108 S.Ct. 148, 98 L.Ed.2d 104 (1987); Haffer v. Temple University, 678 F.Supp. 517, 539 (E.D.Pa.1987).

In Guardians Association v. Civil Service Commission, 463 U.S. 582, 103 S.Ct. 3221, 77 L.Ed.2d 866 (1983), the Supreme Court held that a violation of Title VI itself requires proof of discriminatory intent. However, a majority also agreed that proof of discriminatory effect suffices to establish liability when a suit is brought to enforce the regulations promulgated under Title VI, rather than statute itself. See also Alexander v. Choate, 469 U.S. 287, 293–294, 105 S.Ct. 712, 716, 83 L.Ed.2d 661 (1985); Latinos Unidos de Chelsea v. Secretary of Housing, 799 F.2d 774, 785 n. 20 (1st Cir.1986).

Plaintiffs' amended complaint explicitly alleges both violations of Title IX and its implementing regulations. This Court finds no persuasive reason not to apply Title VI's substantive standards to the present Title IX suit. * * *

The Title IX implementing regulations, like the regulations promulgated under Title VI, to which Title IX is frequently compared, are consistent with this interpretation of the comprehensive reach of the statute. Several Title IX regulations specifically prohibit facially neutral policies. * * *

Based upon a reading of the Title IX regulations, as well as the decisions that apply them, the Court finds that Title IX regulations, like the Title VI regulations at issue in *Guardians,* prohibit testing practices with a discriminatory *effect* on one sex. Consequently, plaintiffs need not prove intentional discrimination.

* * *

Applying the Title VII formulations to this Title IX case as modified to take into account "educational necessity," this Court finds that plaintiffs have demonstrated a likelihood of success on the merits. Plaintiffs have met their burden of establishing a *prima facie* case through persuasive statistical evidence and credible expert testimony that the composition of scholarship winners tilted decidedly toward males and could not have occurred by a random distribution. * * * Defendants have failed to attack plaintiffs' evidence of statewide disparate impact but have instead focused in an *ad hoc* fashion on individual schools and counties. In a case alleging statewide discrimination, such a focus does not rebut plaintiffs' statewide *prima facie* case.

Plaintiffs, moreover, have established that the probability, absent discriminatory causes, that women would consistently score 60 points less on the SAT than men is nearly zero. * * * Defendants concede that at least half of this differential cannot be explained away by "neutral" variables. Based upon the totality of evidence, then, this Court finds that plaintiffs have demonstrated that the State's practice of sole reliance upon the SAT disparately impacts young women.

Thus, to prevail, defendants must show a manifest relationship between use of the SAT and recognition and award of academic achievement in high school. The Court finds that defendants have failed to show even a reasonable relationship between their practice and their conceded purpose. The SAT was not designed to measure achievement in high school and was never validated for that purpose.

* * *

* * *

Plaintiffs have offered an alternative to sole reliance upon the SAT: a combination of GPAs and SATs. The SED's use of this alternative in 1988 sharply reduced the disparate impact against females caused by the use of the SAT alone. A significantly greater number of female students received scholarships in 1988 than in each prior year in which the SED relied solely upon the SAT. * * * Defendants concede that females had a greater opportunity to receive scholarships under the combination system. Defendants also concede that grades are the best measure of high school achievement within the walls of a single school. Instead, they argue that since there is a disparity among schools and their grading systems it is both unfair and impossible to use grades as part of the scholarship eligibility determination. Defendants plan instead to develop a statewide achievement test. While this Court does not dispute the apparent advantages of a statewide achievement test—if indeed a valid test can be developed—it does not agree that pending the implication of such a test, use of grades would be either unfair or infeasible.

While a combination system—using both GPAs and SATs—is not a perfect alternative, it is the best alternative presently available. The SED is concerned that students in academically superior high schools not be disadvantaged by the use of GPAs. This concern is addressed by the combination system because in effect grades would be weighted by SATs. The SAT component which cannot properly itself measure achievement serves to balance the grade component that does. In this way, the SED's concern that use of grades alone will deprive good students in superior high schools of scholarships is ameliorated. * * * More importantly, the combination system would be "fair" in the larger sense of the word, because it would better advance the state's goal of awarding high school performance and would better provide *all* students—not just male students or students from selective schools—with an equal opportunity to compete for prestigious state scholarships.

* * *

Faced with a conflict between the SED's administrative concerns on the one hand, and the risk of substantial discriminatory harm to plaintiffs on the other, the Court has little difficulty in concluding that the balance of hardships tips decidedly in plaintiffs' favor. See Mitchell v. Cuomo, 748 F.2d 804, 808 (2d Cir.1984). The Court finds that plaintiffs have offered a feasible alternative to sole reliance upon SATs. Accordingly, the Court finds that plaintiffs have demonstrated a likelihood of success on the merits of their Title IX claim and, thus, a preliminary injunction is warranted.

b. *Equal Protection*

Alternatively, a preliminary injunction is warranted because plaintiffs also have established a likelihood that they will succeed on their equal protection claim. The classification of scholarship applicants solely on the basis of SAT scores violates the equal protection clause of the Fourteenth Amendment because this method is not rationally related to the state's goal of rewarding students who have demonstrated academic achievement.

Under the lowest standard of equal protection review—the "rational relationship standard"—"[t]he State may not rely on a classification whose relationship to an asserted goal is so attenuated as to render the distinction arbitrary or irrational." City of Cleburne v. Cleburne Living Center, 473 U.S. 432, 446, 105 S.Ct. 3249, 3257, 87 L.Ed.2d 313 (1985). Although considerable deference is given to the decisions of legislators and state administrators under the rational basis test, the test "is not a toothless one." * * * In a long line of cases, the Supreme Court has applied rational basis scrutiny to strike down legislation where the permissible bounds of rationality were exceeded.

* * *

For the reasons stated above, the SED's use of the SAT as a proxy for high school achievement is too unrelated to the legislative purpose of awarding academic achievement in high school to survive even the most minimal scrutiny. The evidence is clear that females score significantly below males on the SAT while they perform equally or slightly better than males in high school. Therefore, the SED's use of the SAT as the sole criterion for awarding Regents and Empire Scholarships discriminates against females and, since such a practice is not rationally related to the legislative purpose, it unconstitutionally denies young women equal protection of the laws and must be enjoined on that ground as well.

* * *

Id., 709 F.Supp. at 360–64. In footnote 39 of his opinion, Judge Walker brushed aside the defendants' reliance on Justice O'Connor's opinion in Watson v. Forth Worth Bank & Trust, set forth in the Casebook at p. 981, concerning the quantum of proof needed for disparate impact cases, on the ground that she spoke only for a plurality of the Court. Now that her opinion has been accepted by a majority in Wards Cove Packing Co. v. Atonio, set forth supra at p. 114, is *Sharif* no longer good law? A notewriter argues that, although *Sharif* significantly expanded Title IX, *Wards Cove* does not impair its holding. See Recent Cases, 103 Harv.L.Rev. 806 (1990). Do you agree?

C. SEXISM AND SEXUALITY IN ACADEMIC LIFE

1. SEXUAL HARASSMENT

Page 875. Add to Note 2:

In Bougher v. University of Pittsburgh, 713 F.Supp. 139 (W.D.Pa.1989), the court flatly rejected in scathing terms a plaintiff's effort to build on a Title VII model to establish a claim of "hostile environment" sexual harassment under Title IX.

> Plaintiff does not state, nor do the facts allege, a Title IX claim against Pitt. Even accepting plaintiff's uncorroborated allegations as true (and leaving aside such overwrought prose as "instead of being her mentor Dr. Melia became her tormentor" [3]), she does not allege the denial of any benefit by Pitt to her on the basis of sex. For that matter, she does not allege defendant Melia discriminated in any respect either. There is therefore, no *quid pro quo* claim. The plaintiff's complaint and evidence begin and end with an alleged consensual sexual relationship which began in 1976 when she was over twenty-one years old and ended at the latest in 1983, more than two years prior to the filing of this complaint.
>
> An extensive recital of plaintiff's evidence is not necessary. She portrays herself as the victim of a lecherous professor [4] from whom she took a single course in rhetoric in 1976. She does not assert that her association and alleged sexual relationship caused her to be denied any academic benefit unless she agreed to have a continuing relationship with him. She complains rather that the relationship which in retrospect was "unwelcome" and "violative" but which at all times was consensual, "went sour" after she called defendant Melia at his family residence, but that defendant, though now cold and distant emotionally, still intruded on her life.
>
> For this intrusion, she seeks to hold Pitt responsible.
>
> Defendant Melia is not alleged at any point after 1976 to have had any official role as plaintiff's advisor or teacher. At most, he is alleged to have abandoned a paper that Melia and plaintiff were co-authoring, forcing plaintiff to complete it at some inconvenience to her Christmas vacation.
>
> Melia's work on the paper is not alleged to be in any way related to any duty or office held by him.
>
> Plaintiff, desirous of stating a claim, ignores judicial precedent and blandly blurs fundamental distinctions between Title VII of the Civil

---

[3]. This is only a sample of what is submitted by way of legal memorandum. We exhort the trial bar to leave the writing of romantic prose to those who are qualified for it, and remember that nouns and verbs, rather than conclusory adjectives, are the stuff of which clear thought and persuasive argument is made.

[4]. "The Lecherous Professor" is the title of a book co-authored by an expert witness proffered by plaintiff. It is an anecdotal account of the author's research into sexual relationships between male faculty members and female students.

Rights Act of 1964, an exercise by Congress of its power under the Commerce Clause to regulate employment conditions, and Title IX of the Education Amendments of 1972, an exercise by Congress under the Spending Clause to eliminate the use of federal funds in certain discriminatory educational programs. See Guardians Association v. Civil Service Commission, 463 U.S. 582, 596, 103 S.Ct. 3221, 3229, 77 L.Ed.2d 866 (1983) (opinion of White, J. announcing the judgment of the Court) for the inappropriate nature of a damages remedy.

Plaintiff begins by assuming her conclusions—that what defendant Melia was allegedly guilty of is sexual harassment for which Pitt is responsible, and that sexual harassment, construed as any sexual involvement between a Pitt employee and a student, violates Title IX. Both assumptions are incorrect. Under Title VII, the Equal Employment Opportunity Commission of the Department of Labor, as an exercise of its agency expertise in interpreting and administratively enforcing Title VII, has promulgated, at 29 C.F.R. § 1604.11 guidelines for defining sexual discrimination in employment. Included in the guidelines, upheld as an exercise of agency discretion within the agency's area of expertise in Meritor Savings Bank v. Vinson, 477 U.S. 57, 65, 106 S.Ct. 2399, 2405, 91 L.Ed.2d 49 (1986), is the "hostile environment" definition of sexual harassment:

> Unwelcome sexual advances * * * *and other verbal or physical conduct* of a sexual nature * * * constitute sexual harassment when * * * (3) such conduct has the purpose or effect of unreasonably interfering with an individual's work performance or creating an intimidating, hostile or offensive working environment. (emphasis added)

29 C.F.R. § 1604.11(a)(3) (1988). Plaintiff, aside from asking the Court to interpret the meaning of "unwelcome" to include "it used to be welcome, but now it's not", is also asking the court to transfer wholesale the EEOC guidelines into an area for which they were not drafted, for enforcement directly by the judiciary without administrative review by the OCR, and in ignorance of Title VI, 42 U.S.C. § 2000d, after which Title IX was patterned, *Cannon v. University of Chicago,* supra, and the procedural provisions of which Title IX adopts. 34 C.F.R. § 106.71.

Title IX prevents gender discrimination in a federal program's distribution of benefits. It also clearly reaches what has been defined as *quid pro quo* sexual harassment by a recipient of Federal funds, since without administrative interpretation this clearly violates Title IX by conditioning benefits on the basis of impermissible criteria. But to suggest, as plaintiff must, that unwelcome sexual advances, from *whatever* source, official or unofficial, constitute Title IX violations is a leap into the unknown which, whatever its wisdom, is the duty of Congress or an administrative agency to take. Title IX simply does not permit a "hostile environment" claim as described for the workplace by 29 C.F.R. § 1604.11(a)(3).

* * *

Id., at 144–45. On appeal, the Third Circuit found it "unnecessary" to reach the question whether evidence of a hostile environment is sufficient to sustain a claim of sexual discrimination in education in violation of Title IX, holding instead that most of the alleged events plaintiff cited to establish her case occurred prior to the applicable limitations period and those few that fell within the 180 day period prior to the filing date were insufficient to create a cause of action. Bougher v. University of Pittsburgh, 882 F.2d 74, 77 (3d Cir.1989).

Page 876. Add to Note 4:

In 1989, the Association of American Law Schools adopted a "Statement of Good Practices by Law Professors in the Discharge of Their Ethical and Professional Responsibilities." The following two paragraphs are included in the Section titled "Responsibilities to Students:"

> Discriminatory conduct based on such factors as race, color, religion, national origin, sex, sexual orientation, disability or handicap, age, or political beliefs is unacceptable in the law school community. Law professors should seek to make the law school a hospitable community for all students and should be sensitive to the harmful consequences of professorial or student conduct or comments in classroom discussions or elsewhere that perpetuate stereotypes or prejudices involving such factors. Law professors should not sexually harass students and should not use their role or position to induce a student to enter into a sexual relationship, or to subject a student to a hostile academic environment based on any form of sexual harassment.

> Sexual relationships between a professor and a student who are not married to each other or who do not have a preexisting analogous relationship are inappropriate whenever the professor has a professional responsibility for the student in such matters as teaching a course or in otherwise advising a student as part of a school program. Even when a professor has no professional responsibility for a student, the professor should be sensitive to the perceptions of other students that a student who has a sexual relationship with a professor may receive preferential treatment from the professor or the professor's colleagues. A professor who is closely related to a student by blood or marriage, or who has a preexisting analogous relationship with a student, normally should eschew roles involving a professional responsibility for the student.

D. LAW SCHOOLS

Introductory Note

Women as Law Students and Professors

Page 882. Add to footnote 17:

See also Klein, The View From My Corner of The World: A Personal Comment on the Process of Becoming a Lawyer, 22 Akron L.Rev. 471 (1989).

Page 883. Add to footnote 25:

See also Angel, Women in Legal Education: What It's Like to be Part of a Perpetual First Wave or the Case of the Disappearing Women, 61 Temple L.Rev. 799 (1988); Chused, The Hiring and Retention of Minorities and Women on American Law School Faculties, 137 U.Pa.L.Rev. 537 (1988).

Page 883. Add to text following footnote 25:

Richard Delgado and Derrick Bell present a disturbing picture of the quality of life experienced by law professors of color, both men and women, in American law schools. See Delgado & Bell, Minority Law Professors' Lives: The Bell–Delgado Survey, 24 Harv.Civ.Rts.Civ.Lib.L. Rev. 349 (1989).

Page 887. Add to footnote 18:

See also Symposium on Women and Legal Education—Pedagogy, Law, Theory, and Practice, 38 J.Leg.Ed. 1 (1988); Torrey, Casey & Olson, Teaching Law in a Feminist Manner: A Commentary From Experience, 13 Harv.Wom.L.J. 87 (1990).

Chapter V

WOMEN AND CRIME

A. RAPE

1. STATUTORY RAPE

Page 907. Add to Note 5:

See also Pineau, Date Rape: A Feminist Analysis, 8 Law & Philosophy 217 (1989), making the point that in cases of date rape, "what is really sexual assault is often mistaken for seduction."

2. FORCIBLE RAPE

Page 919. Add to Note 4:

See also Comment, Abolishing the Marital Rape Exemption: The First Step in Protecting Married Women From Spousal Rape, 35 Wayne L.Rev. 1219 (1989).

Page 921. Add before Text Note:

THE FLORIDA STAR v. B.J.F.
Supreme Court of the United States, 1989.
491 U.S. ___, 109 S.Ct. 2603, 105 L.Ed.2d 443.

JUSTICE MARSHALL delivered the opinion of the Court.

Florida Stat. § 794.03 (1987) makes it unlawful to "print, publish, or broadcast * * * in any instrument of mass communication" the name of the victim of a sexual offense.[1] Pursuant to this statute, appellant The Florida Star was found civilly liable for publishing the name of a rape victim which it had obtained from a publicly released

---

1. The statute provides in its entirety:

    "Unlawful to publish or broadcast information identifying sexual offense victim.—No person shall print, publish, or broadcast, or cause or allow to be printed, published, or broadcast, in any instrument of mass communication the name, address, or other identifying fact or information of the victim of any sexual offense within this chapter. An offense under this section shall constitute a misdemeanor of the second degree, punishable as provided in § 775.082, § 775.083, or § 775.084." Fla.Stat. § 794.03 (1987).

police report. The issue presented here is whether this result comports with the First Amendment. We hold that it does not.

I

The Florida Star is a weekly newspaper which serves the community of Jacksonville, Florida, and which has an average circulation of approximately 18,000 copies. A regular feature of the newspaper is its "Police Reports" section. That section, typically two to three pages in length, contains brief articles describing local criminal incidents under police investigation.

On October 20, 1983, appellee B.J.F.[2] reported to the Duval County, Florida, Sheriff's Department (the Department) that she had been robbed and sexually assaulted by an unknown assailant. The Department prepared a report on the incident which identified B.J.F., by her full name. The Department then placed the report in its press room. The Department does not restrict access either to the press room or to the reports made available therein.

A Florida Star reporter-trainee sent to the press room copied the police report verbatim, including B.J.F.'s full name, on a blank duplicate of the Department's forms. A Florida Star reporter then prepared a one-paragraph article about the crime, derived entirely from the trainee's copy of the police report. The article included B.J.F.'s full name. It appeared in the "Robberies" subsection of the "Police Reports" section on October 29, 1983, one of fifty-four police blotter stories in that day's edition. The article read:

> "[B.J.F.] reported on Thursday, October 20, she was crossing Brentwood Park, which is in the 500 block of Golfair Boulevard, enroute to her bus stop, when an unknown black man ran up behind the lady and placed a knife to her neck and told her not to yell. The suspect then undressed the lady and had sexual intercourse with her before fleeing the scene with her 60 cents, Timex watch and gold necklace. Patrol efforts have been suspended concerning this incident because of a lack of evidence."

In printing B.J.F.'s full name, The Florida Star violated its internal policy of not publishing the names of sexual offense victims.

On September 26, 1984, B.J.F. filed suit in the Circuit Court of Duval County against the Department and The Florida Star, alleging that these parties negligently violated § 794.03. * * * Before trial, the Department settled with B.J.F. for $2,500. The Florida Star moved to dismiss, claiming, *inter alia,* that imposing civil sanctions on the newspaper pursuant to § 794.03 violated the First Amendment. The trial judge rejected the motion. * * *

2. In filing this lawsuit, appellee used her full name in the caption of the case. On appeal, the Florida District Court of Appeal *sua sponte* revised the caption, stating that it would refer to the appellee by her initials, "in order to preserve [her] privacy interests." 499 So.2d 883, 883, n. * (1986). Respecting those interests, we, too, refer to appellee by her initials, both in the caption and in our discussion.

At the ensuing day-long trial, B.J.F. testified that she had suffered emotional distress from the publication of her name. She stated that she had heard about the article from fellow workers and acquaintances; that her mother had received several threatening phone calls from a man who stated that he would rape B.J.F. again; and that these events had forced B.J.F. to change her phone number and residence, to seek police protection, and to obtain mental health counseling. In defense, The Florida Star put forth evidence indicating that the newspaper had learned B.J.F.'s name from the incident report released by the Department, and that the newspaper's violation of its internal rule against publishing the names of sexual offense victims was inadvertent.

At the close of B.J.F.'s case, and again at the close of its defense, The Florida Star moved for a directed verdict. On both occasions, the trial judge denied these motions. He ruled from the bench that § 794.03 was constitutional because it reflected a proper balance between the First Amendment and privacy rights, as it applied only to a narrow set of "rather sensitive * * * criminal offenses." * * * At the close of newspaper's defense, the judge granted B.J.F.'s motion for a directed verdict on the issue of negligence, finding the newspaper *per se* negligent based upon its violation of § 794.03. * * * This ruling left the jury to consider only the questions of causation and damages. The judge instructed the jury that it could award B.J.F. punitive damages if it found that the newspaper had "acted with reckless indifference to the rights of others." * * * The jury awarded B.J.F. $75,000 in compensatory damages and $25,000 in punitive damages. Against the actual damage award, the judge set off B.J.F's settlement with the Department.

The First District Court of Appeal affirmed in a three-paragraph *per curiam* opinion. 499 So.2d 883 (1986). * * *

The Florida Star appealed to this Court. We noted probable jurisdiction, * * * and now reverse.

II

The tension between the right which the First Amendment accords to a free press, on the one hand, and the protections which various statutes and common-law doctrines accord to personal privacy against the publication of truthful information, on the other, is a subject we have addressed several times in recent years. Our decisions in cases involving government attempts to sanction the accurate dissemination of information as invasive of privacy, have not, however, exhaustively considered this conflict. On the contrary, although our decisions have without exception upheld the press' right to publish, we have emphasized each time that we were resolving this conflict only as it arose in a discrete factual context.

The parties to this case frame their contentions in light of a trilogy of cases which have presented, in different contexts, the conflict between truthful reporting and state-protected privacy interests. In *Cox*

Broadcasting Corp. v. Cohn, 420 U.S. 469, 95 S.Ct. 1029, 43 L.Ed.2d 328 (1975), we found unconstitutional a civil damages award entered against a television station for broadcasting the name of a rape-murder victim which the station had obtained from courthouse records. In *Oklahoma Publishing Co. v. District Court,* 430 U.S. 308, 97 S.Ct. 1045, 51 L.Ed.2d 355 (1977), we found unconstitutional a state court's pretrial order enjoining the media from publishing the name or photograph of an 11-year-old boy in connection with a juvenile proceeding involving that child which reporters had attended. Finally, in *Smith v. Daily Mail Publishing Co.,* 443 U.S. 97, 99 S.Ct. 2667, 61 L.Ed.2d 399 (1979), we found unconstitutional the indictment of two newspapers for violating a state statute forbidding newspapers to publish, without written approval of the juvenile court, the name of any youth charged as a juvenile offender. The papers had learned about a shooting by monitoring a police band radio frequency, and had obtained the name of the alleged juvenile assailant from witnesses, the police, and a local prosecutor.

Appellant takes the position that this case is indistinguishable from *Cox Broadcasting.* * * * Alternatively, it urges that our decisions in the above trilogy, and in other cases in which we have held that the right of the press to publish truth overcame asserted interests other than personal privacy, can be distilled to yield a broader First Amendment principle that the press may never be punished, civilly or criminally, for publishing the truth. * * * Appellee counters that the privacy trilogy is inapposite, because in each case the private information already appeared on a "public record," * * * and because the privacy interests at stake were far less profound than in the present case. * * * In the alternative, appellee urges that *Cox Broadcasting* be overruled and replaced with a categorical rule that publication of the name of a rape victim never enjoys constitutional protection. * * *

We conclude that imposing damages on appellant for publishing B.J.F.'s name violates the First Amendment, although not for either of the reasons appellant urges. Despite the strong resemblance this case bears to *Cox Broadcasting,* that case cannot fairly be read as controlling here. The name of the rape victim in that case was obtained from courthouse records that were open to public inspection, a fact which Justice White's opinion for the Court repeatedly noted. * * * Significantly, one of the reasons we gave in *Cox Broadcasting* for invalidating the challenged damages award was the important role the press plays in subjecting trials to public scrutiny and thereby helping guarantee their fairness. * * * That role is not directly compromised where, as here, the information in question comes from a police report prepared and disseminated at a time at which not only had no adversarial criminal proceedings begun, but no suspect had been identified.

Nor need we accept appellant's invitation to hold broadly that truthful publication may never be punished consistent with the First

Amendment. Our cases have carefully eschewed reaching this ultimate question, mindful that the future may bring scenarios which prudence counsels our not resolving anticipatorily. See, *e.g., Near v. Minnesota ex rel. Olson,* 283 U.S. 697, 716, 51 S.Ct. 625, 75 L.Ed. 1357 (1931) (hypothesizing "publication of the sailing dates of transports or the number and location of troops"); see also *Garrison v. Louisiana,* 379 U.S. 64, 72, n. 8, 74, 85 S.Ct. 209, 215, n. 8, 216, 13 L.Ed.2d 125 (1964) (endorsing absolute defense of truth "where discussion of public affairs is concerned," but leaving unsettled the constitutional implications of truthfulness "in the discrete area of purely private libels"); * * *. Indeed, in *Cox Broadcasting,* we pointedly refused to answer even the less sweeping question "whether truthful publications may ever be subjected to civil or criminal liability" for invading "an area of privacy" defined by the State. * * * Respecting the fact that press freedom and privacy rights are both "plainly rooted in the traditions and significant concerns of our society," we instead focused on the less sweeping issue of "whether the State may impose sanctions on the accurate publication of the name of a rape victim obtained from public records—more specifically, from judicial records which are maintained in connection with a public prosecution and which themselves are open to public inspection." * * * We continue to believe that the sensitivity and significance of the interests presented in clashes between First Amendment and privacy rights counsel relying on limited principles that sweep no more broadly than the appropriate context of the instant case.

In our view, this case is appropriately analyzed with reference to such a limited First Amendment principle. It is the one, in fact, which we articulated in *Daily Mail* in our synthesis of prior cases involving attempts to punish truthful publication: "[I]f a newspaper lawfully obtains truthful information about a matter of public significance then state officials may not constitutionally punish publication of the information, absent a need to further a state interest of the highest order." * * * According the press the ample protection provided by that principle is supported by at least three separate considerations, in addition to, of course, the overarching " 'public interest, secured by the Constitution, in the dissemination of truth.' " * * *

First, because the *Daily Mail* formulation only protects the publication of information which a newspaper has "lawfully obtain[ed]," * * * the government retains ample means of safeguarding significant interests upon which publication may impinge, including protecting a rape victim's anonymity. To the extent sensitive information rests in private hands, the government may under some circumstances forbid its nonconsensual acquisition, thereby bringing outside of the *Daily Mail* principle the publication of any information so acquired. To the extent sensitive information is in the government's custody, it has even greater power to forestall or mitigate the injury caused by its release. The government may classify certain information, establish and enforce procedures ensuring its redacted release, and extend a damages remedy against the government or its officials where the government's mishandling of sensitive information leads to its dissemination. Where information is entrusted to the government, a less drastic means than punishing truthful publication almost always exists for guarding against the dissemination of private facts. * * *

A second consideration undergirding the *Daily Mail* principle is the fact that punishing the press for its dissemination of information which is already publicly available is relatively unlikely to advance the interests in the service of which the State seeks to act. It is not, of course, always the case that information lawfully acquired by the press is known, or accessible, to others. But where the government has made certain information publicly available, it is highly anomalous to sanction persons other than the source of its release. * * *

A third and final consideration is the "timidity and self-censorship" which may result from allowing the media to be punished for publishing certain truthful information. * * * *Cox Broadcasting* noted this concern with over-deterrence in the context of information made public through official court records, but the fear of excessive media self-suppression is applicable as well to other information released, without qualification, by the government. A contrary rule, depriving protection to those who rely on the government's implied representations of the lawfulness of dissemination, would force upon the media the onerous obligation of sifting through government press releases, reports, and pronouncements to prune out material arguably unlawful for publication. This situation could inhere even where the newspaper's sole object was to reproduce, with no substantial change, the government's rendition of the event in question.

Applied to the instant case, the *Daily Mail* principle clearly commands reversal. The first inquiry is whether the newspaper "lawfully obtain[ed] truthful information about a matter of public significance." * * * It is undisputed that the news article describing the assault on B.J.F. was accurate. In addition, appellant lawfully obtained B.J.F.'s name. Appellee's argument to the contrary is based on the fact that under Florida law, police reports which reveal the identity of the victim of a sexual offense are not among the matters of "public record" which the public, by law, is entitled to inspect. * * * But the fact that state officials are not required to disclose such reports does not make it unlawful for a newspaper to receive them when furnished by the government. Nor does the fact that the Department apparently failed to fulfill its obligation under § 794.03 not to "cause or allow to be * * * published" the name of a sexual offense victim make the newspaper's ensuing receipt of this information unlawful. Even assuming the Constitution permitted a State to proscribe *receipt* of information, Florida has not taken this step. It is, clear, furthermore, that the news article concerned "a matter of public significance," * * * in the sense in which the *Daily Mail* synthesis of prior cases used that term. That is, the article generally, as opposed to the specific identity contained within it, involved a matter of paramount public import: the commission, and investigation, of a violent crime which had been reported to authorities. * * *

The second inquiry is whether imposing liability on appellant pursuant to § 794.03 serves "a need to further a state interest of the highest order." * * * Appellee argues that a rule punishing publication furthers three closely related interests: the privacy of victims of sexual offenses; the physical safety of such victims, who may be targeted for retaliation if their names become known to their assailants; and the goal of encouraging victims of such crimes to report these offenses without fear of exposure. * * *

At a time in which we are daily reminded of the tragic reality of rape, it is undeniable that these are highly significant interests, a fact underscored by the Florida Legislature's explicit attempt to protect these interests by enacting a criminal statute prohibiting much dissemination of victim identities. We accordingly do not rule out the possibility that, in a proper case, imposing civil sanctions for publication of the name of a rape victim might be so overwhelmingly necessary to advance these interests as to satisfy the *Daily Mail* standard. For three independent reasons, however, imposing liability for publication under the circumstances of this case is too precipitous a means of advancing these interests to convince us that there is a "need" within the meaning of the *Daily Mail* formulation for Florida to take this extreme step. * * *

First is the manner in which appellant obtained the identifying information in question. As we have noted, where the government itself provides information to the media, it is most appropriate to assume that the government had, but failed to utilize, far more limited means of guarding against dissemination than the extreme step of punishing truthful speech. That assumption is richly borne out in this case. B.J.F.'s identity would never have come to light were it not for the erroneous, if inadvertent, inclusion by the Department of her full name in an incident report made available in a press room open to the public. Florida's policy against disclosure of rape victims' identities, reflected in § 794.03, was undercut by the Department's failure to abide by this policy. Where, as here, the government has failed to police itself in disseminating information, it is clear under *Cox Broadcasting, Oklahoma Publishing,* and *Landmark Communications* that the imposition of damages against the press for its subsequent publication can hardly be said to be a narrowly tailored means of safeguarding anonymity. * * * Once the government has placed such information in the public domain, "reliance must rest upon the judgment of those who decide what to publish or broadcast," *Cox Broadcasting,* * * * and hopes for restitution must rest upon the willingness of the government to compensate victims for their loss of privacy, and to protect them from the other consequences of its mishandling of the information which these victims provided in confidence.

That appellant gained access to the information in question through a government news release makes it especially likely that, if liability were to be imposed, self-censorship would result. Reliance on a news release is a paradigmatically "routine newspaper reporting techniqu[e]." *Daily Mail,* * * *. The government's issuance of such a release, without qualification, can only convey to recipients that the government considered dissemination lawful, and indeed expected the recipients to disseminate the information further. Had appellant merely reproduced the news release prepared and released by the Department, imposing civil damages would surely violate the First Amendment. The fact that appellant converted the police report into a news story by adding the linguistic connecting tissue necessary to transform the report's facts into full sentences cannot change this result.

A second problem with Florida's imposition of liability for publication is the broad sweep of the negligence *per se* standard applied under the civil cause of action implied from § 794.03. Unlike claims based on the common law tort of invasion of privacy, see Restatement (Second) of Torts § 652D (1977), civil actions based on § 794.03 require no case-by-case findings that the disclosure of a fact about a person's private life was one that a reasonable person would find highly offensive. On the contrary, under the *per se* theory of negligence adopted by the courts below, liability follows automatically from publication. This is so regardless of whether the identity of the victim is already known throughout the community; whether the victim has voluntarily called public attention to the offense; or whether the identity of the victim has otherwise become a reasonable subject of public concern—because, perhaps, questions have arisen whether the victim fabricated an assault by a particular person. Nor is there a scienter requirement of any kind under § 794.03, engendering the perverse result that truthful publications challenged pursuant to this cause of action are less protected by the First Amendment than even the least protected defamatory falsehoods: those involving purely private figures, where liability is evaluated under a standard, usually applied by a jury, of ordinary negligence. * * * We have previously noted the impermissibility of categorical prohibitions upon media access where important First Amendment interests are at stake. * * * More individualized adjudication is no less indispensable where the State, seeking to safeguard the anonymity of crime victims, sets its face against publication of their names.

Third, and finally, the facial underinclusiveness of § 794.03 raises serious doubts about whether Florida is, in fact, serving, with this statute, the significant interests which appellee invokes in support of affirmance. Section 794.03 prohibits the publication of identifying information only if this information appears in an "instrument of mass communication," a term the statute does not define. Section 794.03 does not prohibit the spread by other means of the identities of victims of sexual offenses. An individual who maliciously spreads word of the identity of a rape victim is thus not covered, despite the fact that the communication of such information to persons who live near, or work with, the victim may have consequences equally devastating as the exposure of her name to large numbers of strangers. See Tr. of Oral Arg. 49–50 (appellee acknowledges that § 794.03 would not apply to "the backyard gossip who tells 50 people that don't have to know").

When a State attempts the extraordinary measure of punishing truthful publication in the name of privacy, it must demonstrate its commitment to advancing this interest by applying its prohibition evenhandedly, to the smalltime disseminator as well as the media giant. Where important First Amendment interests are at stake, the mass scope of disclosure is not an acceptable surrogate for injury. A ban on disclosures effected by "instrument[s] of mass communication" simply cannot be defended on the ground that partial prohibitions may effect partial relief. * * * Without more careful and inclusive precautions against alternative forms of dissemination, we cannot conclude that Florida's selective ban on publication by the mass media satisfactorily accomplishes its stated purpose.

III

Our holding today is limited. We do not hold that truthful publication is automatically constitutionally protected, or that there is no zone of personal privacy within which the State may protect the individual from intrusion by the press, or even that a State may never punish publication of the name of a victim of a sexual offense. We hold only that where a newspaper publishes truthful information which it has lawfully obtained, punishment may lawfully be imposed, if at all, only when narrowly tailored to a state interest of the highest order, and that no such interest is satisfactorily served by imposing liability under § 794.03 to appellant under the facts of this case. The decision below is therefore

Reversed.

JUSTICE SCALIA, concurring in part and concurring in the judgment.

I think it sufficient to decide this case to rely upon the third ground set forth in the Court's opinion, * * * that a law cannot be regarded as protecting an interest "of the highest order," * * * and thus as justifying a restriction upon truthful speech, when it leaves appreciable damage to that supposedly vital interest unprohibited. In the present case, I would anticipate that the rape victim's discomfort at the dissemination of news of her misfortune among friends and acquaintances would be at least as great as her discomfort at its publication by the media to people to whom she is only a name. Yet the law in question does not prohibit the former in either oral or written form. Nor is it at all clear, as I think it must be to validate this statute, that Florida's general privacy law would prohibit such gossip. Nor, finally, is it credible that the interest meant to be served by the statute is the protection of the victim against a rapist still at large—an interest that arguably would extend only to mass publication. There would be little reason to limit a statute with that objective to rape alone; or to extend it to all rapes, whether or not the felon has been apprehended and confined. In any case, the instructions here did not require the jury to find that the rapist was at large.

This law has every appearance of a prohibition that society is prepared to impose upon the press but not upon itself. Such a prohibition does not protect an interest "of the highest order." For that reason, I agree that the judgment of the court below must be reversed.

JUSTICE WHITE, with whom THE CHIEF JUSTICE and JUSTICE O'CONNOR join, dissenting.

"Short of homicide, [rape] is the 'ultimate violation of self.'" *Coker v. Georgia,* 433 U.S. 584, 597, 97 S.Ct. 2861, 2869, 53 L.Ed.2d 982 (1977) (opinion of WHITE, J.). For B.J.F., however, the violation she suffered at a rapist's knifepoint marked only the beginning of her ordeal. A week later, while her assailant was still at large, an account of this assault—identifying by name B.J.F. as the victim—was published by The Florida Star. As a result, B.J.F. received harassing phone calls, required mental health counseling, was forced to move from her home, and was even threatened with being raped again. Yet today, the Court holds that a jury award of $75,000 to compensate B.J.F. for the harm she suffered due to the Star's negligence is at odds with the First Amendment. I do not accept this result.

The Court reaches its conclusion based on an analysis of three of our precedents and a concern with three particular aspects of the judgment against appellant. I consider each of these points in turn, and then consider some of the larger issues implicated by today's decision.

I

The Court finds its result compelled, or at least supported in varying degrees, by three of our prior cases: * * *. I disagree. None of these cases requires the harsh outcome reached today.

Cox Broadcasting reversed a damage award entered against a television station, which had obtained a rape victim's name from public records maintained in connection with the judicial proceedings brought against her assailants. While there are similarities, critical aspects of that case make it wholly distinguishable from this one. First, in *Cox Broadcasting,* the victim's name had been disclosed in the hearing where her assailants pled guilty; and, as we recognized, judicial records have always been considered public information in this country. * * * In fact, even the earliest notion of privacy rights exempted the information contained in judicial records from its protections. See Warren & Brandeis, The Right to Privacy, 4 Harv.L.Rev. 193, 216–217 (1890). Second, unlike the incident report at issue here, which was meant by state law to be withheld from public release, the judicial proceedings at issue in *Cox Broadcasting* were open as a matter of state law. Thus, in *Cox Broadcasting*, the State-law scheme made public disclosure of the victim's name almost inevitable; here, Florida law forbids such disclosure. See Fla.Stat. § 794.03 (1987).

These facts—that the disclosure came in judicial proceedings, which were open to the public—were critical to our analysis in *Cox Broadcasting*. The distinction between that case and this one is made obvious by the penultimate paragraph of *Cox Broadcasting:*

> "We are reluctant to embark on a course that would make *public records generally available to the media* but would forbid their publication if offensive * * *. [T]he First and Fourteenth Amendments will not allow exposing the press to liability for truthfully publishing information *released to the public in official court records. If there are privacy interests to be protected in judicial proceedings, the States must respond by means which avoid public documentation or other exposure of private information* * * *. Once true information is disclosed in public court documents open to public inspection,* the press cannot be sanctioned for publishing it." * * *

Cox Broadcasting stands for the proposition that the State cannot make the press its first line of defense in withholding private information from the public—it cannot ask the press to secrete private facts that the State makes no effort to safeguard in the first place. In this case, however, the State has undertaken "means which avoid [but obviously, not altogether prevent] public documentation or other exposure of private information." No doubt this is why the Court frankly admits that "*Cox Broadcasting* * * * cannot fairly be read as controlling here." * * *

Finding *Cox Broadcasting* inadequate to support its result, the Court relies on *Smith v. Daily Mail Publishing Co.* as its principal authority.¹ * * *

More importantly, at issue in *Daily Mail* was the disclosure of the name of the perpetrator of an infamous murder of a 15-year-old student. * * * Surely the rights of those accused of crimes and those who are their victims must differ with respect to privacy concerns. That is, whatever rights alleged criminals have to maintain their anonymity pending an adjudication of guilt—and after *Daily Mail*, those rights would seem to be minimal—the rights of crime victims to stay shielded from public view must be infinitely more substantial. *Daily Mail* was careful to state that the "holding in this case is narrow * * * there is no issue here of privacy." * * * But in this case, there is an issue of privacy—indeed, that is the principal issue—and

---

1. The second case in the "trilogy" which the Court cites is *Oklahoma Publishing Co. v. District Court,* * * *. But not much reliance is placed on that case, and I do not discuss it with the degree of attention devoted to *Cox Broadcasting* or *Daily Mail.*

As for the support *Oklahoma Publishing* allegedly provides for the Court's result here, the reasons that distinguish *Cox Broadcasting* and *Daily Mail* from this case are even more apt in the case of *Oklahoma Publishing.* Probably that is why the Court places so little weight on this middle leg of the three.

therefore, this case falls outside of *Daily Mail's* "rule" (which, as I suggest above, was perhaps not even meant as a rule in the first place).

Consequently, I cannot agree that *Cox Broadcasting,* or *Oklahoma Publishing,* or *Daily Mail* require—or even substantially support—the result reached by the Court today.

II

We are left, then, to wonder whether the three "independent reasons" the Court cites for reversing the judgment for B.J.F. support its result. * * *

The first of these reasons relied on by the Court is the fact "appellant gained access to [B.J.F.'s name] through a government news release." * * * "The government's issuance of such a release, without qualification, can only convey to recipients that the government considered dissemination lawful," the Court suggests. * * * So described, this case begins to look like the situation in *Oklahoma Publishing,* where a judge invited reporters into his courtroom, but then tried to forbid them from reporting on the proceedings they observed. But this case is profoundly different. Here, the "release" of information provided by the government was not, as the Court says, "without qualification." As the Star's own reporter conceded at trial, the crime incident report that inadvertently included B.J.F.'s name was posted in a room that contained signs making it clear that the names of rape victims were not matters of public record, and were not to be published. * * * The Star's reporter indicated that she understood that she "[was not] allowed to take down that information" (*i.e.,* B.J.F.'s name) and that she "[was] not supposed to take the information from the police department." * * * Thus, by her own admission the posting of the incident report did not convey to the Star's reporter the idea that "the government considered dissemination lawful"; the Court's suggestion to the contrary is inapt.

Instead, Florida has done precisely what we suggested, in *Cox Broadcasting,* that States wishing to protect the privacy rights of rape victims might do: "respond [to the challenge] by means which *avoid* public documentation or other exposure of private information." * * * By amending its public records statute to exempt rape victims' names from disclosure, Fla.Stat. § 119.07(3)(h) (1983), and forbidding its officials from releasing such information, Fla.Stat. § 794.03 (1983), the State has taken virtually every step imaginable to prevent what happened here. This case presents a far cry, then, from *Cox Broadcasting* or *Oklahoma Publishing,* where the State asked the news media not to publish information it had made generally available to the public: here, the State is not asking the media to do the State's job in the first instance. Unfortunately, as this case illustrates, mistakes happen: even when States take measures to "avoid" disclosure, sometimes rape victims' names are found out. As I see it, it is not too much to ask the press, in instances such as this, to respect simple standards of decency and refrain from publishing a victim's name, address, and/or phone number.²

Second, the Court complains that appellant was judged here under too strict a liability standard. The Court contends that a newspaper might be found liable under the Florida courts' negligence *per se* theory without regard to a newspaper's scienter or degree of fault. * * * The short answer to this complaint is that whatever merit the Court's argument might have, it is wholly inapposite here, where the jury found that appellant acted with "reckless indifference towards the rights of others," * * * a standard far higher than the *Gertz* standard the Court urges as a constitutional minimum today. * * * B.J.F. proved the Star's negligence at trial—and, actually, far more than simple negligence; the Court's concerns about damages resting on a strict liability or mere causation basis are irrelevant to the validity of the judgment for appellee.

But even taking the Court's concerns in the abstract, they miss the mark. Permitting liability under a negligence *per se* theory does not mean that defendants will be held liable without a showing of negligence, but rather, that the standard of care has been set by the legislature, instead of the courts. The Court says that negligence *per se* permits a plaintiff to hold a defendant liable without a showing that the disclosure was "of a fact about a person's private life * * * that a reasonable person would find highly offensive." * * * But the point here is that the legislature—reflecting popular sentiment—has determined that disclosure of the fact that a person was raped is categorically a revelation that reasonable people find offensive. And as for the Court's suggestion that the Florida courts' theory permits liability without regard for whether the victim's identity is already known, or whether she herself has made it known—these are facts that would surely enter into the calculation of damages in such a case. In any event, none of these mitigating factors was present here; whatever the force of these arguments generally, they do not justify the Court's ruling against B.J.F. in this case.

2. The Court's concern for a free press is appropriate, but such concerns should be balanced against rival interests in a civilized and humane society. An absolutist view of the former leads to insensitivity as to the latter.

This was evidenced at trial, when the Florida Star's lawyer explained why the paper was not to blame for any anguish caused B.J.F. by a phone call she received, the day after the Star's story was published, from a man threatening to rape B.J.F. again. Noting that the phone call was received at B.J.F.'s home by her mother (who was baby-sitting B.J.F.'s children while B.J.F. was in the hospital), who relayed the threat to B.J.F., the Star's counsel suggested:

"[I]n reference to the [threatening] phone call, it is sort of blunted by the fact that [B.J.F.] didn't receive the phone call. Her mother did. And if there is any pain and suffering in connection with the phone call, it has to lay in her mother's hands. I mean, my God, she called [B.J.F.] up at the hospital to tell her [of the threat]—you know, I think that is tragic, but I don't think that is something you can blame the Florida Star for." * * *

While I would not want to live in a society where freedom of the press was unduly limited, I also find regrettable an interpretation of the First Amendment that fosters such a degree of irresponsibility on the part of the news media.

Third, the Court faults the Florida criminal statute for being underinclusive: § 794.03 covers disclosure of rape victims' names in "instrument[s] of mass communication," but not other means of distribution, the Court observes. * * * But our cases which have struck down laws that limit or burden the press due to their underinclusiveness have involved situations where a legislature has singled out one segment of the news media or press for adverse treatment, see, *e.g., Daily Mail* (restricting newspapers and not radio or television), or singled out the press for adverse treatment when compared to other similarly situated enterprises, * * *. Here, the Florida law evenhandedly covers all "instrument[s] of mass communication" no matter their form, media, content, nature or purpose. It excludes neighborhood gossips, * * * because presumably the Florida Legislature has determined that neighborhood gossips do not pose the danger and intrusion to rape victims that "instrument[s] of mass communication" do. Simply put: Florida wanted to prevent the widespread distribution of rape victims' names, and therefore enacted a statute tailored almost as precisely as possible to achieving that end.

Moreover, the Court's "underinclusiveness" analysis itself is "underinclusive." After all, the lawsuit against the Star which is at issue here is not an action for violating the statute which the Court deems underinclusive, but is, more accurately, for the negligent publication of appellee's name. * * * The scheme which the Court should review, then, is not only § 794.03 (which, as noted above, merely provided the standard of care in this litigation), but rather, the whole of Florida privacy tort law. As to the latter, Florida does recognize a tort of publication of private facts. Thus, it is quite possible that the neighborhood gossip whom the Court so fears being left scot-free to spread news of a rape victim's identity would be subjected to the same (or similar) liability regime under which appellant was taxed. The Court's myopic focus on § 794.03 ignores the probability that Florida law is more comprehensive than the Court gives it credit for being.

Consequently, neither the State's "dissemination" of B.J.F.'s name, nor the standard of liability imposed here, nor the underinclusiveness of Florida tort law require setting aside the verdict for B.J.F. And as noted above, such a result is not compelled by our cases. I turn, therefore, to the more general principles at issue here to see if they recommend the Court's result.

III

At issue in this case is whether there is any information about people, which—though true—may not be published in the press. By holding that only "a state interest of the highest order" permits the State to penalize the publication of truthful information, and by holding that protecting a rape victim's right to privacy is not among those state interests of the highest order, the Court accepts appellant's invitation, * * * to obliterate one of the most note-worthy legal inventions of the 20th–Century: the tort of the publication of private facts. W. Prosser, J. Wade, & V. Schwartz, Torts 951–952 (8th ed. 1988). Even if the Court's opinion does not say as much today, such obliteration will follow inevitably from the Court's conclusion here. If the First Amendment prohibits wholly private persons (such as B.J.F.) from recovering for the publication of the fact that she was raped, I doubt that there remain any "private facts" which persons may assume will not be published in the newspapers, or broadcast on television.

Of course, the right to privacy is not absolute. Even the article widely relied upon in cases vindicating privacy rights, Warren & Brandeis, The Right to Privacy, 4 Harv.L.Rev., at 193, recognized that this right inevitably conflicts with the public's right to know about matters of general concern—and that sometimes, the latter must trump the former. * * * Resolving this conflict is a difficult matter, and I do not fault the Court for attempting to strike an appropriate balance between the two, but rather, for according too little weight to B.J.F.'s side of equation, and too much on the other.

I would strike the balance rather differently. * * *

* * *

I do not suggest that the Court's decision today is radical departure from a previously charted course. The Court's ruling has been foreshadowed. In *Time, Inc. v. Hill,* 385 U.S. 374, 383–384, n. 7, 87 S.Ct. 534, 539–540, n. 7, 17 L.Ed.2d 456 (1967), we observed that—after a brief period early in this century where Brandeis' view was ascendant—the trend in "modern" jurisprudence has been to eclipse an individual's right to maintain private any truthful information that the press wished to publish. More recently, in *Cox Broadcasting,* * * * we acknowledged the possibility that the First Amendment may prevent a State from ever subjecting the publication of truthful but private information to civil liability. Today, we hit the bottom of the slippery slope.

I would find a place to draw the line higher on the hillside: a spot high enough to protect B.J.F.'s desire for privacy and peace-of-mind in the wake of a horrible personal tragedy. There is no public interest in publishing the names, addresses, and phone numbers of persons who are the victims of crime—and no public interest in immunizing the press from liability in the rare cases where a State's efforts to protect a victim's privacy have failed. Consequently, I respectfully dissent.

Notes on B.J.F.

1. Did Justice Marshall give adequate weight to B.J.F.'s privacy claim? A notewriter argues that "[a]lthough the majority * * * appeared to balance the claims of privacy and press freedom, it undercut the evenhandedness of its balancing test by giving little weight to interests other than those of the press." The Supreme Court—Leading Cases, 103 Harv.L.Rev. 137, 265 (1989). What approach would have been better? The notewriter suggests that "[a]n approach that gave more weight to the state's interests in protecting rape victims' privacy and safety, and in

encouraging victims to report rapes to the police, would have set a better standard for the future." Ibid.

2. But what if the rape victim wants to tell her story to the public? Nancy Ziegenmeyer, a rape victim, sought out Geneva Overholser, editor of The Des Moines Register, to disclose the details of her experience. The story, which ran on the front page of the Register for five consecutive days, attracted national attention and has been widely praised. Said Overholser, "I think Nancy Ziegenmeyer will help make the day come sooner that we will treat rape more like other crimes." The New York Times, March 25, 1990, at A1, col. 1.

C. WOMEN AND THE CRIMINAL JUSTICE SYSTEM

1. WOMEN AS DEFENDANTS

Page 956. Add to Note 4.

See also Littleton, Women's Experience and the Problem of Transition: Perspectives on Male Battering of Women, 1989 University of Chicago Legal Forum 23, asking (and beginning to answer) the very complex and dangerous question: "What would legal doctrine and practice look like if it took seriously a mandate to make women safer *in* relationships, instead of offering separation as the *only* remedy for violence against women?" Id., at 52.

Page 958. Add to Note 5:

Restraining orders issued under C.C.P. § 548 now endure for 3 years unless terminated earlier by the court. (1990 Supp.)

†